MANAGEMENT DEVELOPMENT

INFO LINE

TIPS, TOOLS, AND INTELLIGENCE FOR TRAINERS

AN INFOLINE COLLECTION

ASTD Press is an internationally renowned source of insightful and practical information on workplace learning and performance topics, including training basics, evaluation and return-on-investment, instructional systems development, e-learning, leadership, and career development.

Infoline is a real got-a-problem, find-a-solution publication. Concise and practical, *Infoline* is an information lifeline written specifically for trainers and other workplace learning and performance professionals. Whether the subject is a current trend in the field, or tried-and-true training basics, *Infoline* is a complete, reliable trainer's information resource. *Infoline* is available by subscription and single copy purchase.

Ordering information: Books published by ASTD Press, single issues of *Infolines*, and *Infoline* subscriptions can be purchased by visiting our website at store.astd.org or by calling 800.628.2783 or 703.683.8100.

Library of Congress Control Number: 2009931553

ISBN-10: 1-56286-713-X
ISBN-13: 978-1-56286-713-3

ASTD Press Editorial Staff
Associate Editor: Justin Brusino
Interior Design and Production: Kathleen Schaner

Printed by Midland Information Resources, Davenport, Iowa

Management Development

An *Infoline* Collection

Editor
Justin Brusino

Graphic Production
Kathleen Schaner

Be a Better Manager

Issue 0607

Be a Better Manager

AUTHOR

Tora Estep
Associate Editor, ASTD Press
American Society for Training
& Development
1640 King Street
Alexandria, VA 22313-2043
Phone: 703.683.8138
Email: testep@astd.org.

**Manager, Acquisitions &
Author Development**
Mark Morrow

Associate Editor, ASTD Press
Tora Estep

Editorial Consultant
Deborah Tobey

Copy Editor
Ann Bruen

Production Design
Kathleen Schaner

Managing Well

Managers are crucial to the success of organizations. While organizational leaders design forward-thinking strategies, managers make those strategies happen. Given the forces acting on organizations—such as globalization, outsourcing, the upcoming retirements of the Baby Boomer generation—organizations have to reinvent themselves as flexible learning organizations that can attract and retain the best and the brightest to stay competitive. Managers have a powerful role to play in that reinvention.

And yet, despite its importance, management development often receives less attention than leadership development. Where does this leave managers? Especially new or young managers who have been promoted up from the ranks because of skills in their functional areas? Often alone and unskilled in management techniques, floundering between the excesses of the micromanager whose employees feel second-guessed all the time and the passive, acquiescent manager whose employees struggle and whose goals go unachieved. And in the face of the changing business environment and manager role, even trained and experienced managers may need some additional development.

If you find yourself in the position of manager (or aspire to find yourself there) and feel that you could stand to learn some useful management practices and skills, this *Infoline* is for you. Although the list is not comprehensive, this issue describes a selection of competencies widely considered to be important for managers, including

- business management
- people management
- process management
- communication
- personal effectiveness.

Note that this issue is not intended to be a replacement for traditional management development; it is a guide to help you identify areas for improvement and plan for development as well as a supplement to any formal learning programs offered by your organization.

Prepare for Development

As a manager, you are a busy person. You don't have time to waste on learning what you already know or on competencies that don't have an impact on your work. However, constant learning is a hallmark of a great manager. The way to balance learning and a lack of time is to start by identifying your strengths and weaknesses. When you know your strengths, you will be better able to capitalize on them, and when you know your weaknesses, you can prepare an individual development plan (IDP) to improve them. To prepare for your development, follow these steps:

1. Complete the self-assessment in the sidebar *Management Competencies Self-Assessment.*

2. Select three or four of your lowest-scoring competencies and think of a time when lacking skills in these areas cost you or your organization. Describe the costs; this could include personal emotional costs, such as stress, or organizational costs, such as the loss of a high-performing employee and financial costs. From highest to lowest, rank order the selected competencies based on their costs.

3. Starting with the first competency on your rank-ordered list, prepare an IDP to address them, using the job aid at the end of this *Infoline*.

Develop Your Managerial Competencies

Once you have identified where you could use some improvement and determined which competencies have caused the most pain in the past, your next step is to improve your skills. The following sections provide brief overviews of the competencies as well as some tools, practices, and habits that can be useful in your quest to become a better manager. Feel free to skip some competencies and focus on others.

Management Competencies Self-Assessment

Consider the following statements and rate yourself on them according to the following key: (5) This is a real strength; (3) I have adequate skills in this area; (1) I could use some improvement in this area. Then add up your scores for each competency. Circle the three or four competencies with the lowest scores to focus on and assign priority to them (A, B, C).

Business Management	5	3	1	Priority (A, B, C)
I can describe my organization's goals and competitive environment.				
I understand principles of finance, budgeting, and accounting.				
I am skilled at preparing strategic plans that align with organizational goals.				
I understand relevant business regulations and procedures in my organization's industry.				
BUSINESS MANAGEMENT TOTAL:				
People Management				
I use an effective process to hire employees.				
I work with my employees to identify performance goals for them that align with the organization's goals.				
I am comfortable delegating work to my employees.				
I enable my employees to achieve their performance goals and more through effective coaching and motivation techniques.				
PEOPLE MANAGEMENT TOTAL:				
Process Management				
I run effective meetings that achieve their stated goals.				
I understand how change affects people and how to help them to embrace it.				
I am skilled at planning, organizing, and controlling work.				
I use resources effectively.				
PROCESS MANAGEMENT TOTAL:	5	3	1	

Communication	5	3	1	Priority (A, B, C)
I communicate well orally.				
I withhold judgment until I have completely and accurately heard what someone intends to say.				
I regularly provide both constructive and positive feedback that is specific and immediate.				
I communicate well in writing.				
COMMUNICATION TOTAL:				
Personal Effectiveness				
I practice excellent time management skills.				
Each day, I choose to first work on tasks that are highest priority to the organization and to me.				
My work space is well organized, and I always know where to find documents I need.				
I use effective problem-solving and decision-making processes.				
PERSONAL EFFECTIVENESS TOTAL:				

Business Management

According to Lisa Haneberg in "Reinventing Middle Management," today's managers "see themselves as business owners" and "know that they create and represent the organization; they establish the work context." In light of this, the need for a broad understanding of the organization as well as specific knowledge of business regulations and procedures becomes clear. The following are some examples of business knowledge you should know.

■ *State of the Business*
As a manager, you need to understand your organization's

● *business model,* which describes how an organization plans to serve its customers and its employees and includes both strategy and implementation plans

● *business objectives,* which state what your organization wants to accomplish; for example, a business objective might be to increase

profitability by five percent in the next year with the launch of a new product

● *factors that affect organizational growth,* including the competitive environment and the industry as well as the current culture and values of an organization

● *business drivers,* which are the internal (for example, product development) and external forces (for example, government or technology) that direct an organization's strategy, goals, business needs, and performance needs.

To complete the picture of the state of the business, you also need to understand corporate success measures and how the organization defines and measures success. All these factors determine how you will link your department's goals and objectives to overall business goals and objectives.

Basic Accounting Terms

To work effectively with your accounting department or with executives in the organization, you need to understand and learn to use basic accounting terminology.

- *Assets* refer to economic resources—in other words, what a company owns—that may be expressed in monetary terms.

- *Liabilities* are the debts or expenses a company owes.

- *Equity* is the value of the owners' or shareholders' portion of the business after all claims against it.

- *Balance sheet* is a statement of the firm's financial position, including assets, liabilities, and equity (liabilities + equity = assets).

- *Income statements* explain revenues, expenses, and profits over a specified period of time (revenues - expenses = net income).

- *Chart of accounts* is the listing of account lines maintained in the general ledger.

- *Cost-benefit analysis* is a comparison that weighs the costs of a training activity against the outcomes achieved and is carried out to determine the return-on-investment.

- *Expenses* are the costs incurred in the process of earning revenues and conducting business.

- *Incurred expenses* are the expenses in which obligations have been fulfilled but not paid.

- *Operating expenses* are expenses that relate directly to business operations, not to providing products or services.

- *Revenue* is the money a company earns by providing goods or services to its customers.

- *Financial statements* are the four statements that show the end results of an organization's financial condition: balance sheet, income statement, statement of cash flows, and statement of owners' equity.

Some ways you can identify these components of your organization include

- reviewing the organization's mission and vision statements and its annual report

- reviewing strategic plans (these will often be confidential) and talking to executives about the strategic direction of the organization

- maintaining knowledge of your industry through trade papers, conferences, and so forth.

■ *Budgeting and Accounting*

Creating a good budget is more than an annual event designed to document spending; it's a working plan that guides fiscal decisions. A well-designed and executed budget forms the foundation for developing next year's budget.

Although budgeting is often referred to as a process, in reality it's part of a larger accounting system (for some basic accounting terms, see the sidebar at left). A typical accounting system includes three steps:

1. Budget design and development (forecasting).

2. Budget execution (expense tracking, monitoring, and management).

3. Reporting and reconciliation.

In an optimal planning process, you would design a budget based on the business plan, not on other factors, such as available revenue to fund the plan or previous spending levels. The assumption is that business goals justify the expenditures. Note that it is good practice to work with your organization's accounting department to learn their preferences in terms of processes and documentation; this may help you to avoid having to redo your work.

■ *Organizational Structure*

Organizational structure refers to both formal and informal reporting structures as well as ways that information moves across the organization and work gets done. You can learn about formal structures from organization charts, but understanding informal structures requires personal observation and keeping your ear open. However, knowing the informal ways that things get done in an organization can be very powerful. For example, knowing who influences whom can be useful knowledge if you need to get something done.

■ *Strategic Planning*

Strategic planning can be defined as the process of systematically organizing the future, a process in which managers and other professionals use past experience as a filter for future decisions. When creating a strategic plan for your department, focus attention on department outcomes that link with the overall organization's mission and strategic plan and address these questions:

- Where is my department now?

- Where does my department want to go?

- How will my department get there?

- What are my department's strengths and weaknesses?

You can develop a strategic plan by using a four-phase process (see the sidebar *Strategic Planning* at right). Use strategic planning as a tool to accomplish more things that are critical to your department and to the overall business strategy. For that reason, don't think of strategic planning as a one-time event; it should be an ongoing process.

■ *Business Regulations*

Another important component of the business management competency is knowledge of business regulations and ethics. These may include

- employment law and regulatory requirements
- civil rights legislation
- workplace safety
- securities and financial reporting
- information technology compliance
- union relations
- intellectual property
- corporate policies and procedures
- ethical standards.

You can find information about these regulations through your human resources department, government websites, and any professional associations that you may belong to.

Strategic Planning

As a manager, you must be able to turn organizational goals into department goals. The way to do this is to carry out strategic planning for your department. Use this four-phase model to help you.

Phase	Task
1. Formulation	• Identify organizational mission, vision, and values. • Develop department mission, vision, and value statements based on this organizational review.
2. Development	• Conduct an analysis of strengths, weaknesses, opportunities, and threats (SWOT). • Establish strategic goals (two to three years to attain). • Identify strategies to attain those goals.
3. Implementation	• Establish long-term measurable goals to achieve strategies. • Establish short-term objectives (six months to a year) for each goal. • Create action plans to achieve those objectives. • Allocate resources to work toward those objectives. • Motivate employees to achieve those objectives.
4. Evaluation	• Review strategies. • Measure actual performance against strategies, goals, and objectives. • Take corrective action.

For more information on strategic planning, see "Managing the Strategic Planning Process," *Infoline* No. 259710, and "Strategic Planning for Human Resource Development," *Infoline* No. 259206.

Hiring Checklist

Hiring top performers is the culmination of effective recruitment and advertising, interviewing, and selecting. The following four areas cover the basics of the process.

Area 1: Requirements

☐ Focus on the few key attributes you are looking for.

☐ Have a plan. You must see how your employee needs link to the strategic plan of the organization.

☐ Look for *organizational* fit—not just job fit.

☐ Specify the job. Be clear about what the job entails.

Area 2: Hiring System

☐ Plan and prepare for interviews. Eliminate unnecessary duplication of questions, practice your approach, and test your questions beforehand.

☐ Develop the same basic questions for each interview so there will be a basis for comparison later on.

☐ Use both open-ended and closed-ended questions in an interview. Plan on talking about 25 percent of the time and listening about 75 percent of the time.

Area 3: Basics

☐ Be a good host. For example, make the interviewee feel welcome and offer refreshment.

☐ Make sure the interview and hiring processes are clear up front.

☐ Hone your interviewing skills and review federal guidelines for interviewing.

Area 4: Value-Added System

☐ Relate the interview to values and vision, not just to job experience.

☐ Meet across functions with people who will work with this person.

☐ Have a way to compare meaningful notes afterward.

Adapted from E. Stewart Hickman's "Hiring and Retaining Top Performing Employees," Infoline No. 250011.

People Management

The ability to manage people well is a crucial competency for managers, especially given that the job of managers is to achieve the goals of the department and the organization through the work of other people. Furthermore, it has become a truism that people don't leave organizations; people leave managers. How people are managed is a crucial factor in retaining employees.

For these reasons, it's important to develop strong people management skills. Some of these are discussed in the following sections.

Hiring and Retaining

How well your people perform starts with how well you selected them in the first place, and there are effective processes you can learn to interview candidates and hire the right employees (see the sidebar *Hiring Checklist* at left for an overview of an effective hiring process).

To prepare to interview candidates, ask yourself three questions:

1. What will make a candidate suitable for this job?

2. What are the signals that a candidate may be suitable for the job?

3. What are the signals that a candidate may not be suitable for the job?

Preparing an answer to the first question in advance will enable you to answer the second two during the interview itself. Although you will use the job description as a resource, note that the first question refers to more than job requirements; it refers to the culture of your organization and your department. In other words, what kind of person represents a good fit?

Once you have hired the right person, you need to work to retain that person. Losing employees is costly and disruptive to the smooth functioning of your department. One way to do this is to model your department on organizations with good track records for retention, which share certain characteristics. They

- value their workers

- tie workforce initiatives to organizational strategies

- understand the importance of employee growth and development

- link training to operations

- provide training and development for everyone

- use competencies

- track, measure, and evaluate their initiatives.

Managing Performance

Managing employees' performance goes beyond completing a performance review once or twice a year. Although formal performance reviews are an important tool in developing individual goals that will enable the department and ultimately the organization to achieve their goals, managing employees' performance should take place on a far more frequent basis, ideally weekly, or even daily.

This high level of engagement has become increasingly rare, according to Bruce Tulgan in "The Under-Management Epidemic," and represents a fear on the part of managers to appear to be the dreaded micromanager. Tulgan notes "that these under-managers often think they are being 'good guys' by soft-pedaling their authority, but their failure to provide leadership causes so many problems that they are not being good guys at all."

Tulgan describes these six characteristics of highly successful and engaged managers:

1. They know a lot about their employees' work, including how much, how fast, and how hard.

2. They have regular meetings with every employee, ideally once a day, but at a minimum, once a week, to talk about how the job is going.

3. They write everything down in a manager's notebook, which is a running log of employee meetings.

4. They do a lot for their employees—for example, provide training opportunities, recognition, different schedule arrangements—but they expect a lot in return.

5. They link rewards to specific instances of high performance.

6. They consider high performance to be the only option and work hard to achieve it through clear performance expectations, regular feedback, coaching for development, frank discussions, planning, and termination, if required.

Delegating

Delegation is often billed as a time-saving mechanism for the manager, but its benefits don't stop there. Successful delegation maximizes an organization's output, while producing competent employees, balanced budgets, and promotable managers. "Managers who delegate properly will always accomplish more than those who refuse to let go of projects their subordinates should be doing," says Eugene Raudsepp in "How to Delegate Effectively." Delegation has two goals: First, to free you up from routine tasks so that you can focus on more big-picture strategic tasks and, second, to develop employee skills so that they are learning and preparing for future tasks and positions.

Here is an effective process for delegating tasks:

- Decide what to delegate by identifying tasks that someone else can do just as well. (However, remember to always retain tasks related to overall planning, policy making, goal setting, budget supervision, confidential information, and subordinate relations.)

- Pick the right person for the task. To do this, consider your subordinates' characteristics, skills, and interests. The perfect assignment will challenge, but not overwhelm, your employee.

- Plan carefully and explain clearly. Communicate your priorities (speed or quality, for example), expected results, and performance criteria.

- Delegate both responsibility and authority. Make sure the employee has what he or she needs to get the job done. In the area of authority, that may mean contacting others with whom the employee will be working, requesting their cooperation, and letting them know the employee has full authority to complete the task.

- Monitor progress regularly, especially with employees who are undertaking unfamiliar assignments.

- Delegate a whole project. The employee will gain far more satisfaction and learn more from carrying out a complete project than he or she will from doing bits and pieces. If that isn't possible, explain the relevance of his or her contribution to the overall project.

- Encourage your employee. Provide constructive feedback and coaching as required.

- Evaluate the project together with the employee. Correct mistakes privately and tactfully, and reward success generously.

Motivating

Motivation is defined as a psychological force that determines what a person chooses to do, how hard he or she works, and how persistent he or she is in the face of a challenge. Understanding a variety of motivational theories and the different ways that different people are motivated is crucial to the successful work of a manager. The following two influences have a great effect on the motivation of your employees and should also be considered when integrating motivation into work planning, performance feedback, and relationship building:

■ *Management Recognition*
Instead of coming from some nebulous, ad hoc committee or corporate institution, the most valuable recognition comes directly from a person's manager. The sidebar *Rewarding Employees* provides a sampling of ways that you can reward your employees.

■ *Performance Incentives*
Your employees want to be recognized for the jobs they were hired to do. The most effective incentives are based on job performance—not on non-performance-related praise such as attendance.

Developing People

According to Haneberg, today's effective managers create work environments in which employees thrive. One important way to accomplish this is to provide challenging opportunities to learn and grow as well as to provide coaching and feedback.

To be a successful coach, you need to demonstrate certain behaviors, such as supporting employees' needs, creating choices, seeking commitment, and providing avenues of self-expression. Work toward a balance between being supportive and caring and being clear and direct about what is expected of the employee. Two categories of coaching behaviors are effective in developing employees: supporting behaviors and initiating behaviors.

Supporting behaviors demonstrate caring, concern, and acceptance and lead to reduced tension and more open communication. Examples include

- collaboration on solutions to problem areas
- help and assistance where needed
- concern about worker's needs and objectives
- empathy.

Initiating behaviors encourage the employee to discuss the work situation. A manager's initiating behaviors include

- providing feedback and analysis of issues
- clarifying goals and expectations
- planning solutions and changes
- outlining consequences of employee actions.

Process Management

Three processes are familiar to most managers: meeting management, change management, and project management. The following sections will describe some effective methods and tools to carry these out.

Meeting Management

Ineffective meetings that don't achieve their goals are some of the biggest time and money wasters in organizations today. Furthermore, they waste employee commitment and energy.

To make the most of meeting time, you need to do some planning and preparation. Before the meeting, you should

- determine what the meeting should accomplish

- identify who needs to be there and what he or she needs to do to prepare for the meeting

- prepare an agenda

- identify any tools you may need (whiteboards, markers, and so forth)

- invite participants, providing them with a description of what the meeting should achieve as well as any pre-work to accomplish.

At the time of the meeting, you should

- ensure that you have the space and tools that you need

- start on time

- introduce the participants to each other

- explain why you are meeting

Rewarding Employees

Research into why talented people stay in organizations is the basis for the following ways to show your employees that you appreciate them:

■ **Private Time With You**
Have lunch with an employee and ask questions like, "What can I do to keep you on my team?" "What might make your work life easier?" "What can I do to be more supportive to help you?"

■ **Frank Talk About the Future**
Hold a career conversation in a quiet, private place—off-site, if possible. Ask the following questions to start: "What do you enjoy most about your job? The least?" "Which of your talents have I not used yet?" "What jobs do you see yourself doing in the future?"

■ **Potential Growth**
Let employees choose from a list of potential projects, assignments, or tasks that could enrich their work.

■ **Submit to Pruning**
Ask the employee with whom you never agree to engage in some straight talk about how you can work together better. Listen carefully and don't defend yourself. Then take a step toward changing at least one behavior.

■ **A Unique Perk for Fun**
Give an employee a "kicks" coupon that entitles him or her to spend up to X amount of money to take a break or have some fun at work. It could involve the whole team.

■ **Blending Work and Passion**
Have a "Passion Breakfast" for all employees, a team, or one on one. Ask, "What do you love to do?" "At work?" "Outside of work?" Brainstorm and commit to helping them build more of what they love into their workday.

■ **Genie in a Bottle**
Ask an employee to write down six ways he or she would like to be rewarded. Anything goes. The only rule is that half of the ideas have to be low or no cost.

■ **A Chance to Download**
Give 12 coupons for listening time—one for each month, in which an employee can talk about anything for 20 minutes. Your job isn't to understand, just to listen.

Adapted from Beverly L. Kaye and Sharon Jordan-Evans's "The ABCs of Management Gift-Giving," Training & Development, December 2000.

- forecast the meeting process

- explain the ground rules

- display enthusiasm.

During the meeting, use meeting facilitation skills to keep to the agenda, ask all participants to contribute, and park topics that are not on the agenda.

And always follow up meetings by typing up notes and distributing them to everyone who participated, planning to follow up on commitments made in the meeting, and plan for a follow-up meeting to ensure that commitments are being upheld.

Change Management

Organizations make the decision to change for business reasons. But how change is implemented is based on "people reasons." It is important for managers to understand reactions to change and how to implement change effectively.

An organization's people are a critical component in ensuring that any organizational change initiative is successful. Management consultant, futurist, speaker, and prolific author Karl Albrecht described the *personal change response cycle* to help individuals work though the progressive psychological phases of change response, which are as follows:

■ *Threat*
In this phase, individuals are afraid to change the status quo because of fear of the unknown or fear of a state worse than the status quo.

■ *Problem*
At this point, individuals perceive change to be a lot of work and problems. Because they no longer know the rules, it's difficult for them to complete their jobs.

■ *Solution*
Overcoming the problems perceived in the previous phase starts to reveal some of the benefits of the change.

■ *Habit*
As old operating procedures are forgotten, the new become the norm.

Individuals progress through these phases at different rates. Your job as manager is to help people work through them as efficiently as possible. To do this, some of the tasks you have to achieve are to

- define the tasks that need to be done

- create management systems to help accomplish the tasks

- develop strategies for gaining commitment from employees

- develop communication strategies

- invite employee participation in the development of new processes and policies

- assign employees, resources, experts, and consultants to manage the change

- study present conditions

- collect data on employee attitudes toward the change

- create models of the end state

- state the goals of the transition and clearly describe the end state.

Project Management

Project management consists of planning, organizing, and controlling work. The goal of project management is to deliver a project that is on time, within budget, meets the required performance or specification level, and uses resources wisely. A project manager plans for a project's needs and then organizes and controls project resources as it progresses. Your tasks in managing projects are defined in the following sections.

■ *Defining the Project and Goals*

Regardless of the specific project goals and end deliverables, you, as project manager, are responsible for

- ensuring that the project work, and only the approved project work, is completed (scope)

- ensuring that the project schedule is planned, communicated, and monitored

- tracking an initial project budget and expenses incurred as the project progresses

- measuring and monitoring that the project deliverables meet the specified quality guidelines and standards

- scheduling and managing the appropriate use of resources.

■ *Project Planning*

The next task is establishing a plan for how the project will be accomplished. These are the steps in this process:

1. Select a strategy for achieving the objective.

2. Divide the project's tasks into subtasks and units (the work breakdown structure [WBS]).

3. Determine the standards for measuring the accomplishment of each subtask (specifications).

4. Develop a time schedule and sequence for performing tasks and subtasks (Gantt charts and program evaluation review technique [PERT] charts—also known as the critical path method [CPM]).

5. Estimate costs of each task and subtask and compile the entire project's cost budget (if not determined).

6. Design the staff organization needed to fulfill tasks and subtasks, including the number and kind of people required, their duties, and any necessary training.

7. Develop policies and procedures that will be in effect during the project's life cycle.

8. Acknowledge predetermined parameters imposed by the customer or organization, such as military standards or specifications.

Then carefully detail and document each element.

■ *Staffing a Project and Project Roles*

During the planning process, you compiled the tasks and subtasks that need to be performed. An important element of planning is finding and using the correct personnel to perform these tasks. Usually, in the interests of cost, time, and availability, you can find the personnel for a project within the organization. However, project managers often have the option of hiring expertise from outside the organization; hiring a consultant, for example, may be the best way to obtain the required skills without hiring full-time employees.

■ *Managing a Project*

You can use a variety of tools to prepare schedules and track work on a project. The following are three of the most important:

- The WBS not only identifies tasks, subtasks, and units of work to be performed, but also assists in estimating and tracking costs of each of these elements. A WBS represents a graphical hierarchy of the project, deliverables, tasks, and subtasks.

- A project's timeframe is derived from the plan and the WBS. The project manager lists the WBS components, arranges them in sequence, and determines how the elements mesh to form a milestone chart. Timeframe data is mapped into a chart called a Gantt chart, which graphically displays the time relationships of the project's steps and key checkpoints or deliverable dates, known as milestones. It's a valuable tool for project managers in planning, monitoring, and controlling projects.

- PERT and CPM charts are two widely used network-diagramming techniques. Network diagrams plot a sequence of activities (predecessor and successor tasks) to illustrate the interrelationships among activities and resources. PERT and CPM are also used to calculate the project duration.

Communication

Communication is an important competency in all areas of a manager's job, from presenting plans to executives, to interacting with subordinates, to communicating change initiatives, and more. Some facets of communication that a manager must master include presenting, listening, and giving feedback.

Presenting

In business, presentations are a fact of life. They can range from brief presentations to the executive team to a series of talks that constitute a training program. In any case, giving a presentation can be pretty frightening. *Communication Basics*'s authors Judy Jenings and Linda Malcak provide four steps to presentation success:

1. Focus on the participants. Find out who will be there and why, what they need to know and how they want to hear it, what makes them feel comfortable or uncomfortable.

2. Focus on the content. Now that you know who will be there, you know what kind of information they need and want to hear and how they prefer to hear it. Especially try to find out what the audience's pain points are and how what you have to say can relieve those pain points.

3. Focus on the structure of the presentation. Now that you know whom you are talking to and what you need to say to them, it's time to prepare your roadmap for how you are going to say it. Create an agenda that shows you where you stop and start, where you move on to a new topic, and where you provide breaks (if necessary). Then practice. And practice some more.

4. Finally, follow your plan. If you have focused on the right things by following the other three steps, then you can carry off your presentation with confidence.

Listening

The ability to listen well may be one of the most underappreciated and most powerful communication skills that anyone could have. Lyman K. Steil's sensing, interpreting, evaluating, and responding (SIER) model of listening is an effective method to ensure that you take full advantage of the ability to capture the full gist of that person's message before you respond. A brief description of the model follows.

■ *Sensing*

To listen effectively, you must first receive the message accurately. That means being silent and allowing yourself to hear what the other person has to say. But hearing the words is only one component of sensing the other person's message. You've also got to pay attention to the person's body language, tone of voice, and pattern of breathing.

■ *Interpreting*

Successful sensing lays the groundwork for the interpreting stage of the Steil SIER model. This is the stage in which you interpret the speaker's meaning. Considering the variety of meaning in words and the different ways that people use body language, this may be the most difficult stage of listening. To help you interpret correctly, rephrase what the speaker has said or ask for further clarification.

■ *Evaluating*

Only after you have fully sensed and interpreted the message are you in the position to evaluate it. This involves understanding your own reaction to the message: Did you like it? Dislike it? Think it was poorly argued? Think it was complete or incomplete?

■ *Responding*

The final stage of the model is responding. However, people often skip ahead to this point without taking the time and the focus to gather important information from the message along the way.

Giving Feedback

Feedback is a learned skill. Mastering its use can help you

- learn continually
- strengthen your communication skills
- develop more effective relationships
- improve your decision-making capabilities
- take advantage of opportunities for growth.

In your role as a manager, feedback is important in coaching, delegating, and managing performance. The sidebar *Giving Feedback* at right describes an effective feedback process.

Personal Effectiveness

Personal effectiveness is what enables you to stay organized, use your time effectively, and stay on top of your work.

■ *Time Management*
One way to get control of how you use your time is to keep a log of what you do for several days by writing down each task change that you make. Then review the log and determine if there are any obvious time wasters and work to eliminate them.

In "A Get-Real Guide to Time Management," Donna J. Abernathy cites research into time thieves that include telephone calls, drop-in visitors, lack of necessary resources, personal disorganization, indecisiveness, an inability to say no, procrastination, paperwork, and management by crisis. Once you have identified your biggest time wasters, determine ways to eliminate or minimize their effect. For example, if phone calls are your greatest time thief, set aside a portion of the day during which you send all calls into voicemail.

■ *Planning*
Closely related to time management skills are planning and prioritizing skills. To get the most of your time, practice focusing on the things that really make a difference at work. Abernathy describes the following categories to help you sort your work:

- A priorities: If you had nothing to do today, what should you work on that would improve your productivity in one to four weeks? What items on your to-do list are most closely related to organizational goals and strategies?

- B priorities: What things must be done today? Can you delegate any of them?

- C priorities: What things should be done today or tomorrow? Can you delegate any of them?

- D priorities: What things should you not do at all? (This may be the time to delegate, or you may want to let go of the item altogether.)

Giving Feedback

To be effective, feedback must be expressed in a manner that helps the receiver hear the message while keeping the relationship intact. To accomplish these goals, you must do the following:

■ *Show consideration*
One of the objectives of feedback is to help someone, not hurt someone. For that reason, you need to give feedback with care. To show consideration while giving feedback

- monitor your behavior
- practice active listening
- express concern and caring.

■ *Withhold judgment*
To reduce the receiver's resistance to feedback, make sure that you withhold judgment. Don't evaluate the behavior, don't assume its intent, but do describe specific behavior and its effects or consequences.

■ *Deliver at an appropriate time*
Most feedback literature states that you should give your message immediately after the behavior takes place or the next time there is a potential for recurrence. Generally speaking, this is the right approach to take. However, there are occasions when waiting is appropriate. One example is when either you or the receiver may lose emotional control. Another example is when the physical setting is inappropriate.

■ *Provide freedom to change or not*
It is important to acknowledge that the receiver is free to change or not. That decision belongs solely to him or her. However, make the effects of the behavior clear, because these effects may not be what the receiver intended. In addition, make clear what the consequences of continuing the behavior will be, whether positive or negative.

■ *Check for readiness*
Ideally, you should give feedback only when the receiver is mentally, emotionally, and physically ready to receive it. Feedback tends to work best when the receiver is open to it. However, circumstances aren't always ideal, and you may need to give feedback even when the receiver doesn't want to hear it. In those cases, double check your motivation: Do you want to give feedback, or are you just angry and want to sound off?

■ *Check for clarity*
Finally, check with the receiver to make sure that the message he or she received is the one that you intended to send.

Adapted from Holly DeForest, Pamela Largent, and Mary Steinberg's "Mastering the Art of Feedback," Infoline No. 250308.

■ *Organization Skills*

According to David Allen in *Getting Things Done,* "[h]aving a total and seamless system of organization in place gives you tremendous power because it allows your mind to let go of lower-level thinking and graduate to intuitive focusing, undistracted by matters that haven't been dealt with appropriately." One way to free up your mind for higher-level thinking is to empty your in-box regularly and use an efficient process.

Allen describes a simple process to empty your in-box regularly (and it applies to email also):

● Pick up or open the first item first. Don't look at any other items.

● Decide if you have to do anything with the item (whether now or later). If not, determine if you want to throw it out or file it for reference and do so immediately.

● If you do have to do something, determine exactly what that is, including any substeps. The action you decide on should be the next possible thing that you can do. For example, if you have received a tax form, and you realize that you need to file your taxes but you haven't received your W-2s, your next step may be to call your human resources department to get a copy.

● Then, determine how to do it. If it's an action that will take less than two minutes, do it immediately. If it will take longer than that, decide whether to delegate the task or do it yourself. If you need to do it, put a reminder into your schedule and file the paperwork. Never put anything back into your in-box.

■ *Problem Solving and Decision Making*

Solving problems and making decisions make up much of the day-to-day work of managers. Here is a six-step method for doing this that enables you to consider multiple options:

1. Define the problem. Simply stated, a problem is a discrepancy between what is and what should be. State the problem in the form of a question; for example, "How can we reduce the number of errors on the production line?"

2. Analyze the problem.

3. Establish a checklist of criteria use in evaluating potential solutions.

4. List all possible alternatives (it can be helpful to get input from employees who are also involved in the problem).

5. Select the alternative that aligns best with the checklist of criteria and determine how to implement the solution.

6. Implement the solution. Monitor and evaluate the solution to ensure that it solves the problem.

■ *Influencing*

Basically, influence is communicating with the purpose of gaining support for your ideas. To exert influence over others, there are two habits you must develop. First, seek to understand what the other person wants (his or her priorities) and how he or she operates.

Second, examine how your own priorities may blind you to options. Although it is difficult to be objective, doing so liberates you to be more effective with others by enabling you to base discussions on organizational priorities.

When you can listen to others and understand what they want and what you should avoid, you will be able to predict more accurately their priorities and influence their decision making.

Move Forward

This *Infoline* provided a self-assessment to help you identify areas where you could use some improvement as a manager and brief overviews of some management competencies. This is only a beginning. As a manager, you must learn to embrace continual self-development. Start by identifying a competency or a skill to work on, practice the steps provided in this *Infoline* related to that skill, and look to the references and resources for more information. This is just your first step toward becoming a better and more efficient manager.

References & Resources

Articles

Abernathy, Donna J. "A Get-Real Guide to Time Management." *Training & Development*, June 1999, pp. 22-25.

Buckingham, Marcus. "What Great Managers Do." *Harvard Business Review*, March 2005, pp. 70-79.

Gosling, Jonathan, and Henry Mintzberg. "The Five Minds of a Manager." *Harvard Business Review*, November 2003, pp. 54-63.

Haneberg, Lisa. "Reinventing Middle Management." *Leader to Leader*, Fall 2005, pp. 13-18.

Hogan, Robert T., and Jorge E. Fernandez. "Syndromes of Mismanagement." *Quality and Participation*, Fall 2002, pp. 28-31.

Kaye, Beverly L., and Sharon Jordan-Evans. "The ABCs of Management Gift-Giving." *Training & Development*, December 2000, pp. 51-52.

Liccione, William J. "Balanced Management: A Key Component of Managerial Effectiveness." *Performance Improvement*, February 2005, pp. 32-38.

Lippitt, Mary. "How to Influence Leaders." *Training & Development*, March 1999, pp. 18-22.

McCrimmon, Mitch. "How Not to Waste Money on Leadership Development." *OD/Leadership News*, March 2006. Available at http://www.astd.org/astd/publications/newsletters/od_leadership_news.

McLagan, Patricia. "Management by Intent." *Leader to Leader*, Fall 2004, pp. 12-15.

Mittler, James E. "It's Management Quality That Matters—Not Style." *Quality and Participation*, Fall 2002, pp. 19-21.

Raudsepp, Eugene. "How to Delegate Effectively." *Machine Design*, April 20, 1995, p. 11.

Tulgan, Bruce. "The Under-Management Epidemic." *HRMagazine*, October 2004, pp. 119-122.

Books

Allen, David. *Getting Things Done: The Art of Stress-Free Productivity.* New York: Penguin Group.

ASTD (American Society for Training & Development). *ASTD Learning System.* Alexandria, VA: ASTD Press, 2006.

Blanchard, Ken, and Steve Gottry. *The On-Time, On-Target Manager.* New York: HarperCollins, 2004.

Blanchard, Kenneth, Patricia Zigarmi, and Drea Zigarmi. *Leadership and the One-Minute Manager.* New York: William Morrow, 1985.

Flaherty, Jane S., and Peter B. Stark. *The Competent Leader: A Powerful and Practical Tool Kit for Managers and Supervisors.* Amherst, MA: HRD Press, 1999.

Haneberg, Lisa. *High Impact Middle Management.* Avon, MA: Adams Media, 2005.

———. *Coaching Basics.* Alexandria, VA: ASTD Press, 2006.

Handy, Charles. *21 Ideas for Managers.* San Francisco: Jossey-Bass, 2000.

Jenings, Judy, and Linda Malcak. *Communication Basics.* Alexandria, VA: ASTD Press, 2004.

Radde, Paul O. *Supervising: A Guide for All Levels.* Austin, TX: Learning Concepts, 1981.

Russell, Jeffrey, and Linda Russell. *Strategic Planning Training.* Alexandria, VA: ASTD Press, 2005.

Steil, Lyman K., and Richard K. Bommelje. *Listening Leaders™: The Ten Golden Rules to Listen, Lead & Succeed.* Edina, MN: Beaver's Pond Press, 2004.

Infolines

Battell, Chris. "Effective Listening." No. 250605.

Darraugh, Barbara. "Coaching and Feedback." No. 259006 (revised 1997).

DeForest, Holly, Pamela Largent, and Mary Steinberg. "Mastering the Art of Feedback." No. 250308.

Estep, Tora. "Meetings That Work!" No. 250505.

Gaines, Kathryn. "Leading Work Teams." No. 250602 (revised 1998).

Gilley, Jerry W. "Strategic Planning for Human Resource Development." No. 259206.

Grosse, Eric F. "Interview Skills for Managers." No. 250206.

Hickman, E. Stewart. "Hiring and Retaining Top-Performing Employees." No. 250011.

Lauby, Sharlyn J. "Motivating Employees." No. 250510.

Verardo, Denzil. "Managing the Strategic Planning Process." No. 259710.

Wircenski, Jerry L., and Richard L. Sullivan. "Make Every Presentation a Winner." No. 258606 (revised 1998).

Younger, Sandra Millers. "How to Delegate." No. 259011 (revised 1997).

Job Aid

Better Manager IDP

To prepare your IDP, determine where you require additional development using the Management Competencies Self-Assessment. Write the competencies down in the following table. Then rank them. Give the one that is costliest to you and/or your organization the number 1, the next costliest the number 2, and so forth.

Competency Area	Description of Costs (Personal and/or Organizational)	Rank Order
Business Management		
People Management		
Process Management		
Communication		
Personal Effectiveness		

Next, create a table with the following headings to prepare your IDP (you can use a word processing program, a spreadsheet program, or simply write by hand—whatever format is most comfortable for you). Leave plenty of space to write your goals. In the first column, write the name of the management competency. In the second column, identify activities to help you improve your skills in the competency area. Make sure that these follow the SMART goal format: they should be **s**pecific, **m**easurable, **a**ttainable, **r**ealistic, and **t**ime bound. Use the third column to keep track of progress on your goals. In the fourth column, list some ways to apply your new knowledge or some new habits to form that will improve your skills in this competency. The first rows have been filled in with an example to help you get started. Aim to make some progress every day, even if it is something minor like purchasing a book on a relevant topic.

Competency Area	Goals (Are they SMART?)	Progress	Ideas for Application
Process Management	Complete change management training offered through the organization's training department by 5/12.	Change management course completed 5/12	Prepare communication strategy to help people transition to the new paradigm.
	Read *Infoline* on meeting management by 6/18.	In progress	Prepare an agenda for every meeting.
	Complete project management training offered by training department by 8/15.	Submitted training request to training department	

The material appearing on this page is not covered by copyright and may be reproduced at will.

Leadership Development

Issue 0508

Leadership Development

AUTHOR
Lou Russell
Russell Martin & Associates
6326 Rucker Road, Suite E
Indianapolis, IN 46220
Tel: 317.475.9311
Email: info@russellmartin.com

Lou Russell is president and CEO of Russell Martin & Associates. She is the author of *The Accelerated Learning Fieldbook, Project Management for Trainers, IT Leadership Alchemy,* and *Leadership Training*. A popular speaker, Russell addresses national and international conferences such as the Project Management Institute, Project World, and LotuSphere. She holds a computer science degree from Purdue University—where she taught database and programming classes— and a master's degree in instructional technology from Indiana University.

Associate Editor
Tora Estep
testep@astd.org

Copy Editor
Ann Bruen

Production Design
Kathleen Schaner

Manager, Acquisitions and Development, ASTD Press
Mark Morrow

Learning Leadership

A vast number of leadership books occupies shelves in stores, so a need clearly exists. But what's driving that need? Here are just a few realities facing organizations today:

- The complexity of work has increased due to rising time and cost constraints, ever-changing technological options, and a highly competitive business climate.

- Leaders are juggling multiple projects, while acting as leader, developer, and implementer.

- Situations are demanding more resources, but organizations are shrinking to cut costs.

- Many employees cannot prove their people investments provide a positive return.

- Many people, rewarded for being gifted, find themselves in management positions without any training or resources. Nor have many been exposed to good leadership examples.

- Workers are stressed and tired. Extended work hours and virtual home offices have become the status quo.

To manage these situations and more, organizations need leaders who believe that the most important thing is growing the people they lead and who maintain focus on those people. Successful leadership involves managing yourself and your relationships to move toward a specific goal. This *Infoline* will show you the most effective ways to lead while allowing the people you lead to master their own skills and continue to grow.

The sidebar *10 Competencies for Effective Leadership* enables you to assess yourself against a list of competencies organized into three categories: knowing yourself, working with others, and integrating it all. You must grow leadership competencies in this order. You can't work with others until you know yourself. You can't integrate the right person with the right job at the right time unless you work well with others. More information about each competency follows.

Knowing Yourself

The first category of knowledge that a leader must have is self-knowledge. Read on to learn about the competencies of self-awareness and resiliency.

1. Self-Awareness

Leadership grows from what already exists within you. As you look inward, you slowly accumulate "material" that develops into self-awareness and provides the base from which you'll create and grow the leader within you. Leaders are branded by the stories and legends others tell of their leadership style. Authentic leaders ensure that their leadership legend is close to their true character.

How do you get inside yourself and explore whether the right stuff is there and can be expressed through your actions? It requires the commitment to venture into the uncharted territory of self and create a map that will guide you toward authentic leadership. To create this map, reflect on your:

- values, purpose, and vision
- strengths and weaknesses
- behaviors as they reflect your values
- sense of accountability for your actions
- desire to learn.

2. Resiliency

You live in a world of change, experiencing frightening conditions nearly every day. Some examples:

After a great lunch, you've gained the trust of a client. Returning to your desk, you find an email from a colleague to this client, blasting him for something you know was a miscommunication. There goes that relationship!

One of your project managers confessed that his project is running six months behind. He's afraid to challenge the added customer requirements. He's hoping you will inform the customer.

10 Competencies for Effective Leadership

Consider the following list of competencies. For each phrase under the competency, assess your competency as high, medium, or low. Then, give yourself an overall assessment score for the competency. Although you will want to work on all the competencies, pay special attention to those competencies that you scored lowest on.

Knowing Yourself

This category is all about knowing yourself, especially your strengths and weaknesses.

1. Self-awareness.

The following activities are involved in developing your self-awareness:

- develop clarity of personal values, purpose, and vision
- develop a personal branding strategy
- demonstrate authenticity by acting according to values
- take accountability for personal and leadership actions
- know and trust your intuition
- learn to learn.

2. Resiliency.

To increase your resiliency, learn to

- jump in and get things started
- seek opportunities for improvement and development
- build off of others' ideas for the benefit of the decision
- maintain an appropriate, empowered attitude
- persist in managing and overcoming adversity
- act proactively in seeking new opportunities
- prioritize items by effectively using time management.

Working With Others

This category involves many of the abilities identified as the biggest problems in corporate assessment programs.

3. Interpersonal skills.

Interpersonal skills are critical for working effectively with others. To develop these skills, learn to

- understand, appreciate diverse perspectives and styles
- participate and contribute fully as a team member
- demonstrate empathy and understanding
- build trust and demonstrate trustworthiness.

4. Communication skills.

Another key skill for leaders is the ability to communicate well. Some practices for improving those skills are to

- adapt to your audience to help others learn
- express intention concisely in written communications
- collaborate and clearly articulate intention verbally
- listen for understanding
- manage flow of communication or information.

5. Employee development.

A leader is only as good as his or her people. To develop your employees, you need to

- motivate employees to high performance
- coach for development and improved performance
- appreciate and respect diverse values and needs
- delegate tasks that allow employee development
- select appropriate staff to fulfill specific project needs.

Successfully navigating changing terrain demands a certain mindset. Those who thrive have a capacity for dealing with challenges. Their capacity stems from a blending of perspective and skill.

Resiliency is all in your head—literally. Think of it as a puzzle for which you hold all of the pieces. The behaviors you characterize as resiliency stem

from the way you view the world. Resiliency is about more than recovering from setbacks—it is also about discovering the hidden opportunities.

Resiliency skills—attitude, vision, creativity, crisis decision making, and proactive behavior—blend together to form a critical leadership competency. Reflect on your abilities in each of these areas,

6. Vision creation and actualization.

A strong vision enables a leader to stay on course. To develop and actualize a vision, learn to

- create a clear, inspiring vision of the desired outcome
- align the vision with broader organizational strategies
- translate the vision into manageable action steps
- influence and evangelize
- use individual motivators and decision-making styles
- facilitate win-win solutions.

Integrating It All

Integration is the most advanced form of leadership. It's the ability to match the right person and skill set with the right job opportunity at the right time.

7. Customer orientation.

Customer orientation enables organizations to successfully match their output with customer needs. To develop a customer orientation, learn to

- understand and use customer needs and expectations
- gather customer requirements and input
- partner with customers
- set and monitor performance standards.

8. Strategic business acumen.

Strategic business acumen is critical to the success of any professional leader. To enhance your acumen, you need to

- demonstrate the ability to ethically build support
- think of the effects of actions and decisions
- operate with an awareness of marketplace competition.

9. Project leadership.

Skillful project leadership keeps projects and organizations on track. To develop your project leadership skills, learn to

- build cohesive, high-performing teams with purpose
- set, communicate, and monitor objectives
- gain and maintain buy-in from sponsors, customers
- prioritize and allocate resources
- manage multiple, potentially conflicting priorities
- maintain effective, interactive, and productive teams
- manage budget and project progress
- manage risk versus reward and ROI equations
- balance standards with need for exceptions in decision making
- align decisions with needs of business and values
- align decisions with customer and business pace.

10. Change management.

Change is endemic in the business environment. To succeed, organizations must change continually. Managing change well is an important key to leadership. Learn to

- identify and implement appropriate change initiatives
- understand cost/benefit and ROI of change initiatives
- manage transition with employees
- demonstrate and build resilience in the face of change.

maximize those in which you're strong and seek enhancement for the less-developed abilities. Each element is beneficial individually, but when bonded together, they are truly powerful.

Think of a change that surprised you. Then think about how you approached it. The following tips can help you improve your resiliency in any setting.

■ *Remember to Pack Your Attitude*
The power of attitude is evident when you consider your past experiences. At times, you were convinced you couldn't get the job done, and the end result reflected your diminished approach. You may also have experienced times when you approached a difficult task positively, and, once again, the results were evident.

Considering the world's complexity and your struggle for accomplishment, it may be disheartening to realize that you actually control very little. All you can truly master is yourself—your thoughts, feelings, and viewpoint of the world and its challenges.

When you react to adversity, you are reacting to your feelings about that event, rather than the event itself. And while you may not be able to control what happens, you do have some control over your emotions.

The key lies in the interpretation of the issue that is obstructing your path to success. Choosing to see such issues as *challenges* triggers a different response than seeing them as *problems*. Problems weigh you down and cause stress. Challenges energize you, because a challenge can be a test of your abilities—one for which you crave a victory.

■ *Don't Look Where You Don't Want to Go*
Creating and holding a clear vision of your hopeful outcome in a challenging situation is key to personal resiliency. When trying to avoid disaster, remaining focused on the disaster is a surefire way to become embroiled in it. Focus instead on where you *do* want to go. An inspiring vision elicits strong connection and commitment from believers. In uncertain times, vision provides a hopeful direction, positive sense, and dedication to persevere through the challenges.

■ *Flex With the Flow*
While attitude helps to continue striving, and vision provides a sense of direction and hope, your ability to flex your problem-solving muscles is one of your most powerful navigational tools.

Creative thinking is a process that involves thinking differently. The creative process begins with a question, and the trick to seeing different possibilities is to ask the right question. The questions you ask often limit your thinking. Consider the team of engineers with the problem of a truck lodged in an underpass. True to their profession, they began taking measurements and figuring extensive calculations. They debated about how to best apply the exact amount of force at the correct angle to free the truck. A small boy turned to one of the engineers and asked, "Why don't you just let the air out of the tires?"

■ *Learn to Manage the Mess*
As you think about resiliency in response to adversity, ask yourself:

● "How do I choose the most appropriate action?"
● "How do I establish clear priorities in chaos?"

In a high-pressure, chaotic situation requiring quick decision making, where does "What do I do?" mentally place you? It plants you right in the middle of the chaos. Being mentally in the middle means that it's all swirling around you, making it easy to be influenced by the emotion of it all—and that's exactly where you don't want to be, at least until you have clarified your priority actions.

Recent studies on decision-making processes among emergency personnel suggest a different approach to choosing priority actions. Instead of "What do I do?" they ask, "What's going on?" This shift of focus from self to scene makes a tremendous difference on the responder's mental capacity for clear, prioritized decision making. Being on the outside of the scene allows you to assess the situation, stay connected to top-level priorities, and choose the most appropriate course of action.

■ *Eddy Out*
The attention of performers in an organization is usually divided among three modes: operational, strategic, and reflective. Most of you spend your time in operational mode, which is where you do what needs to be done. Strategic mode is where you divert attention to looking ahead. You spend time planning, playing out possible operational scenarios, anticipating problems, being proactive in creating potential solutions, practicing continuous learning, and building your team's organizational communities. Many of you ignore strategic mode until the neglect creates an operational issue. Reflective mode involves looking back and considering the lessons you've learned. Reflective mode typically gets little time and attention, though it holds tremendous value.

Eddying out is about creating space for strategy and reflection and recognizing the value of each. Certainly you need to focus your energies on operational mode, which serves your customers and organizations. Yet you know that failure to plan and learn dooms you to repeat the same mistakes.

Working With Others

After you have mastered the skills, knowledge, and attitudes of knowing yourself, you are prepared to move on to working with others. The skills involved in this category are interpersonal skills, communication skills, employee development, and vision creation and actualization.

3. Interpersonal Skills

You are defined by your connections with others. You are leaders, friends, colleagues, strangers, or even hermits due to your relationships. Leadership is relationship. Leadership is influence; it is directing the energies of others and supporting their growth toward personal and organizational goals.

Interpersonal relationships are the vehicles through which you inspire performance toward your organizations' goals. While there are other ways to induce performance—like coercion, intimidation, and manipulation—they carry costs.

Healthy relationships have certain ingredients:

- a foundation of trust

- a sense of caring or concern for each other's well-being and success

- some common values and shared goals

- respect and acceptance of others, even during disagreement

- the ability to manage conflicts (see the sidebar *Managing Conflict* at right for tips).

Trust is the foundation upon which interpersonal relationships are built and is essential for forming and maintaining effective relationships. Trust is based upon your opinion about a person and may be shaped by several factors:

- credibility—the degree of skill, knowledge, and experience you believe the individual has

- consistency—the degree to which you believe you can anticipate the individual's performance based upon past experiences

---

Managing Conflict

The emotion surrounding conflict blinds you from alternative interpretations. Openness about the root issues of conflict is needed to overcome what can otherwise undermine relationships. Communication is the key to managing conflict, and most conflicts result from insufficient or ineffective communication.

If carried out effectively, all parties can move beyond the conflict using trust, respect, and open communication to strengthen the relationship. The following are some tips that can help you to manage conflict:

- Focus on the facts of the situation; be wary of acting on assumptions or behavioral observations that are open to interpretation.

- Use *I* statements instead of *you* statements, which tend to put people on the defensive.

- Seek to understand the other person's position before expressing your own. By demonstrating your willingness to listen, you encourage them to listen to you.

- Frame the conflict as a mutual challenge and express your willingness to explore creative win-win solutions.

- communication—the degree to which ongoing information provides the reassurance you need to accept that your trust is deserved.

Lack of trust can undermine interactions, making those relationships little more than transactions. Everyone believes he or she is trustworthy, but if that were true, trust would be a non-issue.

However, trust is an issue that often undermines effective leadership. It is a fragile dynamic that exists between individuals and entities. Difficult to establish, easily shaken, and extraordinarily hard to repair once violated, it requires care. As leaders seeking to leverage your employee and customer relationships to maximize performance and create new opportunities, you need to nurture trust.

4. Communication Skills

Interpersonal communication needs to be an intentional act. Think about how unintentional communication creates trouble. You communicate to accomplish a specific purpose, and that purpose must be clear for communication to be effective.

Think of intention as the heart of the interaction. Ask what you intend to achieve through the exchange. As communication occurs, there may be multiple intentions at play. The sidebar *Communicating Effectively* describes the five basic intentions of communication.

■ *Content and Feeling*

Every message you send, whether verbal or written, has two components: the content and the feeling. Content is the "what," the core or intention of the message you're sending. Feeling is the "how," referring to the way the message is packaged. The packaging of the message affects the interpretation of its content. For example, consider the question: Why did you do it that way?

Read the question as if you were asking it with curiosity. Now read it aloud again as if you were asking someone who has taken a stupid approach to a simple task. Notice the difference? It's the same content packaged in a different context.

The words you choose have the smallest influence upon the message. Tone of voice influences the message significantly more. And, depending on the context of the exchange, body language, such as facial expression and body posture, weighs in as the greatest influence.

■ *Communications Media*

You can send messages through a variety of communication media or channels, including face-to-face, written, and telephone. Any of these methods of communication can range from formal to informal. The context and the audience determine the level of formality you should adopt.

Written communication also has degrees of formality. Email tends to be the current preferred communication channel. However, the convenience of email as a written form of communication makes it dangerous. Many people are careless with email communications, overlooking the intentions of their messages and sending thoughts that can be misinterpreted. Unless carefully crafted, email lacks a clear feeling, so the reader must apply her own tone of voice interpretation to the words. Problems occur when the receiver's tone doesn't match the sender's.

■ *Interference*

Interference takes many forms and can originate from the sender, the receiver, or within the environment of the exchange. Sources include:

● assumptions—beliefs you hold about others or those held about you

● time pressures—taking the time to express your message clearly and correctly and allowing the receiver the time to receive and process the message

● mental models—the unconscious interpretations held about the situation under discussion; your mental map of the situation

Communicating Effectively

There are five basic intentions underlying most communication interactions:

1. Informing—to share information or insight.

2. Persuading—to influence a perspective on an issue.

3. Understanding—to create common understanding of an issue or perspective.

4. Deciding—to apply a combination of informing, persuading, and understanding to facilitate a choice between options.

5. Inspiring action—to apply a combination of informing, persuading, and understanding to drive desired action.

Think of a difficult conversation that you have been avoiding. What type of communication do you need to initiate? Using the list above, how can you focus your communication?

- differences of style—misalignment between the communication needs of the receiver and the approach of the sender

- noise and distraction—environmental and psychological factors that distract and inhibit the message from accurate delivery or reception.

■ Ability to Listen

As a leader, you have an additional responsibility for clear, intentional communication. Leadership communication relies upon a style that's the fundamental opposite of the bullhorn approach. It's grounded in the leader's ability to listen.

Quality listening begins with the receiver recognizing intention around the interaction—why the message carries significance—and connecting with the intention of the sender.

The first rule of listening is *Stop Talking*. This is not as obvious as it seems. Even though your mouth may be shut, you may continue to talk to yourself inside your head and merely go through the motions of listening. How do you know when you're being listened to? Effective listeners

- provide eye contact

- maintain an interested and open body posture

- encourage the speaker with both verbal and nonverbal support

- use "door opening" questions to reveal a safe environment and sincere interest

- ask genuine questions to gain deeper understanding of the message sender's perspective

- reflect back their understanding through summary and empathy.

5. Employee Development

The challenge of a leader as a coach is to uncover what the starting place is for each person and then move each from *where he is* to *where he can go*. The coaching you do with your staff should focus on present challenges and future opportunities.

Avoid bringing up problems from the past that were not addressed. Focus on the present—or at least the very recent past—and future.

As a leader of the person being coached, you care about behavioral goals and are not neutral about the behavior you expect from your staff. You can help an employee set appropriate goals, but if she makes choices that are not consistent with corporate strategy, you're responsible for encouraging her to rethink her behavior. If she fails to reach behavioral alignment, you must take action.

Creating goals takes practice. Coach people to think of goals as fluid. Though some goals may stay quite stable, others may become inappropriate. This is completely normal and necessary and does not indicate faulty planning. The ability to build new goals quickly is a characteristic of resiliency. Goals are an essential aspect of coaching because they allow you to

- determine the right first step
- measure progress to encourage momentum
- identify when a goal is met
- know when a goal has changed or is irrelevant.

Coaching is like a mirror, and it's generally wise to reflect back what you think the employee has said. Encourage exploration through active listening with carefully designed, probing questions. If asked what you think about something, always turn the discussion back to the person: "I'm not sure. What do you think?" If you're talking more than 30 seconds, you're no longer coaching; you're telling. The language you use as a coach communicates your true feeling about the person. Remember to serve as a mirror using these guidelines:

- Avoid directing the discussion. Symptom: "No, that's the wrong goal."

- Avoid analysis and interpretation. Symptom: "Yes, I know which part bothers you the most!"

- Describe the future in the present. Symptom: "What will your relationship be like?"

- Push to the end result. Symptom: "Is promotion what you want in the end?"

If you're also the supervisor of the person you're coaching, you'll have to give and receive feedback in ways that maintain the integrity of the relationship, but fully address the issues. Think of feedback as navigational information designed to help people navigate performance situations. Believing that feedback is bad news prevents it from being useful, but letting someone know about behavior that interferes with productivity is imperative for improvement. Think of giving feedback as something you do to help.

Many people often find it difficult to give others positive feedback. Make a habit of catching people being good, because as much learning occurs by reinforcing good behavior as it does from constructive feedback.

Feedback should be given as soon after the occurrence as possible. Keep the focus on how you perceive the situation, using *I* instead of *you*, which keeps the conversation from coming across as judgmental. Seek to understand. Your interpretation of the situation may not be complete, so allow the person the opportunity to share his side of the story before you share your own.

Coaching effectiveness can be measured by looking at the 4Ss:

1. Speak the truth.

Coaches must speak the truth to the best of their knowledge. Opinions are not effective.

2. Suspend judgment.

It's almost impossible to avoid interpretation, and two people can interpret the same conversation differently. "Did you get the report done?" spoken out of concern for the other's stress level, can be interpreted as "What is taking you so long?" Always look for multiple interpretations. Teach the person you're coaching how to notice his own interpretations by modeling this behavior.

3. Stick to facts.

Restrict the discussion to facts, and avoid sharing feelings or hearsay. Although you will discuss facts and feelings of the person being coached, you must suspend judgment to listen effectively.

4. Self-respect.

A coach needs self-respect to have the strength to suspend judgments and feelings. Coaching is about her, not you, and successful focus on the person being coached requires you to be secure.

As you coach your staff, finding your own coach may be helpful. Working with a coach not only allows you to learn more about coaching, but also helps you model the type of growth you'd like to see in your staff.

6. Vision Creation and Actualization

Value, purpose, and vision are the essential building blocks of your character and the source of your being. Authentic leadership grows from a clear sense of these elements and carefully aligning your actions with what they represent.

Your values provide the support for your purpose and vision. An example of how values can affect your work is presented in the sidebar *Working With Values* at right. Purpose answers *why* (Why am I a leader? What is the purpose behind my energies and focus?), while vision focuses on *how* (How do I focus my energies in ways that fulfill my purpose?). With a clear purpose, you can define the path you'll follow. Your actions must align with your values—you must "walk your talk."

Purpose may be grand and nearly untouchable, but vision should be more concrete with solid, attainable steps. It makes you define how you'll choose to use your role to fulfill your purpose. Outlining vision in limited timeframes helps you keep it real. However, given the rapidly changing world, your vision must be dynamic and flexible.

Integrating It All

Integration represents the most advanced level of leadership and comes only after you have mastered knowing yourself and working with others. The competencies in this category include:

- customer orientation
- strategic business acumen
- project leadership
- change management.

7. Customer Orientation

Customer service is not a new field; in fact, companies spend a great deal of money on customer service workshops. Still, many professionals do not see customer service as their job. They don't think they have problems with their customer service (although they can clearly explain how others do). They cannot relate to most customer service training materials, which are typically written for call centers or geared to external customers.

Customer orientation is imperative because the ability of an organization to adapt to a customer-centric philosophy will determine its ability to help the overall business compete. Honoring the customer is also the best defense against the threat of outsourcing. Take valuable staff with less natural communication competency and partner them with people who have more customer orientation.

Leaders must deal with the whole problem of customer orientation, not just the easy fixes. The first step is to get the team to challenge their flawed beliefs through workshops or facilitation. The sidebar *Meeting the Customer* describes how to challenge some historical assumptions about customer service.

While workshops or facilitation create awareness, incentives must also be changed. The compensation of all employees should be tied to customer survey results, and feedback should include key customers. Leaders must be the first to attend the workshops, include customer feedback in their performance reviews, and be held financially accountable for the survey results. When organizations fail to create customer orientation in their ranks, it's usually because they have chosen to exclude the leadership from the efforts, signaling to the staff that the initiative is a facade.

Working With Values

Suppose that one of your values has to do with learning. Behind this value is the belief that all people have potential for growth and, therefore, potential for adding value to the organization. You identified your purpose as supporting that growth and nurturing the contribution of your people. As a vision for fulfilling this purpose, you might choose to implement some of these steps:

- Get to know each team member individually to better identify his professional interests, strengths, and aspirations.

- Facilitate a process for development planning and encourage team members to identify development needs and grow professional skills.

- Sponsor training sessions to help team members enhance their skills.

- Provide regular, consistent performance reviews, while improving your own coaching and feedback skills.

- Create a safe environment in which team members can stretch their abilities (and fail occasionally) as a means of professional growth.

- Model growth and a learning attitude.

Customers judge their relationships with providers through their interpretation of critical moments of truth—small contacts like emails or voicemails. Most of you don't think about these moments nor invest a lot of time in doing them well. Different communication styles and needs can drive this type of disconnect. Consider auditing the critical moments of truth, and ask the following questions:

- Do you have a set of guidelines for proper email use and voicemail responses?

- Have you checked the voicemail of your direct reports to see how a customer would feel leaving a message?

- Have you called your own?

- Do your staff members make eye contact?

Meeting the Customer

Anyone who thinks her job is to deliver a specific product, like a software package, behaves differently toward the customer than does a person who believes that her job is to help customers do their job more effectively. Before customer orientation can be improved, some deeply held, historical assumptions must be challenged. Your staff must be clear who their customer is and what their business need is.

Answer these questions each time you begin a relationship:

- What is your product?
- Who is your customer?
- What value do you provide to your customer?
- What competition do you have?

- Do they speak to the business people?

- Do they ever invite them to lunch?

- How can you get your people closer to their customers?

Consider the following checklist for leaders and staff for creating a customer partnership:

- ☐ Model good customer orientation behavior.

- ☐ Do not accept anything less from your team.

- ☐ When there is a problem, spend more time, not less, communicating with the customer.

- ☐ Use jargon minimally or not at all.

- ☐ Adapt your style to each unique customer when communicating.

- ☐ Listen actively.

- ☐ Ask lots of questions and help the customer explain his need.

- ☐ Do not jump to a solution in the middle of the customer's sentence. Delay new judgment, interpretation, and technology conclusions.

- ☐ Understand the customer's world and context.

- ☐ Clarify the customer's expectations whenever decisions are made.

- ☐ Set mutual milestones and measurements.

- ☐ Say no when you need to.

- ☐ Don't use *but*; substitute *and*. Example: "...but that solution isn't stable" becomes "...and because that solution may not be stable enough...."

- ☐ Use *I*, not *you*. Example: "*I need help understanding that*" versus "*You need to tell me more about that.*"

- ☐ Customize delivery of the communication and the frequency to the needs of each customer.

8. Strategic Business Acumen

The work done by teams is important only when it helps the larger organization. A leader can only contribute when he understands the business. Business acumen demands the ability to

- build and sell a vision
- plan strategically
- grow and nurture a network of advocates
- decode complex business problems.

The most productive approach is to manage the scope of the information you need by filtering it through your organization's vision. This defines the criteria for the type of business and technology knowledge you need to acquire and to what degree. It should drive your hiring and staff development activities. It helps you develop a strategy to find the resources you need.

Living the vision requires an understanding of the value proposition. Who is the customer? What price (time, money, and other resources) is the customer willing to pay? Learning about the business through networking (and politics) requires a mindset change for most leaders. Building strategic business acumen is real, credible work. It is not brown nosing, selling out, or wasting time.

Plan to devote time to building a set of future states (scenarios) with your team. By telling the story of these future states, teams begin to see how the day-to-day actions can cause any one of the scenarios to happen. The benefits of scenario planning include the following:

- As project teams discuss future states, they create a shared vision.

- Planning forces teams to consider what they hope will never happen.

- Each individual on a project team influences the future of the project with his beliefs and assumptions. Discussing future states unveils inconsistent mental models within the team.

- Forcing teams to face the possibility of trouble in the beginning makes it more likely they will plan for it and recognize it early should it occur. Brainstorming glitches before the project influences the way teams build their project estimates. Instead of estimating best-case completion, they estimate more realistically.

- Project glitches trigger emotions, sending project members into fight-or-flight mode. Physiologically, the blood flow to the brain is rerouted to the heart and appendages so people don't think well. Many bad project decisions have been made because of emotional reactions. By working through some of the emotion in the scenario planning sessions, individuals are more likely to respond rationally when surprises occur. They've had some time to think about it, accelerating their reaction to the problems and saving valuable time.

After possible futures are considered, the team can choose a strategy that steers toward the desirable scenario. They may initiate activities to guard against the negative scenarios. Where that's not possible, the best strategy is to create high-level contingency actions. Normally, this type of session occurs when an organization needs to review its beliefs and examine where it wants to be. It is great for team building and clarifying vision.

Note the importance of maintaining flexibility. Effective leaders have flexible plans—and today's business world demands both flexibility and a plan.

Effective leaders do not tie their egos to the plan; they know that the plan is temporary and are prepared to abandon the current plan and adopt a new one when needed. To novices, this may appear to be chaos, but a flexible structure is a key attribute of an effective leader.

9. Project Leadership

Leaders need to apply strong project management techniques to their own work, because the nature of their work is project oriented. Leaders also need to grow the project-management abilities of those to whom they delegate. This provides a systematic way to translate a business need into manageable, well-planned actions.

Four things characterize a project:

1. A beginning and an end.

2. One or more deliverables, with criteria that determine whether the deliverables are acceptable.

3. Temporary resources, including resources that may not be fully available to the project team and some that may be on a part-time basis. For more on managing resources, see the job aid at the end of this *Infoline*.

4. Constraints, which are time, budget, and people, but may be other dimensions as well.

All these represent challenges. For example, the actual beginning of a project may be unclear. Tasks that begin as quick fixes often evolve into projects (sometimes on their own). Companies are notorious for projects that never end, and the difference between development, production, and maintenance is often just a matter of semantics. These types of challenges demand strong leadership, from the project manager who owns the planning, organizing, and control of the project, and from the executives who prioritize and fund project work.

Prioritizing work is critical; saying *no* to work is as critical as saying *yes*. Filtering through a shared vision can accomplish this. If you do not believe the plan is possible, you're probably right. Be honest with yourself and anyone trying to coerce you into a schedule that you do not think is possible.

Projects seem to work best when there is a single project manager. However, this is not always feasible, and many companies use multiple project managers. This does add the risk of different visions and strategies, so roles must be designed clearly to keep the project managers aligned. Often, subdividing the role of the real project manager into categories like technical project manager, training project management, and customer area project manager can help a business map the right competencies to the right role. Constant communication between these project managers is critical. It works best when there is a hierarchy with a single real project manager at the top.

If you are playing the role of a project manager on a large, mission-critical project, you will find it difficult to also play the role of a supervisor or leader. Both of these roles demand a lot of attention. When this is reality, and there is nowhere to delegate either of the roles, plan to dedicate time chunks to ensure that both get proper attention.

To enhance the chances of project success, build a project charter (see the sidebar *Planning the Project* at right). Then the project team can build the project plan by

- creating the schedule
- creating the work breakdown structure
- assigning resources
- exploring environmental factors
- organizing Gantt charts
- compiling project management software
- creating the budget.

A project never goes exactly as planned. Most projects will require a shift in strategy. Think of the plan as the strategy—when you notice the project charter is changing, your strategy will change as well. You will have a *new* project plan, but you will still *have* a project plan.

Anticipating all the events that will occur in a project is impossible. It is also impossible to freeze the customers' needs because business and technology changes are ongoing. Don't get too attached to the project plan. This is not to say that you will make every change requested. Your focus needs to remain squarely on the project stakeholders who have requested that you meet the project objectives to meet the business objectives. This is a critical concept—it is not *your* project, it is *their* project. They make the decision as to when to change the plan to reflect a new need, and you implement the changes. Project managers trying to fight the needs of the business as it changes will expend a great deal of energy on futility. Managing well requires that the project manager implement her communications plan and share information about the trade-offs.

10. Change Management

Leadership is a process of transformation, taking what is and making it what it can be. Change is hard. The challenge of change stems from its uncertainty. What will it be like on the other side of this change? How will this change affect you? Will you find a comfortable place in the changed world? You can't know the answers to these questions until you complete your journey through the change and see firsthand how the new way works and whether you're comfortable there.

To fully understand the challenges of this journey, you must make a careful distinction between two terms: *change* and *transition*. People often say that change is difficult, but that's not actually true. Change is change—it is not good, bad, difficult, or easy. Transition, the human process of adapting to change, is where the difficulty comes in.

Change is an external event, a shifting of circumstances in the world. How change affects you depends upon the transitional process and the insights, beliefs, and attitudes you bring to it.

Well-known transitional process authority William Bridges describes transition as unfolding over three distinct stages: endings, neutral zone, and new beginnings.

■ *Endings*

According to Bridges, before something new can begin, the old must end. Even in situations where you are discontented and where the new beginning is alluring, you can still be reluctant to let go. The knowledge or expectation of what comes after the ending—the neutral zone—brings about this struggle. You don't like endings because they inevitably launch you into limbo, a place in between the way you know and are leaving behind and the way you are coming to know but have not yet arrived at. This explains much of the change-averse behavior you see in yourself and those around you.

■ *Neutral Zone*

At this stage of transition, you have managed to tear yourselves loose from what you were used to and are now lost. You may ask defining questions:

● Who am I? (Who are we?)
● Where am I (are we) going?
● Why am I (are we) on this road?
● How do I (we) fit in the new way?

The neutral zone seems like a fine place to avoid if at all possible, but the reality is that you need this time. This in-between state pushes you to ask important but rarely considered questions, to explore, to learn, to create vision, to rekindle energy, and ultimately to emerge somewhat transformed. The neutral zone is a time of reflection and introspection, of learning about your world, and of defining your place within it. Without this stage of the process, you may not be able to change with the changes around you.

■ *New Beginnings*

New beginnings is the stage of the journey where you "find your feet" again and begin moving forward. It is still a time of learning, fueled by hopeful optimism and a sense of direction. There may still be some grieving for the old way, especially in times of challenge, but this mostly takes the form of memories rather than a longing to return. New beginnings can be exciting times, filled with energy, discovery, innovation, and a sense of creating the future.

Planning the Project

Leaders can increase the chance of success for a project by making sure there is a project charter at the beginning, which answers the following questions:

● Why is the company doing this project? Why is it important to the business?

● What is the scope of the project? Where are the boundaries?

● What are the constraints and priorities of the project?

● What are the risks associated with this project?

● Who are the stakeholders? Who is the key internal customer contact?

● What are the alternatives for success? What is the cost-benefit analysis?

Think of a project you are currently working on or about to start. Answer the project charter questions. What did you discover that will change the way you approach this project?

With this basic understanding of the individual journey through change, you now have an idea of what it means to implement organizational change. Organizations are communities of people, and organizational change is all about supporting your people through the transitional process. The challenge is that each member of your organization will respond differently.

As organizations struggle to adapt and recreate themselves, forgetting about the people element involved in creating change is easy. The organization cannot successfully institute change without bringing its people along. Management can make all the decrees that it pleases, but people ultimately bring about the change. And they do so only when they are ready, having moved through transition at their own pace.

How do you support and facilitate the transitional journey? Consider these key elements:

- Vision—People need to know where they are going, even if the broader vision remains cloudy and is clarified only a step at a time. Vision helps manage the uncertainty and adds confidence for navigating the vast unknown.

- Skills—People need a skill base compatible with the challenge of moving through change and skill development in the areas necessary for success upon arrival at the new beginning.

- Incentives—People need to understand the need for change and what is in it for them.

- Resources—People need physical, human, informational, and psychological-emotional resources to support their journey.

- Action plan—People need a clear sense of day-to-day action with measurable milestones worthy of celebrating upon accomplishment.

These elements work together to support the organization and its people in creating lasting change. In addition, to navigate change successfully, you also will need to carry out some general support activities to facilitate people's journey through change:

- Create ownership. When people understand the driving force and have some say in how the change will unfold, the impact of the change is minimized and accepted more readily.

- Communicate. Leaders often think they have adequately communicated the vision and the change strategy. In reality, they need to send the message continually through different channels to help people stay connected with it.

- Manage the ending. Letting go of the old way is similar to the classic grieving process: shock, anger, and denial. Create opportunities for people to express their grief and recognize that grieving is a step along the road to acceptance.

- Respect diversity. Recognize and allow for differences among people that will cause them to move through the transition in a different fashion, at a different pace, and with different needs. This reality requires some balance, as there may be people already at the doorstep to the new beginning while others are only just letting go of the old way. Be clear, but realistic, as to your performance expectations and provide the appropriate support to each person.

- Coach. Accept that in times of change, leaders need to become coaches, providing support. Clarify the vision for each performer, help her see her connection to it, and provide navigational feedback.

- Foster a learning environment. Change often forces people to try new things, and a learning curve must be expected. Create an atmosphere for learning: Make it safe for people to try and fail, facilitate a positive learning attitude, and model learning behaviors.

This combination of competencies, which proceeds from a basis of understanding yourself to learning to work with other people to integrating all the pieces, will help you in your leadership journey through chaos and change. Good luck!

References & Resources

Books

Allen, David. *Getting Things Done: The Art of Stress-Free Productivity.* New York: Viking Press, 2001.

Barnes, B. Kim. *Exercising Influence: A Guide for Making Things Happen at Work, at Home, and in Your Community.* Berkeley, CA: Barnes & Conti, 2000.

Bridges, William. *Managing Transitions: Making the Most of Change.* Cambridge, MA: Perseus, 1991.

Campbell, Joseph. *The Hero With a Thousand Faces.* Princeton, NJ: Princeton University Press, 1972.

Covey, Stephen. *The 7 Habits of Highly Effective People.* New York: Simon and Schuster, 1990.

Galwey, W. Timothy. *The Inner Game of Work.* New York: Random House, 1999.

Gardner, Howard. *Frames of Mind: The Theory of Multiple Intelligences.* New York: Basic Books, 1985.

———. *Multiple Intelligences: The Theory in Practice.* New York: Basic Books, 1993.

Goleman, Daniel. *Emotional Intelligence: Why It Can Matter More Than IQ.* New York: Bantam Books, 1997.

———. *Primal Leadership: Realizing the Power of Emotional Intelligence.* Boston, MA: Harvard Business School Press, 2002.

Goss, Tracy. *The Last Word on Power: Re-invention for Leaders and Anyone who Must Make the Impossible Happen.* New York: Currency/Doubleday, 1995.

Greenleaf, Robert. *Servant Leadership: A Journey Into the Nature of Legitimate Power and Greatness.* Mahwah, NJ: Paulist Press, 1977.

Herrmann, Ned. *The Whole Brain Business Book.* New York: McGraw-Hill, 1996.

Jones, Laurie Beth. *The Path: Creating Your Mission Statement for Work and for Life.* New York: Hyperion, 1998.

Michalko, Michael. *Thinkertoys: A Handbook of Business Creativity for the '90s.* Berkeley, CA: Ten Speed Press, 1991.

Nonaka, Ikujiro, and Hirotaka Takeuchi. *The Knowledge-Creating Company: How Japanese Companies Create the Dynamics of Innovation.* New York: Oxford University Press, 1995.

Russell, Lou. *The Accelerated Learning Fieldbook: Making the Instructional Process Fast, Flexible, and Fun.* San Francisco: Jossey-Bass/Pfeiffer, 1999.

———. *Project Management for Trainers: Stop "Winging It" and Get Control of Your Training Projects.* Alexandria, VA: ASTD Press, 2000.

Russell, Lou, and Jeff Feldman. *IT Leadership Alchemy.* Upper Saddle River, NJ: Prentice Hall, 2002.

Senge, Peter. *The Fifth Discipline: The Art and Practice of the Learning Organization.* New York: Currency/Doubleday, 1990.

Senge, Peter, et al. *The Fifth Discipline Fieldbook: Strategies and Tools for Building a Learning Organization.* New York: Currency/Doubleday, 1994.

Thiagarajan, Sivasailam "Thiagi," and Ethan Sanders. *Performance Intervention Maps: 36 Strategies for Solving Your Organization's Problems.* Alexandria, VA: ASTD Press, 2001.

Thiagarajan, Siversailam "Thiagi," and Glenn Parker. *Teamwork and Teamplay: Games and Activities for Building and Training Teams.* San Francisco: Jossey-Bass/Pfeiffer, 1999.

Thomsett, Rob. *People and Project Management.* Upper Saddle River, NJ: Yourdon Press, 1980.

Treacy, Michael, and Fred Wiersma. *The Discipline of Market Leaders: Choose Your Customers, Narrow Your Focus, Dominate Your Market.* Cambridge, MA: Perseus, 1997.

Job Aid

Steps to Properly Manage Resources

Strategic planning involves converting lessons learned from scenario planning into a project plan. The project plan includes basic plan components: tasks, dependencies, estimates, resource allocations, and milestones. The project plan is usually the one that is communicated to customers and staff because it's more pragmatic than the scenario plan, although the scenario plan is useful for managing customer and staff expectations.

Proper management of resources is critical to the success of your project. Most projects involve multiple roles and skill sets, some used temporarily from inside organizations, and some rented from outside consulting firms. Managing temporary resources requires strong, pragmatic leadership. In many cases, project managers do not have hire or fire control over these resources and often cannot completely control their day-to-day tasks. The organizations to which they report directly can yank these resources at any time. This kind of resource insecurity requires leadership with strong planning, organizing, and control, including contingency plans. The following figure represents a model for remembering the phases of managing a project: define, plan, manage, and review. To ensure that you maintain control over your projects, follow the steps in each stage of managing a project.

Dare to Properly Manage Resources!

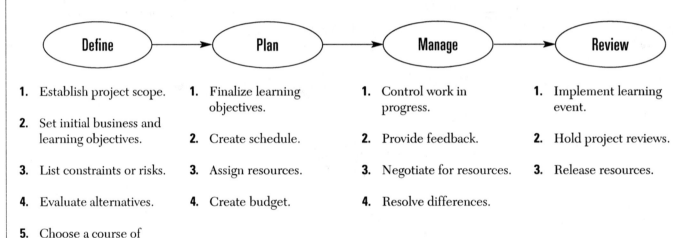

Define	Plan	Manage	Review
1. Establish project scope.	1. Finalize learning objectives.	1. Control work in progress.	1. Implement learning event.
2. Set initial business and learning objectives.	2. Create schedule.	2. Provide feedback.	2. Hold project reviews.
3. List constraints or risks.	3. Assign resources.	3. Negotiate for resources.	3. Release resources.
4. Evaluate alternatives.	4. Create budget.	4. Resolve differences.	
5. Choose a course of action.			

Strategic Planning 101

Issue 0610

Strategic Planning 101

AUTHORS

Jeffrey and Linda Russell

Tel: 608.274.4482
Email:
RCI@RussellConsultingInc.com
Website:
www.RussellConsultingInc.com

Jeff and Linda are co-owners of Russell Consulting, Inc., a consulting and organizational development firm specializing in leadership, strategy, and change. They have authored six management books, most recently *Change Basics* (ASTD Press, 2006) and *Strategic Planning Training* (ASTD Press, 2005). Linda and Jeff consult internationally, and Jeff is a sought-after presenter at national and international conferences.

Editorial Staff for *Infoline*

**Manager, Acquisitions
& Author Development**
Mark Morrow

Editorial Manager
Jacqueline Edlund-Braun

Contributing Editor
Stephanie Sussan

Copyeditor
Alfred Imhoff

Production Design
Kathleen Schaner

Thinking and Planning Strategically

Quick! Without looking for that card stashed in your desk drawer, what is your company's vision statement? And what are the key points of its strategic agenda? Are you drawing a blank on both?

Well, join the club! Though most companies have a well-crafted strategic vision statement and strategic plan, there is often a gap between these ideal words and what people know and do. Why do these words often fail to engage those on the front line?

Before exploring answers to these provocative questions, let's define "strategic planning." The word "strategy" comes from the Greek *strategos*—"the art of the commander-in-chief; . . . of projecting and directing the larger military movements and operations of a campaign" *(Oxford English Dictionary, or OED)*. This definition distinguishes *strategy*—as the larger effort to win the war—from the *tactics* of winning a battle.

The *OED* defines "planning" as an "organized method according to which something is to be done; a scheme of action; the way in which it is proposed to carry out some proceeding." Combining these concepts gives us a complete definition: *Strategic planning is conceiving the overall vision to achieve an organization's goals and then devising a formal method to transform these goals into results.*

We also need to define another term: "strategic thinking." The *OED* defines "thinking" as "the act of conceiving in one's mind, exercising one's mind, and to form or have an idea in one's mind; to imagine, conceive, or picture." Therefore, *strategic thinking is conceiving or imagining the organization's ideal state (vision) and possible methods for achieving this vision.*

Because an effective strategic plan depends on good strategic thinking, organizations must develop strategic thinkers as much as strategic plans. Although strategic planning strives to translate vision into results, strategic thinking helps discern what we need to do differently to achieve this vision. So while strategic *planning* presents a formal plan to realize a desired future, strategic *thinking* enables us to develop a strategic plan and then spontaneously discover new ideas that may lead us to change the original plan in unanticipated ways.

In *The Rise and Fall of Strategic Planning*, Henry Mintzberg, a McGill University management professor and severe critic of strategic planning, argues that strategic planning is too often merely strategic programming—projecting into the future what we already know. Thus, he argues that formal planning "by its very analytical nature, has always been dependent upon the preservation and rearrangement of established categories. . . . But real strategic change requires not merely rearranging the established categories, but inventing new ones." Also: "planning cannot generate strategies, [but] given viable strategies, it can program them . . . [and] make them operational." (Quotations from *Harvard Business Review* article summarizing Mintzberg's book.) For more on Mintzberg's criticism of strategic planning, see the sidebar *First, Kill All the Planners!*

How can we meet the challenge posed by Mintzberg to create a strategic plan that moves our organization forward innovatively? This *Infoline* offers pointers on creating an effective and vibrant strategic plan. Thus, like a strategic plan, this *Infoline* doesn't provide you with answers so much as a map of future possibilities with keys for reading it that will help your organization move ahead creatively.

Value of Thinking Strategically

Strategic *thinking* strives to identify, explain, and learn from what is occurring *now* and integrate these insights into a formal plan. Strategic thinking means spontaneously discovering innovative strategies that a more formal plan could never have envisioned.

A strategic plan is only effective if it responds to what is happening *now*, not what the plan may have presented as a likely future. A strategic plan is best at translating *deliberate* strategies based on a SWOT analysis (a structured way of examining an organization's strengths, weaknesses, opportunities, and threats; see below) into action. But a strategic plan is less effective for identifying and integrating emerging strategies. This is where *strategic thinking* plays a central role.

First, Kill All the Planners!

Henry Mintzberg, author of *The Rise and Fall of Strategic Planning*, highlights several strategic planning issues.

He contends that for too long planners have been at the helm of the strategic-planning process without enough room for the intuitive and creative world of ideas that lays beyond planners' bailiwick of analysis and synthesis. He further argues that formal planning does not, and should not, create strategy as much as it seeks to program the actual strategy created by others.

Mintzberg lays out the three key roles for planners in support of strategy:

● **Planners as strategy finders.** Planners should not develop strategy—this being the purview of executives and managers—but they can help the organization's leaders find innovative ways to move the strategy forward. Planners can ferret out solutions in places where managers may not have the time or inclination to look.

● **Planners as analysts.** The quality of strategy formulation, which is the work of an organization's leaders, depends on their awareness of information on the organization's environment— such as shifts in consumer buying habits and emerging new competitors. But leaders often are too enmeshed in daily operational details to pay attention to this crucial information. This is where planners can best serve the organizational strategy— by gathering and analyzing data and feeding their insights to leaders, who can then consider these findings in formulating strategy.

● **Planners as catalysts.** Strategic planners can encourage innovative, intuitive strategic thinking. Although planners never form strategy, they can seek to ensure that the planning process is provocative and future oriented. As contrarian catalysts, they can engage leaders and managers in questioning conventional wisdom, thinking about the "unthinkable," and breaking out of their conceptual ruts.

Although Mintzberg doesn't exactly ask you to *kill* your planners, he does invite a radical rethinking of the planner's role, which is, in a sense, killing them off—and then giving them new life with a new purpose. So instead of killing your planners, help them find a new vision of service to your organization's executive leadership and line managers—those who will actually develop strategy.

Strategic thinking is a key competency that leaders, managers, supervisors, and front-line employees need to develop to enable the organization to identify and take advantage of emerging issues. It involves backing off from the concerns of the moment, finding a larger context, and then taking a fresh look at oneself, the organization, customers, co-workers, and the environment from this long-range vantage point.

This larger context helps everyone know

● the *purpose* or aim of your organization (its vision and goals)

● the purpose, role, and value of each employee's work contribution

● the core guiding values or beliefs described in the strategic plan that identify the expectations for each employee's attitudes and behaviors

● the current and future needs of customers (internal and external)

● what is occurring in the organization's environment (internal and external).

See the sidebar *Elements of Strategic Thinking* for additional thoughts on the factors that help create a strategic-thinking mindset.

With people at every organizational level thinking and then acting strategically, an otherwise static strategic plan is more likely to become dynamic. And employees are more likely to make the best decisions and act within the strategic framework.

Strategic thinkers are always asking the big questions. When people become strategic thinkers, they help create the organization's long-term future by identifying emerging issues, challenges, and opportunities that were unforeseen when the formal plan was developed. Strategic thinkers routinely challenge the organization to rethink the strategies expressed in its formal strategic plan.

As an organization works to implement strategy, it faces the challenge of how to encourage often-unorthodox strategic thinkers to voice their insights and even allow them to then *act* strategically in their daily work. Some of these insights simply move the organization toward the vision it has already expressed in its larger strategy. But other insights may call for a fundamental retooling of the strategic plan. The best organizations enable strategic thinkers to translate both types of insights into action.

Sustaining long-term organizational success requires a constantly evolving plan that still stays true to its larger vision. A plan that fails to integrate emerging insights may be worse than no plan. And if an organization sticks to a strategic plan that couldn't possibly anticipate emerging trends, it may miss the need to confront an emerging threat.

Purpose of a Strategic Plan

Why have a strategic plan? There is little reason to invest the considerable time and energy required to create a plan if you don't have a clear purpose for doing it. Thus the plan must be anchored to a fundamental business necessity, and it must likewise meet a critical business requirement. There are several common business reasons for an organization to create a strategic plan, including the need to

- Clarify and facilitate the emergence of a consensus on the organization's strategy. The strategic-planning process can help the organization's employees find answers to the big questions about its purpose, meaning, and value.

- Communicate this strategy to all levels of the organization—and to its diverse stakeholders and customers.

- Strengthen the fit between departmental and personal goals and the organization's overarching vision.

Elements of Strategic Thinking

- **Hold ideal future in your mind.** Strategic thinking begins with a clear image of the desired long-range future for the organization. With this vision in mind, decisions and actions are more likely to be shaped by this overarching goal.

- **Consider organization's core values.** While the vision describes the end state that individuals strive to create over time, core values speak to the moment. These values—when clearly defined and accepted by people at all levels of the organization—are more likely to lead to strategic decisions and actions because they speak to today's concerns.

- **Continuously look for opportunities and threats.** The strategic thinking mindset depends on a keen awareness of the environment. Strategic thinkers always have their antennae up—discovering opportunities by being open and receptive to new information—and thus can detect potential threats in advance.

- **Search for patterns and relationships.** Strategic thinkers recognize the patterns between events and circumstances—for example, they will be the first to detect an emerging pattern of customer requests. They can then help begin the conversation on the meaning of such nascent trends for the organization and how to best respond from a strategic perspective.

- **Recognize connections.** Strategic thinkers are deeply aware of interrelationships between actions and events. They recognize that every action within a system (such as lowering prices to attract new customers) may or may not have its desired effect (such as an increase in new business) but will always have *unintended* consequences (such as attracting different kinds of customers). Strategic thinkers have great respect for this *rule of unintended consequences*.

- **Act on vision, values, environment, and connections.** Strategic thinking integrates the elements described above into a holistic strategic perspective that shapes how the individual makes each decision in the moment.

- Identify and align strategic initiatives, so the strategic actions of one part of the organization don't conflict with those of another (for example, so the team-based incentive pay system developed by operations doesn't conflict with the knowledge-based incentive program developed by human resources).

- Guide decision making by leaders, managers, and staff.

- Help set parameters for the allocation of resources and the annual/operational budgeting process.

- Measure and evaluate the organization's progress in implementing its strategy and moving toward its vision.

- Identify organizational assets and strengths—the foundation for the organization's past success.

- Identify opportunities where the organization can improve and learn—areas that pose potential vulnerabilities, risks, or lost opportunities.

- Guide human resource skill- and knowledge-building efforts—to ensure that the leaders, managers, and staff have the competencies that enable effective organizational performance.

- Increase the probability that the organization will stay relevant to the marketplace. Although nothing ensures an organization's long-term success, a strategic plan engages the organization in the big questions that challenge it to remain abreast of a changing world and marketplace.

Developing an Effective Plan

The process of developing a strategic plan involves these basic steps:

- Assess the organization and its environment.

- Discover or create a shared vision for the organization's future and the core values that will help it realize this vision.

- Identify strategies and detailed operational plans that move the organization from where it is to where it aspires to be.

These simple steps can be elaborated into a full model for developing the strategic plan that involves four stages. Each stage requires a way of thinking and a set of activities to achieve specific outcomes or deliverables.

■ Stage 1: Assess the Organization

The first stage of developing a strategic plan involves gathering information on the organization, its performance, its strengths and vulnerabilities, its history, the external environment in which it operates today, and the environment it is likely to face in the future.

This stage looks at the organization's experience with previous strategic plans and operational goals, which provides insight into its culture and helps employees learn if it has a history of realizing or missing its strategic targets.

Even more important than examining the organization's historical record of successful strategy or goal attainment is conducting a SWOT analysis—a structured way of looking at both the internal and external aspects of the organization. In the first part of the analysis, employees look *internally* at the organization's assets or strengths (S for short) and its weaknesses (W). This internal assessment develops an awareness of both those factors that help sustain the organization's success and also those that, if not addressed, might erode its future success.

The second part of the SWOT analysis concerns the *external* environment. Employees look at the opportunities (O) presented by forces outside the organization that may enable or facilitate its future success—if seized. Then they examine the threats (T) posed by outside forces that, if not understood and addressed, might jeopardize the organization's success.

(See the back of this issue for a job aid that can help you conduct a SWOT analysis.)

Key stage 1 deliverables: A clear description of the organization's internal capacities (strengths and weaknesses) and of the external forces that will likely have an impact on its ability to seize future opportunities.

■ *Stage 2: Define Vision and Identify Values*
In the second stage of the strategic-planning process, employees and other stakeholders create a vision for the organization—describing the future they want to create or accomplish. This vision becomes truly *shared* to the extent that it resonates with these employees who can pursue it.

Along with this shared vision, at this stage employees also develop a set of guiding principles and core values that will support the vision by identifying model attitudes and behaviors for everyone on the organization's staff.

Key stage 2 deliverables: A clear and compelling vision that is widely shared throughout the organization and a set of guiding principles and core values that employees and other stakeholders can use every day to guide their decision making and actions.

■ *Stage 3: Identify the Strategic Agenda*
The first stage of the process described the beginning state, and the second stage defined the desired end state. The third stage describes how to move from the beginning to the end state—the strategic agenda. There is no scientific formula for how to determine and pursue this agenda, because there are no roadmaps for formulating strategy.

But strategy formulation is central to every plan. It is the stage in the process when the organization decides to pursue some strategies and abandon others. The sources for the strategic agenda run the gamut from the intuitive hunch of a charismatic leader to a realistic analysis of the competition to the results of the SWOT analysis.

Deciding what strategies to pursue is perhaps the most difficult stage of the strategic-planning process, partly because simply gathering more data or talking to a greater number of people will not help organizational leaders or employees decide what to do. Henry Mintzberg's strongest criticism of strategic planning is that it has largely failed to provide insight into strategy formulation.

Key stage 3 deliverables: A strategic agenda that will drive departmental, work unit, and team actions toward the organization's vision. For each item on the agenda, target outcomes and goals have been determined to ensure organizational accountability.

■ *Stage 4: Develop and Monitor Plan*
The fourth and final stage uses the broader strategic agenda that was identified in the third stage to push performance accountability deep into all levels of the organization. For each item on the agenda, functional units are designated that will take the lead or coordinate work toward the strategic goal.

Sometimes, a strategic initiative is the responsibility of a particular organizational unit (such as human resources for a capacity-development initiative). Other times, every functional unit is expected to pursue a strategic goal within its area (such as building partnerships with internal and external customers). In both cases, to ensure accountability, these operational plans—which are revised annually, or more often as needed—specify such measurable outcomes as deliverables, timelines, and resource use for each goal.

This stage also ensures that the plan stays dynamic and responsive to changing conditions. To keep the plan this flexible, it must have inherent capacities for checking progress, assessing emerging issues, and periodically challenging the strategic agenda.

Key stage 4 deliverables: A comprehensive operational plan that translates the strategic vision (from the second stage) and the strategic agenda (from the third stage) into actions and results at the level of the individual work of employees. There are also a built-in mechanism to periodically assess the plan's effectiveness and relevance and a method to integrate flexible innovation into the plan.

Components of an Effective Plan

Once an organization has worked through the four stages described above, it will have a thoughtful, comprehensive strategic plan articulating an ideal vision and how to achieve it. The parts of this strategic plan, while varying depending on each organization's history and culture, will often include the following elements:

● **Vision statement,** a description of the *ideal* future of the organization and the outcomes it hopes to create for its stakeholders. The vision describes the end state—the ideal final destination for the organization and the people it serves. See the sidebar *Recipe for a Compelling Vision.*

● **Mission statement,** a description of who the organization serves and how the organization will structure itself to accomplish its preferred future. This statement translates the aspiration of the vision into specific dimensions while emphasizing the organization's distinctiveness. The mission informs employees, customers, suppliers, regulators, and other key stakeholders about the organization's primary purpose. The statement, which also describes the *structure* and *strategy* the organization will use to achieve its vision, delineates the organization's essential purposes and audience.

● **Core beliefs, principles, and values,** statements of belief that guide individual actions throughout the organization. These values describe how individuals should think, act, and interact. In some environments, a compelling vision and clearly defined core beliefs are all that are needed to encourage people to do the right thing every day.

● **Strategic agenda,** a description of the key goals that the organization needs to pursue to close the gap between the *ideal* and *real* worlds, which commonly comprises five to eight strategic priorities. One way to shape the strategic agenda is the balanced scorecard—described by Robert Kaplan and David Norton in *The Balanced Scorecard*—a suite of interrelated measures for translating strategy into action.

● **Critical success factors,** broad measures indicating that the organization is making progress toward the vision (such as an increase in market share in all product lines). These factors, often identified as *leading indicators,* form an early warning system that enables the organization to shift resources, priorities, and actions to ensure that it stays on track toward its vision.

These, of course, are parts of a theoretical plan. Although your organization's plan may not distinguish between vision and mission, might be silent on core beliefs, or may not identify critical success factors, what matters most is that your plan *gets results.* The structure, components, and depth of the plan matter less than the fact that it helps people make strategic decisions every day and moves the organization toward realizing its vision.

Maximizing Participation

Traditionally, an organization has looked exclusively to its executive leaders or board of directors to discern its vision and set its strategic agenda. But today, in times of tumultuous change, organizations need an inclusive strategic-planning process involving as many employees' heads and hearts as possible.

Wide stakeholder participation in the strategic-planning process provides diverse insights and perspectives from people at different levels of the organization. What a front-line employee sees and understands about the environment in which the organization operates may be starkly different from what a unit manager perceives, and their viewpoints may dramatically differ from those of the CEO. Unless the planning process includes a mechanism to capture these diverse perspectives, the organization may fail to discover essential knowledge about the real-world environment, emerging customers' needs, actual organizational capacities, and the like.

If this failure occurs, the strategic plan loses its relevance inside the organization (for instance, "this doesn't accurately describe the internal challenges we face") and outside it ("the plan really missed the ball on seeing the impact of this new technology on customer buying preferences").

Individual contributors to the strategic-planning process—such as those on the front line, supervisors, and department managers—should never have a veto over the final say in crafting the vision statement or in selecting the strategic agenda, but their voices must be heard. The goal of participation is not to make people feel good or to create a democratic workplace (which would be untenable for most organizations); it is simply to gather information essential to the organization's future—which will not be identifiable until *after* it's been gathered.

Wide participation is useful if the organization can integrate these diverse viewpoints and essential knowledge to help paint a more accurate portrait of its internal assets and vulnerabilities and the external opportunities and threats that it must face to move toward a successful future.

One effective method for developing the strategic plan is to create a cross-functional strategic-planning development team that plays a key coordinating role in gathering data (for the first and second stages of the process) and then guides strategy formulation. This team would have members from and work closely with the executive leadership and the board of directors to manage the entire process. They would play a key role in ensuring that the final deliberative body—the group that establishes the vision and strategic agenda—has rich and comprehensive information upon which to base their decisions.

Recipe for a Compelling Vision

At its best, vision transforms aspirations into daily behaviors at all levels of the organization by motivating and inspiring people to act on it. So how do you make your vision compelling? A compelling vision

- **Captures imaginations and engages spirits.** It connects with people's hopes and aspirations. To the extent it taps into a dream in which they can individually participate, it pulls them forward.

- **Inspires people to excellence.** It gives people a reason to strive to do their best in their day-to-day work.

- **Provides focus in an ever-changing world.** A vision is a place to return when faced with uncertainty or challenge. When people aren't sure what to do, the vision gives them guidance.

- **Enables people to evaluate their actions.** An effective vision enables people to see each day whether they are making decisions, acting, and achieving results that will help fulfill the vision.

- **Challenges people to unite toward a common goal.** A bold vision should spur people to focus their individual and collaborative energies in ways that require extraordinary effort.

With these ingredients, you make the vision truly compelling by taking these three steps:

- **Involve your people.** A vision cannot be imposed; it needs to be discerned through an organization-wide dialogue. The more the vision reflects the collective aspirations of all those who will be pursuing it, the more it will be truly shared and the more compelling people will find it.

- **Make it meaningful.** For the vision to have power over people's daily thoughts and behaviors, it must speak to their hearts. The vision must unfold through a process that reaches deeply into the organization to empower people to discover a shared purpose that puts their work in a new light.

- **Be bold.** Benjamin Disraeli, the British statesman, said that "success is the child of audacity." A compelling vision proposes a profoundly different future.

Then stand back and let people get to work!

W. Edwards Deming, the founder of the modern field of quality and productivity improvement, often heaped scorn on those who sought employee participation in process improvement only for participation's sake. His point was not to discourage participation but to urge planners to focus on the *purpose* of participation: better information and more comprehensive knowledge leading to better decisions and actions. Taking his advice and maximizing participation to gather divergent perspectives in your strategic-planning process can significantly strengthen the quality of the data available for crafting the vision and deciding on the strategy.

Overcoming Barriers to Implementation

Even if your organization has a strategic plan and is filled with strategic thinkers at every level, this does not guarantee that the plan will achieve the desired outcomes. Every organizational leader and those leading the strategic-planning effort should be keenly aware of a number of common barriers to implementing plans.

Plan's development failed to use an inclusive process to integrate diverse perspectives. A successful planning process finds ways to gather divergent viewpoints from all levels of the organization. Though the plan may be written by the top leaders, they need to listen to people on the front line.

There was a failure to create a truly shared strategic vision and plan—one that taps into the hopes, dreams, aspirations, and passions of employees at every level. With this failure—closely related to the first barrier—a plan will be considerably less effective because it will not engage people, capture their imagination, or compel them to work in a new and significantly different way.

Leaders failed to develop strategic-thinking skills throughout the organization. Strategic thinking enables people at every level to make effective decisions and act independently on behalf of the organization's vision, guiding values, and strategic agenda. When people are strategic thinkers, the organization ends up spending less time managing and controlling them and more time supporting innovative contributions from its staff. And without these strategic thinkers throughout the organization, there will likely be fewer "eyes and ears" on the lookout for emerging issues, serendipitous opportunities, and new information that should be fed back into the plan, leading to renewed strategies and priorities.

Strategic vision and agenda are impractical. Considerable effort is made to create a bold, compelling, attractive, audacious vision. This vision gets people excited about the future. But when it comes to enacting this vision, it collapses in platitudes. For a plan to be workable, to directly guide the work of employees at all levels, the vision and its supporting strategic agenda must be translated into concrete, doable steps. People need to see that progress toward the vision is possible day in and day out.

Performance standards and accountability are lacking. Closely related to the problem of having an impractical vision and strategic agenda is the issue of measurement and accountability. Many strategic plans fail because they have neglected to define specific performance standards that can clearly measure progress toward each strategic agenda issue. And without these performance standards, accountability suffers; how can we hold departments, teams, and individuals accountable to the plan if we don't know what progress even looks like?

Method for tracking performance focuses more on *tactical* than on *strategic* measures. In the absence of strategic performance standards, the organization at all levels tends to focus on what's working or not working *now*—the things that can more easily be counted, inventoried, tallied, crossed-off, and so forth. This reinforces short-term tactical thinking and behaviors while shifting the focus away from strategic and long-term thinking and actions. The key challenge for organizations serious about implementing their strategy is to develop clear measures that focus on strategic outcomes rather than operational or tactical ones.

Planners fail to make plan dynamic. Every strategic plan should be published in three-ring binders that allow flexibility to revise the plan as it is implemented. As new information is gained from the strategic thinkers throughout the organization, this information is shared, discussed, and debated; and if it has merit, it is integrated into the dynamic, ever-evolving plan. The traditional plan is a static document that reflects the thinking at the moment of its creation. A truly innovative plan is continually evaluated, challenged, refreshed, updated, and revised to reflect what people are seeing and learning. An effective strategic plan may establish a three- to five-year planning horizon, but it is routinely adjusted to reflect emerging issues and insights.

Chaos and complexity theories are a fascinating field of study that examines the pervasive uncertainty in the world and the difficulty of predicting the future of a system (and thus complicates the ability to plan for the future). Chaos theory holds that while the future is unknowable, the future of a system tends to follow a natural pattern that becomes evident only at a distance and over time, and especially if the observer gains a systems perspective. See the sidebar *When the Unexpected Happens.*

Planners fail to link vision and strategic plan with performance expectations. Too often, annual budgets and operational plans reinforce *business as usual* and don't reflect the priorities of the strategic plan. Preexisting organizational processes that are used to set goals, establish performance standards, evaluate performance, and ensure accountability need to be anchored to the outcomes, goals, and priorities given in the strategic plan. Without this strong link, people's behavior will revert back to what they did yesterday. But a strong link will reinforce strategic action.

Method for allocating resources isn't tied to the strategic plan. For the strategic plan to be deeply felt and acted upon throughout the organization, all operational and fiscal planning must be tied to the plan's strategic priorities. Money, resources, and employee energy should be focused on what the plan says matters most toward advancing the vision and realizing the organization's goals.

Planners fail to understand the organization's culture and its past behavioral patterns (for instance, "we ignore strategy from the top" or "the organization's track record on goal attainment is spotty"). If these cultural and historical elements—key drivers of behavior at all levels of the organization—aren't faced when the plan is crafted, the plan likely will encounter resistance and apathy that may jeopardize implementation.

Acting on the Plan

Imagine that your organization has successfully developed a strategic plan. After all the hard work involved in gathering data, analyzing the environment, crafting a compelling vision statement, and making the tough choices on the strategic agenda, a comprehensive strategic plan for the future is now in your hands!

Your executive leadership team and the cross-functional team that facilitated the entire strategic-planning process worked well together to gather essential knowledge and insights to craft a plan that presents a strong vision for moving the organization in a new direction. So now what do you do?

This is where the going gets the toughest. Although writing a vision statement and deciding on the strategic agenda can be invigorating, transforming *aspirations* into *action* can be extremely difficult. And the more the plan challenges the status quo of where the organization is today, the more difficult it will be to implement.

When the Unexpected Happens

The challenge of any strategic plan is how to ensure that it stays relevant in the face of unpredictable events. For example, what if your organization was a police department for a large city and you had just completed your vision and strategic plan on September 10, 2001? You couldn't have known that the next day would bring a revolutionary transformation in perceptions of outside threats and security challenges.

Because the future is unknowable—no strategic plan or SWOT analysis can predict it—your strategic-planning process must be dynamic and flexible. You also will need to develop strong strategic thinking skills that will enable the eyes and ears of the organization to detect changes occurring in the chaotic world around us.

In fact, there has been quite a bit of interest in the ideas of *chaos* and *complexity* as they relate to the world of organizations. These two overlapping theories—*chaos* and *complexity*—offer a way of looking at the natural world and, by extension, organizations, from a perspective that seeks out patterns and relationships. The main thesis of the chaos and complexity theories is that while the future is unknowable, all living systems tend to follow patterns that, if we could see them, might enable us to better understand the future behavior of the system.

There are a number of excellent guides to understanding these new sciences, particularly Margret Wheatley's *Leadership and the New Science,* Ralph Stacey's *Managing the Unknowable,* and *Surfing the Edge of Chaos,* by Richard Pascale, Mark Millemann, and Linda Gioja. These books suggest that an organization's response to chaos has less to do with having a strategic plan than with how it detects and responds to information in its environment. The heart of this new way of looking at the world and its implications for strategic planning and thinking can be summarized thus:

- **Status quo is death.** Stability and equilibrium are the enemies of long-term organizational success. Stability should never be the goal of strategic planning and strategic thinking—at best, stability codifies yesterday's success. The future holds new and perhaps profoundly different challenges than those of yesterday or today.

- **Future is unknowable.** Innovative strategies take an organization into the uncharted waters of open-ended change, where success involves discovering the destination as you go.

- **Organizations are dynamic systems.** With their dynamic, nonlinear feedback and the like, the upcoming directions of these systems are unpredictable and *unplannable!*

- **Chaos is not the absence of order.** When observed over time and at a distance, a "chaotic" living system actually conforms to boundaries and patterns. So while you can't predict the future of a system, you can imagine paths it may follow.

- **Organizations are self-organizing systems.** When dynamic systems are faced with radical amounts of change, they often are pulled apart (such as IBM in the late 1980s). But if they can find a way to reorganize into a more responsive, adaptable form—as around new fields of information (the new IBM of today), they can survive, even thrive, in their reincarnation.

- **In a living system, people focus on issues, challenges, and aspirations.** Instead of trying to control an organization to achieve stability, leaders, managers, and staff can explore emerging issues that will challenge people to envision a tantalizing future while focusing on what they can learn today and capitalize on tomorrow.

- **Complex learning leads to future success.** An organization's ability to survive over the long term depends on the ability of its members to question mental models (paradigms), build new models, and devise new ways to work together that encourage diversity.

- **Informal networks and political behavior are the wellspring of new ideas and directions.** Innovative ideas emerge through the capacity of individuals to use informal networks and engage in political behavior to highlight and promote innovation. Organizations must develop people's capacities for effective influence and persuasion.

There are three steps an organization should take to act on the plan: establish accountability, monitor implementation, and integrate the plan into the organization's structure.

■ *Establish Accountability*
The first step is to begin establishing *general* and *specific* accountability for moving the plan forward.

General accountability should be established by asking each department or organizational unit to develop its own strategic and operational plans based on the new strategic vision and agenda. If, for example, a key organizational strategy is to develop a stronger partnership with suppliers, then each department would develop its own response to this issue. Thus each department might identify its own key suppliers and then develop a plan to strengthen partnerships with these suppliers.

Specific accountability to the strategic plan is established by assigning key strategic initiatives to particular departments. These lead departments would be expected to take primary responsibility for moving a strategic issue forward on behalf of the entire organization. For example, if one organizational strategy is to broaden the competencies and skills of high-value-added positions in the company, the human resources department might be assigned the lead role in enacting this strategy. Although other organizational units might have specific roles in addressing this issue (the departments that manage these high-value-added positions might develop professional development plans for people in these positions), human resources would still take the lead.

■ *Monitor Implementation*
The second step to ensure that the strategic plan is acted on is to charge the team or workgroup that worked with the leadership to create the strategic plan with a continuing role as the plan unfolds: to monitor its implementation and give quarterly progress updates. Too often, the daily operational and tactical challenges facing any organization have a tendency to crowd out strategic thinking and action. Steven Covey, author of *The 7 Habits of Highly Effective People* and *First Things First*,

cites the work of Charles Hummel who calls this the "tyranny of the urgent." To mitigate the effects of this tyranny, the strategic-planning development team can help keep the plan vibrant, dynamic, and a high priority by

- communicating general and specific expectations to organizational leaders and departments

- monitoring plan implementation

- tracking results against expectations

- advocating for the plan as the framework for decision making and action

- highlighting general and specific accountabilities to ensure follow-through and performance results

- asking periodically about the plan's ongoing relevance

- suggesting changes to the plan's priorities and strategies based on emerging data, insights, changes in the environment, and the like

- reporting to the larger organization on the progress that the plan is making on the critical success factors and toward the strategic vision.

■ *Integrate Plan into Organization's Structure*
The third step is to aggressively integrate the plan into every aspect of the organization's infrastructure, which requires a deep commitment by the leadership to making the plan the basis for everything that happens in the organization. This integration at a minimum includes

- department operational planning and goal setting

- annual budgeting

Transforming Strategy into Results

The plan is finally done. What happens next? A good strategic plan lays out a desired path of action for departments, teams, and individuals throughout the organization. The plan provides clear expectations and accountability, reinforces and rewards desired behaviors and actions, and ensures an ongoing assessment of both success in implementing it and the continuing need to strategically rethink and revise it. The figure below displays the critical connections between the *formation* of the strategic plan and its elements, and the *implementation* of the plan.

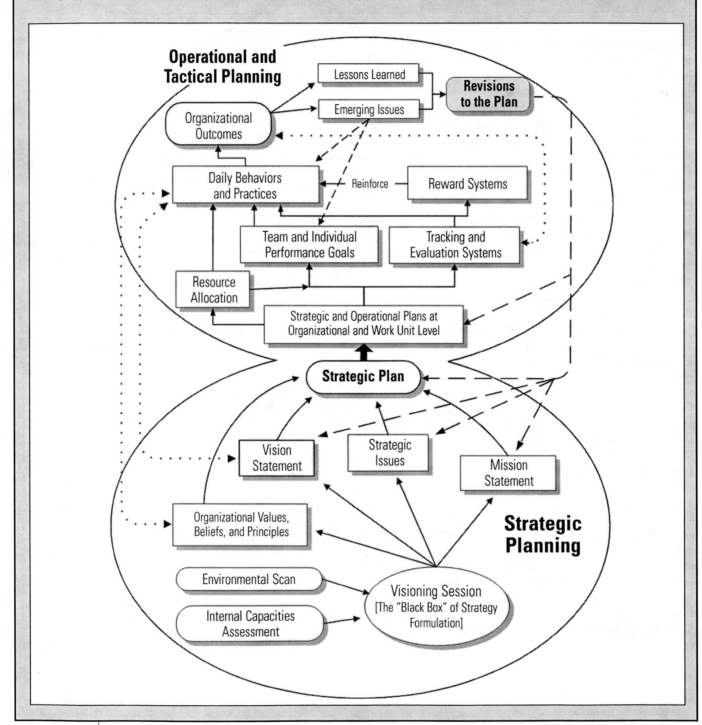

- quality-improvement initiatives—including international standards certification, six sigma programs, and so forth

- recruitment and selection strategies

- new employee orientation

- employee development initiatives

- individual performance management systems—including performance goal setting, performance coaching, and performance reviews

- capital and facility planning

- research and development

- marketing/branding

- organizational communications—Web- and print-based methods

- information technology planning

- organization-wide, department, team, and individual performance incentive programs (variable pay)

- succession planning

- strategic alliances and partnership agreements.

See the sidebar *Transforming Strategy into Results* for a graphical depiction of the relationship of these two worlds: strategy and operations.

Gauging Plan's Effectiveness

The true test of a strategic plan is how well it helps the organization achieve its strategic vision and thus succeed in fulfilling its overarching purpose. Strategic planning won't guarantee an organization's success—nothing can do that—but it is a useful method for asking big questions and transforming the answers into results for the organization and its stakeholders, investors, and customers.

References & Resources

Articles

Courtney, Hugh, Jane Kirkland, and Patrick Viguerie. "Strategy under Uncertainty." *Harvard Business Review,* November-December 1997, pp. 66-79.

Hamel, Gary. "Strategy as Revolution." *Harvard Business Review,* July-August 1996, pp. 69-82.

———. "Innovate Now!" *FastCompany,* December 2002, pp. 115-124.

Kaplan, Robert S., and David P. Norton. "Using the Balanced Scorecard as a Strategic Management System." *Harvard Business Review,* January-February 1996, pp. 75-85.

———. "The Office of Strategy Management." *Harvard Business Review,* January 2006, pp. 72-80.

———. "The Balanced Scorecard." *Harvard Business Review,* January 2006, pp. 172-180.

Kim, W. Chan, and Renée Mauborgne. "Charting Your Company's Future." *Harvard Business Review,* June 2002, pp. 76-83.

Mankins, Michael C., and Richard Steele. "Turning Great Strategy into Great Performance." *Harvard Business Review,* July-August 2005, pp. 64-72.

———. "Stop Making Plans; Start Making Decisions." *Harvard Business Review,* January 2006, pp. 76-84.

Mintzberg, Henry. "The Fall and Rise of Strategic Planning." *Harvard Business Review,* January-February 1994, pp. 107-114.

Porter, Michael. "What Is Strategy?" *Harvard Business Review,* November-December 1996, pp. 61-78.

Books

Brown, Shona, and Kathleen Eisenhardt. *Competing on the Edge: Strategy as Structured Chaos.* Boston: Harvard Business School Press, 1998.

Collins, James. *Good to Great: Why Some Companies Make the Leap and Other's Don't.* New York: HarperCollins, 2001.

Collins, James, and Jerry Porras. *Built to Last: Successful Habits of Visionary Companies.* New York: HarperBusiness, 1994.

Covey, Steven. *The 7 Habits of Highly Effective People.* New York: Simon and Schuster, 1989.

Covey, S., A. Roger Merrill, and Rebecca R. Merrill. *First Things First: To Live, to Love, to Learn, to Leave a Legacy.* New York: Simon and Schuster, Fireside Book, 1994.

de Geus, Arie. *The Living Company.* Boston: Harvard Business School Press, 1997.

Kaplan, Robert S., and David Norton. *The Balanced Scorecard.* Boston: Harvard Business School Press, 1996.

Mintzberg, Henry. *The Rise and Fall of Strategic Planning.* New York: Free Press, 1994.

Mintzberg, Henry, Bruce Ahlstrand, and Joseph Lampel. *Strategy Safari: A Guided Tour through the Wilds of Strategic Management.* New York: Free Press, 1998.

Nadler, Gerald, and Shozo Hibino. *Breakthrough Thinking.* Rocklin, CA: Prima Publishing, 1990.

Pascale, Richard T., Mark Millemann, and Linda Gioja. *Surfing the Edge of Chaos: The Laws of Nature and the New Laws of Business.* New York: Crown Business, 2000.

Russell, Jeffrey, and Linda Russell. *Strategic Planning Training.* Alexandria, VA: ASTD Press, 2005.

Schwartz, Peter. *The Art of the Long View.* New York: Doubleday Currency, 1991.

Senge, Peter M. *The Fifth Discipline.* New York: Doubleday Currency, 1990.

Senge, Peter M., Charlotte Roberts, Richard Ross, Bryan Smith, and Art Kleiner. *The Fifth Discipline Fieldbook.* New York: Doubleday Currency, 1994.

Stacey, Ralph D. *Managing the Unknowable.* San Francisco: Jossey-Bass, 1992.

———. *Strategic Management and Organisational Dynamics.* London: Prentice Hall / Financial Times, 2003.

Stacey, Ralph D., Douglas Griffin, and Patricia Shaw. *Complexity and Management.* London: Routledge, 2002.

Wheatley, Margaret J. *Leadership and the New Science.* San Francisco: Berrett-Koehler, 1992.

Infolines

Larsen, Non Gesche. "Implementing Strategic Learning." No. 250210.

Marquardt, Michael. "16 Steps to a Learning Organization." No. 259602.

Solomon, Cynthia. "Cultural Audits: Supporting Organizational Success." No. 250412.

Titcomb, T.J. "Chaos and Complexity Theory." No. 259807.

Verardo, Denzil. "Managing the Strategic Planning Process." No. 259710.

Younger, Sandra M. "How to Develop a Vision." No. 259107.

Zulauf, Carol. "Systems Thinking." No. 259703.

SWOT Analysis

No matter how you approach strategic planning, a central part of your work is to analyze the environment in which your company operates. A SWOT analysis—SWOT meaning strengths, weaknesses, opportunities, and threats—presents a simple structure for examining both your internal environment (strengths and weaknesses) and external environment (opportunities and threats). Post-It Notes are a great tool when conducting a SWOT analysis—whether you are working alone or with a strategic planning team. Post-It Notes also enable you to form groups of related ideas within each SWOT dimension. Use the space below to capture and then prioritize your ideas from the Post-It Note exercise that reflect the key environmental factors shaping your strategy.

Internal strengths: What does our organization do well?

Reflect on different dimensions of your organization (for example, communication, planning, performance management, culture, technology, the employees, leadership, reward systems, and organizational structure). Within these areas, where is your organization strongest? What are its assets? Of which aspects do you feel proudest?

1.

2.

3.

4.

5.

Internal weaknesses: Where is our organization most vulnerable?

Reflect on different dimensions of your organization (for example, communication, planning, performance management, culture, technology, the employees, leadership, reward systems, and organizational structure). Within these areas, where is your organization most vulnerable? What are its weaknesses? What creates the greatest frustration for you and others?

1.

2.

3.

4.

5.

(continued on next page)

SWOT Analysis (continued)

External opportunities: What, in the outside environment, might enable our success?

Reflect on changes that are occurring in different dimensions of the external environment (for example, demographic, social, economic, technological, political, cultural, and market niche). Within these areas, what opportunities do you see occurring or emerging that, if you took advantage of them, would enable you to achieve your vision? What changes in the outside world could hold great promise for you—if you found a way to prepare for and respond to them?

1.

2.

3.

4.

5.

External threats: What, in the outside environment, might prevent us from achieving our vision?

Reflect on changes that are occurring in different dimensions of the external environment (for example, demographic, social, economic, technological, political, cultural, market niche, and so forth). Within these areas, what threats or challenges do you see occurring or emerging that, if you failed to address them, would prevent you from achieving your vision? What changes in the outside world could threaten your future—unless you find a way to prepare for and respond to them?

1.

2.

3.

4.

5.

How to Delegate

Issue 9011

How to Delegate

AUTHOR:

Sandra Millers Younger
Consultant
San Diego, California

Editorial Staff for 9011

Editor
Barbara Darraugh

ASTD Internal Consultant
Cathy Fisk

Revised 1997

Editor
Cat Sharpe

Contributing Editor
Ann Bruen

Designer
Steven M. Blackwood

All About Delegation

With computers in their laps, phones on their dashboards, and faxes at their fingertips, information-age training managers may be tempted to shun traditional business methods. One key to management success, particularly in today's high-tech, high-pressure business arena, is the tried and true act of delegation. In fact, those who accept Peter Drucker's classic definition of management as "accomplishing tasks through others" insist that effective training managers must first be skillful delegators.

In essence, delegation is the process of transferring responsibility and decision-making authority from a supervisor to a subordinate. In day-to-day practice, that translates to making the best use of any organization's most valuable resource—people.

Although some management experts describe various levels of delegation, others distinguish between staff participation and true delegation. Theoretically, they say, participation emphasizes equality and conformity, while delegation—whether gathering information, recommending solutions, or taking complete charge of a project—encourages individual autonomy and achievement. From a pragmatic point of view, participation involves sharing authority, while delegation demands relinquishing authority—a much tougher, yet essential, task.

This issue of *Infoline* focuses on delegation in the strictest sense of the word. It explains the dual benefits of delegating that accrue in both time management and employee development. It counters typical objections, helps determine which tasks should and shouldn't be given away, steers around obstacles, and offers a clear-cut, step-by-step approach to successful delegating. Most important, it presents delegation as a valuable skill to be learned.

Delegation: Art or Science?

Business literature is full of references to the "art of delegation." Differing managerial styles and people skills ensure that each supervisor's approach to delegating is a unique one. And, as with any craft, creativity and practice can yield winning results. But most management experts say the actual process of delegation can be dissected, labeled, explained, and replicated—just like any scientific procedure.

Is delegation an art or a science? The most effective delegators prove it's a combination of both. Just as great musicians must master scales and technique before interpretation, great delegators rely on both the rules and their own leadership finesse.

Why Delegate?

Delegation is most often billed as a time-saving mechanism for managers, but its benefits don't stop there. Successful delegating maximizes a company's output while producing competent employees, balanced budgets, and promotable managers. "Managers who delegate properly will always accomplish more than those who refuse to let go of projects their subordinates should be doing," says Eugene Raudsepp, president of Princeton Creative Research, Inc.

History confirms Raudsepp's premise. Among the nation's top bosses—our 41 presidents—skillful delegators, including Lincoln, Wilson, Eisenhower, and the Roosevelts, are praised for effective administrations, while "lone rangers" such as Cleveland, Harding, Polk, and Carter are criticized for lackluster performances.

From the Oval Office to the training office, effective delegation offers a wealth of benefits:

■ *More discretionary time for managers*
Supervisors freed from the tyranny of trivia can concentrate on the "big picture," rightfully dedicating their skills and expertise to strategic planning, policy making, and goal setting.

■ *Competent, motivated employees*
Workers mentored through increasingly difficult assignments grow in confidence, professionalism, and job satisfaction, contributing to efficiency, high morale, and low turnover within an organization.

■ *Bottom-line savings*
Proper delegation contributes to overall efficiency by ensuring that each job is completed at the lowest and least expensive level.

■ *Praise and promotion for the manager*
Department heads known for their capable staff and consistent production gain a reputation as shrewd managers, ripe for promotion. But supervisors who render themselves indispensable by failing to groom successors may be passed over.

■ *Fewer work disruptions*
Competent employees, groomed by delegation, can carry on the work of the department even in the manager's absence.

■ *Department recruitment*
Skillful delegators attract proficient employees, eager for a challenge.

■ *Trust between managers and subordinates*
Cooperating successfully on delegated assignments opens channels of communication and understanding.

Resisting Delegation

Despite these weighty arguments in favor of delegation, most managers resist sharing their work with others. "If you want something done right, you have to do it yourself" becomes their battle cry. It's natural that managers well on their way up the corporate ladder have mastered many tasks in their climb. They may even be the resident experts in their departments, capable of doing almost any job better and faster than their subordinates.

Yet those who try to do everything often accomplish nothing. President Jimmy Carter, for example, was so obsessed with detail he even monitored scheduling of the White House tennis courts. But in an August 1979 congressional poll, two-thirds of respondents rated Carter's performance below average, citing lack of leadership as his primary weakness.

The pressures of the presidency are so intense, in fact, that failure to delegate can kill an executive. James K. Polk's management philosophy was "to supervise the whole operation of the government," even to the point of meeting daily with Washington's street repairmen. Although he was only 49 when elected, Polk emerged from the White House an old man at 53 and died of heart failure 15 weeks later.

Considering the obvious advantages of delegating, why are many managers reluctant to entrust parts of their jobs to subordinates? According to Eugene Raudsepp, managers cite several reasons for their reluctance to delegate:

"What if they screw it up?" The corollary to "if you want it done right…," this excuse reflects a perfectionist manager's distrust of subordinates and fear of responsibility for their failures. Others dread dealing with an employee who hasn't performed well. Managers who invest time training their staff through effective delegation, however, are rewarded with competent, trustworthy employees. And savvy managers realize that delegation, like any worthwhile endeavor, involves a degree of risk.

"I've always done that job before." New managers, especially, may feel insecure in their new role. Missing the sense of competence and achievement they'd acquired in their former position, they may retreat to the comfort of old routines.

"I'm in charge here." Some managers insist on maintaining total control of their departments, making all the decisions and taking all the credit for success. By withholding information and authority from their subordinates, these despots ensure no one else sees the "big picture" but themselves.

"I can do the job twice as fast myself." Managers need to realize that time spent monitoring a delegated project is a long-term investment bound to pay off—in employee competence and time savings.

"They might do too good a job." Insecure or paranoid managers may fear losing their position to a rising young star. Some may try to hide talented subordinates in low-visibility jobs or squelch their ideas and enthusiasm with excessive criticism.

"I need to pull my share of the load." Some managers are afraid their supervisors will see them as lazy or weak if they give away work. Others hesitate to risk ill will by "imposing" on subordinates.

"My boss doesn't delegate." Managers often emulate their own mentors. Those who have never seen effective delegation in action probably haven't learned how to use it themselves.

"That job is mine!" Managers often retain lower-level jobs they consider prestigious or enjoyable.

"I need more to do." Workaholic managers may insist on hoarding projects just to feed their habit.

Public relations executive Nancy Hicks suggests these warning signs may indicate it's time to delegate:

Overwhelming managerial workload. Are you holding on to duties that someone else could do just as well as you?

Staff malaise. Do you sense a lack of creative energy among your staff? Are you hoarding new assignments and challenges that could bolster their enthusiasm?

Not breaking new ground. Have your job responsibilities remained unchanged, despite potential for professional growth? Can you give up some old responsibilities to make room for new ones?

The Critical Switch

Underlying these excuses, suggests Dale McConkey, author of *No Nonsense Delegating,* lurks a more fundamental reason why more managers don't delegate: Many of them simply don't know what they should be doing. They don't understand how their new management tasks differ from old technical duties or even previous lower-level management duties.

Giving Up the Solo Act

Entrepreneurs whose growing businesses catapult them into the role of CEO may find it particularly hard to hand over their pet projects to others.

"The entrepreneurial personality is not conducive to delegation," says Oksana Exell of the Canadian Federation of Independent Business. "Entrepreneurs by definition like to be in control—they take great pride in their independence and their gut sense of what's right—characteristics that make them poor team players and even poorer delegators." But reality dictates the necessity of sharing the work to ensure the survival of both the entrepreneur and his or her young company.

Seasoned business people offer these suggestions to fledgling CEOs:

Recognize the danger signs. Don't wait until crisis management becomes a way of life. It's time to delegate when there's not enough time for both day-to-day duties and long-range planning.

Decide what to delegate. Until you can afford enough employees to delegate all but high-level planning and goal setting, stick with what you're good at, and delegate in areas where you're not strong. A person who enjoys interpersonal relations might do well to hire an office manager and concentrate on sales, while a math wizard might prefer to keep the books and hire a sales manager.

Choose the right person. Thin through your requirements to define what type of personality and qualifications you're looking for. If you're not ready to take on a full-time employee, consider hiring consultants or outside advisors.

Keep the troops on track. Convince your employees you're serious about delegating. Back up a new manager's authority by refusing to impinge on his or her assigned area. Provide positive coaching and feedback, and request regular progress reports.

Check the bottom line. If profits are increasing, you know that your people are doing a good job and your experiment in delegation has been a success.

Adapted from Handing Over the Oars of Power, *by Carla Furlong* (Canadian Business, *October 1987).*

Are You Working On the Wrong Job?

Management expert Dale D. McConkey, author of *No Nonsense Delegation,* offers these clues to help identify managers who haven't yet made the "critical switch" from doing to supervising.

Managers are working on the wrong job, McConkey says, if they:

- hold daily staff meetings
- approve routine expenditures
- approve actions covered by established procedures
- roam the office for an hour or more daily
- require their people to copy them on all correspondence
- attend meetings that should be handled by subordinates
- become excessively involved in customer complaints
- retain detailed knowledge of everything in their office
- check that all lights are out at the end of the day
- believe they can do things better than subordinates
- lack planning and organizing skills
- don't know what and when to delegate
- fail to make expectations clear
- give detailed instructions to subordinates
- require frequent status reports
- delegate parts of a project rather than the whole project
- overrule decisions made by subordinates
- keep parts of their old job because they enjoy them
- concentrate on technical rather than conceptual skills
- emphasize hours worked rather than results achieved
- are perfectionists
- resist change and new ideas
- don't accept risks
- hate to admit mistakes or the need for help
- fear subordinates will show them up
- fear they won't have enough to do if they delegate
- attract followers rather than leaders
- don't train their people
- withhold credit when credit is due
- blame subordinates for all mistakes
- criticize subordinates in front of others
- gloss over poor performance
- follow a nebulous open-door policy
- spend too much time socializing with their people
- don't ask people to do things they won't do themselves
- correct others' mistakes for them
- make major decisions without consulting their people

These same individuals would quickly cry foul if a professional football coach insisted on suiting up, jogging out onto the field, and replacing the star quarterback. They'd frown with disapproval if a symphony conductor left the podium and demanded the guest artist's violin. And they'd scream in protest if the neighborhood soccer coaches sidelined the kids and took the field themselves.

Yet many managers—frustrated and confused by a lack of manager training—cling to their old jobs instead of moving on to new duties. In the process, they short-circuit both their own and their employees' development, while undermining overall departmental efficiency. These muddled managers may even become hopelessly discouraged and leave the organization, despite their innate potential for management success.

McConkey dispels this confusion by drawing a heavy line between "doing" and "managing." "Doing," he says, involves hands-on accomplishment of a task or project, while "managing" ensures that tasks are accomplished through planning, organizing, delegating, and controlling. McConkey explains these differences more fully by comparing the primary duties of lower- and higher-level jobs:

Higher Level
Planning
Broad thinking/action
Future oriented
Concepts
Priority matters

Lower Level
Executing
Narrow scope
Present oriented
Techniques
Routine

Though each manager's job includes aspects of both "doing" and "managing," each successive promotion requires a supervisor to give up more and more "doing" while assuming more and more "managing." Nothing is as essential to a manager's present and future success, McConkey claims, as this "critical switch."

From a psychological angle, the critical switch asks managers to examine their needs for self-esteem, control, and approval. Faced with a new position and new management duties, successful managers shift their source of self-esteem from their own technical accomplishment to the overall performance of their staff. They realize it's no longer necessary to be the best salesperson or technician. Their new goal is being the best manager.

Effective managers also learn to accept less direct control in technical areas. Though it may sometimes be uncomfortable, the process of relinquishing authority and control of the "doing" is necessary to free managers for their new "managing" duties.

Finally, mature managers realize that everyone runs into conflicts while directing people toward mutual goals. Managers must be prepared to settle such disputes, accepting the fact that not everyone will agree with their solutions and that some may even dislike them for it. Thorough training can help prepare future managers for new duties by explaining these crucial aspects of effective managing. In return, savvy managers who can shift smoothly into new positions bring benefits to themselves, their employees, and the company as a whole.

Deciding What To Delegate

Delegation is not abdication. Despite the value of delegating as a management technique, not all tasks should be given away. But knowing which jobs to farm out and which to keep is crucial to success. The rule of thumb suggested by most management experts is: "Never do anything someone else can do for you" or, in economic terms, "Never do anything that can be done just as well by someone who is paid less."

To apply this advice, McConkey suggests that managers examine what they really should be doing at their current management level, sort their activities into "managing" and "doing" categories, and develop a plan for gradually transferring the "doing" tasks to capable subordinates. Managers should always retain broader management duties, such as overall planning, policy making, goal setting, and budget supervision, as well as work that involves confidential information or supervisor-subordinate relations. And managers can never delegate away ultimate responsibility for the failure or success of their subordinates.

The following questions also may help managers evaluate whether or not to delegate a given task:

- How important is this job?

- Can I risk mistakes?

- Is anyone else besides me qualified and available to handle this task?

- If no one else is trained, can someone be trained to take over the job in the future?

- Will someone on my staff greatly benefit from the experience of completing this project?

- Am I avoiding the delegation of this job?

Step-by-Step Delegating

Though personal management styles differ, those individuals who have mastered the art of delegation invariably attribute their success to the following principles:

Pick the right person. In order to delegate effectively, managers must know their subordinates—their characteristics, interests, and skills. Raudsepp suggests compiling a comprehensive inventory of each employee's capabilities by reviewing personnel files, recalling previous performance levels, and scheduling personal interviews. Matching the right task to the right person maximizes chances of success and allows subordinates to develop at a comfortable pace. The perfect assignment will challenge, but not overwhelm, employees and offer them a chance to stretch beyond their present skills to attain a realistic goal.

Plan carefully; explain clearly. Envision the project, from start to finish, in your own mind. Then clarify the assigned task for your subordinate. Communicate your priorities (quality or speed?), the results you expect, and the criteria you'll use to evaluate performance. Be sure the employee understands and shares your vision, perhaps by asking him or her to repeat your explanation or by writing down important points. Less-experienced employees may require more guidance than seasoned staff, but keep the project's structure as loose as possible to encourage initiative and creativity. Focus on results, not operational details.

Delegate both responsibility and authority. Don't hamstring your subordinates. Be sure they have the ability to complete their assignments, including access to all necessary resources.

Set a schedule of checkpoints and deadlines. To ensure success, managers must monitor progress and redirect the effort if necessary. Employees undertaking unfamiliar assignments will need closer supervision than those who have already mastered their task. Investing this extra time in one-to-one employee training is the secret to cultivating top-notch staff members capable of saving the manager's time and the company's money.

Delegate the whole job. Subordinates will learn more and gain extra job satisfaction from completing an entire project rather than bits and pieces of someone else's job. Pride of ownership contributes to commitment and success. If for some reason you can't delegate an entire job to one individual, explain the relevance of his or her contribution to larger projects or organizational goals.

Be an encourager. Express confidence in your staff. Keep criticism constructive, directed at the task and not at the employee.

Evaluate. Discuss the finished project with your employee, focusing on results. Note suggestions for improving the delegation process. Correct failure tactfully and in private; reward success generously and in public. Recognition, increased responsibility, and greater authority are powerful motivators.

Choosing the Best Person

Picking the right person or persons to accomplish a delegated task requires an orderly selection process. Joseph T. Straub, in his article "Do You Choose the Best Person for the Task?" suggests that to properly analyze the task and the available candidates, you should consider the following factors:

How close is the deadline? Rush jobs require a worker who will do the task well—and on time.

How much coordination is needed? Delegate jobs that require cooperation to consensus-builders, not to your independent, less diplomatic employees.

How much innovation is involved? Innovative tasks should be assigned to workers who are creative. Routine jobs, on the other hand, should be assigned to those who enjoy detail-oriented work.

What else should you consider? Weigh enthusiasm and ambition as well. Choose employees who like to acquire new skills and are anxious to grow and meet new challenges. Have any of your employees asked to take on new assignments?

What if several people are qualified? There are three alternatives when faced with this dilemma:

1. Let the employees decide among themselves who will get the job. This will enable them to gain experience in compromise and group dynamics. Clarify, however, that by offering them this choice, you are not relinquishing your supervisory position.

2. Pick the person yourself, being careful to explain your choice to the others, assuring them that you will give them the next assignments that arise. This minimizes claims of favoritism or discrimination.

3. Choose a team of equally qualified workers.

What if there is no clear choice? Consider giving the job to the person who seems to need the experience the most, or who possesses the skills that the particular job requires.

● Discuss the assignment in depth with the candidate or candidates you have selected, expressing your belief that they will be up to the challenge. Be prepared to train less-qualified employees but stress that the responsibility for accomplishing the task is theirs.

Provide Authority

According to Robert Nelson, in *Empowering Employees Through Delegation,* a delegated task must be accompanied by a delegated level of authority. Too little authority limits choices the employee can make when attempting to accomplish the task. Too much authority can make a manager uneasy about the employee making costly mistakes. The solution, he says, is to determine ahead of time the appropriate level of authority for each delegated task using the following levels:

Level A (no authority). Use this level as infrequently as possible when the task is especially important or difficult, or the employee is inexperienced, and the manager is justified in retaining all authority. Characteristics of this level include:

- Manager determines employee's responsibilities and goals.

- Manager plans project and sets performance standards and communicates them to employee.

- Employee consults regularly with manager to report progress.

- Employee consults manager on all problems encountered.

Level B (minimal authority). Use this level as the employee gains experience and is ready for greater latitude. It gives the employee some input but enables the manager to stay informed and to intervene if necessary. It is characterized by the following:

- Manager determines employee's responsibilities, but manager and employee together set goals and performance standards and develop project plans.

- Employee consults regularly with manager to report progress.

- Employee consults manager on difficult problems.

Level C (medium authority). Use this level when the manager trusts the employee to make some decisions. It affords the employee greater latitude but lets the manager intervene when problems arise. Characteristics of this level include:

- Manager determines employee's responsibilities.

- Employee sets goals, develops project plans, and sets performance standards, then seeks manager's approval before continuing.

- Employee consults regularly with manager to report progress.

- Employee consults manager on difficult problems only when employee thinks it necessary.

Determining Whom To Hire

A venture capital company has a won a contract with a major computer company to develop a new product to scan circuit boards to detect construction errors. The recently promoted manager of software development is asked to help with a presentation to potential investors, citing what type of people they will need to develop the software, how many people they will need, and how long it will take to develop software for the computer company.

The manager's first step is to divide the types of software needed into three categories: most difficult, requiring someone with experience and creativity; moderately difficult, requiring someone with a fair amount of experience to determine what tools are useful; and least difficult, requiring some who can accomplish well-defined tasks.

There are various staffing alternatives available to the manager:

- Hire all inexperienced professionals, who will require a lot of on-the-job training. Salaries will be lower, but the process will take longer and require a lot of the manager's time.

- Hire all experienced professionals, which would be costly, require less time for training and management, but risk the manager's having less control over the final outcome.

- Hire a mix of experienced and inexperienced workers, leaving the experienced people to develop the difficult software and using the inexperienced ones to develop the less demanding software.

Problem: What is the best strategy for hiring the software development team? Hire all experienced professionals who have worked for years in the areas needed? Hire all inexperienced software personnel who will require training? Hire approximately equal numbers of experienced and inexperienced personnel? Hire more inexperienced personnel than experienced ones? Or hire more experienced than inexperienced people.

Solution: Hire more experienced software developers than inexperienced personnel. This is the best approach for a small start-up company. It will bring in highly qualified professionals to act as equals in determining design strategies. Training time for new professionals will be kept to a minimum. The manager can delegate high levels of authority to the experienced personnel and low levels to the new ones.

Adapted from Robert B. Nelson, Empowering Employees Through Delegation, *New York: Irwin, 1994.*

Level D (complete authority). Use this level when the employee has demonstrated competence in the type of assigned task. The manager has minimal interaction with the employee, save for status reports, and gains more discretionary time for other tasks. It is characterized by the following:

- Manager and employee together determine the employee's responsibilities.

- Employee sets goals and performance standards and develops project plans.

- Employee consults with manager only to give regular status reports.

Overcoming Obstacles

In addition to following the preceding guidelines for delegation, another way to ensure success is to be aware of the common pitfalls of the process and to know how to avoid them.

■ *Faulty communication*
Most delegating failures can be traced to misunderstandings between managers and subordinates. Clear directions and proper monitoring are crucial to success. Detail-oriented micromanagers defeat the purposes of delegation by wasting their valuable time and discouraging subordinates.

Employees can't function with a nagging supervisor hanging over their shoulders. Those who are never trusted with meaningful work become discouraged and may even leave. Conversely, vague directions and loose reporting procedures ("keep me posted") leave too much to chance.

Steer a safe course between the shoals by requesting regular progress reports and asking specific questions to pinpoint progress. And don't be afraid to suggest corrections along the way in order to keep the project focused and on course.

■ *Reverse delegation*
Delegation breaks down when a manager, for whatever reason, takes the job back. Bosses who renege on assignments or allow subordinates to delegate tasks back to them cheat themselves of extra time and their subordinates of the opportunity to develop professionally. Recheck to be certain your employee has access to sufficient resources to compete the assigned task, but restrict personal input to support

and feedback. "I'll get back to you on that," frees employees of their problems and commits you to respond, while "what are the alternatives?" and "what do you recommend?" lob the ball back into their court where it belongs.

Perfectionist, controlling "super managers" must learn to accept risks and imperfection rather than jerk jobs away from employees in the process of learning. Bosses should avoid answering tough questions, assuming difficult work, or suggesting easy solutions for subordinates temporarily stumped by a challenging assignment.

■ *Dumping dirty work*
Delegation should not be seen as an opportunity to unload tedious or distasteful tasks. Bosses who abuse their subordinates by farming out busywork, while keeping the most rewarding parts of a project for themselves, will pay a heavy price in low morale, high turnover, and reduced organizational efficiency.

■ *Emotional judgments*
Managers who let feelings cloud professional objectivity when matching projects and subordinates may overlook shortcomings in people they like or strengths in people they dislike. Playing favorites can result in too much work for some and resentment in others. Again, knowing your staff is the key to avoiding this pitfall.

■ *Glory-grabbing*
Some managers are tempted to take credit when a subordinate successfully completes a delegated task. But nothing is more demoralizing than to watch others win praise for your work. By contrast, subordinates whose accomplishments are recognized within the department and mentioned to supervisors up the line will be motivated toward continued growth and success. The most effective delegators take full blame when their people fail but give full credit when they succeed.

When Delegation Bogs Down

When an employee fails to perform a delegated task well, the response of his or her manager is critical to the future success of not only the employee but of the manager and other employees as well. Joseph T. Straub, in his article entitled "What Should You Do If Delegation Doesn't Work," suggests four steps a manager should follow to minimize confusion and resentment when delegation bogs down.

1. Talk before you act. Meet with the employee privately to explain why the work is unacceptable and to review performance standards. Ask the employee for solutions to the problem. Is lack of training, or a lack of sufficient authority, hampering the employee's performance?

2. Achieve closure on the conference. End the meeting with a clear understanding of where you go from there. Will you take back part of the task? What exactly is the employee expected to accomplish? Agree on standards to be met and arrange a timetable for follow-up.

3. Back up your words with actions. Monitor future performance carefully. Watch for possible anxiety or defensiveness on the part of the employee.

4. Delegate more work as performance improves. Restore duties that may have been taken back previously or add new elements to the job as warranted. Do this slowly so that the employee can integrate the new tasks into the work routine gradually and successfully.

Evaluating Delegation

Robert B. Nelson suggests that two questions must be answered when evaluating a delegated task:

1. Was the job completed properly and in a timely manner?

2. What could be done to better accomplish a similar task in the future?

The Delegator's Dozen

Dick Lohr, president of the Institute of Management & Sales Techniques, Inc., of Grafton, Virginia, teaches managers how to delegate effectively by following 12 developmental steps that he calls "the delegator's dozen."

1. Set a clear objective.

2. Select a delegatee, but not necessarily your best employee. Ask for volunteers.

3. If necessary, train the employee for the task. Delegation should increase confidence; so select a task that will stretch, but not break, the worker.

4. Ask the employee for ideas. He or she may have a different approach to the problem. This also ensures that the employee understands the task being assigned.

5. Assign the task and explain why that particular employee has been chosen.

6. Provide guidance. This doesn't mean telling the employee how to accomplish the task, but rather supplying needed facts and suggesting possible ways to achieve the goal.

7. Devise a "contract" to establish how much access the employee will have to company resources, how often you will follow up, and how the employee's performance will be evaluated.

8. Establish a budget and appropriate deadlines.

9. Maintain control over all aspects of the assignment.

10. Provide feedback—both positive and negative.

11. Evaluate the project when it is completed.

12. Identify the lessons you have learned—both managers and employees benefit from delegation.

Reprinted with permission from Industry Week *(February 6, 1995). Copyright Penton Publishing, Inc., Cleveland, Ohio.*

Use the following criteria for your evaluation:

■ *Compare results with initial goals*
Measure project accomplishment against the intended objectives. Did the employee understand the assignment, and did he or she have the proper authority to complete it? Did the manager clearly communicate objectives?

■ *Assess employee performance*
Objectively evaluate results with goals, ignoring personality factors. Note the quality of the results and the efficiency with which they were accomplished. Was the employee resourceful in overcoming problems and successful in obtaining the cooperation of others?

■ *Discuss evaluation with the employee*
Good evaluation contains both positive and negative feedback, always starting with the positive. Make sure that negative information is constructive and offered as a means of helping the employee improve performance. Emphasize solutions and ways to better approach future assignments. Be specific, and always hold performance reviews in private.

Don't permit the discussion of mistakes to discourage the individual from undertaking new tasks in the future. Suggest what could be done to avoid similar mistakes, seeking input from the employee.

■ *Evaluate the manager's role*
Managers must provide the proper atmosphere for employees to accomplish delegated tasks well. They should involve employees in the planning process, communicate their desires clearly; secure employee agreement with goals and standards; follow through on promised support; and properly evaluate employee responsibilities upon job completion.

■ *Reward outstanding performance*
Managers must recognize good performance so that employees know that their work is appreciated. Failure to do so undermines the organization's effectiveness and risks the loss of good employees.

■ *Hold employees accountable*
Just as rewarding good performance is critical, so is identifying and responding to poor performance. Failure to act will perpetuate inadequate performance and undermine the efficiency of the entire work force.

Delegation Quiz

Take the following test to find out if you delegate effectively. For each statement, mark the answer that most accurately describes your actual behavior or attitude and then check your score.

1 = Always	2 = Usually	3 = Sometimes
4 = Rarely	5 = Never	

	1	2	3	4	5	Score
1. Delegation to me means handing over responsibility for results together with the requisite authority and decision-making power.	☐	☐	☐	☐	☐	_____
2. No matter what the delegated task, I try to make it seem like a challenge.	☐	☐	☐	☐	☐	_____
3. I tend to delegate to the subordinate who has the best experience with a similar task.	☐	☐	☐	☐	☐	_____
4. I refrain from giving advice when delegating.	☐	☐	☐	☐	☐	_____
5. I have full confidence in my subordinates' abilities to shoulder increasingly more difficult responsibilities.	☐	☐	☐	☐	☐	_____
6. I make sure important decisions on delegated tasks remain with me.	☐	☐	☐	☐	☐	_____
7. I insist tasks be done according to the methods I have outlined.	☐	☐	☐	☐	☐	_____
8. I make sure controls are built into all tasks and projects I delegate.	☐	☐	☐	☐	☐	_____
9. I am willing to admit some of my subordinates are able to do the job as well, or better, than I can.	☐	☐	☐	☐	☐	_____
10. I make sure to acknowledge good performance.	☐	☐	☐	☐	☐	_____
11. When I have to criticize, I do it fairly.	☐	☐	☐	☐	☐	_____
12. I feel I must be in control of delegated tasks all the time.	☐	☐	☐	☐	☐	_____
13. My subordinates defer all decisions on problems to me.	☐	☐	☐	☐	☐	_____
14. I find work slows down when I am out of the office.	☐	☐	☐	☐	☐	_____
15. I am reluctant to give feedback when a subordinate turns in poor work.	☐	☐	☐	☐	☐	_____
16. Daily operations are so time consuming I have little time left over for long-range planning.	☐	☐	☐	☐	☐	_____

	1	2	3	4	5	Score
17. I am constantly harassed by unexpected emergencies.	☐	☐	☐	☐	☐	_____
18. Many of my tasks are beyond what my subordinates can handle.	☐	☐	☐	☐	☐	_____
19. My subordinates are not sufficiently motivated to perform well.	☐	☐	☐	☐	☐	_____
20. I am bothered by unfinished business.	☐	☐	☐	☐	☐	_____
21. I have to keep close control of every detail to have a job done right.	☐	☐	☐	☐	☐	_____
22. I expect perfection of myself in everything I do.	☐	☐	☐	☐	☐	_____
23. I am willing to accept complicated work that is less than perfect.	☐	☐	☐	☐	☐	_____

1 = Agree	2 = Disagree

	1	2	Score
24. I am often bogged down in endless detail.	☐	☐	_____
25. I frequently put in overtime.	☐	☐	_____
26. I often take work home evenings or weekends.	☐	☐	_____
27. There have been times I have taken back a task midstream without explanation.	☐	☐	_____
28. I work harder than most people in my department.	☐	☐	_____
29. My subordinates seldom come to me to present their ideas.	☐	☐	_____
30. My subordinates seldom show any initiative.	☐	☐	_____
31. I seldom ask a subordinate to do something I would not be willing to do.	☐	☐	_____
32. I often handle routine work in order to appear busy.	☐	☐	_____
33. Some of my subordinates are out to get my job.	☐	☐	_____
34. If I were promoted today and had to name a successor, I would have little trouble choosing one.	☐	☐	_____
35. If I were to leave my company today, my department would continue to function properly.	☐	☐	_____
36. I am often amazed at the incompetence of my subordinates.	☐	☐	_____

Reprinted with permission, Machine Design, *by Eugene Raudsepp, © 1989.*

Scoring

	1	2	3	4	5
1.	6	4	2	1	0
2.	0	1	3	4	5
3.	1	2	3	4	5
4.	1	2	3	4	5
5.	6	5	3	1	0
6.	1	2	3	4	5
7.	0	1	3	5	6
8.	6	5	3	1	0
9.	6	5	3	1	0
10.	6	5	3	1	0
11.	6	5	3	1	0
12.	1	2	3	4	5
13.	0	2	4	5	6
14.	0	1	2	3	5
15.	1	2	3	4	5
16.	0	1	3	4	5
17.	1	2	3	4	5
18.	1	2	4	5	6
19.	1	2	3	4	5
20.	1	2	3	4	5
21.	0	1	3	4	6
22.	1	2	3	4	5
23.	5	4	3	1	0

	1 = Agree	2 = Disagree

	1	2
24.	1	4
25.	2	4
26.	2	4
27.	3	5
28.	3	5
29.	1	5
30.	0	5
31.	2	4
32.	1	4
33.	2	5
34.	5	1
35.	5	1
36.	1	5

If you scored **136-185,** congratulations, you obviously know how to delegate tasks and responsibilities to your subordinates.

If you scored **74-135,** you sometimes do a good job of delegating. However, some of your attitudes and behaviors are acting as barriers to good delegation.

If you scored **30-73,** there seem to be serious weaknesses in your delegation skills that need attention.

Reprinted with permission, Machine Design, by Eugene Raudsepp, © 1989.

References & Resources

Articles

Abbott, Pat. "Delegating." *Telephone Engineer & Management,* vol. 81, March 15, 1987, p. 120.

Anders, Geoffrey T. "Duties You Should—and Shouldn't—Delegate." *Medical Economics,* August 15, 1988, pp. 182-191.

Axley, Stephen R. "Delegate: Why We Should, Why We Don't and How We Can." *Industrial Management,* vol. 34, September/October 1992, pp. 16-19.

Baughman, Rowland G. "The Art of Becoming Unnecessary." *Management World,* November-December 1988, p. 26.

Berk, Joseph M., and Susan H. Berk. "Delegating Effectively." *Manage,* vol. 39, January 1987, p. 8.

Brunsman, Roger. "Who's In Charge When You're Absent?" *Supervisory Management,* vol. 39. April 1994, p. 3.

Bushardt, Stephen C., Aubrey Fowler Jr., and Eric P. Fuselier. "Delegation, Authority, and Responsibility." *Akron Business and Economic Review,* vol. 19, Spring 1988, pp. 71-78.

Calano, Jimmy, and Jeff Salzman. "How Delegation Can Lead Your Team to Victory." *Working Woman,* vol. 14, August 1989, pp. 86-87+.

Callarman, William G., and William W. McCartney. "Reversing Reverse Delegation." *Management Solutions,* vol. 33, July 1988, pp. 11-15.

Caudron, Shari. "Delegate for Results." *Industry Week,* vol. 244, February 6, 1995, pp. 27-30.

Conroy, Robert M., and John S. Hughes. "Delegated Information Gathering." *Accounting Review,* January 1987, p. 50.

Davidson, Jeffrey P. "Successful Staff Motivation Hinges on Enthusiastic Delegators." *Data Management,* vol. 24, June 1986, pp. 17-19.

Deeprose, Donna. "Working Smarter: Managing Multiple Priorities." *Trainer's Workshop,* vol. 6, July/August 1992, pp. 1-48.

Dimma, William A. "On Leadership." *Business Quarterly,* Winter 1989, p. 17.

Dinsmore, Paul C. "Delegating Responsibility and Authority." *Trainer's Workshop,* vol. 6, 1991, pp. 4-48.

Dorgan, William J., III. "Delegating Means Not Dumping!" *Modern Machine Shop,* March 1989, p. 120.

Dowd, Ann Reilly. "Learning from Reagan's Debacle." *Fortune,* vol. 115, April 1987, pp. 169-172.

Feferman, Richard N. "The Case Plan: An Effective Aid in Delegation." *Legal Economics,* vol. 12, March/April 1986, pp. 30-31.

Feinstein, Selwyn. "Delegator-Managers Are Out: Companies Now Seek Hands-On Executives." *The Wall Street Journal,* April 5, 1988, p. 1.

Firnstahl, Timothy W. "Delegating Your Life Away!" *Nation's Restaurant News,* February 9, 1987, p. 7.

Flamholtz, Eric G., and Yvonne Randle. "How To Develop a Managerial Mindset." *Working Woman,* vol. 13, April 1988, pp. 26-30.

Forbes, Paul M. "Fourth Management Skill: Delegating." *National Petroleum News,* June 1989, p. 66.

Furlong, Carla. "Handing Over the Oars of Power." *Canadian Business,* vol. 60, October 1987, pp. 100-101.

Hicks, Nancy. "How to Delegate." *Public Relations Journal,* vol. 44, June 1988, pp. 31-32.

Hoagland, Pamela R. "Delegation for the Busy Administrator." *Journal of Reading,* vol. 32, March 1989, pp. 550-551.

Horton, Thomas R. "Delegation and Team Building: No Solo Acts Please." *Management Review,* vol. 81, September 1992, pp. 58-61.

Iaconetti, Joan. "Seven Delegating Mistakes—and How to Avoid Them." *Working Woman,* vol. 12, July 1987, pp. 24-27.

Kirby, Jess. "Delegating: How To Let Go and Keep Control." *Working Woman,* April 9, 1990, p. 42.

Klock, Joe. "Delegation: An Art or a Science?" *Real Estate Today,* November/December 1989, p. 67.

Knippen, Jay, and Thad B. Green. "Delegation: What Are the Outcomes of Ineffective Delegation?" *Supervision,* March 1990, p. 7.

Labich, Kenneth, and Kate Ballen. "The Seven Keys to Business Leadership." *Fortune,* vol. 118, October 24, 1988, p. 58-70.

Leana, Carrie R. "Power Relinquishment Versus Power Sharing: Theoretical Clarification and Empirical Comparison of Delegation and Participation." *Journal of Applied Psychology,* vol. 72, May 1987, pp. 228-233.

Longenecker, Clinton O. "The Delegation Dilemma." *Supervision,* vol. 52, February 1991, pp. 3-5.

Luquire, Sharon. "Learn to Hand Off Work Gracefully." *RN,* July 1989, p. 19.

Maihafer, Harry J. "The Rewards and Dangers of Overdelegating Authority." *The Wall Street Journal,* September 28, 1987, p. 32.

Marini, Richard A. "Letting Go: The Secret to Power Is Delegating." *Success,* vol. 35, June 1988, pp. 40-41.

Marquand, Barbara. "Effective Delegation." *Manage,* vol. 45, July 1993, pp. 10-12.

Mayo, Edward J., and Lance P. Jarvis. "Delegation 101: Lessons from the White House." *Business Horizons,* vol. 31, September-October 1988, pp. 2-12.

McConkey, Dale D. "Whose Job Are You Working On?" *Business Quarterly,* vol. 51, March 1987, pp. 39-42.

References & Resources

McCullough, Rose V. "A Three-Step Process for Effective Delegation." *Rough Notes,* vol. 130, April 1987, pp. 39-40.

———. "Delegation: A Not-So-Simple Skill Which Requires Planning, Objectivity." *Rough Notes,* vol. 129, February 1986, pp. 45-47.

McVicker, Mary Frech. "Delegating Can Be Good for Managers, Employees." *Contractor,* November 1988, p. 57.

Metz, Alex. "Improve Productivity Through Delegation." *Transportation & Distribution,* vol. 33, January 1992, pp. 25-26.

Molloy, Francis S. "The Delicate Art of Delegation." *Journal of Forms Management,* vol. 12, February/April 1987, pp. 19-21.

Morgan, Dennis F. "Delegating for Time." *Records Management Quarterly,* vol. 21, July 1987, p. 35.

Morgan, Rebecca L. "Guidelines for Delegating Effectively." *Supervision,* vol. 56, April 1995, pp. 20-21.

Nelson, Robert B. "Empowering Employees Through Delegation." *Small Business Reports,* vol. 19, June 1994, pp. 56-58.

———. "Mastering Delegation." *Executive Excellence,* vol. 7, January 1990, pp. 13-14.

Nilson, Carolyn. "How To Use Peer Training." *Supervisory Management,* vol. 35, June 1990, p. 8.

Nisbet, Michael A. "The Art of Delegation." *Canadian Banker,* vol. 95, September/October 1988, pp. 36-37.

Pollock, Ted. "Secrets of Successful Delegation." *Production,* vol. 106, December 1994, pp. 10-11.

———. "When You Must Give an Unpleasant Assignment." *Production,* vol. 107, April 1995, p. 11.

Raudsepp, Eugene. "How To Delegate Effectively." *Machine Design,* vol. 61, April 20, 1989, pp. 117-120.

Rozek, Michael. "Giving Away Work." *USAir Magazine,* July 1990, pp. 24-29.

Russell, Anne M. "How To Manage a Grand Project." *Working Woman,* December 1989, pp. 73-75.

Sandage, Suanne M. "The Art of Delegating." *Real Estate Today,* October 1988, pp. 45-46.

Savary, Suzanne. "Ineffective Delegation—Symptom or Problem?" *Supervisory Management,* vol. 30, June 1985, pp. 27-33.

Schilit, W. Keith, and Howard M. Schilit. "Improving Your Time Management Skills." *Journal of Accountancy,* vol. 162, July 1986, pp. 116-121.

Schwartz, Andrew E. "The Why, What, and to Whom of Delegation." *Management Solutions,* vol. 32, June 1987, pp. 31-38.

Smith, Perry M. "20 Guidelines for Leadership." *Nation's Business,* vol. 77, September 1989, pp. 60-61.

Solomon, Jolie. "1960s Political Term Resurfaces in Business ('Empowerment' Becoming a Management Buzzword)." *The Wall Street Journal,* November 20, 1989, p. 81.

Stevens, Mark. "Cardinal Sins of Management." *Nation's Business,* vol. 78, February 1990, pp. 53-54.

Straub, Joseph T. "Delegation Dilemma: What Should You Do If It Doesn't Work?" *Supervisory Management,* vol. 34, August 1989, pp. 7-10.

———. "Do You Choose the Best Person for the Task?" *Supervisory Management,* vol. 37, October 1992, p. 7.

———. "What Should You Do If Delegation Doesn't Work?" *Supervisory Management,* vol. 39, November 1994, p. 3.

Swindall, Linda. "Delegate, Delegate." *Working Woman,* vol. 10, July 1985, pp. 18-23.

Thomas, William C. "Delegation—A Skill Necessary in School-Based Management." *NASSP Bulletin,* vol. 73, September 1989, p. 30.

Tracey, William R. "Deft Delegation." *Personnel,* vol. 65, February 1988, p. 36.

Treese, Lorett. "Teach Employees Not To Bring You Their Problems." *Supervision,* vol. 50, March 1988, pp. 6-8.

Vinton, Donna. "Delegation for Employee Development. *Training & Development Journal,* vol. 41, January 1987, pp. 65-67.

Wojcik, Joanne. "Changing Times at Small Firms: Risk Managers Delegate More." *Business Insurance,* May 7, 1990. p. 52.

Yate, Martin. "Delegation: The Key to Empowerment." *Training & Development,* vol. 45, April 1991, pp. 23-24.

Books

Galbraith, Jay R. *Designing Complex Organizations.* Reading, MA: Addison-Wesley, 1973.

Nelson, Robert B. *Empowering Employees Through Delegation.* Burr Ridge, IL: Irwin, 1994.

Percival, Nora, ed. *Practicing the Art of Delegation.* New York: American Management Association, 1969.

Steinmetz, Lawrence L. *The Art and Skill of Delegation.* Reading, MA. Addison-Wesley, 1976.

Job Aid: Keys to Success in Delegating Tasks

Successful delegating can be broken down into three major areas: deciding what to delegate, to whom to delegate, and providing guidance. The following "keys" can help you delegate effectively.

1. Decide what to delegate.

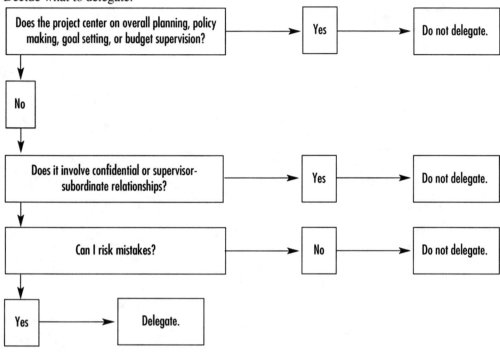

2. Decide to whom to delegate the project.

    a. Who among your subordinates is qualified and available? _____

_____

    b. Who can be trained to complete the project? _____

_____

    c. Who will benefit most, in terms of career development, from completing the project? _____

_____

3. Define the project.

- Clarify project goals and expected results.
- Establish priorities.
- Explain the criteria for evaluation.
- Establish a project schedule.
- Monitor progress.
- Reward results.

Leading Work Teams

Issue 0602

Leading Work Teams

AUTHOR

Kathryn Gaines
Leading Pace, LLC
6105 Twain Drive
New Market, MD 21774
Tel: 301.865.2960
Fax: 301.865.3688
Email: kgaines@
leadingpace.com
Website: www.LeadingPace.com

Kathryn Gaines has served as a management and organizational consultant, coach, and trainer for 15 years. She partners with client groups to improve performance, results, commitment, and accountability in the workplace. Gaines specializes in developing leadership and teamwork.

Associate Editor, ASTD Press
Tora Estep
testep@astd.org

Editor
Sabrina E. Hicks

Editorial Consultant
Chris Battell

Copy Editor
Ann Bruen

Production Design
Kathleen Schaner

Manager, ASTD Press
Mark Morrow

Leading Teams

Everyone works on teams. You work with co-workers within your department, with clients and customers, across organizational functions, and on temporary committees. Such collaboration is mandatory to achieve organizational goals. One benefit of the team structure is that you have the opportunity to hone your leadership skills, whether or not you hold the title of "team leader."

Every element of a team's success depends on its leadership processes: planning, clarifying roles, building relationships, accomplishing tasks, negotiating conflicts, navigating changes, making decisions, and solving problems. To complicate matters, the structure of today's workforce is complex:

- a team leader may work in a different time zone than his or her team members

- team members may report to more than one leader in a matrix operating structure

- a team, working on a knowledge-intensive project, may have a leader who has less technical expertise than some of his or her team members.

Cross-functional teams and geographically dispersed organizations—these are just a few of the current workplace trends that make the traditional command-and-control leader obsolete. Traditional conceptions of leadership focus on the top leader in the hierarchy selling a clear, compelling picture of the future to everyone in the organization. Present day notions of leadership center on a team of workers discovering a shared vision of the future. The best teams are those in which each member expresses some type of leadership—either formal or informal—to achieve team goals.

If you find yourself in a formal position of leadership, it's your responsibility to cultivate leadership—at all levels. Empowering all members of a team is important because, although you are the designated team leader, you may not be the expert, and you certainly won't always have the answers.

By becoming more engaged in leadership, with or without formal authority, you contribute greater value to, and have more impact on, your team.

Engaging in Leadership

Leadership is a process of influencing others to work toward the shared goals of the team. It is a collaborative relationship built through communication and influence behaviors.

While not everyone is a leader in the formal, traditional sense of the word, everyone shares an obligation as a member of a team. You have the responsibility to speak up, take action, and show initiative to mobilize your team to achieve results.

This *Infoline* will guide you in the application of basic leadership principles in a team setting. Whether you don the title of team leader or are one of many team members participating in the leadership processes, this *Infoline* offers tips and tools to help you

- break through barriers to effectively engage in leadership

- influence your team members by building and sustaining respect, trust, and credibility

- understand and strengthen the five core leadership behaviors and skills:
  — employing a *pulling* communication style
  — conveying information clearly and credibly
  — facilitating group learning and insight
  — envisioning an inspiring future
  — advocating action

- assess your skills and identify areas for improvement.

Basic Building Blocks

Respect, trust, and credibility are the fundamental building blocks of leadership. These basic elements inspire commitment and enlist the cooperation necessary to mobilize others to work together toward shared goals. Identifying, developing, and using behaviors that build respect, trust, and credibility can sometimes be challenging. You'll notice these behaviors in how you treat people and how you relate to others. But influence is not developed overnight. It takes time to build relationships and establish your reputation.

Obstacles to Leadership

To fully engage in leadership, you must first identify what obstacles are in your way. Consider how your perceptions, beliefs, and experiences could interfere with your participation in leadership.

☐ I am reluctant to speak up or take initiative because I do not feel that it is "my place." I worry that I will be seen as stepping outside the proper boundaries of formal authority.

☐ I have a formal position of leadership, but I do not want to be seen as pushy or aggressive.

☐ I have a formal position of leadership, but I am worried that I do not have the "right" answer or solution.

☐ I do not believe that it is my responsibility to participate in leadership unless I am officially given the title or position. Isn't that why people in formal leadership positions are paid more and given higher status?

☐ I am unwilling to accept the responsibility of engaging in leadership. It is not a risk I need to take. After all, isn't leadership the obligation of those in formal leadership positions?

☐ I do not participate in leadership because my team or organization does not provide any rewards or incentives for doing so.

☐ I do not participate in leadership because my team or organization punishes those who do so.

☐ I no longer participate in leadership. I have tried to do so in the past, but I ended up either overloaded or unappreciated. I felt exploited or taken for granted.

☐ I have tried to engage in leadership without formal authority. Others did not respond positively. I am afraid or unwilling to try again.

☐ I would like to participate in leadership; however, I am uncertain how to do it, so I just let it go.

Respect

If people respect you, they

● listen to what you have to say
● take you seriously
● seek your input
● demonstrate that they value your contributions.

But, respect is reciprocal. One way to gain respect is by showing respect to others. To build respect on teams, you should listen, support, and follow.

■ *Listen to Understand*
Demonstrate respect by listening to understand, not to respond. Using classic active listening behaviors (such as reflecting and paraphrasing) is an excellent way to do that.

■ *Ask Questions*
Convey an interest and a sense of value in others by asking questions (instead of giving answers) and taking the time to explore and probe to reach a deeper understanding. When you invest the time to fully understand what your team members are saying, you show not only that you care but also that you are open and objective.

■ *Do Real Work*
Directing, telling, advising, and ordering from the sidelines won't motivate modern work teams. But if you get down to business and put forth real effort—shoulder to shoulder—with your teammates, you'll inspire them. That shows respect.

■ *Provide Opportunities*
Another strategy for building respect is to provide opportunities for others to lead you. If you are secure enough to step aside and let someone who has more expertise lead the way, you show that not only are you open to learning from others but also that you respect your teammates. It also helps to admit your mistakes.

Trust

Respect is relatively easy to secure. You can convey it immediately as you interact with others. Trust is more difficult to build. Occasionally, people are generous and will trust you until there is some reason not to trust. Most of the time, however, people will trust you only after repeated positive experiences. Trust comes down to a simple mathematical equation: trust = your actions + your words.

● Do you do what you say that you're going to do?

● Have you established a reputation of following through on your promises—enough to make co-workers believe that you're likely to continue to do so in the future?

The level at which you are able to build trust with team members coincides with the consistency between your actions and your words.

■ *Walk the Talk*

One way to strengthen a connection is by making sure that your practices and behaviors align with your espoused values and beliefs.

■ *Assume the Best*

Another way to engender trust is by being predisposed to trust others. If you give people the benefit of the doubt, and are open and trusting of others, then others will more likely perceive you as trustworthy.

■ *Set High Expectations*

Finally, holding yourself and your teammates to the same high standards will help everyone achieve the consistency and fairness needed to build trust.

Credibility

Credibility inspires in others the conviction that is essential for influence and leadership. Respect and trust are both elements of credibility, but they are not the whole picture. Cultivate credibility by demonstrating that you have competence, sincerity, and integrity.

Leadership Skills Inventory

Consider each influence and leadership skill listed below in connection with your own behaviors and capabilities. Rate your strengths and opportunities for development.

1 = Strong   2 = Average   3 = Needs Development

1.	Listens openly to understand.	1	2	3
2.	Poses questions rather than tells information.	1	2	3
3.	Reports observations objectively.	1	2	3
4.	States position, thoughts, and feelings openly and objectively.	1	2	3
5.	Conveys information clearly and credibly.	1	2	3
6.	Offers group process feedback.	1	2	3
7.	Facilitates group learning and insight.	1	2	3
8.	Envisions an inspiring future.	1	2	3
9.	Advocates for action.	1	2	3

■ *Competence*

Stemming partly from technical expertise and education, competence also comes from the work experiences you bring to the team. In both respects, a sign of competence is not only being capable, but also being aware of your weaknesses and blind spots: Know what you do not know.

■ *Sincerity*

Credibility also comes from sincerely valuing the interests of others. It is built through honest, open, and authentic communication. Do you really care about those you lead and serve? Are you able to convey that care and interest sincerely?

■ *Integrity*

One way to demonstrate integrity and build credibility is by acknowledging and utilizing the strengths of your teammates. You're more apt to be viewed as credible if you are not threatened by their talents and expertise, and are willing to empower them. You must know when to step aside and allow others the chance to lead.

If people believe that you have a solid, moral character, their best interests at heart, and strong capabilities or expertise, then they're likely to see you as credible. Credibility, paired with trust and respect, is fundamental to leadership. The use of threats, rewards, coercion, or raw power will gain only compliance, not commitment.

Influence Behaviors and Skills

Leadership is not about being heroic, popular, powerful, or famous; it's about being wise, confident, and unafraid to do the right thing for those you serve. Leadership is a way of communicating (the act of speaking up) and behaving (how you speak up). Not only do you need to understand the characteristics that are necessary to influence others, but also you must practice certain behaviors. To have influence, you must increase your chances that people will be receptive to what you have to say. Connect their interests and goals with the needs and directions of the team, and you'll do just that.

Two communication skill sets are fundamental to influence. The first set—pulling communication—pertains to understanding; the second—authentic communication—concerns being understood and motivating others to action.

"Pulling" Communication Style

To best communicate with your team, it is better to "pull" than to "push."

A *pulling style* of communication means listening without providing an immediate response or reaction. It involves paraphrasing, reflecting, asking questions, and probing to get beyond the surface of the statement. Not only does a pulling approach provide a better understanding of the other person's needs, position, and situation, but also it conveys respect and demonstrates openness and objectivity. This approach prevents you from leaping to conclusions and helps you check your assumptions.

In contrast, a *pushing style* of communication involves telling, advising, directing, and giving information. Pushing is almost always met with resistance, especially if you don't have formal authority. If you're trying to influence a person or a group of people to move in a certain direction, then a pushing style is likely to be too forceful and create unproductive resistance. For example, if you disagree with a team member, your typical pushing responses might include

● evaluating, attacking, or judging his or her position

● offering data or arguments to explain why his or her position won't work

● telling him or her what should be done instead

● providing warnings or making threats about what will happen if the team goes in that direction.

Such responses create an adversary for you and inspire push-back from your team. In addition, your team might view you as a poor leader or a difficult team member. But you can avoid all that by using a pulling style of communication to demonstrate your respect, openness, and understanding. Such behavior increases the likelihood that your teammates will accept your position, and it helps to build a more collaborative, influential relationship.

You've probably heard of the pulling style of communication before. It is similar to Peter Senge's (known for his work on the learning organization and author of the book *The Fifth Discipline*) notion of balancing inquiry and advocacy. If you take a position and dig in your heels to defend it, then you get caught in destructive, unproductive interactions. If you're too forceful and pushing in your style of communicating, you're going to turn people off, construct walls, and limit your opportunities to influence others. Even if co-workers initially do what you want or fail to voice any opposition because they are intimidated, you still haven't succeeded in inspiring commitment or building ownership. In the long term, you fail to influence and lead.

Naturally, the pulling style of listening and working to understand is only half of the leadership equation. If you did nothing except observe, listen, and ask questions, you would merely serve as a facilitator—with minimum influence. You won't be valued as a contributor. You might understand others (an essential element of being influential), but you won't be understood or make an impact. To be influential, you need to convince others to discover or recognize what the team can do collaboratively to succeed. Only when the team is motivated to act together to achieve common goals have you achieved "leadership." For that, you need to be able to assert a clear, credible position.

Authentic, Inspiring Communication

The second skill set centers on the ability to state thoughts and perceptions directly, honestly, and objectively without attacking, judging, controlling, or threatening others. This skill must be paired up with communication that inspires others to action.

Authentic, inspiring communication behaviors include

- stating your position, thoughts, and feelings openly and objectively

- conveying information clearly and credibly

- facilitating group learning and insight

The Push–Pull Communication Continuum

The next time a co-worker brings a nontechnical problem to your attention, try to resist the urge to provide a solution straightaway (that's an outdated form of leadership). Instead, try the following pulling communication behaviors:

- Paraphrase and reflect back to your co-worker his or her description or feelings about the situation.

- Ask open-ended questions: "Tell me more about that." "Could you elaborate further?" "Could you help me understand better?"

- Summarize key points and continue to probe further with questions such as, "What else do you think could be going on?" or "What might be some other things contributing to this?"

- Ask your co-worker, when you're confident that you share a deeper understanding of the problem, "What do you think would help turn this situation around?" or "How do you think we should address this?"

Avoid or minimize the following pushing communication behaviors:

- telling co-workers what to do
- offering advice
- providing recommendations or solutions
- giving information
- sharing your own experiences.

If you use pushing behaviors to address a problem, you risk losing a chance to provide your co-worker with a learning opportunity. In addition, he or she probably won't feel as committed to the solution if it is provided by someone else.

Essential Components of Authentic Communication

It takes practice to state your position clearly and objectively, without judgment. Listed below are the six essential components necessary for authentic communication with your team.

- Influence others in a direct, positive way—not with tricks, coercion, or manipulation.

- Practice an active and initiating (rather than reactive) mode of behavior.

- Exhibit self-expression in which you stand up for your needs and wants without denying the needs and wants of others and without experiencing undue anxiety or guilt.

- Possess a nonjudgmental attitude that minimizes the use of labels, stereotypes, and prejudices.

- Take responsibility for yourself by not making other people responsible for who you are, what you do, and how you think and feel.

- Communicate wants, dislikes, and feelings in a clear, direct manner without threatening and attacking.

- envisioning an inspiring future

- advocating action.

You must possess self-awareness and self-control to make use of this skill set. You must also be able to assess and diagnose the situation and adapt your communication behaviors to the context.

■ Convey Information Objectively

You must be able to objectively relay information about what you observe, think, feel, want, or need. You can achieve that in several ways:

- report your observations and experiences without judgment or evaluation

- own your perceptions and feelings by using "I" statements

- describe the impact of specific team member behavior you observe or experience, which includes praise and encouragement for positive contributions.

In addition, you must acknowledge the needs, perceptions, thoughts, and positions of others. Empathizing and recognizing the constraints, frustrations, or obstacles other team members face is one way to show you understand; thus, you encourage others to be more understanding of your position and needs.

If you are aware of the needs and interests of others, you can use that knowledge to appeal to what is important to them and build influence toward meeting the overall needs of the team. Use these authentic communication skills individually or combine them. Remember, these skills are not just for team meetings; you can use them in one-on-one scenarios also.

When you effectively use these behaviors, you create communication that is clear, direct, and understood by others. However, you are not engaging in leadership until others are moved to act on behalf of the common goals of the team. Facilitating learning and awareness, envisioning an inspiring future, and advocating for action are ways to participate in leadership.

■ *Facilitate Learning and Awareness*

If you frame a problem or point out an issue, invite the team to reflect upon it (consider its causes and impact), and respond to it in some way, you've facilitated learning and awareness. The following are pulling communication behaviors that help to facilitate awareness:

● Solicit the team's perceptions first. Let each member speak to his or her behaviors by asking, "What do you notice about what is going on with the group now?" or "What are others observing or feeling right now?"

● Report your observations. Focus the team's attention on a specific pattern that you notice in the group. Don't overload team members, and don't become the judge or evaluator. State, "What I saw happening was…" or "What I heard (team member X) say was…." Most important, don't forget to offer praise, encouragement, and recognition for positive dynamics and contributions.

● Ask questions to verify your perception. Find out if the team agrees with you by asking, "Did anyone else see or hear that?" "Am I off target?" "Is there another way to interpret that?"

● Clarify the implications of the identified pattern. Find out what your team members think the impact of that pattern or behavior will be by asking, "What impact does that behavior have on the team's ability to perform?"

● Present possible solutions, and ask the team to prioritize or assess them. You facilitate learning and awareness by offering process comments that encourage team members to pay attention to how they interact and relate to others. Process comments should include statements that praise, support, and encourage the team.

Envision an Inspiring Future

Because constant, turbulent change is a daily reality for most organizations, the view of the future is often blurred. It's easy to lose sight of your ultimate destination. The steps below use pulling communication behaviors and group facilitation to encourage discussion and clarification of your team's shared vision.

1. Distribute sticky notes, index cards, or slips of paper to each team member.

2. Pose the following question to the team: "It is one year from now. We have succeeded at achieving our mission. Describe what it looks like and what is going on. What's it like to work on this team?"

3. Ask each person to write down one description or idea per sticky note or piece of paper.

4. Collect all the ideas and begin reading them out loud to the team, posting them on a wall or board, and grouping them into like categories.

5. Once all of the ideas are posted, invite everyone to silently review and move the items until the team is satisfied with how the ideas are organized and categorized.

6. As a group, title each category. This will reveal the central elements of the team's shared vision.

7. Based on these elements, the team can craft a powerful, compelling picture of the future.

With this ultimate vision in mind, the team will make decisions, allocate resources, and take action. If it is not motivating, inspiring, shared, and understood by all, the team is not likely to achieve its potential.

Case Scenario: Leadership as a Team Attribute

You are a research physician employed by a global pharmaceutical company. You are serving on a cross-functional drug development team. The project team comprises biologists, chemists, statisticians, marketing professionals, and regulatory affairs officers. You are the only M.D. on the team.

The team has spent considerable time, money, and other resources to develop a compound that showed great promise in the early stages of clinical development. However, as further testing was performed, the drug proved to have only slight positive effects. Because so much had been invested in early testing and development of the drug, the team leader decided to press forward. He is convinced that the drug will be this year's breakthrough blockbuster and feels that his career as a project leader and his future with the organization is riding on its success. Earlier in the development process, preliminary data suggested the weak positive effects of the drug. The team leader refused to take the data seriously and transferred to another team the individual who pointed out the data.

The drug is now far into the final development stage, and, as you review the results from several clinical trials, you come across disturbing information that points to serious, though non-life-threatening, side effects of this drug. You are questioning the payoff of taking this drug through full development.

Discussion

1. Which response below is closest to how you would handle the situation—not how you think you should handle it?

Option A: Speak up adamantly at the next meeting. Share your concerns and doubts with the team. Point out the potential costs and impact of the team's decision. Demand that the team reconsider its decision and take the findings more seriously.

Option B: Schedule a one-to-one meeting with the team leader. Share your concerns and doubts with him. Point out the potential costs and impact of the team's decision. Appeal to the possible impact on his career if this drug is a failure. Ask him to reconsider the decision and to take the findings more seriously.

Option C: Let this one go. You need to pick and choose your battles. You have reported the data from the clinical trials. It is the team leader who is ultimately responsible and accountable. Why should you stick out your neck and risk being transferred from the team?

Option D: Refuse to work on this project. Resign from the team on ethical grounds.

Option E: Pose some questions for the group at the next meeting. Point out your concerns and doubts by raising them as questions for the team. Seek the team's input and reaction.

2. What is the potential impact of each option on you, on the team, and on the organization?

Option A: This approach uses a *pushing* style of communication that gives information, tells people what to do, and can often be seen as aggressive. The team leader might view it as an attack and could be threatened by this approach. This response could easily create a defensive, adversarial climate on the team, rather than an open, collaborative climate. The team could be less open to your arguments and naturally resist if you push or demand too adamantly. The team leader might transfer you from the team as he did the other team member who voiced opposition. Bottom line: The team is not likely to listen or seriously consider the issues you raise.

Option B: This approach allows the team leader to save face. Depending on your relationship with the team leader, it could be a direct and honest way of bringing up your concerns. But this "behind closed doors" approach still incorporates a pushing style of communication. Even if you use a respectful tone, the team leader could view this as a direct challenge. The team leader could be less open to your arguments and naturally resist if you push or demand too adamantly. The team leader might transfer you from the team as he did the other team member who voiced opposition. Bottom line: The team leader is not as likely to listen or seriously consider the issues you raise. There's a good chance that this will never be brought up with the rest of the team.

Option C: This approach might seem the safest and most comfortable. It is also the most passive. As the only physician on the team, it is critical to consider your responsibility for ensuring the clinical safety of the drug under development. This approach will protect you, but what are the implications for patients and other stakeholders? As with all options, it is important to weigh the costs and benefits.

Option D: This response makes your position clear, but what result does it achieve? The team is likely to feel relieved that one more obstacle is moved out of its way. Team members are likely to continue on the path they've chosen. Bottom line: Nothing is likely to change, and you will have abdicated any responsibility.

Option E: This approach puts the concerns on the table and offers them to the team for consideration. It strikes a nice balance between an aggressive and a passive response. It does not abandon responsibility, but it is not pushy or domineering. This is the action that most closely resembles leadership. It puts the spotlight on the issue and offers it to the entire team to own and handle.

The Next Step

There are no clear-cut right or wrong answers. All situations requiring leadership are complex and values-based. You need to consider your intentions, the potential impact of your actions, the larger goals of the team, and the costs and benefits of every alternative.

Although there is no magic recipe, there are some important ingredients. You need to strike a balance between forceful, aggressive behavior and passive, laissez-faire behavior. Your objective is to influence the decisions and actions of the team in ways that move the team toward achieving its overall goals. You need to know how and when to intervene. Consider where on the continuum your response would fall: Do you use more of a pushing or pulling communication style?

You also might need to identify and challenge your assumptions about leadership. For example, as the physician on this team, would you feel an obligation to act or speak up, or do you feel it is the sole responsibility of the designated team leader? Would you worry about stepping on toes because you are not the official leader? Do you feel that it is your right to speak up or intervene?

■ *Envision an Inspiring Future*
A shared vision of the future can motivate people to work together toward a common goal. Any person can help his or her team envision an inspiring future by appealing to the shared values, needs, and priorities of the team. Invite the team to begin creating its shared vision of the future by describing an ideal or imagined scenario for the group. Another approach is to pose a question to the group: "What does success look like for us?" The objective is to have a clear, shared understanding of an inspiring vision of the future.

■ *Advocate Action*
Ultimately, leadership is not happening if people are not influenced to take action to achieve the common goals of the team. Advocating action is a key leadership skill. Use one of the following approaches to inspire action:

● Argue for a specific course of action. Take a position and present reasons and arguments for why the team should pursue that course of action. Lay out the costs and benefits or the pros and cons. Appeal to the needs, priorities, values, and emotions of the team. Assuming you have established credibility with the group, you will persuade them.

● Prompt the team to closure. Encourage the group to make a decision or take action, but not necessarily in a particular direction. This approach uses communication skills reviewed earlier (such as providing process comments, reporting observations, and posing questions). It can often be as simple as saying: "We seem to be going back over the same ground here. Are we ready to make our final decision?"

● The third approach combines aspects of the first two approaches. It involves building dialogue and group discussion in order for the team to reason through alternatives and make a choice. Asking the following questions provides an opportunity for the team to think through the application of each approach:

— What actions are you advocating?
— Who are the stakeholder groups that will be affected?
— What are their needs, priorities, values, and expectations?

Stages of Team Development

Teams go through predictable stages of development, and different types of leadership are needed at each stage. The text below describes the characteristics of each stage and lists the various leadership skills required to help a team progress to the next stage. By identifying what stage your team is in, you'll be able to pull from the broad range of leadership capabilities to meet the needs of the team.

Stage: Forming

Team members discover what behaviors are acceptable to the group during the forming stage. For newly established groups, this is a stage of transition: from individual to team member. The forming stage is a time in which members will test behaviors and dependence on formal or informal group leadership—especially for teams with new leadership, a new mission, or new members. Other characteristics of this stage are:

- identification of tasks and decisions about how the group will accomplish those tasks

- decisions on the type of information needed and how it will be used

- participation that is hesitant

- tests of behavioral expectations and ways to handle behavioral problems

- feelings of initial attachment to the team

- discussions of problems peripheral to the task

- complaints about the organizational environment

- suspicion, fear, and anxiety about the new situation

- minimal work is accomplished (people are not clear about objectives, and there can be false starts).

Leadership Needed

- Provide more direct, hands-on leadership.

- Pay attention not only to the tasks but also the relationships.

- Dedicate time to define the mission, goals, boundaries, resources available, and roles.

- Allocate space for the group to begin building trust and open communication. (Team members need to get to know one another better; clarify hopes and fears about the team; and understand each other's strengths, needs, and expectations.)

- The tools that are essential to the forming stage are ice-breakers, team builders, team norms and ground rules, a strategic or operational plan, and role descriptions.

Stage: Storming

During the storming stage, team members may become aggressive or overzealous as a way to express their individuality and resist the group. Members recognize that the team's task is demanding, and they respond emotionally to the perceived requirements for self-change and self-denial. This is particularly relevant for cross-functional teams in which team members over-identify with their function or discipline and cultivate an "us/them" mindset, rather than a "we" mindset. Other characteristics of this stage are:

- in-fighting, defensiveness, and competition

- establishment of unattainable goals

- disunity, increased tension, and jealousy

- resistance to task demands because they are perceived to interfere with personal needs

- polarization of group members

- fluctuations of relationships and reversals of feelings

- concern over excessive work

- establishment of pecking orders

- low to moderate work accomplished because energy is spent on resistance and conflict.

Leadership Needed

- Provide active, hands-on leadership if you are in a formal leadership position.

- Be less directive and more facilitative than in the forming stage.

- Use process comments and facilitation behaviors to help the team surface, discuss, and resolve the dynamics that are diverting energy from the real purpose of the team.

- Expect the storming stage. It is normal, so you should schedule the time needed to work through it.

- Recognize that charging forward, without dealing with this stage, means that you bog down the team and detract from productivity.

Stage: Norming

The norming stage is when you notice team members accepting the team, team norms, their roles, and the idiosyncrasies of fellow members. Emotional conflict is minimized as the team norms and relationships are developed. Other characteristics of this stage are:

- an attempt to achieve maximum harmony by avoiding conflict

- a high level of intimacy (characterized by team members confiding in each other, sharing personal problems, and discussing team dynamics)

- a new ability to express emotions constructively

- a sense of team cohesiveness with a common spirit and goals

- the establishment and maintenance of team boundaries

- moderate work accomplishment.

Leadership Needed

- Use a hands-off, facilitative leadership style.

- Spotlight issues and conflicts that the team may be avoiding or ignoring for the sake of cohesion.

- Continue to provide feedback to the group, but do it on a process level rather than task level.

- Recognize that the team will see directive, task-oriented communication as mistrust and micro-management.

- Continue to offer praise and make sure that the team members know you are there to support them and advocate for them.

Stage: Performing

Now that the team has established its interpersonal norms, it enters the performing stage. It is capable of diagnosing and solving problems and making decisions. Other characteristics of this stage are:

- insight into personal and interpersonal processes
- constructive self-change
- a great deal of work is accomplished.

Leadership Needed

- Formal leadership recedes into the background as a leader-aware team is cultivated.

- Team members lead themselves and each other.

- Leadership emerges collectively, and team members step into and out of leadership roles as needed.

- Formal leaders do not abdicate leadership responsibilities; they continue to offer support, advocacy, and feedback.

Although the stages are described as separate and distinct, it's important to remember that you'll experience a considerable degree of overlap. In fact, you'll often notice elements of one stage present in every other stage. However, it's the dominant behaviors that determine the developmental stage of the team.

During the life cycle of the team, it's common to add or lose members, get a new mission or task, or experience a change in leadership. Any of those events will cause some change in the team development cycle and will require reassessment and modification of behavior. In general, when a significant change occurs, it's likely that the team will move backward through the development stages. A good leader will notice the effect of a change on a team and will modify his or her behavior to reflect the appropriate stage of the team.

Identify a Stage

- Consider your work team. What stage of team development seems most predominant? What behaviors do you see?

- How can you help the team successfully negotiate that stage? What does the team need?

— What emotional or persuasive appeals could you use to connect with those needs, values, priorities, or expectations?
— How will this course of action benefit the stakeholders?
— What are the potential risks or costs of this course of action for each stakeholder group?
— How will you avoid or minimize those risks or costs? How are they outweighed by the benefits?
— How does this course of action compare with alternatives?
— How can you establish your credibility with stakeholders in order to convince them to take this action? What knowledge, experience, sincerity, or integrity do you bring to the argument?

If the team is persuaded or inspired to act, then securing or providing needed resources to support the action can be another way of exerting leadership.

Leadership in Action

All leadership behaviors are communication and influence activities. None relies on formal authority or position power. Any member of a team, organization, or community—regardless of title, rank, or position—can use these behaviors and engage in leadership. But it's not simple or easy. Leadership is a complex process that requires skill-building, practice, experience, perceptiveness, and flexibility. You must overcome obstacles, develop capabilities, diagnose each situation skillfully, and become adept at combining the correct mix of skills to suit the context. After reading this *Infoline*, you should have the information and resources you need to engage in leadership on work teams.

References & Resources

Articles

Barry, D. "Managing the Bossless Team: Lessons in Distributed Leadership." *Organizational Dynamics,* vol. 21 (1991), pp. 31-47.

Dotlich, D.L., and S.H. Rhinesmith. "The Unnatural Leader." *T+D,* March 2005, pp. 27-30.

Goldstein, M. "Building Speak-Up in Corporations." *T+D,* July 2005, pp. 37-42.

Hollander, E.P. "Leadership, Followership, Self, and Others." *Leadership Quarterly,* vol. 3 (1992), pp. 43-54.

Hollander, E.P., and L.R. Offerman. "Power and Leadership in Organizations: Relationships in Transition." *American Psychologist,* vol. 45 (1990), pp. 179-189.

Manz, C.C., and H.P. Sims Jr. "Superleadership: Beyond the Myth of Heroic Leadership." *Organizational Dynamics,* vol. 19 (1991), pp. 18-35.

Marion, R., and M. Uhl-Bien. "Leadership in Complex Organizations." *Leadership Quarterly,* vol. 12 (2001), pp. 389-418.

Pearce, C.L., and H.P. Sims Jr. "Shared Leadership: Toward a Multi-Level Theory of Leadership." *Advances in Interdisciplinary Studies of Work Teams,* vol. 7 (2000), pp. 115-139.

Raelin, J. "Preparing for Leaderful Practice." *T+D,* March 2004, pp. 64-70.

———. "The Myth of Charismatic Leaders." *T+D,* March 2003, pp. 46-52.

Schwarz, R. "Becoming a Facilitative Leader." *T+D,* April 2003, pp. 51-58.

Walston, S.F. "Courage Leadership." *T+D,* August 2003, pp. 58-60.

Books

Badaracco, J.L. Jr. *Leading Quietly: An Unorthodox Guide to Doing the Right Thing.* Boston: Harvard Business School Press, 2002.

Bennis, W. *On Becoming a Leader.* Reading, MA: Addison-Wesley, 1989.

Bergman, H., K. Hurson, and D. Russ-Eft. *Everyone a Leader: A Grassroots Model for the New Workplace.* New York: Wiley & Sons, 1999.

Block, P. *Stewardship: Choosing Service Over Self-Interest.* San Francisco: Berrett-Koehler, 1993.

———. *The Empowered Manager: Positive Political Skills at Work.* San Francisco: Jossey-Bass, 1987.

Cohen, A.R., and D.L. Bradford. *Influence Without Authority.* 2nd edition. San Francisco: Jossey-Bass, 2005.

Drath, W. *The Deep Blue Sea: Rethinking the Source of Leadership.* San Francisco: Jossey-Bass, 2001.

References & Resources

Hakim, C. *We Are All Self-Employed: A New Social Contract for Working in a Changing World.* San Francisco: Berrett-Koehler, 2004.

Heifetz, R.A. *Leadership Without Easy Answers.* Cambridge, MA: The Belknap Press of Harvard University Press, 1994.

Hesselbein, F., M. Goldsmith, and R. Beckhard, eds. *The Leader of the Future: New Visions, Strategies, and Practices for the Next Era.* San Francisco: Jossey-Bass, 1996.

Huszczo, G.E. *Tools for Team Leadership: Delivering the X-factor in Team Excellence.* Palo Alto, CA: Davies-Black, 2004.

———. *Tools for Team Excellence: Getting Your Team Into High Gear and Keeping It There.* Palo Alto, CA: Davies-Black, 1996.

Katzenbach, J.R., and D.K. Smith. *The Wisdom of Teams: Creating the High Performance Organization.* New York: HarperCollins, 1993.

Kouzes, J.M., and B.Z. Posner. *Credibility: How Leaders Gain and Lose It, Why People Demand It.* San Francisco: Jossey-Bass, 1993.

———. *The Leadership Challenge.* San Francisco: Jossey-Bass, 1995.

Lencioni, P. *The Five Dysfunctions of a Team.* San Francisco: Jossey-Bass, 2005.

———. *Overcoming the Five Dysfunctions of a Team.* San Francisco: Jossey-Bass, 2002.

Marquardt, M. *Leading With Questions: How Leaders Find the Right Solutions by Knowing What to Ask.* San Francisco: Jossey-Bass, 2005.

Raelin, J.A. *Creating Leaderful Organizations: How to Bring Out the Leadership in Everyone.* San Francisco: Berrett-Koehler, 2003.

Senge, P.M. *The Fifth Discipline: The Art and Practice of the Learning Organization.* New York: Doubleday, 1990.

References & Resources

Infolines

Butruille, S.G. "Listening to Learn; Learning to Listen." No. 258806 (revised 1997).

DeForest, H., P. Largent, and M. Steinberg. "Mastering the Art of Feedback." No. 250308.

Russell, L. "Leadership Development." No. 250508.

Sindell, M., and T. Hoang. "Leadership Development." No. 250101.

Thomas, S.J. "Developing Thought Leaders." No. 250410.

Job Aid

An Action Plan for Engaging in Team Leadership

Use this worksheet to develop a personal action plan to help you participate in leadership on your team.

Topic/Skill	Potential obstacles and challenges	How I will strengthen and develop this element	Resources needed and how I will access them	Target date
Basic building blocks: respect, trust, credibility				
Listening openly to understand				
Posing questions rather than telling or giving information				
Reporting observations objectively				
Stating my thoughts and position directly and openly				
Conveying information clearly and credibly				
Facilitating group learning and insight				
Envisioning an inspiring future				
Advocating action				

How to Resolve Conflict

Issue 0104

How to Resolve Conflict

AUTHORS

Phoebe A. Sheftel
Email:
psheftel@windsorassociates.com

Matthew Bennet
Email:
mbennet@windsorassociates.com

Windsor Associates
PO Box 432
Ardmore, PA 19001
Tel: 610-896-9909
Web: www.windsorassociates.com

Windsor Associates provides environmental and public policy mediation and facilitation, and organizational development for governmental, corporate, and community groups.

Editor
Cat Sharpe Russo

Managing Editor
Stephanie Sussan

Production Design
Kathleen Schaner

Workplace Conflict

Mention the terms *conflict* and *mediation* and most people think of labor negotiations. Over the past number of years, conflict-resolution techniques have been embraced by many individuals and organizations to reach collaborative solutions in all types of disputes. There's a reason for this—the philosophies and methods that have emerged from the last several decades of labor negotiation serve as a foundation for creating consensus in the workplace and overcoming conflict.

Examples of workplace situations where conflict management is effective include:

- A firm upgrades its computers, causing feelings of uneasiness and insecurity among employees.

- A business's plan to construct a new facility provokes neighborhood opposition.

- An organization is restructuring and encounters resistance from long-term employees.

- Business partners are dissolving a small firm and want to find a way to get through the process without ending up in court.

- A company wants to use new technology to clean up a waste site, but the government enforcement agency wants to adhere to existing regulations.

What triggers workplace conflict? Anything from a lack of information to competition for limited resources can cause a conflict. Other triggers include miscommunication among employees, change in the workplace environment, and differing values.

How an organization reacts to conflict can result in either a *destructive* or a *constructive* outcome. A destructive tact can divert energy from important issues, decrease productivity, polarize groups and build distrust among co-workers. A constructive take, however, can not only resolve a problem, but can ultimately lead to a higher level of understanding and communication among colleagues.

Conflict Management Theory

There are two schools of thought on producing effective outcomes in conflict situations:

1. The settlement-driven approach.

2. The relationship-focused approach.

Behind both theories lies the principle that the individuals involved in the conflict are the people best positioned to resolve the situation. Through negotiation, they will focus on a resolution that is most beneficial to all parties. When the individuals can not come to a resolution, it is then necessary to call in an outside party, usually referred to as the conflict manager, to facilitate a resolution to the situation. Once a conflict manager has been called in, he or she can focus on helping the participant find a solution based on an underlying issues that caused the conflict.

Since the 1994 publication of *The Promise of Mediation* by Robert A. Baruch Bush and Joseph Folger, many conflict managers have embraced a philosophy of relationship-based mediation, which highlights mending the broken relationship between the disputants, with the understanding that only then will the parties be in a real position to design their own solution. An agreement is seen as a useful outcome, but not the only goal of the process.

This issue of *Infoline* will present the two schools of thought and then focus on a step-by-step approach for applying sound principles of conflict resolution to most situations. This is accomplished by using a conflict manager to help resolve workplace disagreements. In addition, the roles of all participants are clearly defined to help you understand the appropriate behaviors and ensure success to resolving conflict.

Use Communication Skills

A conflict manager ideally accepts differences while maintaining respect for what all the involved parties need. Developing the skills to manage conflict and make it productive is not easy. It requires a willingness to listen and understand others. It also requires practice.

Training for conflict managers basically is a refinement of everyday communication skills. People in a conflict often are looking to win, or at least survive. Many times people are preparing their next arguments rather than listening to what the other person is saying.

In addition to actively listening, it is important to occasionally summarize the thoughts on the floor to let everyone know you have been listening. Don't be afraid to ask questions or involve everyone in the discussion.

Conflict management builds on the basic communication tools. By working with those tools, a strong, productive working environment will develop.

Models for Resolution

Negotiation is the simplest form of settlement. Each of us negotiates in our professional and personal lives, whether it's closing a deal with a client, buying a car, or deciding where the family will take a vacation. How well we negotiate largely depends on our willingness to take the time to prepare for the negotiations. Understandably, the amount of preparation time directly corresponds to the complexity of the negotiation and the importance of the outcome.

If two or more competing or disagreeing parties can reach their own agreement, they may pave the way for a better working relationship in the future. The main goal in direct negotiation is to find a solution to the problem.

The steps in negotiation are:

- The conflicting parties need to clearly define their own objectives and goals.

- The parties must carefully anticipate the other party's needs and underlying interests.

A successful negotiation is based on clearly explaining your own needs and fully understanding the other's interests. Only then is it productive to turn your attention to developing and negotiating settlement options.

Another key step to the process is understanding that you may not get 100 percent of what you desire. Therefore, it is important to come up with an alternative solution that would be acceptable to you. Having a best alternative to a negotiated agreement (BATNA) in your back pocket gives you with options that will keep you from settling for less than you could achieve through negotiation.

Determining your BATNA is key for anyone preparing to participate in a conflict-resolution process. A BATNA, first coined by Roger Fisher and William Ury, authors of *Getting To Yes*, keeps you from settling for an unacceptable agreement. It provides you with an understanding of your alternatives in advance, without setting an inflexible bottom line that may limit your creativity in developing a wholly unanticipated solution.

A well-considered BATNA gives you a tool that is far more effective in negotiations than other external sources of power (wealth, size, position).

Settlement-Driven Approach

In the settlement-driven approach, success often is measured in terms of whether an agreement is reached. For example, if an employee is upset because he says he never receives his messages from the receptionist, a settlement-driven solution could be to have all his calls go directly to his voice mail rather than going through the receptionist. Solving the problem is the driving factor in this approach.

Relationship-Driven Approach

In this approach, the goal is to empower the conflicting parties to create their own solution based on a recognition of each other's interests. In this manner, relationships are mended and individual participants tap into their own creativity to craft a resolution. Using the example posed above, in a relationship-driven approach, a mediator would try to draw out why the receptionist wasn't delivering his messages, and help the employee explain why it was important to get the messages promptly. The theory here is that by helping the disputants understand the motivations behind their actions, they can craft a solution that addresses those needs.

This is the approach that the U.S. Postal Service (USPS) has adopted in its mediation program, called REDRESS (Resolve Employment Disputes, Reach Equitable Solutions Swiftly). The USPS program provides a quick, informal alternative to the Equal Employment Opportunity process of filing a formal complaint. Instead, a professional mediator from outside the USPS is brought in to quickly facilitate a solution to a pending conflict.

The difference between the two approaches is that the former solely seeks to find a solution to the immediate problem, whereas the relationship-driven approach looks to dig out the issues that are causing the conflict. The latter approach may or may not result in a resolution, but it can help build understanding.

Using a Conflict Manager

If direct negotiation between the parties does not work, or if the situation involves a number of people and complex issues—such as an entire division of a company at odds over which new computer program will provide them with the technology to get the job done in the most efficient manner—then the situation calls for employing a conflict manager.

Stakeholders in a conflict may feel they can move forward quickly because they are familiar with the topic. But without the help of a trained conflict manager, they may avoid the uncomfortable step of abandoning their starting positions long enough to explore new solutions. Left on their own, they may unconsciously collude to avoid seeing reality or perpetuate dysfunctional ways of discussing problems.

A conflict manager is a neutral, third party who directs the process, and facilitates a resolution. The conflict manager's objective is to help the conflicting parties meet their needs through an agreement that everyone can live with. This agreement can be settlement-driven, relationship-driven, and often is a combination of both.

The role of the conflict manager is complex. First, he or she must become familiar with the issues behind the dispute. It is misleading to assume that the person with the most authority (such as the boss) should facilitate a collaborative process; it may be more useful to have that person's input as part of the group. (See *Things to Consider When You Select a Conflict Manager* sidebar on the next page.)

When people decide they need someone to help them through a decision-making process, they should look for certain qualities that will enhance that third party's effectiveness. The qualities include:

■ *Neutrality*
While it is nearly impossible to be entirely neutral, the mediator's goal is to conduct the process in an unbiased manner as possible, so that in the end, each participant could say that he or she had been treated fairly and respectfully.

Things to Consider When Selecting a Conflict Manager

Using the following list to tailor your search for a conflict manager will help you find the right person for your situation.

☐ Determine your goals for the process.

☐ Decide if you want a facilitator who will suggest options or one who focuses on helping the participants generate their own ideas.

☐ Get names of members of organizations such as the Association for Conflict Resolution or the International Association of Facilitators, statewide mediation organizations, or consult with a local community mediation center.

☐ Ask the candidates about their training—the number of hours, the credentials of the trainers.

☐ Decide if it is important that the facilitator have knowledge of the subject under discussion or if an unbiased view will help you see things differently. Ask the facilitator what he or she thinks; ethical standards require a person to step down from facilitating when they feel they lack specific qualifications.

☐ Use an interview to get a sense of the facilitator's interpersonal skills, maturity, integrity, and sensitivity. Ask what values and goals the facilitator emphasizes in his or her practice.

☐ Get an understanding of what preparation the facilitator feels is necessary to set the stage for a productive meeting. Discuss who will select the participants and why it might be important to have a neutral party play a role in that process.

☐ Ask which ethical standards the facilitator follows and request a copy of them.

☐ Discuss confidentiality and exactly what that will mean in your situation.

☐ Find out the cost structure—if it is based on an hourly rate or a fixed fee, and whether travel time is included.

■ *Awareness of Bias*

During the preliminary assessment, the facilitator should reflect on any factors that could trigger personal biases and take intentional steps to avoid letting them influence his or her management of the process. This might mean teaming with a co-facilitator who can handle those hot-button issues or personalities. In some cases it can mean stepping aside and offering to help the group find a replacement facilitator.

■ *Ability to Listen*

It is very important that the mediator be able to quickly pick up the information necessary to understand the organization, the conflict, and what caused the conflict within the organization.

■ *Understanding*

Being part of a conflict is a very stressful experience. A conflict manager needs to be understanding of that and work to alleviate some of the stress.

The convener has an important role in this process. The convener is the person who calls in the conflict manager. The convener, who is frequently the highest-level manager for the group involved in the conflict, has several responsibilities, which include:

- making an initial assessment of the situation

- determining the key stakeholders

- interviewing, selecting, and negotiating terms with the conflict manager.

The stakeholders are groups or individuals that have an interest in the conflict. For a conflict to be meaningfully resolved, all of the important stakeholders must be involved in the resolution process.

Using Internal or External Resources

Conflict managers can come from within a company or from an outside source. Both have negative and positive attributes associated with them.

The Internal Conflict Manager

This is an individual from within the organization who is not directly involved with the people in the dispute. This approach combines the benefits of a person who is neutral to the outcome, but who has knowledge of the context.

Please be aware of these potential issues:

- Avoid using a facilitator who reports to one of the parties.

- If the situation involves disputants from outside the organization, the internal facilitator may not be accepted as impartial, no matter how much experience he or she has.

The External Conflict Manager

Using an individual from outside an organization can ensure a non-biased viewpoint, neutrality, and professionalism. When seeking out an external conflict manager, look for someone with training and experience and someone who can promote inquiry and help reveal important underlying issues that need to be addressed. An external mediator can focus on managing the process of conflict resolution, while stakeholders can devote energy to listening, understanding, and finding solutions.

Be aware of these issues when using an external conflict manager:

- It takes time to find a suitable external consultant.

- There is an expense associated with using an external consultant.

- It may be difficult to locate an external conflict manager who understands the frequent, complex, and technical nature of specific conflicts arising in workplace situations.

Managing Conflict

You can opt for a settlement-driven approach or a relationship-focused approach, but whichever approach you select, there are two additional ways to categorize conflict management:

1. **Reactive.** An immediate conflict emerges and dispute resolution methods are employed in an attempt to resolve it productively.

2. **Proactive.** The potential for conflict is identified in an upcoming action. A conflict management strategy is institutionalized to improve the chances for productive dialogue, while minimizing the opportunity for disagreement to halt progress.

Both approaches to conflict management involve similar steps and require similar skills to implement. The well-prepared conflict manager will be conversant in both methods and be prepared to adapt to whatever a situation presents.

Reactive and *proactive* can be value-laden terms, with respectively negative and positive connotations. They are used here merely to draw the distinction between when conflict management strategies are introduced into a situation. Most people tend to expect they will avoid conflict and rely on what they believe are well-conceived strategies to effect change or deal with controversial situations. As a result, most conflict is confronted only after the crisis has erupted.

Reactive Conflict Management

Conflict management in the workplace is inevitable. How it is managed may mean the difference between success and failure. Generally the first step is negotiation. If that fails, the parties will call in a conflict manager to find a solution. Use the following five steps to manage conflict and develop a productive solution.

Step 1: Identify Stakeholders

Identify who is involved and who needs to be involved. Stakeholders can be two individuals, multiple internal parties, or a mix of internal and external parties. Identifying all of the stakeholders up front ensures that you include the right people in any discussions and they become invested in creating the solution.

This step may seem obvious, but it is sometimes overlooked in the haste to resolve an issue. The convener will frequently claim to know who should be involved and want the conflict manager to get on with bringing people together to work out a solution. The best place to start finding out who should be at the table is by asking the parties involved who else needs to be part of the solution.

Setting the Stage

A well-prepared meeting location sets the tone for the group's interaction and helps diffuse polarizing issues.

Choose a neutral setting.

Use round tables to counter a sense of hierarchy.

Set up the room so everyone can see and hear one another.

Plan ways to maximize involvement, such as:

- Break down into smaller groups.

- Pair off people who may be on opposite sides of an issue.

- Have everyone write out ideas on separate cards that you can stick to the wall and rearrange as needed.

Give breaks and include snacks to sustain the group's energy level.

Step 2: Prepare an Assessment

The second step is to develop an understanding of the parties' perceptions of the conflict. This includes discovering:

- reasons why the conflict occurred

- the parties' interest in its resolution

- barriers to its resolution

- strategies for its resolution

- the parties' willingness to participate in a collaborative search for solutions

The assessment is a valuable preparation tool. It helps the conflict manager understand the nature of the issues. Once everyone comes together to work on issues, the conflict manager can use his or her understanding of the underlying conflicts to encourage the parties to consider all the problems and any solutions. The assessment process not only gives the parties their first chance to be heard, but it helps them hear themselves. Explaining their interests to a neutral third party forces the parties to examine their own interests and start thinking about their goals. (See the job aid *Conflict Assessment Tool* at the back of the issue.)

Step 3: Create a Forum

Using the information gathered during the assessment, the conflict manager now designs the forum. This forum can be as simple or as complex as the issues indicate.

The forum might be a single meeting where the parties seek resolution. It might entail multiple sessions, combining large and small group discussions, working groups, one-on-one discussions, agreement writing teams, and more.

Through the forum, the conflict manager provides a structure that responds to the needs of the parties and the situation. (See *Setting the Stage* sidebar on the previous page.)

Step 4: Prepare an Agenda

Although an agenda is important for any meeting, it is particularly important for this process. The conflict will stress the participants. An agenda gives the parties a preview of each step in the process and a sense of what they can expect from the meeting. It is usually a good idea to share, or even create, the agenda with participants before the meeting so they can begin to develop ownership of the process. (See *Sample Agenda* sidebar on the next page.)

Step 5: Conduct the Meeting

After an opening explanation of the meeting's purpose, agenda, and process, the conflict manager will work the parties through the following steps. The complexity of the issue will determine how much time and effort is spent with each stage in the process.

■ *Adopt Ground Rules*
The process of adopting ground rules is the first test of a group's ability to work within a collaborative setting. The guidelines can be as detailed or simple as the group decides, but ground rules should at least cover critical topics like confidentiality and the decision-making process. (See *Ground Rules, Confidentiality and Consensus* sidebar on the next page.)

■ *Identify the Conflicts*
The conflict manager may provide a summary of the issues identified during the initial assessment or ask the parties to name the issues themselves. This is a judgment call for the conflict manager. If you present the points of conflict for the group, it may be a more objective list than the parties would provide. It is essential, however, that you allow the group to modify or add to the list of issues.

Reframe the issues as joint problems, rather than leave them as personalized criticisms or attacks. For instance, turning accusations such as "she never lets me know what's planned for the meeting" and "he doesn't return my calls" into a statement about a shared communication problem helps the parties focus on joint problem solving rather than personal feelings from the past.

Ground Rules, Confidentiality, and Consensus

Setting ground rules and feeling comfortable and secure at the negotiation table can make a huge difference in trying to come to a consensus on the solution to the pending dispute.

Ground Rules

Knowing the expectations for the meeting makes people more comfortable and able to engage in difficult discussions. Ground rules can be as simple or as complex as the group requires. Posting the ground rules for everyone to see makes it easier for the group to police itself and accept responsibility for what happens in the meeting. Here are some sample ground rules:

- Share all relevant information.
- Use questions to test assumptions and inferences.
- Explain the reasons and motivations behind your statements.
- Work as a group and avoid side conversations.
- Disagree with opinions, but don't attack the person.

Confidentiality

Anyone presenting him or herself as a mediator should be aware of the importance of confidentiality. Several states have laws that extend confidentiality privileges to mediators. But even if you are not operating as a mediator, you will find that respecting confidentiality enhances your standing as a person who can be trusted.

The parties may want to include confidentiality as part of their ground rules. A commitment that everything said in a meeting stays in the room, unless everyone agrees otherwise, provides a comfort zone that helps people open up to discussing risky issues or ideas.

Consensus

Consensus is generally defined as an agreement reached by gathering information and viewpoints; discussing; analyzing; reconsidering; and persuading. Consensus does not mean that everyone likes the solution equally well, but it does represent a group's decision to move forward with a proposed solution.

The prospect of one or two participants being able to keep a group from making a decision often leaves people wary of adopting consensus as a decision-making tool. To avoid this, the group may choose to define consensus as an agreement that includes an acknowledgment of minority views.

How an agreement will be implemented has a bearing on the amount of unanimity needed to adopt a decision. Will all the parties need to play a role in carrying out the agreement? If time is taken up front to secure everyone's commitment and agreement, it may avoid later sabotage. If the group is serving in an advisory function, it may be less important to struggle for unanimous consensus.

■ *Record Issues*

It is helpful to use a flipchart to record issues, ideas, and points of discussion. Writing things down in front of the group acknowledges each person's input and ensures that the group memory accurately reflects what was said. It also is useful to have a list of options visible to everyone when the group is making decisions.

■ *Prioritize Issues*

After identifying the points of conflict, have the group decide which issues they need to address first. During this stage, the conflict manager may rely on the wisdom of the group to know what to tackle first, or suggest dealing with a smaller issue to get a sense of accomplishment before facing more complex disagreements.

Getting agreement about where to start is the first step toward resolving the points of conflict. A good conflict manager identifies and amplifies small agreements that the parties make along the way. These small agreements can build momentum for substantial progress.

■ *Share Information*

Now that you have identified and prioritized the points of conflict, your next step is to help the parties develop an understanding of each other's perspectives. As they share information about the motivation behind their positions or demands, parties often begin to understand each other's interests and the basic needs that any solution must take into account. Tailoring solutions to address those fundamental interests, rather than arguing over predetermined positions, is the best path to a mutually beneficial agreement.

■ *Brainstorm Solutions*

After the parties have developed an understanding of each other's interests, they may be ready to discuss solutions. Brainstorming is a good way to open up this process. In brainstorming, you record and recognize all ideas, no matter how outlandish. Postpone evaluation of ideas put forward until the next step. Brainstorming promotes collaborative problem solving by getting the parties to focus on expanding the pie of possibilities, rather than getting entrenched in defensive positions.

Sample Agenda

Use this sample agenda as a guide to create your own. Recognize that full exploration of issues may take more time than you think.

8:30	Opening
	Develop agreement on ground rules
	Identify issues
10:30	Break
10:45	Define, categorize, and prioritize issues
12:00	Lunch
12:45	Share information & brainstorm solutions
	Refine options and define points of agreement
2:30	Break
2:45	Evaluate and reality test solutions
	Confirm agreement
4:00	Debrief and close

■ *Refine Options*

Once the parties have churned out some ideas on how to resolve the problems, the conflict manager helps them evaluate their options. Looking at the positive and negative impacts of various proposals is a good way to explore ways of responding to everyone's interests.

■ *Define Points of Agreement*

As the solutions begin to take shape and the parties begin to find some satisfying options, the conflict manager records tentative agreements. This does not lock parties into a decision, but it does form a working agreement, which you can shape into a long-term solution.

■ *Perform a Reality Check*

As agreements begin to gel, parties often become enthusiastic about their progress. In their eagerness, they may temporarily ignore the reality of implementing these solutions. The conflict manager conducts a reality check, asking questions that make participants think about the real-world challenges of making the agreement work. Working out strategies to handle potential problems in advance may be crucial to an agreement's long-term success.

■ *Confirm Agreement*

After you have refined and tested the agreements, review them a final time to make sure that all parties are comfortable with the solutions proposed. You can document an agreement several ways. The method you select depends on the needs of the parties.

Formal, signed document. One party may draft the agreement, and the others can review it, or the group may appoint a writing team to create the draft.

Summary minutes. The facilitator or a member selected from the group prepares summary minutes of the meeting. This process is less formal, but it allows the parties to the verify points of agreement.

Verbal statement. If the parties wish to agree to certain points, but not have them recorded, they may use a verbal agreement to accompany or replace a written agreement.

Circular Nature of the Process

Even skilled conflict managers frequently find that parties engaged in conflict resolution do not move neatly through these sequential steps to arrive at an agreement. The facilitator occasionally may need to step back and tackle a new issue that emerges late in the process. It even may be necessary to go back to brainstorming options. If the parties get discouraged and start to feel they are not accomplishing much, the facilitator can encourage them by spotlighting the areas where they have gained understanding and already developed options.

A conflict manager must help the participants understand that the agreement is only the beginning. Its implementation may not work out as planned. But the parties should expect that everyone is entering the agreement with their best intentions, knowing that they have built into it a process for dealing with unexpected difficulties.

Proactive Conflict Management

Whether you are using the structure outlined above to manage a hot conflict, or planning proactively for collaborative decision making, the approach hangs on a similar framework. The significant difference between the two approaches is that reactive conflict management often includes the added task of repairing damage already done. Proactive conflict management focuses on developing systems in advance and harnessing the creative potential of conflict.

The best conflict management approach avoids the negatives of conflict. If you know in advance about a need to plan for some change, make a decision, or advise on a new product, you can devote the time to preparation that might not be available in a crisis situation. Most people focus on what happens during the meeting and fail to recognize the importance that preparation plays in the ultimate successful search for a solution. (See *Conflict: Not Always Negative* sidebar on the next page.)

Conflict: Not Always Negative

In a basic conflict resolution training session, the trainer often opens by asking: "What comes to mind when you think about conflict?" Participants typically respond with words like:

- fear
- pain
- destruction
- disagreement
- anger
- discomfort
- flight
- avoid
- loss
- battle
- frustration
- fight
- obstacle
- opportunity

Each of these responses is correct. Everyone has a different reaction to conflict. Judging by the frequency of pessimistic comments, many believe conflict is negative and should be avoided.

The person who associates conflict with opportunity, however, sees things differently. To this individual, conflict provides the chance for change and development. It may shake up systems that need change or modification; it may energize people toward a creative breakthrough that resolves an old problem; it may be just what an organization needs. But you need to know how to manage conflict to get a positive result.

The payoff during the meeting comes from having taken the time up front to:

- secure a real buy-in on the process

- get an understanding of the situation

- identify all the people who should be involved

- get stakeholder input on creating the agenda

- find the best location for the meeting

- coach the participants on how to get the greatest benefit out of the process.

Using a collaborative process for planning and decision making not only ensures that the people who will need to implement the results are involved in developing the outcome, it also generates a creative synergy that can lead to a greater range of options.

Organizations from large federal agencies to small companies are recognizing the benefits that come from having a conflict management system in place. When facilitation and mediation become standard tools for decision making, proactive conflict management is fully integrated into the way of doing business.

Styles of Approach

Regardless of a reactive or proactive approach, conflict managers perceive conflict differently, and have diverse responses to it. While there is no single, best conflict management style, the way you respond can be damaging or helpful, depending on the circumstances.

A skilled conflict manager seeks to understand each person's reaction to conflict. Understanding how this behavior fits into the continuum of conflict management styles is critical to recognizing its impact on a conflict situation.

When faced with a dispute, people may have very different responses. Two university professors Kenneth Thomas and Ralph Kilman, identified the responses as competing, accommodating, avoiding, collaborating, and compromising.

Competing. Using a competitive response, the individual seeks to meet his or her own needs without regard to, and often at the expense of others involved.

Accommodating. Accommodators neglect their own concerns to satisfy the concerns of the other person.

Avoiding. In this response, individuals do not address the conflict. They do not seek to meet their own interests or the interests of the other person.

Collaborating. The collaborator works with the other individual to find a solution that fully satisfies both of their interests.

Compromising. A compromiser seeks to split the difference in a way that partially satisfies both parties.

No response is inherently superior or inferior. There are times when each response is more or less effective. For example, a competitive approach is better than a collaborative approach for handling an emergency. It also may be best to avoid a conflict temporarily in order to let both parties cool down.

Although individuals may have a preferred response to conflict, they might respond differently to a conflict at home than at work. A person's response to conflict is learned behavior, and it changes as a person gains life experience. Understanding one's own preferred response to conflict and its potential positive and negative effects is critical to managing conflict. Learning to recognize the preference of others gives the conflict manager the tools to speak in a way that each participant can hear.

Questions to Draw Out Conflict

Use this job aid to learn more about the issues and interests involved in a conflict.

Information About the Individual

Date and Time:

Name:

Position:

Years with the organization:

Phone number:

Information About the Conflict

What is your understanding of the situation?

What do you believe caused it to occur?

What are the underlying issues that led to the situation?

How has it affected you and your work?

How do you think this situation can be resolved?

What might stand in the way of resolving it?

How would you be willing to help resolve this issue(s)?

Who else should I talk to about this situation?

Conflict Triggers

In addition to learning the preferences of others, a key element to strong conflict management is understanding what can cause a conflict to occur. Conflict develops in ways as diverse as the people involved. Behind the individual expression of wants and needs, however, there are common conditions that trigger conflict. Parties may be blind to the root cause of their conflict because the symptoms of the conflict attract their attention. When questioned, they may focus on surface problems and miss the more fundamental issues. The key to helping the parties resolve their conflict lies in showing them how to recognize and satisfy their basic needs as they deal with their mutual problem.

Skill at recognizing what triggers conflict is an important tool for a conflict manager. Questions that draw out the underlying issues help the groups develop a sense of the real conflict they need to address. As a conflict manager, you must be patient. Also, you must be ready to test initial answers about the cause of the conflict with follow-up questions looking for further explanations and additional causes. By helping people discover the unmet needs behind the particulars of their disagreement, the conflict manager guides the search for solutions. (See *Questions to Draw Out Conflict* sidebar on the previous page.)

Conflict Management Training

Whether the conflict manager is internal or external, training and self-awareness are key criteria for effectiveness. While there are a few states or organizations that certify mediators, most people working in conflict management develop their own credentials. Training in conflict resolution deals with a very specific set of skills.

Training for conflict managers is not so much an indoctrination of mysterious or unusual skills as it is a refinement of communication techniques that we all use most of the time. The problem is that we often focus more on the content of the communication than on the process. People often are already preparing the next argument that will get across their points, and barely listening to what the other person is saying. And even when you think the other person is actively listening, you can expect that the other person will almost always hear something different than what you intended.

The following skills help a conflict manager create a forum where people can really begin to hear and acknowledge what others bring to the table. By modeling these techniques and explaining them to the participants, the conflict manager shows everyone how to take an active role in creating solutions.

■ *Listening*
Listening involves not just hearing words, but understanding their underlying meaning. The conflict manager needs to be able to reframe points so all the participants recognize them as issues worth exploring. Good facilitators model the skill of good listening by acknowledging both the speaker's thoughts and feelings.

■ *Summarizing*
Summarizing information validates the speaker and helps everyone else build an understanding of what the speaker intends by what he or she says. Reframing emotion-laden statements into issues for everyone to consider helps the group focus on the real task.

■ *Ask questions*
Asking questions is an important way to help people talk about and explore issues. Closed questions are useful ways to develop information: "Do you know how much is budgeted for this project?" But open-ended questions give people an invitation to make themselves understood and explain their real interests: "Can you tell us more about what makes funding for that project an important consideration for you?"

■ *Involve all parties in the discussion*
This is essential if the final outcome is to reflect the full range of interests. As facilitator, you should warn people at the beginning of the meeting that you may ask a frequent speaker to hold on to a point to give others a chance to participate, or go around the room to make sure you get everyone's input on an issue.

■ *Deal with emotions*
Dealing with emotions is better than ignoring or squashing them. A simple acknowledgment of personal feelings helps the speaker feel safe in expressing them. An emotional moment might be an appropriate time to allow a few seconds of silence. Avoid the urge to fill the void with talk.

■ *Recognize biases*

This is a critical tool for maintaining impartiality as a conflict manager. Everyone harbors biases that make it hard to keep an open mind. Does the slow speaker leave you anxious to move ahead quickly? Check in with yourself or the group to make sure you are aware of and controlling your biases.

■ *Read body language*

This is just as essential to understanding communication as hearing the spoken words. Research has shown that more than 50 percent of your message comes across nonverbally. Interpreting or questioning body language can often illuminate the essential issues behind a person's statement.

■ *Expand the "pie"*

This is the really creative work of the collaborative process. If two people argue from set positions or bargain down to a middle ground, they may have missed a unique solution that neither could have devised independently. Identifying interests and brainstorming ideas helps tap into the creative possibilities of the collaborative process.

Getting Good Out of Conflict

Conflict is the symptom of a difference in values, perception, or needs. Conflict invites a response. Whether that response takes the form of fighting from an entrenched position or collaboratively creating a mutually beneficial outcome depends on the intentions and skills of the participants.

Conflict management builds on the basic tools that help people communicate and understand each other's needs. By reframing individual positions as shared interests, the parties come to see that a win for you can also be a win for me. When you focus on both sides' energy toward expanding rather than dividing the pie, a solution that is amenable to everyone can be found.

References & Resources

Articles

Caudron, Shari. "Keeping Team Conflict Alive." *Training & Development.* September 1998, pp.48-52.

Falcone, Paul. "Managers at Mediators." *HRMagazine.* December 1999, pp. 140-144.

Guttman, Howard M. "Conflict at the Top." *Management Review.* November 1999, pp. 49-53.

Petesch, Peter, and Joshua Javits. "Mediation's on—Grab a Spoon." *HRMagazine.* April 2000, pp. 163-170.

Stepp, John R., et al. "Interest-based Negotiation: An Engine-Driving Change." *Journal for Quality and Participation.* September/October 1998, pp. 36-41.

"U.S. Postal Service's Conflict Resolution Program Addresses Three-Fourths of All Employee EEO Disputes." *Workforce Strategies.* March 2000, pp. WS-15.

Van Slyke, Eric J. "Resolve Conflict, Boost Creativity." *HRMagazine.* November 1999, pp. 132-137.

Wong, Nancy. "Partners Awaken Cultural Change." *Workforce.* March 2000, pp. 72-78.

Books

Colosi, Thomas R. *On and Off the Record: Colosi on Negotiation.* Dubuque, IA: Kendall/Hunt Publishing, 1993.

Fisher, Roger, and William Ury. *Getting to Yes: Negotiating Agreement Without Giving In.* New York: Penguin Books, 1983.

Fisher, Roger, and Scott Brown. *Getting Together: Building Relationships as We Negotiate.* New York: Penguin Books, 1988.

Bush, Robert A. Baruch, and Joseph P. Folger. *The Promise of Mediation: Responding to Conflict through Empowerment and Recognition.* San Francisco: Jossey-Bass, 1994.

Kaner, Sam, et al. *Facilitator's Guide to Participatory Decision-Making.* Gabriola Island, BC, CA: New Society Publishers, 1996.

Moore, Christopher W. *The Mediation Process: Practical Strategies for Resolving Conflict.* San Francisco: Jossey-Bass, 1996.

Schwarz, Roger M. *The Skilled Facilitator: Practical Wisdom for Developing Effective Groups.* San Francisco: Jossey-Bass, 1995.

Thomas, Kenneth W., and Ralph H. Kilmann. *Thomas-Kilmann Conflict Mode Instrument.* Palo Alto, CA: Consulting Psychologists Press. 1974.

Ury, William. *Getting Past No: Negotiating with Difficult People.* New York: Bantam Books, 1991.

Organizations

Association for Conflict Resolution (ACR) 1527 New Hampshire Avenue, NW; Third Floor; Washington, D.C. 20036 Phone: 202-667-9700 Fax: 202-265-1968 Email: spidr@spidr.org; Web page: http://www.spidr.org/

International Association of Facilitators (IAF) 7630 West 145th Street, Suite 202; St. Paul, MN 55124; Phone: 612-891-3541; Fax: 612-891-1800; Email: iafoffice@igc.org;Web page: www.iaf-world.org

International Association for Public Participation (IAP2); PO Box 10146; Alexandria VA 22310; Phone: (703) 971-0090 or (800) 644-4273 in North America; Fax: (703) 971-0006; Email: iap2hq@pin.org; Web page: http://iap2.org

American Arbitration Association (AAA) 335 Madison Avenue, 10th floor; New York, New York 10017-4605; Phone: 212-716-5800 or 800-778-7879 (Customer Service); Fax: 212-716-5905; Web page: http://www.adr.org/

Infolines

Cassidy, Michael F. "Group Decision Making." No. 9906.

Kirrane, Diane. "Listening to Learn; Learning to Listen." No. 8806. Revised 1997.

Vrooman, Rona J. "Group Process Tools." No. 9407. Revised 1997.

Conflict Assessment Tool

The assessment is a valuable tool. The process gives the parties their first chance to be heard, and it also helps the facilitator begin to understand the issues.

Party/Group Name:	
Names of stakeholders	
What are the issues they identify?	
What is their position on these issues?	
What needs are they trying to satisfy?	
What options do they have to meet those needs?	
What power do they hold over determining the outcome?	
What is their deadline to make a decision?	
How important is a solution to them?	
Where is there room to negotiate?	
What is their BATNA (Best Alternative To A Negotiated Agreement)?	

How to Facilitate

Issue 9406

How to Facilitate

Editorial Staff for 9406

Editor
Barbara Darraugh

Consultant
Don Aaron Carr

Revised 1999

Editor
Cat Sharpe

Contributing Editor
Ann Bruen

Production Design
Anne Morgan

Getting Teams to Work

The EXITS Publishing Company was experiencing difficulties in maintaining inventory on the rapidly increasing sales of a popular how-to book series. The organization wrote, published, marketed, and filled orders, handling all aspects in-house. As a result, this product required input and actions from many different units in the organization:

- *customer service*
- *fulfillment*
- *editing and design*
- *product management*
- *accounting*
- *computer services.*

Although product sales were growing, the product manager frequently heard complaints about the handling of the product from the other area managers. Customer service and fulfillment often ran out of stock and became frustrated when clients ordered an unavailable issue. Accounting had difficulties with the computer reports it received. And the product manager often had to intervene in the process to soothe ruffled feathers and order emergency restocking of the product.

After several years, the organization instituted total quality management and decided to form a quality team to address what was considered to be an inventory problem. Through its total quality management mechanism, the organization brought together managers in each of the departments to discuss the problem. Each of the managers—Sara from customer service, Dan from fulfillment, Paula from accounting, Tom from computer services, and George, the product manager—were very enthusiastic about finally having a forum in which to address a problem that affected them all and that they had been unable to solve individually. They were hopeful that with the tools taught to them during their quality training, easy solutions to their problems would be found quickly and simply. They happily scheduled their first meeting.

At the first meeting, Dan told Sara that she needed to keep better track of orders, that too often his staff received back orders on items in stock and orders for items that weren't in stock. Sara refused to be accountable, noting that the responsibility for

reordering rested with George. An argument broke out between Sara and George, who said he couldn't keep track of the inventory, since he received reports from her sporadically and always too late to help. Sara then attacked Tom, saying the computer generated the late or inaccurate reports.

Tom noted the "garbage in, garbage out" theory of data processing. Paula attacked the computer reports and Tom's handling of them. Sara left the meeting feeling she had been personally attacked, and Tom refused to discuss the computer output further. The two-hour meeting lasted only an hour. No progress had been made, and some fence-mending needed to occur before the managers met again.

Several months later, with no easy solutions in hand, the "team" dreaded each weekly meeting. They had only agreed that nothing had been accomplished, and all felt that the meetings were a waste of time. Territory that had been covered in the first meeting was re-covered endlessly, with each individual protecting his or her own turf. The team members distrusted each other and often attacked one another personally. The group was floundering, and inventory was still out of control.

Unfortunately, this team will continue to meet, possibly for many more months, until one of the members leaves for a different organization and the team dissolves. In the meantime, the team members' interactions outside of the team room have also deteriorated. All in all, this is not what management expected when it instituted the total quality management program and formed the team to look at the problem.

The disastrous effects could have been avoided had management provided the team with a qualified facilitator. The facilitator would have been able to defuse the personality issues, coach the team on the proper tools to use to examine the problem and provide solutions, and conduct refresher or minicourses on the quality tools. This issue of *Infoline* will outline the facilitator's role and his or her necessary skills.

Facilitators and Their Roles

Facilitators are usually individuals who assist teams in their meetings, to enhance the process—how the team works and comes to decisions. Generally, the facilitator is not involved in the process or task being examined: He or she is not a stakeholder and may begin team involvement knowing nothing about what is being discussed. Good facilitators ensure that teams don't get bogged down in personality or process issues and that every individual within the group is heard.

Don Aaron Carr, a consultant who specializes in team training, asserts that a good facilitator possesses "an attitude and philosophy that confirms a position of respect and admiration. Therefore, good facilitators display a high tolerance for ambiguity and conflict, patience and persistence."

Facilitators have a responsibility to both the team and the organization to support the team and integrate it into the organization's mainstream. Carr defines the facilitator's role as the following:

- coaching the team in process, roles, procedures, policies, and goals

- attending team meetings on an as-needed basis to provide feedback to the team leader and members

- acting as a regular consultant to the team leader

- monitoring team dynamics, diagnosing problems, and making appropriate interventions

- promoting the team concept.

These roles contrast with those of the team leader, Carr says, noting that team leaders have the following roles:

- plan meeting agendas and conduct the meeting

- ensure through facilitation techniques that all members are involved in the team

- communicate with management about the team's progress

- consult with the facilitator on team issues.

Since these two roles may overlap, the facilitator and the leader may negotiate which roles they want to play. A leader, for example, may want the facilitator to be present at every meeting to ensure that all team members participate if the leader feels uncomfortable in this team maintenance role. Or the leader may ask the facilitator to run or train the team in the processes involved in idea generation or decision making.

David Quinlivan-Hall and Peter Renner stress the use of a neutral facilitator who guides the group through its process stages. A neutral facilitator helps team leaders prepare the meeting and takes over the process. In this way, he or she allows the team leader to participate in the program.

Quinlivan-Hall and Renner list the following tasks facing facilitators:

Managing the Process

This includes the following:

- striving for consensus
- keeping members on task
- following the agenda
- focusing on problem solving
- controlling the flow of contributions
- rewarding and motivating group members.

Acting as a Resource

This task includes:

● advising on problem-solving methods

● providing on-the-spot training in group-process techniques

● protecting group members from personal attacks.

Remaining Neutral

This includes the following:

● keeping emotionally uninvolved

● keeping out of the spotlight

● becoming invisible when the group is facilitating itself

● keeping silent on content issues.

Skills Required

The facilitator's role, while rather broad, is crucial to the success of the team. A good facilitator basically checks his or her personal concerns and causes at the door. Glenn Varney, president of Management Advisory Associates in Bowling Green, Ohio, suggests that facilitators should have the following skills:

■ Listening
The facilitator needs to be able to listen actively and hear what every team member is saying. "A day spent facilitating is as tiring as a day spent chopping wood," Quinlivan-Hall and Renner note. (For more on listening skills, see *Infoline* No. 8806, "Listening to Learn; Learning to Listen.")

■ Questioning
The facilitator should be skilled at asking questions. Good questions are open ended and stimulate discussion.

■ Sharing
The facilitator should be able to share his or her feelings and create an atmosphere in which team members are willing to share their feelings and opinions.

■ Problem Solving
Facilitators should be skilled at applying group problem-solving techniques. Group problem solving follows this process:

● defining the problem
● determining the cause
● considering alternatives
● weighing the alternatives
● selecting the best alternative
● implementing the solution
● evaluating the results.

■ Resolving Conflict
Conflict among team members should not be suppressed. Indeed, it should be expected and dealt with constructively. This includes barring personal attacks. (For more information on conflict resolution, see *Infoline* No. 0104, "How to Resolve Conflict.")

■ Using a Participative Style
The facilitator should be able to encourage all team members to participate in the meetings.

■ Accepting Others
The facilitator should maintain an open mind and not criticize the ideas and suggestions of the team members.

■ Empathizing
The facilitator should be able to "walk a mile in another's shoes" to understand the team members' feelings, and he or she should be able to express these feelings.

■ Leading
The facilitator must be able to keep the members focused and the discussion on target.

See the self-assessment instrument on the next page to assist facilitators in evaluating their skill levels.

Skill Inventory Self-Assessment Instrument

Glenn Varney provides the following inventory of team and interpersonal management skills to help you determine your strengths and weaknesses and chart your progress.

To What Extent Do You Need to Improve...

	1 (very little)	2	3 (somewhat)	4	5 (very much)
Relationships With Peers and Supervisors					
1. Competing with my peers.	☐	☐	☐	☐	☐
2. Being open with my seniors.	☐	☐	☐	☐	☐
3. Feeling inferior to colleagues.	☐	☐	☐	☐	☐
4. Standing up for myself.	☐	☐	☐	☐	☐
5. Building open relationships.	☐	☐	☐	☐	☐
6. Following policy guidelines.	☐	☐	☐	☐	☐
7. Questioning policy guidelines.	☐	☐	☐	☐	☐
Team Dynamics					
8. Knowing other team members as individuals.	☐	☐	☐	☐	☐
9. Meeting sufficiently often.	☐	☐	☐	☐	☐
10. Supporting open expression of views.	☐	☐	☐	☐	☐
11. Setting high standards.	☐	☐	☐	☐	☐
12. Punishing behavior that deviates from the team norm.	☐	☐	☐	☐	☐
13. Clarifying aims and objectives.	☐	☐	☐	☐	☐
14. Giving information and views.	☐	☐	☐	☐	☐
15. Using status to influence decisions of the team.	☐	☐	☐	☐	☐
16. Delegating to reduce workload.	☐	☐	☐	☐	☐
Relationships With Team Members					
17. Helping others identify problems.	☐	☐	☐	☐	☐
18. Practicing counseling skills.	☐	☐	☐	☐	☐
19. Being distant with some people.	☐	☐	☐	☐	☐
20. Intervening when things go wrong.	☐	☐	☐	☐	☐
21. Being strong when reprimanding.	☐	☐	☐	☐	☐
22. Giving energy to others.	☐	☐	☐	☐	☐
23. Clarifying individuals' objectives.	☐	☐	☐	☐	☐
24. Supporting others in difficulty.	☐	☐	☐	☐	☐
25. Bringing problems out.	☐	☐	☐	☐	☐
26. Supporting risk taking.	☐	☐	☐	☐	☐
27. Being open in assessment of others.	☐	☐	☐	☐	☐
Relationships With Employees					
28. Being known as a person by employees.	☐	☐	☐	☐	☐
29. Being available to employees.	☐	☐	☐	☐	☐
30. Knowing how people feel.	☐	☐	☐	☐	☐
31. Acting to resolve conflicts.	☐	☐	☐	☐	☐

To What Extent Do You Need to Improve...	1 (very little)	2	3 (somewhat)	4	5 (very much)

Relationships With Employees *(continued)*

	1	2	3	4	5
32. Emphasizing communication.	☐	☐	☐	☐	☐
33. Passing information quickly.	☐	☐	☐	☐	☐
34. Emphasizing personal status.	☐	☐	☐	☐	☐
35. Bypassing management structure when communicating.	☐	☐	☐	☐	☐

Working in Groups

	1	2	3	4	5
36. Using a systematic approach.	☐	☐	☐	☐	☐
37. Developing others' skills.	☐	☐	☐	☐	☐
38. Being prompt.	☐	☐	☐	☐	☐
39. Using time efficiently.	☐	☐	☐	☐	☐
40. Listening actively.	☐	☐	☐	☐	☐
41. Openly expressing views.	☐	☐	☐	☐	☐
42. Dominating others.	☐	☐	☐	☐	☐
43. Maintaining good group climate.	☐	☐	☐	☐	☐
44. Dealing constructively with disruptive behaviors.	☐	☐	☐	☐	☐
45. Building informal contacts.	☐	☐	☐	☐	☐
46. Disparaging other groups.	☐	☐	☐	☐	☐
47. Sharing objectives with other groups.	☐	☐	☐	☐	☐
48. Identifying mutual communication needs.	☐	☐	☐	☐	☐
49. Arranging intergroup social events.	☐	☐	☐	☐	☐
50. Acting to resolve conflicts.	☐	☐	☐	☐	☐

Helping Others Improve

	1	2	3	4	5
51. Making time for counseling.	☐	☐	☐	☐	☐
52. Identifying the group's training needs.	☐	☐	☐	☐	☐
53. Setting coaching assignments.	☐	☐	☐	☐	☐
54. Allocating time and money for training.	☐	☐	☐	☐	☐
55. Giving feedback to others.	☐	☐	☐	☐	☐
56. Sharing parts of the job for others' development.	☐	☐	☐	☐	☐

Self-Development

	1	2	3	4	5
57. Setting aside time to think.	☐	☐	☐	☐	☐
58. Visiting other organizations.	☐	☐	☐	☐	☐
59. Discussing principles and values.	☐	☐	☐	☐	☐
60. Taking on new challenges.	☐	☐	☐	☐	☐
61. Attending training events.	☐	☐	☐	☐	☐
62. Knowing when and how to use specialists.	☐	☐	☐	☐	☐

Participant Guidelines

Don Aaron Carr presents the following guidelines for effective team facilitation:

- Contract with the team on your roles and responsibilities up front.

- Don't take on the team's work (for example, recording or scribing).

- Intervene to satisfy the team's needs, not your own desire to be heard.

- Give team members time to correct problems themselves before intervening.

- Once you've said your piece, be quiet.

- Do more asking than telling.

- Facilitate the leader so the leader can facilitate the team.

- Don't repeat feedback the team has already discussed.

- Be willing to take risks.

- Be willing to be wrong.

©1994 by Don Aaron Carr.
Used with permission.

Appropriate Interventions

The word *intervention,* Carr says, is derived from a Latin word meaning to "interfere with the affairs of others." This is a good description of the kinds of actions facilitators are charged with taking. The facilitator, Carr notes, "performs an intervention whenever he or she decides to shift from that of a passive observer to that of an active participant or change agent."

Most frequently, interventions are focused on process, not on individuals or content. Carr maintains that there are four different types of interventions:

1. Interventions that cause the team to examine its dynamics and improve its performance.

2. Interventions that encourage member participation.

3. Interventions that encourage problem solving and decision making.

4. Interventions that ensure compliance with procedures, policies, ground rules, and requirements that define the process within the organization.

Active interventions alter the flow of events. They may quicken the development of the team, change the course of the discussion, increase the team's energy, or help the team become more aware of how it is functioning.

The facilitator should not intervene unless there is a reason for it—the intervention should alter what the team is doing or make available some additional information. Facilitators should intervene when the team wanders off track, when two team members are in conflict, when an individual isn't participating or is angry, or when the leader becomes autocratic.

Interventions, Carr continues, are made at four points in group process: before the meeting, during the meeting, at the end of the meeting with the team, and at a postmeeting coaching session with the leader. Timing an intervention depends on both the facilitator's style and the needs of the situation. Situational considerations include:

■ *Felt Need*

If the team is floundering and experiencing discomfort with its inability to move forward, the team may ask the facilitator to take some immediate action. If a felt need doesn't exist, Carr recommends not intervening, because the intervention might disrupt the group process. Carr also recommends that facilitators follow the "five-minute rule": Wait five minutes before intervening to see if the team corrects itself.

■ *Danger*

If an interaction occurs during a team meeting that would be difficult to repair later, the facilitator may intervene immediately—for example, if the team leader puts down a team member and the team shows no signs of addressing the interaction.

■ *Impact*

An immediate intervention has the greatest impact, but it may have to be repeated several times before the team begins to self-monitor. But beware of intervening every few minutes.

■ *Repeats*

If the facilitator intervenes with the same comment several times and the team doesn't act on it, the facilitator should mention the problem in a coaching session with the team leader.

How to Intervene

Knowing how to intervene in a group's process is key to the facilitator's success. David Quinlivan-Hall and Peter Renner in *In Search of Solutions* present 25 facilitator interventions and some guidance on when to use them. A few samples follow:

Describe process obstacles. If nothing is happening, the facilitator can describe the next step and perhaps encourage the contributions of several group members.

Encourage participation. The facilitator, Quinlivan-Hall and Renner note, should "establish a participative climate at the start of the meeting and maintain it throughout."

Stages and Phases

The work objective of an effective facilitator is to put himself or herself out of a job. It is easier to reach this end if the facilitator knows the stage of group development the team happens to be in. J. William Pfeiffer and Arlette C. Ballew have made several suggestions for the appropriate level of intervention in the various phases of group growth:

■ *Forming*

This is the "polite" phase. The facilitator's approach may be highly directive, instructing the group on what is to be done and how to do it. The facilitator intervenes by structuring getting-acquainted exercises, reviewing agenda items, and exploring similarities among members. During the later part of this phase, facilitators offer the group members the opportunity to set their own standards and identify each individual's reason for belonging to the team. Their task should be clarified, and the group members should be committed to it.

■ *Storming*

This is the "power" stage: who has it, who wants it, and who is doing what to get it. The facilitator's job in this stage is to create a common language and manage conflict: "Too little control can allow chaos, while suppression of all conflict can lead to apathy," Pfeiffer and Ballew point out. The facilitator engages in relationship-building activities, such as support, praise, encouragement, and simply paying attention.

■ *Norming*

This is the "positive" stage. The group comes together and works as a team. The team becomes self-monitoring. The facilitator can help the group share ideas, monitor or lead group problem-solving and decision-making tools, and provide feedback. Depending on the team, the facilitator may now become a consultant, attending only when the team feels his or her presence is needed, or working to blend in with the group.

■ *Performing*

This is the "proficient" stage. The facilitator turns over responsibility for decisions and implementation to the group and engages in both low-task and low-maintenance behaviors. He or she becomes "invisible."

■ *Adjourning*

This is the final phase. The team accomplishes its goal and disbands. The facilitator may help the team celebrate its success, debrief it on what worked and what did not, and help group members let go.

Roles Members Play

Team members can take on behaviors that hinder the group process. The following chart identifies several of these behaviors, explains why team members may behave that way, and tells what you can do about it.

Roles	Why It Happens	What to Do
Heckler	Probably good natured most of the time but is distracted by job or personal problems.	• Keep your temper under control. • Honestly agree with one idea, then move on to something else. • Toss a misstatement of fact to the group to turn down. • Talk privately with the person as a last resort to determine what is bothering him or her.
Rambler	One idea leads to another and takes this person miles away from the original point.	• When there is a pause for breath, thank him or her, refocus attention, and move on. • In a friendly manner, indicate that "We are a little off the subject." • As a last resort, use your meeting timetable. Glance at your watch and say, "Time is limited."
Ready Answer	Really wants to help, but makes it difficult by keeping others from participating.	• Cut it off tactfully by questioning others. Suggest that "we put others to work." • Ask this person to summarize. It keeps him or her attentive and capitalizes on his or her enthusiasm.
Conversationalist	Side chatter is usually personal in nature but may be related to the topic.	• Call by name and ask an easy question. • Call by name, restate the last opinion expressed, and ask his or her opinion of it. • Include in the discussion.
Personality Problems	Two or more individuals clash, dividing your people into factions and endangering the success of the meeting.	• Maximize points of agreement; minimize disagreements. Draw attention to the objective at hand. • Pose a direct question to an uninvolved member on the topic. • As a last resort, frankly state that personalities should be left out of the discussion.
Wrong Track	Brings up ideas that are obviously incorrect.	• Say, "That's one way of looking at it," and tactfully make any corrections. • Say, "I see your point, but can we reconcile that with our current situation?" • Handle tactfully because you will be contradicting him or her. Remember, all members of the group will hear how you respond to each individual, and you can encourage or discourage further participation.

Roles	Why It Happens	What to Do
Quiet One	Bored	Gain interest by asking for opinion.
	Indifferent	Question the person next to him or her. Then, ask the quiet one to comment on the view expressed.
	Timid	Compliment this person the first time he or she contributes. Be sincere.
	Superior	Indicate respect for this person's experience, then ask for ideas.
Bungler	Lacks the ability to put good ideas into proper order; has ideas, but can't convey them and needs help.	Don't call attention to the problem. Say, "Let me see if we are saying the same thing." Then, repeat the idea more clearly.
Mule	Can't or won't see the other side; supports own viewpoint no matter what.	• Ask other members of the group to comment on the ideas. They will straighten him or her out. • Remind the person that time is short, and suggest that he or she accept the group consensus presently. Indicate your willingness to talk with him or her later. Then, follow up.
Talker	Highly motivated	Slow this person down with some difficult questions.
	Show-off	Say, "That's an interesting point. Now, let's see what the rest think of it."
	Well informed	Draw upon his or her knowledge, but relay to the group.
	Just plain talkative	In general, for all overly talkative folks, let the group take care of them as much as possible.
Griper	Has a pet peeve, gripes for the sake of complaining, or has a legitimate complaint.	• Point out that the objective at hand is to operate as efficiently and cooperatively as possible under the present circumstances. • Indicate that you will discuss his or her personal problem privately at a later date. • Have another member of the group respond to his or her complaint.

Use body language. Facilitators can sit away from the table to indicate noninvolvement or move to the table when intervening in the process. "Moving closer to someone who is 'under fire' from the group gives this person support," they claim, while "moving close to a noisy, disruptive person usually results in a quieting down."

Discourage personal attacks. The facilitator may need to remind individuals of one of the first tenets of team building: "Examine the process, not the person." If one group member begins to attack another, the facilitator needs to step in to refocus the discussion on the issue.

Suggest a process. The facilitator should be able to instruct or run certain processes, such as idea generating and decision making, in order to move the group along.

Encourage equal participation. Facilitators need to observe the group to notice who is talking and who is being quiet. The trick is to draw out the wallflowers and shut up those who monopolize the conversation, without offending either.

Suggest a break. Taking a spontaneous break can end a deadlock or simply reenergize the group. Refreshment breaks are common, but others work just as well, including a "seventh-inning stretch," moving to small groups for several minutes, taking a five-minute "joke break," or bringing in a guest speaker.

Summarize. If the group has presented many alternatives, and those alternatives have generated much discussion, the group may get lost. Summarizing the problem and several of the alternatives may help the group refocus and keep moving.

Have the group manage the process. During the group's maturity, the facilitator may appropriately turn some of his or her duties over to the group. This indicates both trust and respect for the team and its interactions.

Debrief the group. A debriefing requires all team members to look at what is happening. It should be done at the end of the meeting and may be useful at natural breaks in the meeting agenda. Facilitators may take several approaches:

Objective: What happened here?

Reflective: How do you feel about what happened?

Interpretive: What did you learn from what happened?

Decision making: What do you want to do with this information for the next time?

Search for common threads. If the group is wandering, the facilitator may stop the meeting and ask members to search for what the solutions or problem definitions have in common. "With the common elements identified," Quinlivan-Hall and Renner assert, "focus is achieved for the next steps."

Present a straw man. During a break, the facilitator may develop, or suggest that someone else develop, a draft problem description or solution—the straw man. Encourage the team to criticize the plan, attack it, and pull it apart. "Only by picking it apart, adding to, and changing it, will the group develop ownership of it," the authors say.

Act stupid. Team members who are uninvolved may not understand what is happening or what someone else is saying, but may not, for many reasons, want to volunteer their ignorance. The facilitator may help these individuals by asking for clarification of issues, problems, terminology, or anything else that may get in the way of consensus later in the process. Remember, Columbo always got his criminal.

Get specific. Similar to acting stupid, getting specific can clear up hard-to-grasp issues, problems, and solutions.

The Power of Observation

All interventions have one thing in common: The facilitator has provided the proper feedback and timed the intervention to alter what the group is doing somehow. This means that the facilitator has paid careful attention to what the group as a unit is doing, as well as the interactions between individual team members.

The key tool in observing the group is listening. Listening shows interest in the individual speaking and respect for the other person's experience. According to Carr, there are three types of effective listening:

1. Passive listening, where one has no interaction with the speaker, such as listening to the radio or a cassette.

2. Attentive listening, where one has some interaction with the speaker, such as listening for content to lectures in class or taking notes in a meeting.

3. Active listening, where one has a high level of interaction with the speaker, listening for content, meaning, and feelings.

Facilitators listen actively throughout the meeting. They observe who talks and for how long, whom individuals look at when they talk, who supports whom, any challenges to group leadership, nonverbal communication, side conversations, and nonparticipation. They watch for individual reactions to what is being said in order to provide coaching. Facilitators may ask questions, restate what has been said, summarize positions, or reflect a speaker's feelings. They may also keep track of the different roles team members play.

Many facilitators find it helpful to develop a chart to "keep score" of the team members' different behaviors. Although these are helpful, the facilitator should get the team's permission to use it, especially in the early stages when team members may not trust each other completely. If the facilitator springs the results on the team at the end of the meeting, team members may feel spied on and resent the tracking. A sample form with more detailed instructions is shown in the sidebar on the next page.

The chart attempts to quantify the contributions of team members in two broad areas: task and maintenance. Task functions facilitate the group in selecting, defining, and solving a common problem; maintenance functions alter or maintain the way in which group members interact. The chart also records any antigroup roles adopted by team members. Facilitators may want to chart the following behaviors:

Task Activity

Initiating. Proposing tasks or goals, defining the problem, suggesting a procedure or ideas for solving the problem.

Information seeking. Requesting facts, seeking relevant data about a problem, asking for suggestions or ideas.

Clarifying. Clearing up confusion, indicating alternatives and issues, giving examples.

Summarizing. Restating suggestions, synthesizing ideas, offering a decision or direction for the team to accept or reject.

Consensus testing. Setting up straw men to see if the team is near conclusion, checking to see how much agreement has been reached.

Maintenance Activity

Encouraging. Being friendly, recognizing others.

Expressing group feelings. Sensing moods, feelings, relationships with others, sharing feelings.

Harmonizing. Reconciling disagreements, reducing tensions, getting others to explore their differences.

Keeping Track

Many facilitators use checklists to track the behaviors—both good and bad—of team members. This allows the facilitator to provide accurate feedback at the end of the meeting. Keeping track of the team members' behaviors can make criticism specific, objective, and, therefore, easier to take. And it helps to know everyone on the team is receiving the same type of commentary.

But keep in mind that checklists could make team members uncomfortable. If you make such a list, do it with the team's approval and agreement on how the data will be used and discussed.

The checklists are generally a row-and-column grid. If group process is being monitored, the facilitator may put the team's rating in the second column. The facilitator then keeps a tally of how many times an individual engages in a particular behavior. For example, the team members may feel that, as a group, they interrupt each other too much. The facilitator may be asked to monitor that one aspect and report to the team members at the end of the meeting. Conversely, many facilitators use the tally sheet as a confidence-builder by tracking various desirable leadership behaviors and reporting them back. A sample grid follows:

Roles	Members									
Task Activity										
Initiator										
Information Seeker										
Clarifier										
Summarizer										
Consensus Tester										
Information Giver										
Maintenance Activity										
Encourager										
Expresser of Group Feelings										
Harmonizer										
Compromiser										
Gatekeeper										
Standard Setter										
Coach										
Collaborator										
Individual Activity										
Blocker										
Avoider										
Digressor										
Recognition Seeker										
Dominator										

Compromising. Admitting error, disciplining one-self to maintain group cohesion.

Gatekeeping. Trying to keep communication channels open, suggesting procedures to induce discussion of group problems.

Setting standards. Expressing standards to achieve, applying standards to evaluate the group and its output, evaluating frequently.

Coaching and consulting. Working with team members and management outside of meetings.

Individual Activity

Blocking. Interfering with group progress by arguing, resisting, disagreeing, or beating a dead horse.

Avoiding. Withdrawing from the discussion, daydreaming, doing something else, whispering, leaving the room.

Digressing. Going off the subject, filibustering, discussing personal issues.

Other areas may also be observed that help the team function better. The facilitator may want to customize the list to suit the organization's culture or team environment. Among these other areas are:

- group rules
- clarity of ideas
- handling group problems
- favoritism
- group status
- sensitivity to needs of the group
- positive or negative body language
- seating arrangements
- tension
- program planning
- hidden agendas
- invisible committees
- making others aware of their own contributions.

Feedback

These above categories also provide a framework for individual and group feedback. Gaining permission from the team members to keep track of their behaviors and explaining what impact these different behaviors have on the group will help the facilitator give useful feedback. In general, feedback should be:

■ *Descriptive*
Feedback is intended to provide others with a reading of what we are experiencing. For facilitators, this may mean pointing out someone's reaction to the action or statement of another, such as "What happened when you failed to post an agenda for the meeting?"

■ *Specific*
General feedback makes no value judgment of the person the facilitator is attempting to help: "I noticed you stared out the window when Bonnie was talking. It appears to me you may not be listening to Bonnie."

■ *Mindful of the Needs of Both Parties*
Feedback, especially when it is being given by the facilitator, should not be aimed at relieving one person's feelings or at relieving the facilitator's own feelings. Such feedback, Carr notes, tends to be destructive or hurtful, cuts off or reduces communication, and does little to change the behavior. (See *Infoline* No. 9006, "Coaching and Feedback," for more information about feedback.)

Facilitators also observe how teams make decisions. Edgar H. Schein notes that observing how decisions are made helps the facilitator "assess the appropriateness of the method to the matter being decided on." Decisions made by groups are "notoriously hard to undo," Schein continues, adding that "often we can undo the decision only if we reconstruct it and understand how we made it and whether this method was appropriate." He lists some group decision-making methods:

Plop. Group decision by omission. "I think we ought to introduce ourselves." Silence.

Self-authorized agenda. Decision by one. "I think we should introduce ourselves. I'm John Smith."

Handclasp. Decision by two. "I wonder if it would be helpful if we introduced ourselves." "I think so. I'm John Smith."

Does anyone object? Decision by minority—one or more. "We all agree that introductions are appropriate."

Voting. Decision by majority.

Polling. "Let's see where everyone stands. What do you think?"

Consensus taking. Test for opposition, or find out if the opposition feels strongly enough to block the implementation of a decision. "Can you live with this?"

References & Resources

Articles

Allcorn, Seth. "Understanding Groups at Work." *Personnel*, August 1989, pp. 28-36.

Bettenhausen, Kenneth L. "Five Years of Group Research: What We Have Learned and What Needs to Be Addressed." *Journal of Management*, June 1991, pp. 345-381.

Cooper, Colleen, and Mary Ploor. "Challenges That Make or Break a Group." *Training & Development Journal*, April 1986, pp. 31-33.

Crapo, Raymond F. "It's Time to Stop Training…and Start Facilitating." *Public Personnel Management*, Winter 1986, pp. 433-449.

Driskell, James E., et al. "Task Cues, Dominance Cues, and Influence in Task Groups." *Journal of Applied Psychology*, February 1993, pp. 51-60.

Head, Thomas C. "Impressions on What Makes a Good Facilitator from a Frustrated Teamplayer." *Organization Development Journal*, Winter 1992, pp. 61-63.

Kaczmarek, Patricia S. "Planning and Conducting Facilitated Workshops—Part 2: Conducting the Session." *Performance and Instruction*, January 1993, pp. 31-34.

Kaye, Beverly. "Advisory Groups on the Seven Cs." *Training & Development*, January 1992, pp. 54-59.

Kochery, Timothy S. "Conflict Versus Consensus: Processes and Their Effect on Team Decision Making." *Human Resource Development Quarterly*, Summer 1993, pp. 185-191.

Levine, John M., and Richard L. Moreland. "Progress in Small Group Research." *Annual Review of Psychology*, vol. 41 (1990), pp. 585-634.

Rogelberg, Steven G., et al. "The Stepladder Technique: An Alternative Group Structure Facilitating Effective Group Decision Making." *Journal of Applied Psychology*, October 1992, pp. 730-737.

Sugar, Steve. "The RAT Race: An Exercise in Group Dynamics." *Performance & Instruction*, August 1990, pp. 13-17.

Thiagarajan, Sivasailam. "Secrets of Successful Facilitators." *Journal for Quality & Participation*, 1992, pp. 70-72.

Thornton, Paul B. "Teamwork: Focus, Frame, Facilitate." *Management Review*, November 1992, pp. 46-47.

Varney, Glenn H. "Helping a Team Find All the Answers." *Training & Development Journal*, February 1991, pp. 15-18.

Weingart, Laurie R. "Impact of Group Goals, Task Component Complexity, Effort, and Planning on Group Performance." *Journal of Applied Psychology*, October 1992, pp. 682-693.

Weingart, Laurie R., et al. "The Impact of Consideration of Issues and Motivational Orientation on Group Negotiation Process and Outcome." *Journal of Applied Psychology*, June 1993, pp. 504-517.

Williams, Bill. "Ten Commandments for Group Leaders." *Supervisory Management*, September 1992, pp. 1-2.

Books

Dimock, Hedley G. *Groups: Leadership and Group Development*. San Diego: University Associates, 1987.

Fox, William M. *Effective Group Problem Solving*. San Francisco: Jossey-Bass, 1987.

Heron, John. *The Facilitator's Handbook*. New York: Nichols Publishing, 1989.

Kayser, Thomas A. *Mining Group Gold: How to Cash In on the Collaborative Brain Power of a Group*. El Segundo, CA: Serif Publishing, 1990.

Mink, Oscar G., et al. *Groups at Work*. Englewood Cliffs, NJ: Educational Technology Publications, 1987.

Nutt, Paulo C. *Making Tough Decisions*. San Francisco: Jossey-Bass, 1989.

Quinlivan-Hall, David, and Peter Renner. *In Search of Solutions: Sixty Ways to Guide Your Problem-Solving Group*. Vancouver: PFR Training Associates, 1990.

Ulschak, Francis L., et al. *Small Group Problem Solving*. Reading, MA: Addison-Wesley, 1981.

Infolines

Darraugh, Barbara. "Coaching and Feedback." No. 9006 (revised 1997).

Kirrane, Diane E. "Listening to Learn; Learning to Listen." No. 8806 (revised 1997).

Sheftel, Phoebe A., and Matthew Bennet. "How to Resolve Conflict." No. 0104.

Intervention Starters

Interventions during facilitation often take the form of questions the facilitator asks of the group. The text discusses four forms of questions: objective, reflective, interpretive, and decision making. Following are suggested openers for each type of intervention.

Objective

What happened?

Do we need to get back on track?

Have we strayed from the topic?

Do we need to take a break?

Summarize the group's activity.

Reflective

How do you feel?

Would you like to say something?

Maybe we misunderstood our roles.

I'm sorry it appears that way.

How would you like me to provide feedback?

Hey, you wanted an enforcer!

Interpretive

What did you learn?

Is this what the team thinks?

What are the specifics?

What's our common ground?

Do you understand the other's point of view or work process?

Decision Making

What do you want to do?

The material appearing on this page is not covered by copyright and may be reproduced at will.

Meetings That Work

Issue 0505

Meetings That Work

AUTHOR

Tora Estep
ASTD
1640 King Street
Box 1443
Alexandria, VA 22313-2043
Tel: 703.683.8138
Email: testep@astd.org

Contributing Editor
Tora Estep
testep@astd.org

Editorial Consultant
Chris Clarke-Epstein

Copy Editor
Ann Bruen

Production Design
Kathleen Schaner

**Manager, Acquisitions and
Author Relations, ASTD Press**
Mark Morrow

Meetings 1-2-3

Do you love meetings? Are they a chance to see your pals and catch up on the latest office gossip? Are they an opportunity to take a nap on company time, take a break from the work that keeps piling up on your desk, stretch your legs, and see a fresh set of walls?

Or maybe you can't stand meetings. You seem to spend more than half of your work life in them, and you are sick to tears of them. They waste your time. You rarely seem to do anything productive in them. They only add to your stress by filling your life with conflict and dithering, and they are getting in the way of getting through your workload.

Excessive, non-value-adding meetings aren't just wasting your time, they are wasting the time of your organization. And the money! Next time you are in a meeting that's bogged down in conflict, veering wildly off the topic, and chock full of people having side conversations and snoozing, take a guess at the cost to the organization. Don't forget to include:

- estimated hourly salary of each participant

- estimated hourly cost of benefits for participants (in *50 One-Minute Tips to Better Communication*, Phillip Bozek estimates the cost of benefits at about 33 percent of annual salaries)

- hourly cost of use of facilities

- hourly cost of use of equipment.

Then multiply that by the number of hours you spend in the meeting. That's a pretty hefty number (especially if you imagine it coming out of your own pocket). If you have the same pointless meeting every week or month, imagine the annual cost to your organization. Now you know why meetings have been called "the great white-collar crime of business," wasting about $37 billion annually according to Burt Albert in *Fat Free Meetings*.

But meetings don't have to be a big waste of time and money. Meetings go awry because leaders and participants don't have the skills and knowledge to take advantage of meetings as a precious tool. The value of meetings lies in their power to generate excitement, creativity, and innovation and the opportunity to turn a multiplicity of talents toward solving a problem or making big things happen.

So, if you believe that you'll get great results just by putting a group of talented people together in a room, you are out of luck. You need skills and knowledge to run an effective meeting. Because you want to make the most of your workday—including meetings—this *Infoline* is going to help you turn those long, frustrating, dull-as-dishwater time wasters into productive, exciting events in which you and your co-workers can shine. This *Infoline* will show you a simple, three-step process to eliminate unproductive meetings and to get more value out of the meetings you do have. The steps are:

1. Get ready to meet.

2. Meet.

3. Follow up.

Obvious? Self-explanatory? Maybe, but most people go straight to 2 and never pass 3. All three are critical steps in having effective meetings.

1. Get Ready to Meet

Preparation—here as in so many other areas—is critical for making meetings successful and productive. Next time you want to jump right in and wing it, don't. If you neglect getting prepared, you'll end up with a big sloppy mess of a meeting in which participants don't know what they are supposed to do, get bored, have side conversations, "space out," argue among themselves, and so forth. In other words: The meeting ends being a big waste of time and causes more problems than it solves.

So what's involved in preparing for a meeting? The following points forecast what this section is going to show you to do to prepare for meaningful, valuable meetings. You also can use the job aid at the end of this *Infoline* to help get ready.

1. Determine if having a meeting is such a great idea in the first place. This means you need to figure out what the meeting is supposed to accomplish.

2. Identify who needs to be there and decide what participants need to do.

3. Prepare an agenda.

4. Identify any tools you might need.

5. Invite the participants. You'll let them know when and where and why. Also, you are going to distribute the agenda and let them know what, if anything, *they* need to do to prepare. (Effective meetings also require prepared participants!)

Deciding to Meet

One of the first things you to do before typing up that meeting invitation and distributing it is to make sure that a meeting is really the best use of people's time. Must you have a meeting just because it's Tuesday, or could you convey the same information with a quick email or a few phone calls? Do you actually have something to say?

Have a meeting only when you have a good reason. In "Holding Your Own in Meetings, but Working as a Team," Dianna Booher suggests that you call a meeting when:

- you want to present information to a lot of people quickly, and you don't want to write it

- you want input from others

- you want to gain "buy in"

- you want to motivate and energize your team.

Other good reasons for meetings are planning projects, brainstorming, and problem solving. If you can say "yes" to many of the following questions, then a meeting is probably in order:

☐ Can you state your purpose for meeting?

☐ Is your meeting purpose worth the time and cost of calling in the participants?

☐ Is meeting going to be a more efficient and accurate way to convey information than sending an email or making some phone calls?

☐ Do you really want participants' input and not just a slate of agreements?

☐ Are you going to act on people's input?

☐ Do you have the information that you need to meet productively?

☐ Will you and your participants have enough time to prepare for the meeting?

☐ Are the participants going to be able to work together on the issue?

If after answering these questions you have concluded that a meeting really is the best way to accomplish your objective, then your next step is to determine whom to invite.

Identifying Who Should Come

People's time is a valuable resource, both in terms of what it costs and in terms of what else they can achieve in that time. This is one reason to ensure that the people you ask to the meeting are the people whose contributions will enable the success of your meeting.

Another reason to be selective is that with each new person, group dynamics grow more complex, and achieving meeting objectives becomes trickier. So be choosy about whom you invite. Articulate a reason for each person to be there. Ask yourself some of the following questions:

- Who needs the information you are going to share? Who needs the information firsthand?

- From whom do you need to get firsthand information?

- Who is directly affected by the problem?

- Who can contribute to the achievement of the meeting objectives?

- Who has the authority to approve of a solution or take action?

After you've identified the participants, determine what each person's responsibilities for the meeting will be. Do you need someone to provide specific background information? Do you need someone else to come prepared with suggestions and ideas for discussion? Do you simply need the participants to read a report and be able to discuss it intelligently?

Also determine if you need everyone there for the duration of the meeting, or if someone can simply come for part of it. For example, you may only need someone to give a brief presentation of information and then you can let him or her leave.

Another type of responsibility that you may require of participants is for them to play specific meeting roles such as timekeeper, facilitator, and notetaker. These are discussed in further detail in the sidebar *Meeting Roles* at right.

Whatever you ask of your participants, make sure that you give them a sufficient amount of time to prepare. How many times have you been in a meeting and found that you have information that would have been relevant to the meeting, but you weren't asked to bring it?

Preparing a Meeting Agenda

The next step in preparing for a meeting is to create the agenda. A sample agenda is given in the sidebar *Sample Agenda:* ToadStools *Sales Meeting.* Look at the headings presented in the sample more closely. They are:

● meeting objective(s)
● logistics
● participants and responsibilities
● meeting outline.

■ *Meeting Objective(s)*
In calling the meeting, you probably already have an objective in mind. When you write it down, evaluate it by thinking SMART: Is it specific, measurable, achievable, realistic, and timebound? What meeting outcomes would indicate that you have achieved the meeting's objective? If you consider the *ToadStools* example, the meeting will have achieved its objective when the team has

Meeting Roles

Productive meetings are conducted in an efficient, smooth manner and also are documented for follow-up activities. To accomplish this, you may need the help of three participants to function as timekeeper, facilitator, and notetaker. If the meeting is a regularly scheduled meeting—such as a project status report—assign the roles to a different person each time.

■ *Timekeeper*
Effective meetings start and end on time. To help make that happen, use a timekeeper. The timekeeper notes the amount of time allotted on the agenda for each activity and keeps track of the actual amount of time spent. If the group goes beyond the allotted time for an activity, the timekeeper interrupts (gently) and asks the group to make a decision: Should they continue the activity now or at a later meeting? If a discussion is particularly productive, moving other agenda items to another meeting can be worthwhile, but first gain agreement from participants.

■ *Facilitator*
Facilitation is a highly desirable skill set that requires learning and practice. People often underestimate its importance and difficulty. During a meeting, the facilitator has two main jobs to do: to draw out quiet participants and to prevent other participants from dominating the discussion. To draw out quiet participants:

● ask by name if the person has something to contribute: "Lakshmi, you seem concerned; do you have anything to add?"

● recognize when someone has made a contribution: "That's a good point, how does that affect the situation?"

● ask a question and have everyone respond to it one at a time.

A slightly sneaky way to keep someone from dominating the discussion is to assign that person to be the facilitator. Other ways are to interrupt gently and ask someone else for his or her opinions or remind everyone of the time limits on agenda items.

■ *Notetaker*
The notetaker serves as the official historian for the meeting. Depending on the structure of the meeting, he or she might take notes on a flipchart, in which case the notetaker should periodically check to ensure that points are recorded accurately. Alternatively, the notetaker may keep notes on a pad of paper, use an electronic whiteboard, or photograph flipcharts with a digital camera. In any case, the notes should be typed up and distributed to all participants.

Adapted from "More Productive Meetings," Infoline No. 258710.

Sample Agenda: *ToadStools* Sales Meeting

MadeUpThings, Inc.'s *ToadStools* is a novelty product about the size and shape of a button. Users breathe on the button, and it inflates to become a comfortable cushion that decomposes in about eight to 10 hours. It has been widely sold at outdoor concerts, sporting events, and so forth, but recently sales have declined. Marketing manager Bessie Smith has called a meeting to determine why the sales have been going down and to identify ways to get the product back on track. The following is the meeting agenda.

Meeting Objective(s)

To determine the causes behind the declining sales of *ToadStools* and to identify a few viable solutions to the problem using brainstorming techniques.

Logistics	Participants	Responsibilities
Date: Thursday, October 14 **Time:** 10:00 a.m.–11:00 a.m. **Location:** Conference room 811	Bessie Smith	Meeting leader
	Maria Callas	Present the product history; suggest possible solutions
	Robert Johnson	Timekeeper; read background materials and suggest possible solutions
	Tito Puente	Notetaker; read background materials and suggest solutions
	Dick Dale	Facilitator
	Marian Anderson	Read background materials and suggest possible solutions
	Johnny Cash	Understand background; explain budget limitations

Meeting Outline

The following lists planned meeting activities, their duration, and the person or persons responsible:

- purpose of meeting; introduction of participants (5 minutes; Bessie Smith)
- brief product history (5 minutes; Maria Callas)
- brainstorming session (15 minutes; whole group)
  — process: round robin in which each participant gives one or two suggestions for increasing sales
- identification of basis for evaluating solutions (10 minutes; whole group)
  — process: determine most important criterion for solution (speed, quality, innovation, and so forth)
- evaluation and ordering of solutions based on ranking of criteria (10 minutes; whole group)
- agreement on responsibilities and next steps and conclusions (10 minutes; Bessie Smith)
- question-and-answer session (5 minutes; whole group).

identified two or three viable solutions for improving sales of the product and next steps. It also can be useful to indicate in the objective the methods you will use to achieve your objective.

■ *Logistics*

The logistics heading in your meeting agenda indicates date, time, and location. Pick a date that is far enough out to give participants time to prepare, such as a week in advance. Also, pick a date when everyone can attend. When you are planning your meeting, be sure to consider organizational priorities and events. Is this a good time to start any new initiatives or add to people's workload?

Experts disagree about the best time to have a meeting. Some say avoid having them late in the day or on Friday afternoons when energy levels are low. Others note that people are more likely to stay on task and try to get the work of the meeting done in order to leave early if you have them on a Friday afternoon or just before lunch. However, most agree that Monday mornings and just after lunch are always bad times for meetings!

When you are planning the location of your meeting, consider the following questions:

● How many people are coming?
● Will the people fit comfortably in the room?
● What are you going to do?
● Will you need any special equipment?

The logistics heading on your agenda is also a good area to note any unusual circumstances that the participants should be prepared for. For example, in "Escape From Meeting Hell," Patrick J. Sauer describes meetings in which participants go to the mall to check out the competition's products. For the logistics section in cases like this, it would probably be helpful for the participants to know to bring their coats and comfortable shoes.

■ *Participants and Responsibilities*

You've already identified who needs to attend the meeting. Put their names on the agenda and indicate what they need to do to prepare for the meeting and what responsibilities they will have during the meeting. Also indicate here who will play the roles of timekeeper, facilitator, and notetaker, so that these individuals are ready to carry out these functions when the time comes.

■ *Meeting Outline*

The meeting outline lists the activities that will take place during the meeting. When you are preparing the outline, make sure that you aren't trying to cover too much territory. Keep your activities focused on achieving your objective and prioritize them in terms of importance. Work on your most important tasks first, unless you have one or two minor items that you can quickly clear away.

Your meeting outline also gives an estimated amount of time that the activity should take and indicates who is responsible for each activity. In the *ToadStools* example, Bessie Smith is responsible for the introductory portion of the meeting, while Maria Callas provides a quick overview of the history of the product.

For some activities, it may be helpful to describe the process that you will use to complete an activity. To brainstorm solutions to the *ToadStools* sales decline, each participant will be asked to give a couple of suggestions for increasing sales.

The meeting outline should be complete enough that the meeting could run without you. You won't be able to harness the full effectiveness of the participants if they don't know what is expected of them. However, you shouldn't be married to the agenda either. If a productive discussion is going on, and the time allotted for that activity has elapsed, don't be afraid to ask the participants if they want to continue with the discussion and meet again to go over remaining agenda points.

Identifying Tools

Now that you've prepared the meeting agenda, you can identify the tools that you are going to need. Some tools that you may need include:

● audiovisual equipment
● laptop computer
● overhead projector
● whiteboards
● flipcharts and markers.

You also may need process tools. In "Holding Your Own in Meetings, but Working as a Team," Dianna Booher suggests using props to stop anyone from dominating the conversation. For example, you can place a broken record, a whistle, or a bat in the center of the table and push it in front of anyone who bogs down the meeting. Another idea for keeping people involved is to toss a ball around the room; whoever has the ball must contribute a thought or an idea before throwing it to the next person. This can be helpful for keeping the energy up and for getting quiet participants involved.

Electronic tools form another category of meeting tools. Most commonly used among these are video-conferencing and groupware. In *Cyber Meetings*, James L. Creighton and James W.R. Adams describe the latter as a combination of software and a server that connects meeting participants. Groupware enables people at separate locations to "meet" and work together from the comfort of their own desks, sharing documents as needed.

Inviting Participants

Now that you have everything planned—including what the meeting is going to accomplish, who should be there, and where it's going to be—it's time to send out your meeting announcement. The announcement should contain the following information:

- names of all meeting participants
- your name and phone number
- meeting date
- starting and ending times
- meeting location
- meeting objective(s)
- preparation required by participants
- additional materials for participants to bring.

Once again, be sure to send out the announcement far enough in advance for participants to be able to clear time on their calendars for the meeting and carry out any preparations. If you are asking anyone to carry out specific functions in the meeting—such as make a presentation, or carry out the role of timekeeper, facilitator, or notetaker—give those people additional advance notice.

2. Meet

Bravo! You have completed all your meeting preparation, from determining whether you really need to meet to picking the right participants to creating a solid agenda. Being prepared makes all the difference in the world when it comes to running an effective meeting. It also helps to know how to get a meeting running and keep it going. In this section, you learn about four meeting stages—t minus one, liftoff, the trip, and the landing—and get the tools and tips to successfully get through each stage.

T Minus One

A hallmark of an effective meeting is excellent preparation, and that goes for every component, from the agenda to room setup. Get to the meeting room early enough to make sure that:

- the seating arrangements are the way you would like them to be

- the lighting is appropriate to your needs

- the audiovisual equipment is working properly and you know how to use it

- the visual aids are arranged so that everyone can see them

- you have all the materials that you need: handouts for everyone, extra copies of the agenda, markers for the flipcharts, and so forth.

Use the checklist provided in the sidebar *Pre-Meeting Flightcheck* at right to make sure that everything in the room is ready to go as soon as the first participant arrives.

Liftoff

3-2-1 and liftoff! It's time for your meeting to start. The way you start your meeting sets the tone for the whole meeting. Set the right tone by starting on time, displaying enthusiasm, introducing everyone, explaining why you are meeting, forecasting the process, and explaining the ground rules.

■ Start on Time

Here's a new meeting habit to foster: Start when it's time for the meeting to start, not when everyone who was invited has shown up. And don't restart when latecomers do show up. The people who arrived on time will feel that their punctuality is appreciated and that their time is respected, and the latecomers will get the point. In "We've Got to Stop Meeting Like This," Edward E. Scannell suggests setting an odd start time, such as 2:03 p.m. instead of 2 p.m. He notes that "[p]eople tend remember odd starting times more easily; they tend to be more punctual as well."

■ Introduce Everyone

Make sure that everyone in the group knows one another. Introduce anyone who is new to the group. Also explain why each person is there and indicate who will be playing the roles of timekeeper, facilitator, and notetaker.

■ Explain Reasons for Meeting

As a brief introduction to the meeting, explain the reasons for it and describe what a successful outcome of the meeting would be. Make any appropriate changes suggested for the agenda.

■ Forecast the Process

After you have introduced the desired outcomes of the meeting, explain the process steps that you will take to achieve those outcomes. If you are planning to hold a brainstorming session, explain how the process will work. If you are planning to have a discussion session, explain what your expectations for the discussion are. For example, do you want analysis of a problem, or do you want recommendations for solutions only?

■ Explain the Ground Rules

If necessary, review the ground rules. Considering the professional level of the participants and their previous ability to work together, determine if you need to review rules such as:

● Give everyone the opportunity to speak.
● Show respect for everyone and their opinions.
● Give constructive feedback.
● Accept feedback professionally.

Pre-Meeting Flightcheck

Your meeting is about to start. Run through the following checklist to make sure you have everything you need to minimize disruptions during the meeting.

☐ Have you made enough extra copies of the agenda to distribute to all the attendees in case they forgot theirs?

☐ Are there enough seats for everyone?

If you are planning to have someone take notes on a flipchart:

    ☐ Do you have enough flipchart paper?

    ☐ Do you have markers?

    ☐ Do you have tape, so that the completed sheets can be taped to the wall?

☐ Have you brought a pad of paper and pens for the notetaker in case he or she forgot?

☐ Do you have a timepiece for the timekeeper to use in case he or she doesn't have one?

If you are planning to use a laptop for a presentation:

    ☐ Have you checked that it works?

    ☐ Do you have the files that you need?

If you are planning to use an overhead projector:

    ☐ Have you turned it on and made sure that it works?

    ☐ Do you have the pens you need to mark up transparencies?

☐ If you are planning activities, do you have any additional materials that you need?

☐ If you are planning to use a process tool such as a ball or an item to indicate someone is dominating the conversation, did you bring it?

☐ Other:_____

Running Meeting Activities

When you get a meeting activity under way, the first thing to do is to remember what you are trying to achieve. Keep the purpose of the activity in mind when you run some of the following commonly used meeting activities.

■ *Presenting*

Although in most meetings you probably want to keep presentations to a minimum so that you can capitalize on the energy of the group, presenting is still an important way to get information across. Some tips for giving an effective presentation in your meeting include:

● review your presentation objectives
● relate the content to the meeting objective
● vary the pitch, rate, and volume of your voice
● maintain an appropriate pace
● avoid using fillers
● enunciate clearly and distinctly
● use familiar terms and expressions
● maintain eye contact.

For more on giving presentations, see "Make Every Presentation a Winner," *Infoline* No. 258606.

■ *Discussing*

Use discussions to gather information and opinions from participants. The following guidelines will help:

● Make sure participants are familiar with the issues and topics under discussion. If they don't know the topic, they can't have a productive discussion.

● Moderate, don't dominate. Open the discussion and then invite participation from the group.

● Intervene only to interpret points, to handle disruptive or dominating participants, to encourage quiet participants, and to restart a stalled discussion.

● When appropriate, summarize points made. Restate major points.

■ *Brainstorming*

Use brainstorming sessions to generate new ideas. Follow these steps to unleash participant creativity:

1. Announce the brainstorming ground rules:

   ● All ideas will be accepted.
   ● Discussion of suggestions comes later.
   ● Suggestions will not be criticized.

2. Set an achievable goal and a time limit, for example, 30 ideas in 30 minutes.

3. Announce the topic or problem. An effective way to get people started is to state a question. For example, "How can we increase sales of *ToadStools*?"

4. Keep a written record of ideas on a flipchart. Because ideas will come hard and fast, alternate notetakers.

5. Get everyone involved. If someone is dominating the discussion, ask that person to take notes. If someone is being quiet, encourage his or her participation.

6. When ideas start to come more slowly, review what you have to stimulate more ideas.

■ *Problem Solving*

Use the following process to conduct a useful problem-solving session:

1. Clearly state the problem.

2. State why the problem must be solved.

3. Ask participants to state causes of the problem.

4. Ask participants to offer solutions to the problem.

5. Ask participants to determine the best solution.

6. Ask participants to plan implementation of the solution.

■ *Decision Making*

There are two forms of group decision making: either a majority, or a consensus. A consensus is ideal, but consider how much time it may take to reach. Determine before you start what kind of decision you want to reach.

■ *Display Enthusiasm*

An often-overlooked yet important component in getting a meeting off to the right start is to be energetic and enthusiastic about it. If you aren't excited about the meeting, then why would any of your participants be? Even if the meeting is a routine project update meeting or staff meeting, you can still be excited about getting results and making progress. Get your participants excited to be there and ready to contribute with all their attention and energy.

The Trip

Now that your meeting participants know what they are doing there and are excited to contribute to effective meeting outcomes, you want to keep your meeting running productively. To make the most of the trip, you want to be able to:

● run various meeting activities
● communicate effectively
● keep the meeting on track
● manage conflict.

Run Meeting Activities

You created a great agenda that identifies the activities that are going to achieve your meeting purpose. But are you sure you know how to run those activities? How do you get it started and keep it going? What is the process for brainstorming anyway? The sidebar *Running Meeting Activities* at left describes several common meeting activities and how to make them work for your meeting.

Communicate Effectively

Entire forests have been cut down to produce the books published on the topic of communication (and that's not to say all those books aren't valuable or necessary). So there is a lot of information out there about communicating effectively. But some communication pointers that can be particularly helpful for meetings are to deliver a clear message, watch your nonverbal signals, ask good questions, and listen actively.

■ *Deliver a Clear Message*

Remember that meeting time is valuable time, so learn to get to the point clearly and concisely. Oddly enough, that means that you need to take some time to gather your thoughts, clarify the purpose of what you plan to say, and rehearse before you even open your mouth. To enhance the communication skills of all meeting participants, Peter M. Tobia and Martin C. Becker, in "Making the Most of Meeting Time," recommend encouraging people "to take 'pregnant pauses' before delivering their messages." That little upfront investment of time will yield valuable dividends of clarity and purpose. It will also help you avoid saying "um" and "uh" and using other fillers.

In addition to organizing your thoughts, another aspect of communicating clearly is making your speech intelligible. Speak up. Enunciate. Don't be afraid to overarticulate. Also remember that your tone of voice can either reinforce your words or convey mixed signals. Vary your rate of speed, emphasis, and force in ways that get your point across.

■ *Watch Your Nonverbal Signals*

Your appearance, facial expressions, and body language communicate even when you aren't saying anything. Make sure that you also are in control of those messages by:

● dressing appropriately for the purpose of your meeting (one rule of thumb is to wear the most formal outfit you expect to see)

● avoiding distracting clothing or jingly jewelry

● maintaining an open, neutral facial expression

● maintaining eye contact (this also will help you to recognize if participants are bored or are not understanding something)

● nodding and leaning forward to encourage someone to continue speaking

● leaning back, folding your arms, or breaking eye contact to discourage someone from dominating the discussion

Questioning Tips

Questioning is not an easy skill. However, you can learn some techniques that will help you pose effective questions in meetings. Consider the following tips as you prepare:

- Develop questions when you create the agenda. Review agenda items and identify points where you might want to ask questions.

- Design questions to be brief. If you ask a question that's too long, you'll get the response, "Would you please repeat the question?"

- Ask questions at different difficulty levels. Some questions should require only a yes or no answer (closed). Others should require that a participant answer in greater detail (open). Learn to use different types of questions to further the purpose of your meeting and control difficult behaviors. For example, pose a yes or no question to a dominant participant and ask a question that requires more input of a quiet participant.

- Ask questions of the whole group (open questions).

- Target questions to particular meeting attendees. This enables you to encourage persons who don't respond to group questions to participate.

Adapted from "Effective Classroom Training Techniques," Infoline *No. 250108.*

- keeping your hands still and managing any tics, such as tapping pencils, shuffling papers, cracking your knuckles, and so forth; avoiding creating the impression you are distracted

- sitting upright and leaning slightly forward

- avoiding slouching.

■ Ask Good Questions
Questions are a great tool for effective communication. They can help ensure that everyone shares the same understanding of the issues by surfacing any unclear points. They also stimulate participants to get actively involved in the meeting.

Furthermore, you can use questions to manage the group's interactions. For example, if you have a couple of people off in a corner having a discussion of their own, manage the situation by asking the individuals a direct question to bring them back into the general discussion. This stops side discussions, while preserving the dignity of the speakers if they actually do have an additional point to contribute.

You also can use questions to draw out quiet or shy participants. For example, pose a question and ask each person in turn to give an answer. Another way to use questions to encourage quiet people to participate is to ask that person a simple question and acknowledge his or her contribution:

"Maria, what is the number one customer complaint about the product?"

"The product deteriorates too quickly."

"Great, Maria. Do you have any suggestions for how we could address that complaint?"

Some tips for asking effective questions in meetings are presented in the sidebar *Questioning Tips* at left.

■ Listen Actively
The last—but certainly not least—communication skill that this *Infoline* will address is listening actively. Why does listening matter? Well, for one thing, one of the reasons you presumably called a meeting was to get people's input. And one of the best ways to collect that input is by listening. But, as Diane Kirrane notes in "Listening to Learn; Learning to Listen," *Infoline* No. 258806, effective listening is neither easy nor passive. Some tips for listening effectively include:

- judging content, not delivery

- delaying evaluation: focusing on the speaker, not your response

- listening for ideas

- listening for the feeling behind people's words

- resisting distractions

- exercising your mind by mentally paraphrasing the speaker's words

- keeping your mind open.

Keep the Meeting on Track

OK, your meeting has been running along pretty smoothly: Your activities have gone as planned, and you've used your excellent communication skills to keep the ideas flowing. But now, all of a sudden, the meeting has taken a wrong turn, and it's veering wildly off course. Sunnunta has brought up an unrelated topic, and George and Lori have seized upon it to vent some unrelated frustrations. You are getting confused, and you can see the success of your meeting going down the drain. But don't let that happen! Here's what you can do to take back control or to maintain control in the first place:

■ Be Observant
Clearly, it's better to avoid getting off track in the first place, and the way to do that is to pay attention to behavioral cues in the room. If you are observant, you can often stop the meeting from going off track before it happens. One thing you can do is to note if anyone in particular seems keen to discuss a different topic and keep that person on task. Also pay attention to cues that indicate that attendees may be bored, frustrated, or need a break. You may need to deal with the problem by assigning a new activity, addressing the causes of their frustration, or providing a break.

■ Intervene
If you've noticed that meeting participants are no longer talking about issues related to the agenda, guide them back gently by asking them, "Are we getting off track?" or "We are getting a little off track here, where were we before we started talking about . . . ?"

■ Stick to the Agenda
You put a lot of work into creating the agenda, now stick to it! Call attention to when the meeting is getting off track by asking the timekeeper how much time you have left on the current agenda item, and then continuing with it or moving on.

■ Or, Change the Agenda
You may find that the agenda as you planned it isn't working and is causing people to get off track. If that's the case, remember your meeting objective and identify how best you can achieve it. Even though following the agenda is important, making sure that you achieve your meeting objective is more important.

■ Park It
Discussions in meetings can raise a lot of issues, questions, and ideas that won't contribute to the purpose of the meeting, but are nonetheless valuable. To record such ideas, use a parking lot, which can take the form of a flipchart. When participants bring up useful ideas to explore at another time, tell them to park it. That way you will have a record of and can follow up on those ideas at another time. Individuals also can get unrelated concerns heard and can return to focusing on the topic at hand.

■ Model Behavioral Expectations
If you want to maintain a productive climate in your meetings, you have to model the behaviors you want from meeting participants. Take your process seriously, listen thoughtfully and empathetically, and treat all participants and their contributions with respect. Set an energetic and attentive example.

■ Review Periodically
At appropriate points in the meeting, summarize and review what has been accomplished so far and clarify what remains to be done. This will help you stay on track for achieving your meeting objective.

Manage Conflict

The phrase "managing conflict" may in this instance be a bit of a misnomer. A productive meeting doesn't necessarily quash conflicts, but instead offers an opportunity to air disagreements and use conflict as fuel for innovation. In "Keeping Team Conflict Alive," Shari Caudron describes the value of "good" conflict: ". . . when people are allowed to express their opinions, no matter how disagreeable, magic can occur. More ideas are put on the table, which can lead to more discovery, which can lead to quantum leaps in improvement and innovation. Put simply, conflict is a potent source of creativity—especially in troubled times." Surfacing conflicts enables all participants to air their opinions, which in turns enables all participants to buy in to and fully support eventual solutions. When people aren't given the opportunity to say what's really on their minds, they will resent any decisions that they don't agree to and find ways to avoid following up on their commitments. In the end, you lose because your meeting doesn't produce the outcomes you were aiming for.

To reap the value of conflict, you have to create an environment that allows participants to disagree publicly. In fact, part of your job as meeting leader is to encourage and protect minority opinions. At the same time, you don't want to venture into the area of destructive conflict. How do you strike the right balance? Caudron provides these tips:

● Look for shared goals and win-win situations.

● Clarify, sort, and value differences.

● Gain people's commitment to change their own attitudes and modes of communication when necessary.

● Openly praise participants who are willing to suggest new and different approaches.

● Analyze why conflicts keep occurring. Usually, people aren't fighting about what they say they are fighting about.

● Encourage individuals to take the initiative to change personally.

● Model the kind of behavior that shows a comfort level with conflict.

Some other tips to keep in mind are to encourage the use of "I" statements instead of "you" statements and to depersonalize the conflict. Using "I" statements means turning statements from accusations ("You did this!") into statements of fact or personal feeling ("I felt this way when this happened . . ."). Depersonalizing a conflict involves looking at a problem objectively, without individuals entering the story. Instead of saying, "You scrapped my project," you might say, "The project was scrapped because of budget cuts." Both of these communication behaviors reduce the personal emotional attachment to the problem, which is a source of destructive conflict, and return the focus to the issue itself.

The Landing

The final stage of a meeting is the landing. Ending a meeting well has as much to do with how effective it is as starting it well. What do you want to get done in this stage of the meeting? The following steps wrap up a productive meeting:

1. Summarize.

At the end of the meeting, take a few minutes to summarize and review what you have covered in the meeting. Go over the agenda points and indicate what you covered and what you didn't cover and identify possible items for another meeting.

2. Open up the room for questions.

Allow at least five minutes of question time at the end of your meeting summary to ensure that everyone has the same perception of the meeting as you do and there are no points of confusion.

3. Gain agreements and commitments from all participants.

The meeting should end with all participants agreeing on the contents and outcome of the meeting. In addition, each person should have made a commitment to further action. Make sure that each person is able to state what he or she is going to do and when. Plan to follow up at a later date.

4. Evaluate the meeting.

Periodically distribute an evaluation form to maintain and improve meeting quality. A sample form is available in the sidebar *Meeting Evaluation* at right.

5. End on time (or better yet, a few minutes early)!

Show that you respect your participants' time and end the meeting when the agenda said it would end. If there are agenda points that you didn't get to, plan to have another meeting. If possible, end on a high note by ending a few minutes early. And always thanks your participants for their time and participation!

3. Follow Up

Well, the meeting has adjourned, and you are packing up to leave. You are all finished, right? Of course not. Now you have to follow up on the meeting. Don't forget to:

☐ Type up and distribute the notes from the meeting. Make sure that everyone who attended the meeting gets a copy as well as anyone who is affected by the outcomes of the meeting but didn't need to attend.

☐ Plan to follow up on your commitments. If you said you were going to do something, make sure that you add the task to your to-do list and do it!

☐ Plan for a follow-up meeting to make sure that commitments are being upheld and the purpose of your meeting is being achieved. Also the follow-up meeting will point out if any new problems have surfaced that meeting participants need to solve.

☐ If you distributed an evaluation form, review the comments. Resolve to make improvements as needed.

Now you're done. So take a breath and enjoy the moment. You just had a productive meeting! It was pretty exciting because you got so much done, and the energy of the participants is really going to produce some great outcomes! Keep following these steps, and your meetings will get even more productive as you improve from the feedback you get and as participants get into the habit of making meeting time effective, productive, and energizing.

Meeting Evaluation

Given the amount of time that people spend in meetings, isn't it surprising how seldom the effectiveness of a meeting is evaluated? You evaluate and work to improve almost everything else, why not do the same for meetings? At the end of your meeting, distribute an evaluation form like the one below. If you are holding a regularly occurring meeting, like a weekly project update meeting, distribute the form only once in every four meetings to ensure that meeting quality maintains a high standard.

Meeting Evaluation

To:

From:

Date:

Title/subject of meeting:

Date of meeting:

1. Did the meeting achieve its objective(s)?

2. Was meeting time managed effectively?

3. How well did the meeting leader manage interpersonal relationships? What could be improved?

4. What aspects of the meeting could have been better?

Thanks for your feedback!

References & Resources

Articles

Booher, Dianna. "Holding Your Own in Meetings, but Working as a Team." *Training & Development,* August 1994, pp. 54-63.

Clark, Jim, and Richard Koonce. "Meetings Go High-Tech." *Training & Development,* November 1995, pp. 32-38.

Clarke-Epstein, Chris. "Increase Your ROM (Return on Meetings)." *T+D,* April 2002, pp. 65-67.

Caudron, Shari. "Keeping Team Conflict Alive." *Training & Development,* September 1998, pp. 48-51.

Flores, Luis G., and Janyce Fadden. "How to Have a Successful Strategic Planning Meeting." *Training & Development,* January 2000, pp. 31-34.

Gallagher, Helen. "Breeze Live: Don't Wait for a Meeting to Get Your Point Across." Available at http://www.learningcircuits.org/2004/aug2004/aug04_reviews.htm.

Gilbert, Jennifer. "Become a Meeting Master." *Sales & Marketing Management,* December 2002, pp. 46-51.

Kaplan-Leiserson, Eva. "The Future of Meetings." *T+D,* November 2004, pp. 10-12.

Katz, Sally N. "Power Skills for Effective Meetings." *Training & Development,* July 1991, pp. 53-56.

Sandwith, Paul. "Better Meetings for Better Communication." *Training & Development,* January 1992, pp. 29-32.

Scannell, Edward E. "We've Got to Stop Meeting Like This." *Training & Development,* January 1992, pp. 70-71.

Sauer, Patrick J. "Escape From Meeting Hell." *Inc. Magazine,* May 2004, available at http://www.inc.com/magazine/20040501/escape.html.

Tobia, Peter M., and Martin C. Becker. "Making the Most of Meeting Time." *Training & Development,* August 1990, pp. 34-38.

Books

Albert, Burt. *Fat Free Meetings: How to Make Them Fast, Focused, and Fun!* Princeton, NJ: Peterson's/Pacesetter Books, 1996.

Anderson, Karen. *Making Meetings Work.* Des Moines, IA: American Media Publishing, 1994.

Bozek, Phillip E. *50 One-Minute Tips to Better Communication.* Revised edition. Menlo Park, CA: Crisp Publications, 1998.

Cameron, Esther. *Facilitation Made Easy: Practical Tips to Improve Meetings & Workshops.* 2nd edition. London: Kogan Page, 2001.

Chang, Richard E., and Kevin R. Kehoe. *Meetings That Work!* Irvine, CA: Richard Chang Associates, 1993.

Clarke-Epstein, Chris. *I Can't Take Your Call Right Now, I'm In a Meeting: How to Make Time In Meetings Pay Off.* Wausau, WI: Link Publications, 1998.

Creighton, James L., and James W.R. Adams. *Cyber Meetings: How to Link People and Technology in Your Organization.* New York: AMACOM, 1998.

Howell, Johnna L. *Tools for Facilitating Team Meetings: Easy Ways to Help Plan, Organize, Conduct, and Evaluate Team Meetings.* Seattle, WA: Integrity Publishing, 1995.

Jenings, Judy, and Linda Malcak. *Communication Basics.* Alexandria, VA: ASTD Press, 2004.

Kaye, Steve. *The Manager's Pocket Guide to Effective Meetings.* Amherst, MA: HRD Press, 1998.

Kayser, Thomas A. *Mining Group Gold: How to Cash In on the Collaborative Brain Power of a Group.* 2nd edition. Chicago: Irwin, 1995.

McCain, Donald V., and Deborah D. Tobey. *Facilitation Basics.* Alexandria, VA: ASTD Press, 2004.

Mina, Eli. *The Complete Handbook of Meetings.* New York: AMACOM, 2000.

Mosvick, Roger K., and Robert B. Nelson. *We've Got to Start Meeting Like This! A Guide to Successful Business Meeting Management.* Glenview, IL: Scott, Foresman, 1987.

Orey, Maureen, and Jenni Prisk. *Communication Skills Training.* Alexandria, VA: ASTD Press, 2004.

Infolines

Guillot, Tara L. "Team Building in a Virtual Environment." No. 250205.

Kirrane, Diane. "Listening to Learn; Learning to Listen." No. 258806 (revised 1997).

Plattner, Francis B. "Improve Your Communication and Speaking Skills." No. 259409 (revised 1997).

Sheftel, Phoebe A., and Matthew Bennet. "How to Resolve Conflict." No. 250104.

Spruell, Gerry, ed. "More Productive Meetings." No. 258710 (revised 1997).

Sullivan, Rick, and Jerry L. Wircenski. "Effective Classroom Training Techniques." No. 250108.

Wircenski, Jerry L., and Richard L. Sullivan. "Make Every Presentation a Winner." No. 258606 (revised 1998).

Planning Your Meeting: A Worksheet

You are planning to call a meeting. To help ensure that the meeting is as productive and valuable as it can be, go over this worksheet. You may find you don't even need to call a meeting!

Do You Need to Have a Meeting?

Answer the following questions to determine if a meeting is your best option.

Question	Yes or No?
Can you clearly state the purpose of your meeting?	
Do you want input from others to solve a problem, plan a project, or brainstorm?	
Are you going to act on participants' input?	
Do you need to deliver information to a lot of people but don't want to write it?	
Do you want to motivate and energize your team?	

Did you answer "No" to any (or all) of these questions? If so, stop here. You probably don't need to call a meeting. Consider making some phone calls or sending an email or a memo instead. If you do need to call a meeting, jot down the purpose of your meeting here:

_____

_____

_____

_____

_____

Who Needs to Attend?

Considering what you want to achieve with your meeting, who can make contributions to its success? Who needs to come? List the names of the people you are considering, then note the reason that person should come. If you can't think of a good reason for someone to come, you should probably cross him or her off the list. For optimum efficiency, you probably don't want more than about a half-dozen people to attend, but that does depend somewhat on the kind of meeting you are planning.

Name	Reason to Attend?

Planning Your Meeting: A Worksheet (continued)

Who Needs to Do What?

Now that you have decided whom to invite to the meeting, determine if you need someone to carry out any specific tasks in the meeting, such as presenting information or coming up with some preliminary ideas. Also identify who you want to carry out the roles of timekeeper, facilitator, and notetaker.

Task or Role	Name
Timekeeper	
Facilitator	
Notetaker	

What Facilities or Equipment Are Needed?

To identify the facilities and equipment you might need, answer the following questions:

- Do you have a space that's big enough to comfortably accommodate all the participants?

- Do you need any special seating arrangements?

- Is the meeting going to take long enough to require breaks or refreshments? Should you go off site?

- How are you planning to deliver information or have notes taken?

- Is the equipment that you need to deliver information available in the room or facilities that you have chosen?

What Needs to Get Done?

The last component in planning your meeting is determining what is going to happen. To identify the right agenda items in the right quantity (not too many, not too few), answer the following questions:

- What has to happen to accomplish your objective?

- What is the most important outcome you want from the meeting?

- If meeting time were cut in half for some reason, what would be the first thing removed from the agenda?

- If this is a follow-on meeting, were agenda items left from the last meeting that should be taken care of?

- During which activity are meeting participants going to commit to further action and next steps?

- Are there any minor issues that could be quickly cleared up during this meeting?

Now, list the activities. Mark each activity high priority (H) or low (L). You may still want to keep low-priority activities on your agenda, but you will know where to spend more or less time. If possible, go through high-priority activities first both to capitalize on the energy of the group and to ensure that you cover them.

Activity	Priority (H/L)

Basics of Emotional Intelligence (EI)

Issue 0810

Basics of Emotional Intelligence (EI)

AUTHOR

Lynda C. McDermott
President
EquiPro, International, Inc.
420 Lexington Avenue
Suite 300
New York, NY 10017
Phone: 212.297.6176
Email: lmcdermott@equiproint.com

Lynda McDermott is president of EquiPro International, specializing in improving organizational, leadership, and team development. She is the author of best-selling business books and a certified speaking professional with a master's degree in organizational psychology.

***Infoline* Associate Editor**
Justin Brusino

Copy Editor
Ann Bruen

Production Design
Kathleen Schaner

What Is EI?

We all know a story about someone who was exceptionally intelligent, but who could not make big career strides because he or she lacked good "people skills." We probably also know of someone who is not particularly intellectually gifted but who progressively rose to top-level positions. How do you explain one person's failure and another's success? IQ? Past experiences? Expertise? Perseverance? Political skills? Research from the last two decades suggests that the most successful performers in organizations are alike in one critical way—they all have *emotional intelligence (EI)*.

It is a commonly held belief that employees should leave their emotions outside the workplace. "Don't be so emotional" and "Don't take it personally" are phrases often used by bosses or colleagues with a co-worker who is visibly upset over a situation at work. However, in the last 20 years there has been much research to suggest that emotions are a natural part of the brain's decision-making process and should not be disregarded.

In the early 1990s, psychologists Peter Salovey and Jack Mayer were the first to propose that individuals differ in their abilities to perceive, understand, and use their emotions. They labeled this ability *emotional intelligence*.

The concept of applying emotional intelligence in the workplace was later popularized by the work of Daniel Goleman in his books *Emotional Intelligence* (1995) and *Working with Emotional Intelligence* (1998). Goleman was interested in understanding the EI competencies that support superior work performance.

There continues to be some disagreement between academic researchers (such as John Mayer and Peter Salovey) and practitioners (such as Daniel Goleman and Reuven Bar-On) about what competencies should be included in a definition of emotional intelligence. This *Infoline* does not focus on any one person's definition of emotional intelligence; rather it uses an amalgam of thoughts and ideas.

While there are varying emotional intelligence definitions and models that have been developed over the years, we are defining it as: *Our capacity to recognize our own feelings and those of others and to manage emotions in ourselves and others.*

Emotional intelligence competencies include

- self-awareness
- self-regulation
- motivation
- social awareness
- social skills.

For more detailed descriptions of the competencies, see the sidebar *Emotional Intelligence Competency Definitions.*

This *Infoline* is designed for anyone looking to understand the basics of emotional intelligence with an eye toward improving their abilities. It is also useful for a trainer or coach who wants to develop the emotional intelligence of others. You will learn how

- emotional intelligence is related to work performance

- our brains govern emotional intelligence

- to assess your own and others' emotional intelligence

- to develop emotional intelligence competencies

- to assess and develop a team's emotional intelligence.

The Value of Emotional Intelligence

Many people believe emotional intelligence simply means "being nice" or employing "touchy-feely" management. This is a narrow view. Emotional intelligence is really about understanding yourself and relating to others.

Anyone who wants to ascend the ranks in their organization will have to deal with more and more people. When moving into a leadership position, managing relationships with others is easily as important as planning a budget. Emotional intelligence contributes to other managerial talents such as managing conflict and negotiating.

Even if you do not want to take on a managerial position, research from the last two decades suggests possessing and applying emotional intelligence competencies has a positive impact on job performance. Who doesn't want to work better with their colleagues?

Important EI Findings

Daniel Goleman and countless other researchers have analyzed data from hundreds of organizations across a range of job positions. Here are some of the important findings:

- Emotional competencies are much more important in contributing to work excellence than pure intellect and expertise.

- Emotional intelligence competencies provide a competitive edge for those who want to climb the organizational ladder because they contribute 80 to 90 percent of the competencies that distinguish outstanding leaders from average ones.

- The most successful global companies are run by leaders who display attitudes that include self-confidence, self-control, achievement-orientation, empathy, and teamwork—all components of emotional intelligence.

- Higher degrees of emotional intelligence contribute to the "bottom-line," whether you are a partner in a multinational consulting firm or a cosmetics sales agent.

- Executives who "derail" are often seen as lacking *emotional strength*. They were unwilling to hear and see the reality of a situation and then move to constructively deal with it.

- When it comes to emotional intelligence, both genders appear to have it in relatively equal measurements, although women seem to have significantly stronger interpersonal skills and men appear to have a stronger sense of self.

The bad news is that our own current state of emotional intelligence has been hard-wired as a result of our brain's development and socialization. The good news is that emotional competencies can be developed.

Why We Get Emotional

Our emotional intelligence is a function of the interconnections between the neural systems that are responsible for the intellect and those that are responsible for the emotions. Our emotional brain circuitry runs from the prefrontal area to the amygdala, located on either side of the midbrain. This limbic area of the brain, in moments of high emotion such as anxiety, frustration, or fear is actually stronger than the rest of the brain and can, in fact, "hijack" our ability to reason and problem-solve.

While the amygdala is watching out for signs of danger, the prefrontal lobes have the ability to keep the amygdala's urges restrained so that our response in potentially threatening situations is more measured and skillful. The challenge is to "catch" the amygdala before it overrides the prefrontal lobes.

Emotional Intelligence Competency Definitions

Being emotionally intelligent involves two sets of competencies: personal and social. Each competency has its own skills and behaviors. Knowing these competencies is crucial to understanding and building emotional intelligence.

Personal Competence (Self)

These skills are focused on you and how well you know yourself.

■ *Self-Awareness*
Knowing one's internal states, preferences, resources, and intuitions. This is the foundational skill of emotional intelligence.

- Emotional Awareness: Recognizing one's emotions and their effects.
- Accurate Self-Assessment: Knowing one's strengths and limits.
- Self-Confidence: Having a strong sense of one's self-worth and capabilities.

■ *Self-Regulation*
Managing one's internal states, impulses, and resources.

- Self-Control: Keeping disruptive emotions and impulses in check.
- Trustworthiness: Maintaining standards of honesty and integrity.
- Conscientiousness: Taking responsibility for personal performance.
- Adaptability: Having flexibility in handling change.
- Innovation: Being comfortable with novel ideas, approaches, and new information.

■ *Motivation*
Understanding emotional tendencies that guide or facilitate reaching goals.

- Achievement Drive: Striving to improve or meet a standard of excellence.
- Commitment: Aligning with the goals of the group or organization.
- Initiative: Being ready to act on opportunities.
- Optimism: Having persistence in pursuing goals despite obstacles and setbacks.

Social Competence (Others)

These skills are focused on how well you interact with and understand other people.

■ *Social Awareness*
Being aware of others' feelings, needs, and concerns.

- Empathy: Having an active interest in others and demonstrating that you care.
- Understanding Others: Sensing others' feelings, perspectives, and concerns.
- Developing Others: Sensing others' development needs and bolstering their abilities.
- Service Orientation: Anticipating, recognizing, and meeting customers' needs.
- Leveraging Diversity: Cultivating opportunities through different kinds of people.
- Political Awareness: Reading a group's emotional currents and power relationships.

■ *Social Skills*
Being looked upon favorably by others.

- Influence: Wielding effective tactics for persuasion.
- Communication: Listening openly and sending convincing messages.
- Conflict Management: Negotiating and resolving disagreements.
- Leadership: Inspiring and guiding individuals or groups.
- Change Catalyst: Initiating or managing change.
- Building Bonds: Nurturing instrumental relationships.
- Collaboration and Cooperation: Working with others toward shared goals.
- Team Capabilities: Creating group synergy.

Bruce's Emotional Outburst

Let's look at an example of how our emotions can overtake our brain and cause us to act irrationally.

Meet Bruce, a mid-level manager at a software company. Bruce was furious. His boss caught him off-guard in a meeting with high-level executives by questioning a decision about the product launch that was made several years earlier, when Bruce was a newly appointed team leader. His boss had not been with the company at that time.

Bruce's immediate reaction was to verbally "attack" his boss by angrily replying: "It's easy for people who weren't around then to second-guess things today. You don't have a clue about what the competition was doing to us back then." The rest of the people attending the meeting were shocked by Bruce's outburst.

Bruce was surprised by his boss's question and angry that he hadn't been asked about the product's history earlier instead of getting put on the spot. Bruce felt threatened by his boss's question, and his emotional brain undermined the workings of his intellectual brain. Bruce's amygdala, a limbic brain structure that is on constant alert for danger, commandeered the other parts of Bruce's brain, including rational centers in the neocortex, for an immediate reaction to the perceived threat.

In essence Bruce's amygdala "hijacked" the rest of his brain and caused him to "snap" instead of allowing the prefrontal area to veto his emotional impulse and respond more effectively.

If Bruce had a more well-developed capacity for self-control under stressful situations, he might have taken the spotlight off of himself and calmed down by asking his boss a question. For example, what part of the product launch decision was his boss most interested in hearing about. Then Bruce would have been able to more effectively respond to his boss's specific question with the facts and not with his emotions.

Control Your Emotions

Learning to control our emotions at work or at home is important because:

- Negative emotions—especially chronic anger or deep-seated frustration erode your mental abilities and confidence.

- Emotional distress not only impedes work performance, but also interferes with your ability to read others' emotions accurately, and negatively influences your interpersonal and social skills.

Therefore, one of the first steps in building your overall EI competence is to become more aware of your emotions—being able to describe them at any point in time and to understand their source.

The next step is to move beyond understanding to being able to execute self-control in order to modify your responses to situations so they are more appropriate and effective.

For more information, see the sidebar *Manage Your Emotions*.

Manage Your Emotions

Learning to properly manage your emotions is one of the first steps to improving your emotional intelligence. Anger and anxiety are two of the most common emotions. Authors Jeff Feldman and Karl Mulle offer the following advice to cope with these powerful feelings.

Manage Anger

- **Practice postponing your anger response for small increments of time**—Eventually, you will be able to postpone indefinitely and choose your response.

- **Find the triggers**—Identify the situations and circumstances that tend to trigger your anger response and manage those situations.

- **Mix pleasantness with anger**—Just as oil doesn't mix with water, anger doesn't mix with feelings of pleasantness. This is a behavioral strategy. To manage your anger, do something that makes you feel good.

- **Reframe your anger**—Anger is often a signal to ask yourself the question: What is actually beneath my anger? The primary emotions that tend to drive anger are fear, deep concern, worry, guilt, and hurt. When you use your self-awareness to connect with your primary emotions, you are actually managing your anger by *reframing* it as one of these primary emotions.

- **Choose your battles carefully**—There are things in life that are worth spending your anger energy on, but you have to separate them from the things that are trivial. When you feel angry, your amydgala is not always drawing a clear distinction between a real injustice and a trivial offense.

Manage Anxiety

- **Ask anxiety inventory questions**—Anxiety is an emotion that will tend to narrow your field of perception by making it difficult for you to see what is going on and what your choices are. We often get paralyzed by anxiety because we can't come up with a good answer to a question like, "What do I do?" Instead, we can ask:

  — What is going on here?
  — What's the worst thing that could happen?
  — How likely is it?
  — Is it in or out of my control?
  — Is there anything I can do?

- **Recognize the irrationality of worry**—Much of the time we spend worrying is unproductive, because worry does not actually accomplish anything. It has been estimated that only 10 percent of what we spend our energy worrying about is actually within our control. Focus your worry energy on the things that you can control that are important.

- **Resist using worry as a tool to manipulate others**—Worry can be used as a way to get other people to do what you want them to do. Parents do this all the time with children. A child is expected not to climb a tree because the parent is worried about the potential for an injury. The child complies, not because of understanding the safety issues, but because the child does not want the parent to worry. The parent is unwittingly teaching the child to be manipulated by emotion instead of teaching the child to think about what is or isn't responsible behavior.

From Jeff Feldman and Karl Mulle's, Put Emotional Intelligence to Work, *ASTD Press, 2007.*

Assess Emotional Intelligence

If possessing highly developed emotional intelligence has been shown to determine outstanding job performance in many occupations, including management and professional jobs, wouldn't individuals and organizations want to ensure the development and continuous improvement of EI competencies?

Of course! But this obvious answer is counterbalanced with the following skepticism as to

- whether EI competencies can be measured objectively (as compared with a standardized IQ test)

- whether one can be trained or coached to become more empathetic, more self-confident, more self-aware, and so on.

Rest assured that over the years there has been much progress in the measurement of emotional intelligence. Academics and practitioners may differ on what truly constitutes the components of emotional intelligence, but there is consensus that it can be measured.

Emotional intelligence assessments directly measure your emotional understanding of yourself (insight) and your ability to manage emotional issues effectively. They also measure your facility with interpersonal relationships, such as "reading" people and working with them to achieve a desirable outcome. Knowing where your EI strengths and weaknesses lie shows you where you need improvement and builds your self-awareness.

EI Assessment Methods

If you are planning on having a coach or professional assess your EI competencies, you should be aware of the possible methods that they could utilize. You may also use the list below if you are planning on becoming someone else's EI coach.

- Observation: Noting an individual's behavior and its impact on others in a work or social setting.

- Behavioral event interviews: A specially designed interview that asks an individual to describe in their own words what they said, thought, felt, and did in specific situations.

- Simulation feedback: Individuals participating in case-like situations are given feedback on their roles and behavior.

- Surveys: Paper or online questionnaires that evaluate a person's competency and describe the action he or she would take in specific situations. Many of the more sophisticated assessments require accreditation for their use by internal or external trainers and coaches.

A more formal assessment feedback tool, the Hay/McBer Emotional Competence Inventory (ECI), is accompanied by a booklet entitled *The Development Advisor* that provides development materials (books, articles, and films) and suggests on-the-job development activities that may be used to improve each of the EI competencies that are measured.

Another useful tool is the *Emotional Intelligence Quick Book* by Travis Bradberry and Jean Greaves. This book offers a link to an online assessment that is quick, informal, and cost-effective. This can be a good starting point before turning to one of the more sophisticated assessment instruments.

For more information on emotional intelligence assessment tools, see the sidebar *EI Assessment Instruments*.

Use Multi-Rater Assessments

Assessments, based on a specific EI competency model, provide precise and focused feedback on your emotional intelligence strengths and limitations. Most of the assessments provide for both a self-assessment and multi-rater assessments (360-degree from bosses, direct reports, peers, and others).

It's always a good idea to use a mutli-rater assessment when measuring EI competencies for the following reasons:

- You may not be very aware of your strengths and limitations or have difficulty objectively and accurately evaluating your EI competencies.

- Even if you are skilled at realistically assessing yourself, others may have a different view of your behavior.

The 360-degree view offers a composite profile of your EI competencies, assuming that evaluations are done by people who interact with you on a regular basis. Whatever methodology you select, it is vital that you be clear on what you are intending to measure.

Robert Kabacoff of the Management Research Group, an assessment company, comments on the measurement of emotional intelligence and leadership practices:

"Emotional intelligence measures can help us to gauge an individual's ability to understand and manage their internal emotional life and to understand the emotions of others and thus produce desirable interpersonal outcomes. However, emotional intelligence does not directly assess the leadership practices that are important for organizational effectiveness, such as strategic visioning, effective delegation, and managerial follow-through."

EI Assessment Instruments

There are many organizations that offer assessment instruments for measuring emotional intelligence. Here we highlight three that have been developed by prominent researchers in the field.

EQ-I (Emotional Quotient Inventory). Developed by Reuven Bar-On, this is a self-report instrument in which the score is an outcome of how you respond to the 133 questions that make up the instrument. This assessment measures skills concerning intrapersonal and interpersonal abilities, as well as adaptability, stress management, and general mood areas such as optimism and happiness. The EQ-I is well regarded for selection purposes and career development.

ESCI (Emotional & Social Competence Inventory). Developed by Daniel Goleman and Richard Boyatzis in partnership with the Hay Group, this is a 360-degree assessment instrument compiling responses from a group you invite to offer performance feedback with regard to your degree of emotional intelligence. This instrument aligns with the Goleman model of emotional intelligence and is designed to assess competencies from the four quadrants of self-awareness, self-management, social awareness, and social skills. The ESCI is well suited to individual and organizational development.

MSCEIT. The name of this instrument is taken from its developers, John Mayer, Peter Salovey, and David Caruso (Mayer, Salovey, Caruso Emotional Intelligence Test). Slightly different from an assessment, this instrument is actually a test, with your score being determined by your choosing the best response to each question. The test measures your abilities in perceiving emotions, applying emotions for facilitating thought, understanding emotions, and managing emotions. The MSCEIT is especially useful in understanding your ability or lack of ability in recognizing emotions in others.

From Jeff Feldman and Karl Mulle's, Put Emotional Intelligence to Work, *ASTD Press, 2007.*

Kabacoff recommends performing a combination of assessments on an individual to gauge emotional intelligence, leadership practices, and motivations to get a full picture of a person's abilities.

EI Feedback Process

The feedback reports from these EI assessments indicate the specific emotional competencies that are strengths, and which ones may need development.

For example, you may find that you are perceived to be very skilled in the area of "empathy," but seen as lacking in "self-confidence." You may also discover that you are not seen in the same way by different observer groups or that how you perceive yourself is different from how others see your behavior.

When the EI assessment feedback process is poorly managed, it can lead to resistance to learning and change. Emotional intelligence competencies are closely linked to one's self-esteem; so if the feedback process is not handled with sensitivity and skill, individuals may become defensive and resistant to learning.

In the most effective development processes, participants work with a trained coach or facilitator to help interpret the feedback ratings and identify the focus of any training or development efforts.

Develop EI Competencies

It's true that some people are just born with more emotional intelligence than others. But everyone can build their EI competencies. If fact, there are some data that show emotional intelligence actually improves as we age—it's called *maturity*. But people often resist hearing that they may need to develop more emotional intelligence because emotional intelligence is linked so closely to identity. No one wants to be told that his or her behavior is wrong.

Don't Take It Personally

The interactive habits we have developed over time have contributed to our own perceptions of our success, and we may expect others to just "live with it." When someone suggests that we need to learn to control our temper or to be less blunt in our feedback to others, they are calling into question habits and behaviors that not only define part of who we are, but also what others have come to expect from interacting with us.

To really improve emotional intelligence, you must first learn to not take feedback personally. No matter how exceptional someone's emotional intelligence, we all have faults that can be worked on.

Find Motivation to Improve

Finding the proper motivation helps drive the desire to improve emotional intelligence. Your motivation may be to

- increase your effectiveness in working with others

- increase your potential for promotion

- achieve more fulfilling personal relationships

- improve a bad performance review.

If someone has been scalded by feedback from a boss or significant other or is motivated by threats or a fear of loss, the motivation to change will probably not be sustainable.

The key to motivation is appealing to a person's "hot buttons." The four primary motivators for change are

- money
- power
- status
- popularity.

What motivates you?

If you are looking to drive change in a group of others, find out what motivates each individual. Change motivated by what someone will gain has a much higher chance of being sustained.

Rehearse Your Reactions

One important EI development strategy for overcoming old behavioral habits is to engage in mental rehearsals. This is a process imagining a better way of acting in real-life settings. By cueing up the situation and imagining behaving in a different and more productive way, the prefrontal cortex of the brain becomes acutely focused on these new patterns. Without that practiced new response, a person will act out old and potentially unproductive routines.

For example, before a meeting with colleagues or more senior executives, Bruce (the team leader who had a confrontation with his boss) could imagine someone saying something that might call into question his capabilities, which would lead to him feel upset. By mentally rehearsing for a confrontation, Bruce prepares himself to deliver a more measured response.

Rehearse your own reactions, and take the following steps when faced with a confrontation:

- Use active listening in order to understand the true nature of the statement or question being asked.

- Ask clarifying questions.

- Don't interrupt while the other person is talking.

- Try to be objective and not defensive by trying to understand the other person's point of view.

Positive Visioning

Thinking through how to handle situations that have been problematic in the past greatly improves your ability to learn new skills. For years, sports coaches have used this strategy of "positive visioning" with athletes to help them imagine competing successfully. The brain cells used to mentally practice something are the same brain cells that are used during an actual situation, so the mental practice serves to strengthen the brain connections.

Enlist a Buddy

You may enlist a coach or "buddy" at work to observe your behavior and provide real-time feedback. Regardless of the type of activity, if you are committing to experimentation with new behaviors, you need to find a way to get feedback from others about the progress you are making.

Your EI buddy doesn't have to be a friend. In fact, it is often better to have a buddy that you are not connected to emotionally. If you are too friendly with your chosen "coach," he or she may be reluctant to give constructive feedback and may just tell you what you want to hear. You should look for someone with whom you interact on a daily basis and whom you trust to give you honest, direct, and timely feedback.

Overcome Relapses

Remember, working on your emotional intelligence is particularly difficult because it involves modifying your ingrained behaviors. Having a relapse is common. It's important to not get discouraged and to remain focused on your goals. Keep trying, and you will continually improve as relapses grow less and less common.

See the sidebar, *An EI Success Story*, which describes one woman's journey to improve her emotional intelligence.

An EI Success Story

While attending an off-site leadership development program, Barbara received feedback from an EI coach that indicated that there was a significant "gap" between how she saw herself and how others perceived her behavior at work. More specifically, others saw her as "too opinionated" and "not a good listener." She was also seen as extremely competitive with her co-workers.

Understandably, Barbara was devastated by the assessment and initially reacted defensively. However, working with the coach, she began to understand how she had developed this leadership profile over the years and, frankly, how it had helped her move up the career ladder in tough environments where that type of behavior was rewarded. What she came to understand, however, was that if she wanted to continue to advance she needed to develop her ability to empathize with others and develop her ability to influence and not just "command" others.

Barbara enlisted the help of her EI coach to develop a learning action plan to improve her skills. She knew she needed to practice paying attention to others' feelings and needs. She also needed to watch the impact of her own behavior on those around her. She took the opportunity to learn more about different ways to influence others.

In her role, Barbara was in constant contact with direct reports, peers, and customers so that she had many opportunities to practice new behaviors and ways of interacting. She also enlisted the help of a trusted colleague whom she could bounce ideas off of and who would give her straight feedback on how she was progressing.

In a three-month period, the EI coach solicited feedback for Barbara from her direct reports and peers, who reported that they had seen a real effort on Barbara's part to change her behavior—not, without "relapses." They appreciated her commitment and expected to see her continued progress. After six months, her boss gave her a performance review that favorably reflected her sustained progress.

Barbara, herself, reported that her interactions at work were considerably less stressful and that she was getting more projects completed with more cooperation from others. The positive results she was getting were reinforcing her work effort at building her emotional intelligence.

Why Training Fails

Unfortunately for those of us in the training and development field, training programs designed to teach a broad array of EI skills have a minimum amount of long-term impact. Some of the reasons why these general, one-size-fits-all EI training programs don't work are:

- The learners sent to these programs may not be motivated to learn and change.

- Most training programs appeal to the neocortex area of the brain, which is effective in learning technical or analytical skills or for comprehending concepts—not changing behavior.

- Emotional intelligence improvement requires reshaping behavioral habits learned early in one's life that have grown in strength over time. It is not sufficient to teach the rational definitions of emotional intelligence in a one-day program or even to give examples of how others use emotional intelligence successfully at work. Optimizing the limbic areas of the brain requires thoughtfulness, practice, and continuous feedback.

So then, how do you train and coach for emotional intelligence? As we indicated earlier, you have to start with finding a motivated learner. The most effective training and coaching methodologies for developing EI competencies rely on

- individuals deciding what and how they will change

- experiential learning that comes through role play, group discussion, and simulation

- continuous practice in order to reprogram neural circuits that lead to sustainable changes in habitual patterns of thinking, feeling, and behaving (this is not unlike what it takes to unlearn specific elements of a bad golf swing and replace them with minor changes in stance or hand placement that can make a difference in several golf strokes).

See the job aid, *Emotional Intelligence Development Plan,* at the end of this *Infoline* for help designing an emotional intelligence learning plan for yourself or others.

EI As a Liability

Can you have too much emotional intelligence? Probably not. But there might be a danger in overdoing an EI asset to the point that it stops being an asset and becomes a liability.

For example, if you are too empathetic you may be hesitant to fire anyone. If you are too achievement focused you may constantly change strategies to beat the competition and lose focus. And interestingly enough, although self-awareness is seen as the foundation for emotional intelligence, an overly critical focus on one's self can lead to reduced self-esteem.

Emotionally Intelligent Teams

In the last few decades organizations have placed a greater emphasis on creating teams to make decisions and collaborate on work projects. The assumption is that group synergy creates better decisions and work products than any one talented individual. However, this assumes that the team is truly able to elicit the best ideas of its members and coalesce around decisions and deliverables.

There is evidence throughout the workplace that some groups never achieve this vision of high performance because they cannot manage the dynamics of unproductive arguing, interpersonal competition, and power politics. Essentially, a team of people performs better than individuals only when they exhibit what we have come to define as *emotionally intelligent team behavior.*

While there has been extensive research on how emotional intelligence is directly critical to an individual's effectiveness at work, there has been less research on how the collective emotional intelligence of people who work together can actually improve team performance. We cannot assume that a collection of highly emotionally intelligent people will, by definition, become a highly effective team. Team dynamics, themselves, create an identity for a team that is unique and requires its own type of self-awareness and self-management.

The research of Vanessa Urch Druskat and Steve Wolff has identified that three conditions are essential for a team's effectiveness:

- trust among team members
- a sense of team identity
- a sense of team efficacy.

A team can still function and achieve results if any one of these is missing, but it will not be as effective, and its members will not be as fully engaged or motivated to perform at their highest levels.

Emotional intelligence, as defined by Goleman and others, has primarily focused on personal and social competence. A team is more complex. For a team to demonstrate emotional intelligence, the team needs to be aware of and act upon

- the emotions of all of its members

- the team's own culture and climate

- the emotions toward the team coming from its stakeholders, i.e., those groups and individuals who influence the team's success.

Intelligent Teamwork

One high-performing team adopted these team norms in order to establish a team culture that was conducive to meet both the team and the team members' needs.

- Share information openly within the team and with all key stakeholders.

- When a conflict or disagreement emerges, look first for areas of agreement.

- Faced with challenges, be optimistic and proactive problem-solvers. Don't blame.

- Be advocates for the team and its goals within and outside of the team.

- Heed the maxim: If you're uncomfortable with something, speak up. If you don't agree, silence is not golden. Make proposals, if possible.

- Debate ideas. Don't attack one another.

- Listen actively and without interruption to the contributions of others.

- Have fun and celebrate success.

- When problem-solving or making decisions, respect differences in perspectives.

- Ask quieter team members to speak up and ask those more vocal to give others "air time."

- Deal directly with team members with whom you have a problem. Don't talk "behind their backs."

- Be sensitive to and supportive of one another's needs.

- Periodically assess and give feedback to the team and individuals regarding their effectiveness.

- Validate team members' contributions. Let members know they are valued.

Truly emotionally intelligent teams recognize that emotions are best not suppressed or avoided. They consciously seek out an assessment of the team's and its stakeholders' emotional perceptions and work at building effective relationships within and outside of the team.

Building Team EI

Emotionally intelligent teams take responsibility for defining what success looks like and for behaving in ways that will ensure their success. One way that teams can begin to build their emotional intelligence is by formally establishing team norms, which are explicit expectations of the team regarding the types of behaviors that they believe will create a high-performance team culture.

For some examples of emotionally intelligent team norms, see the sidebar *Intelligent Teamwork*.

Emotionally intelligent teams also continuously monitor individual and group behaviors, to ensure they continue to be in alignment with the norms, and confront the team and its members when they are not.

Highly emotionally intelligent teams also reach outside of the team to try to understand the concerns and needs of their stakeholders and the wider organizational culture and politics. They encourage cross-pollination of ideas with others and monitor whether they are meeting stakeholder expectations.

The team leader plays a critical role in setting the tone and culture for a team, but when a team establishes and holds itself accountable for this process of "self-management," it creates a shared leadership for the team's emotional intelligence. When these core values and norms are jointly owned by the team, the team leader does not even need to be present for these habits to be put into practice.

The EI Journey

Is emotional intelligence sufficient for leading a successful organization, creating a successful relationship, or leading a successful life?

No. It is just one component. Success is determined by the integration of all different types of intelligence: cognitive intelligence, emotional intelligence, and strategic intelligence. The most successful people have developed these capabilities to their fullest and are able to understand which EI competencies are required to be effective.

Still, emotional intelligence is unique because it directly affects how we see ourselves and how we interact with those around us. Understanding and building your emotional intelligence not only enriches your working life but your life outside of the office as well.

References & Resources

External Consultant

Sue Ziegler, CPLP
Senior Training Specialist
U.S. Pharmacopeia

Articles

Charan, Ram, and Geoffrey Calvin. "Why CEOs Fail." *Fortune,* June 1999, pp. 60-75.

Cherniss, Cary, et. al. "Bringing Emotional Intelligence to the Workplace." *The Consortium for Research on Emotional Intelligence in Organizations,* 1998. www.eiconsortium.org/reports/technical_report.html.

Druskat, Vanessa Urch, and Steven B. Wolf. "Building the Emotional Intelligence of Groups." *Harvard Business Review,* March 2001, pp. 81-90.

Goleman, Daniel. "Leadership that Gets Results." *Harvard Business Review,* March 2000, pp. 78-90.

―――. "What Makes a Leader?" *Harvard Business Review,* January 2004, pp. 82-91.

Kahn, Jeremy. "The World's Most Admired Companies." *Fortune,* October 1999, pp. 206-226.

Mayer, John D., and Peter Salovey. "The Intelligence of Emotional Intelligence." *Intelligence,* October 1993, pp. 433-442.

Salovey, Peter, and John D. Mayer. "Emotional Intelligence." *Imagination, Cognition and Personality,* July 1990, pp. 185-211.

Books

Bradberry, Travis, and Jean Greaves. *The Emotional Intelligence Quick Book.* New York: Simon & Schuster, 2005.

Cherniss, Cary, and Daniel Goleman, eds. *The Emotionally Intelligent Workplace: How to Select for, Measure, and Improve Emotional Intelligence in Individuals, Groups, and Organizations.* San Francisco: Jossey-Bass, 2001.

Cherniss, Cary, and Mitchel Adler. *Promoting Emotional Intelligence in Organizations.* Alexandria, VA: ASTD, 2000.

Druskat, Vanessa Urch, Gerald Mount, and Fabio Sala. *Linking Emotional Intelligence and Performance At Work.* Mahwah, NJ: Lawrence Erlbaum Associates, 2006.

Feldman, Jeff, and Karl Mulle. *Put Emotional Intelligence to Work.* Alexandria, VA: ASTD Press, 2007.

Goleman, Daniel. *Emotional Intelligence.* New York: Bantam, 1995.

―――. *Working with Emotional Intelligence.* New York: Bantam, 1998.

Goleman, Daniel, and Annie McKee Boyatzis. *Primal Leadership: Learning to Lead with Emotional Intelligence.* Boston: Harvard Business School Press, 2004.

Hughes, Marcia M., Bonita L. Patterson, and James Bradford Terrell. *Emotional Intelligence In Action: Training and Coaching Activities for Leaders and Managers.* San Francisco: Pfeiffer, 2005.

Lynn, Adele B. *The Emotional Intelligence Activity Book: 50 Activities for Promoting EQ at Work.* New York: AMACOM, 2002.

McDermott, Lynda, William Waite, and Nolan Brawley. *World Class Teams.* New York: Wiley, 1998.

Websites

www.6seconds.org

www.eiconsortium.org

www.haygroup.com

www.mrgconsulting.com

www.talentsmart.com

Emotional intelligence measurement sites:

www.cjwolfe.com

www.eqi.mhs.com

www.essisystems.com

www.haygroup.com/TL

Select Your EI Buddy

The journey to improving your emotional intelligence (EI) can be long and frustrating. It always helps to have an informal coach or buddy to help you through difficult moments and provide you with objective feedback and pointers. This job aid is designed to help you choose who is best suited to help you along the way.

Candidate 1: _____

1. Is this person willing to help me?

   Yes   No

2. Is this person familiar with emotional intelligence competencies?

   Very Much   Somewhat   Not Much

3. Does this person have time to help me?

   Very Much   Somewhat   Not Much

4. Does this person work closely with me on a daily basis?

   Very Often   Somewhat   Not Often

5. Can this person be trusted to give me honest, candid feedback?

   Very Much   Somewhat   Not Much

Additional Comments: _____

_____

Candidate 2: _____

1. Is this person willing to help me?

   Yes   No

2. Is this person familiar with emotional intelligence competencies?

   Very Much   Somewhat   Not Much

3. Does this person have time to help me?

   Very Much   Somewhat   Not Much

4. Does this person work closely with me on a daily basis?

   Very Often   Somewhat   Not Often

5. Can this person be trusted to give me honest, candid feedback?

   Very Much   Somewhat   Not Much

Additional Comments: _____

_____

Candidate 3: _____

1. Is this person willing to help me?

   Yes   No

2. Is this person familiar with emotional intelligence competencies?

   Very Much   Somewhat   Not Much

3. Does this person have time to help me?

   Very Much   Somewhat   Not Much

4. Does this person work closely with me on a daily basis?

   Very Often   Somewhat   Not Often

5. Can this person be trusted to give me honest, candid feedback?

   Very Much   Somewhat   Not Much

Additional Comments: _____

_____

Review your choices carefully. Your ideal buddy is someone who is very familiar with emotional intelligence, works with you often and knows your behavior, has time to help, and will offer you objective feedback.

Emotional Intelligence Development Plan

This job aid outlines the steps you should take if you want to strengthen your emotional intelligence (EI). Because each individual is different, customize this plan to help you achieve your specific emotional intelligence goals. This job aid also can be used by an EI coach to help someone else develop their emotional intelligence competencies.

Step	Description	Action	Your Plan
Step 1	Assess your motive and values for change.	Identify the "what's in it for me" motivator for you to commit to a change process that would improve your emotional intelligence, as well as your job performance or relationships with others.	
Step 2	Obtain EI feedback.	Through some form of EI assessment (such as interviews, observation, multi-rater surveys, and so on), objectively identify how you are viewed by others with whom you interact.	
Step 3	Balance goals of preservation and adaptation.	Identify your EI strengths and where the gaps are between how you would like to be perceived and how others observe you to be behaving today.	
Step 4	Develop an EI action learning plan.	For each EI competency to be developed, identify specific behavioral goals and strategies for improvement, such as reading, formal training, coaching, and so on.	
Step 5	Execute the plan.	Engage in learning and practicing activities to help you achieve your EI goals.	
Step 6	Seek feedback and positive reinforcement.	Enlist the support of people who will give you feedback on your progress.	

The material appearing on this page is not covered by copyright and may be reproduced at will.

Harness the Power of Coaching

Issue 0310

AUTHOR

Jennifer Long
The Source International
950 Logan Street
Denver, CO 80203
Tel: 303.832.4181
Fax: 303.832.1202
jent@thesourceintl.com

Jennifer Long is the senior vice president of program development for The Source International, Australia's number one company in executive skills development and a global leader in skills and performance coaching. She has spent 16 years with the company in the co-development and refining of its proven coaching methodology. She also heads the design and production of all company technology-based learning solutions to complement currently instructor-based courses. Long has incorporated her expertise in directing, improvisation, and production into the dynamic interactive learning that has become the hallmark of The Source. She is currently working on the development of a national network of Source Certified Master Coaches to support the upcoming release of Web-based coaching services.

Managing Editor
Mark Morrow

Contributing Editor
Tora Estep

Copy Editor
Ann Bruen

Production Design
Kathleen Schaner

Harness the Power of Coaching

Why Coaching?

Coaching is a powerful tool in organizational and performance development. But what is coaching and what can it do? And, more to the point, how do you make coaching work for you and your organization?

The claims for what coaching can do—such as increasing productivity, improving quality, strengthening organizations, and retaining best employees—are numerous and may strike anyone inexperienced with coaching with some skepticism. Can coaching really produce such exceptional outcomes?

Darelyn "DJ" Mitsch's book, *In Action: Coaching for Extraordinary Results*, presents a case study in which a global telecommunications firm found that its coaching intervention increased sales productivity by 14 percent, reduced hiring and training costs by 18 percent, reduced customer erosion by 21 percent, and helped to create a positive working environment. Participants also indicated that they would be likely to use the coaching techniques they learned, thus making these outcomes self-perpetuating.

Another case study from the book describes more personal benefits of coaching: A vice president of a national nonprofit organization was not only able to improve his work performance, but also gained "a greater sense of relatedness with his team and a deeper sense of personal well-being that spilled over into his family life." Powerful outcomes such as these are among the many reasons to take advantage of the power of coaching.

But what is coaching exactly? Well, one thing it isn't is a "fix-it" tool. It doesn't fix poor performance; it makes average performance great. It also causes significant improvements in individuals' behaviors and skills. Coaching is a performance development tool with both immediate and long-term effects.

But even if you believe coaching is a core value in your organization, it may not be fully integrated into the culture. Sometimes coaching is merely canonized and not really effective. A functional coaching culture is one of actualization and empowerment and can provide real return-on-investment to your organization. Employees who are coached are more likely to perform at substantially higher levels using

practiced and demonstrated competencies. Experience in the field suggests that employees who are coached correctly change behavior—permanently.

Instilling a coaching culture, as with any culture change, is a long-term strategy for large organizations. Coaching in and of itself is not a strategy. For cultural effect, it must be mapped onto and added as a tool to the larger developmental goals set out by the organization. Coaching a handful of executives to improve strategic or leadership capability does not create a coaching culture. Similarly, teaching mid-level managers to coach others to improve their performance does not a coaching culture make. For a cultural shift in which management incorporates coaching into their management style, your coaching strategy must employ three levels:

1. Experience: Management must be coached one-on-one.

2. Education: Management must be trained to coach.

3. Enactment: Management must be expected to coach others as part of the job.

This *Infoline* will show you how to harness the power of coaching to drive performance development by making coaching a fundamental part of your organization's culture. To foster a coaching culture that will drive performance development, follow these steps:

- Step 1. Align with strategic objectives.
- Step 2. Give a firsthand experience.
- Step 3. Cultivate internal coaches.
- Step 4. Measure the impact.
- Step 5. Talk it up and celebrate.

Step 1. Align With Strategic Objectives

So you've been impressed with all you've heard about coaching, and you are considering adding it to your organization's development strategies. But how do you start? Before you introduce coaching as a development strategy, set the parameters for how to integrate and substantiate it and, most important, determine what you expect to gain from it. How will your organization benefit? Alignment of your coaching development initiative with business goals is important because to bring about cultural change you must work from the top down, and to get the attention of senior management your efforts must demonstrate direct impact on business measures.

You will want to start off with a single coaching program to get the ball rolling. As coaching becomes part of the culture of your organization, you can expand the application of coaching to encompass several development efforts simultaneously.

Focus on What, Not How

Answer specifically why you are choosing coaching. How will you use it and what do you hope to gain from it? The first set of questions to consider is: "What kinds of outcomes are you looking for"; "What will a coaching experience look or be like"; "What do you expect a coach to do for the learners?"

At this point, don't consider any questions about how you are going to implement coaching. You will become better able to answer that type of question after you have outlined what you want to achieve. The following are some examples of what you can do with coaching:

- attain a sustained competitive advantage through better performance in specific target areas or competencies

- diminish the expense of firing and hiring and training new people

- turn around under-performing or derailed executives

- increase knowledge transfer of high performers and exceptional managers

- accelerate leadership capability

- develop a more effective management or leadership succession program

- develop higher-performing project or cross-organizational teams.

Specify what you want coaching to do. Once you have defined the purpose of the initial coaching initiative, evaluate it for the degree of "stretch" it

provides. How significant is the lift in performance? Ask yourself how much the target group being coached will have to change. Will the coaching intervention require a big push in terms of development, or will participants only gain a moderate degree of improvement? What are the stakes? How high are they? How big are the skill gaps? How important is the improvement or change? The correct answer for these questions should be "significant." Remember, you don't coach poor performers to be good; you coach adequate performers to be excellent.

Tie Coaching to Programs

Coaching can be used as a stand-alone development tool for specific individuals as well as in combination with other training programs. However, when targeting a cultural change, the latter use is a far more effective choice. To use coaching effectively, select an existing training program or program initiative waiting to be implemented and integrate coaching into the program design as an additional development tool. Once again, be sure to select the program that will incur the greatest amount of stretch for participants. For example, if your organization has determined it wants to build higher performing cross-organizational teams, and you plan to use coaching to drive significant outcomes in this area, then you must include coaching as part of an advanced teaming training program.

To identify a program that is going to provide a lot of stretch for participants, refer to the needs assessments that identified the original need for training. (For a quick refresher on how to carry out a needs assessment, see the sidebar *Needs Assessment* at right.) Target your use of coaching at the biggest skill gaps and at the highest levels to achieve the greatest levels of performance improvement and the most visibility and support.

Integrating coaching into an existing program serves several purposes. First, inclusion of coaching as a development tool will improve the effectiveness of the program overall. Second, by latching coaching onto an existing program, you support strategic organizational goals as they are expressed in terms of development investment. Third, by latching coaching onto existing development objectives, you raise the visibility of coaching, thus getting the word out about the extraordinary outcomes coaching can achieve. With the word of mouth that

Needs Assessment

Training and development professionals should carry out needs assessments at the outset of any systematic approach to training. The purpose of a needs assessment is to define optimal and actual performance in a given area, identify attitudes within the organization with respect to the performance issue, and determine the root causes of any deficiency to ensure that training actually is a viable solution.

You also can use the data collected in a needs assessment as an aid in determining which program to incorporate coaching into. The program you select for your coaching intervention should address a large gap between actual and desired performance and ideally should be part of a high-profile strategic initiative. The following presents an abbreviated method of carrying out needs analyses adapted from "Be a Better Needs Analyst," *Infoline* No. 258502.

Step 1. Define Your Objectives

Determine the objectives of the analysis. Some objectives for conducting a needs analysis are as follows:

● identify employees who need training

● identify problems, deficiencies, and the root causes and development needs for strategic initiatives

● decide priorities for the upcoming year and for long-range strategic planning

● determine whether training is the best solution

● secure the support and commitment of management in the process of building and evaluating effective training programs

● generate data that will be useful in measuring the effect of the training program

● provide specific recommendations for training programs: scope, methods, frequency, cost, and location

● justify spending to top management by determining the value and cost of training.

Step 2. Identify the Necessary Data

A thorough needs assessment requires information to identify:

● the need
● the solution
● the population requiring training
● the strategies for delivering training.

Know the nature and quantity of information you may need for a useful assessment study. You may need opinions, attitude surveys, financial statements, job descriptions, performance appraisals, work samples, or historical documents from the company's archives.

Step 3. Collect the Data

Choose or design a method for gathering data. Use various combinations of the following methods: interviews, questionnaires, observations, group discussions, key consultations, work samples, records, reports, and tests.

Base structured or formal assessment methods on the necessary data outlined in Step 2. Once you have selected a sample or study group, administer the questionnaires, conduct the interviews, observe performances, and so forth.

Step 4. Analyze and Compile the Data

Compare the new data with past years' information and analyze to uncover problems and related trends or patterns. Confirm results and check for accuracy by consulting with the persons who originally provided the information. Compile the data into a report that points out problems, needs, and weak areas and recommend strategies for improvement.

the coaching intervention will generate, you will find that more people will want to participate in future coaching programs.

Create Impact Objectives

For the effect of coaching to be measurable, the coaching intervention must support specific impact objectives. These are critical if you intend to measure the results of the coaching initiative on business performance. To create impact objectives, determine the expected outcomes of coaching based on the goals and objectives of the training program you have selected. What specifically should improve as a result of the learning and coaching? How is that linked specifically to the business?

Donald Kirkpatrick's fourth level of evaluation measures the impact of a training intervention on business measures. Typical objective Level 4 measures include increased output, cost savings, time savings, or quality improvement. Typical subjective measures include employee satisfaction, employee turnover, increased confidence, customer satisfaction, customer retention, implementation of new ideas, and so forth.

By linking the skills and behaviors that the coaching intervention is designed to address and improve to some kind of Level 4 measure, both the learner and the coach have a point of focus in terms of what specific skills within the competency need to be coached as well as a clear roadmap for on-the-job application.

Step 2. Give a Firsthand Experience

A coaching culture places high expectations on corporate leaders to model coaching as a productive and profitable way to improve performance. Senior management must first embrace coaching as the best way to permanently lift individual performance. At the same time, middle management must learn how to *use* a coach as well as *coach* the development of others. Once established from the top down, coaching cultivates its own standards within the organization by giving rise to expectations of development and self-driven learning.

This is typically where most organizations go wrong. Instead of starting out by giving employees a definitive, firsthand experience of coaching in another competency, they ask management—or leadership-level employees—to coach subordinates as part of their jobs, simply adding coaching to their job descriptions. Without firsthand experience, managers lack a clear understanding of what coaching is; they may get only a detailed list of behaviors that lack real meaning and demonstrated application.

Until a manager has undergone the experience of coaching for development, realizing his or her own capacity as an effective manager-coach is nearly impossible. Having a model from which to work, that is, a live coach, is a more effective stepping stone in shaping the expectation than simply presenting a set of behaviors.

Identify Whom to Target

The learning population you choose affects your degree of success. You may have a specific group in mind, but be sure to start with the group that is most likely to give you the biggest win. You want your first coaching initiative to be successful to ensure that program participants continue to sell the program internally for you. You may want to consider:

- finding coaching champions to participate

- including willing learners who are anxious for training and development

- starting at the management or executive level

- piloting the program first with a small number of participants and allowing for corrective action prior to full rollout.

It's best to start as high up in the organization as you can, because the top levels drive the culture of an organization. However, keep in mind that the people at the top are also the toughest learners. You must deliver a positive, effective experience to sink a root at the top that will impel a cultural shift. Don't waste senior-level employees' time with an unfocused initiative or coaches who can't coach at advanced levels, demand the appropriate amount of discipline, or effectively engage the learner (skills and qualities of an ideal coach are presented in the sidebar *Composite Coach* at right). Both the training program and the coach must be credible.

Composite Coach

Coaches need to have the right blend of skills, abilities, and personal qualities to be effective. In addition to job-related knowledge, working experience at the level they coach, and a clear understanding of expected outcomes, a good coach has the following skills and abilities:

- the ability to recruit players and staff of assistants
- the drive and desire to empower
- a focus on establishing goals and objectives
- planning and organizational skills
- advanced communication skills
- the ability to analyze current performance of skill
- the ability to provide reflective and objective feedback
- the ability to make decisions
- advanced listening skills
- the ability to drive and maintain discipline
- knowledge of measuring performance and progress
- the ability to build relationships
- the capacity to operate effectively under stress.

Some particularly critical skills are:

■ Observational Skills
The coach should be able to spot opportunities for the participant to expand his or her capabilities and improve performance and relate them to the participant.

■ Analytical Skills
The coach should be able to systematically compare actual, current performance with the participant's perception of his or her performance and describe any gap between these levels. In addition, the coach must identify the difference or gap between current and desired levels of performance because this forms the basis of the coaching engagement.

■ Probing Skills
Coaches need to be able to ask the right questions and elicit the responses they need to move development forward. Skillful coaches use the following three methods:

1. Open-ended questions. These encourage the participant to think about the problem, to think about things he or she may not have considered previously to achieve an insight or to draw a conclusion.

2. Closed questions. These guide a discussion into a specific topic or area, or garner specific information when a discussion is too general.

3. Reflective questions. These restate in question form something the participant has said. They are used to prevent any misunderstandings.

■ Feedback Skills
How the coach presents his or her observations can cause the participant to become defensive, angry, or intimidated, or open to discussion about how to improve a difficult situation.

The ideal coach also has the following personal qualities:

- enthusiasm and dedication
- patience
- impartiality
- integrity and honesty
- self-confidence
- genuine concern for the participants
- warmth
- optimism
- resourcefulness
- vision
- conviction
- consistency
- sense of humor
- flexibility
- professional standard of ethics.

Adapted from "Coaching and Feedback," *Infoline* No. 259006.

Evaluating External Coaches

When you start looking for and evaluating external coaches, keep the following considerations in mind.

Brand Recognition

Selecting a vendor based on brand recognition isn't necessarily best. Look instead for the longest substantiated track record of success. You want longevity, demonstrated success, and dedicated individual coaches.

Versatility and Scalability

Versatility and scalability are also part of the strategy. The coaching vendor must have both policy and manpower to meet the needs of your learners. Can your coaching vendor switch coaches to provide the best match at any given point in the learning curve? Does the vendor have enough trained and certified coaches to meet the demands of your development program?

Credibility

Coaches who coach at senior and executive levels should either have worked at that level for at least five years or have substantial coaching training. International Coaching Federation credentialing is also important. Most important, talk to the people cited in the vendor's references.

Quality Control

Coaching requires many meetings with a specific focus and management of multiple participants' track records. To guarantee consistency and quality for every learner, your coaching vendor should be able to bring best practices to the table in terms of process, administration, confidentiality, and professionalism.

Transfer of Capability

Can the coaching vendor transfer the coaching capability to your organization over a reasonable period of time? This capability is critical in terms of long-term, ongoing results as well as cost-effectiveness.

Look at the company organizationally starting at the top. Can you identify a specific project or high-profile team in a specific business unit that would benefit substantially? The executive team handling sales and service is an excellent place to start because this area provides the most discernible and measurable business results. Strategically, it's one of the best places to start building the case for coaching. Look for the highest level group with the widest skill gaps or biggest challenges. *Do not start at the front line.* While this may have a substantial effect on profits or the business in general, it doesn't change the culture of the organization. You will end up with better performing frontline people who leave to take management positions elsewhere.

Once you have identified your pilot group, start with a small program with an eye to build over time. Keep in mind that you are changing culture, which takes time. Work through the organizational structure slowly, allowing one area of the business to gain momentum before working on the next. It's the same strategy pursued in marketing. You want to maintain a vertical with deep penetration before going across the organization. Credible, authentic results must come first, or you undermine the continued effectiveness of coaching by creating a shallow performance change that doesn't take root within the company.

Who Will Coach?

Don't start your first coaching program with an internal coach; instead, find an individual or organization that specializes in coaching to put a program in place. Always remember that coaching is political, especially when you're working at the top of the organization. Coaching by its very nature requires the development of interpersonal skills, which means that coaches teach people to work better with other people. For this reason, third-party coaches with the right expertise are the best option when starting out. The sidebar *Evaluating External Coaches* at left presents what to look for when researching and evaluating potential coaches.

Map of Coaching Events

The following figure is an example of a coaching plan worked out between a coaching company and a client. It shows the various steps of the process, including specific action items. Based on a general outline like this, a more detailed project plan can be worked out to include timelines, scope of work, and budget.

Organizational assessment	**Goals, strategies, and impact maps**	**Coach orientation**	**Client orientation**	**Industrial assessments**
• interview organizational sponsors and key department heads • review corporate dashboard • understand goals and objectives.	Establish • three top goals • exact participants • number of impact maps.	• culture • organizational goals • new material (if any)	• What is coaching? • Getting the best out of coaching. • Understanding the platform.	

Training or development program

Organization debriefs, evaluations, and coach passalongs

Final report and design for future

You hire an outside coach to produce results. By tying the coach to a specific program, he or she has a single point of focus driving each session. You pass responsibility to the coach to maintain mutual accountability in delivering on the impact objectives and to stay on track and on budget. This is neither a loose "see what happens" kind of arrangement, nor a 12- to 24-month commitment working at a broad scope of development. Work with the coach or coaching company to develop a specific plan that details the scope of the work and its objectives, with a budget and timeframes. An example of a coaching plan worked out between a coaching company and one of its client organizations is presented in the sidebar *Map of Coaching Events*. To make a cultural change, you must remain targeted to specifics; otherwise, your outcomes are difficult to verify.

For your coaching program to succeed, you need two things to work for you consistently: objectivity and confidentiality. Objectivity eliminates any internal politics that may be at play when a manager focuses on his or her skill development. Because the coach is an outsider, he or she is unbiased and can focus wholly on the individual's success. There is no hidden or personal agenda.

Confidentiality ensures that all information that comes out in a coaching session stays there. This has to be the case to ensure that the learner fully trusts the coaching relationship. Without trust, no development takes place, and you are wasting your time and company dollars.

What Coaching Is and Isn't

There's lot of confusion about coaching. So let's clear the air about what coaching is and the differences between coaching and mentoring and between coaching and performance management.

Coaching is a practice through which an individual supports the learning or performance improvement of another individual through interactive questioning and other means of active input and support. A coach identifies performance gaps, wins commitment to learning, constructs applied practice, and drives continual application and reflection to actually lift competence. A coaching relationship is built on discipline and trust. A coach is a change agent, responsible for driving behavior and performance change in a supportive yet demanding environment.

Differences From Mentoring

Mentoring is a process to help people with their career development. Mentors provide useful guidance to help an individual achieve the kind of professional achievement he or she seeks. Mentoring differs from coaching in that it is a longer-term process and in that mentors have no responsibility to the participants for personal and professional development. Mentors may provide motivation, connections, and advice, but they do not enable learners to directly and substantially improve their performance.

Differences From Performance Management

If you coach people to change behavior, isn't that performance management? Unfortunately, a lot of coaches are in fact selling performance management. Coaching is different. A manager manages the performance of an employee by getting the employee to take ownership for his or her performance choices and ultimately the outcome of his or her performance. By taking ownership, employees learn to make better choices and thus deliver better performance.

Coaching is about driving performance development. A coach not only confronts the performance issue and gets the employee to own the behavior choice, he or she also works directly with the employee showing *how to apply* a new skill and *enact a behavior.* People can't just change behavior. They must practice the new behavior in real time with someone who knows how it's done.

Make It Mandatory

The coaching experience is the missing link in most training programs. Coaching drives behavior change in the workplace, causes rapid skills development, and builds confidence and motivation in learners. To be effective as a development strategy, it requires methodical integration and full organizational support. Coaching cannot thrive in an organization where it is optional. Coaching cannot simply be placed on a menu of courses from which learners may choose at will.

Coaching requires personal investment in growth, in discipline, and in change of behavior because change is uncomfortable. Many training programs fail to push learners outside their comfort zones. That is what new skills and behaviors do: They force you to act in unfamiliar ways. A coach encourages and supports the change as well as ensures that it actually happens. For consistency and effect, the coaching element of your programs cannot be voluntary, occasional, or undisciplined. Participants in the learning must also participate in the coaching.

Set Participants' Expectations

When you prepare to roll out the coaching program, prepare an orientation session that describes:

● what coaching is and what it isn't (the sidebar *What Coaching Is and Isn't* at left provides some clarification)

● why your organization is investing in coaching

● what the participants can expect from the coaching (the objectives of the coaching)

● what the responsibilities of both coaches and participants will be

● what level of confidentiality they can expect

● what the logistical aspects are.

An important part of the orientation session is to ensure that participants understand their own responsibilities. Personal commitment and accountability of coaches as well as employees drive the success of any coaching program. The following presents the responsibilities of coaches and participants:

Coaches:

- provide and maintain the learning discipline

- conduct and facilitate the coaching session

- present continuous challenges

- function as the primary agent of change by keeping the learner engaged

- provide appropriate assignments to continually stretch the learner

- document progress

- ensure that the coaching process is adhered to

- identify the starting point of the learning and the desired outcomes and measure the progress.

While learners:

- take full ownership of the learning imperative

- commit to achieving the desired result

- drive the learning agenda by identifying the learning areas

- research and complete pre-work to start the learning

- practice continuously in both coaching sessions and assignments

- document practice to be used in coaching sessions.

All participants have their own vision of where they want to go. Learners have complete control of how well they use the coach in moving forward. They must determine the direction of the learning they want to engage in while they are in the program and set the level at which they want to participate.

But a good coach will confront a learner if he or she feels the learner is not invested. The coaches are there to instill the discipline, target the applications, initiate the practice, and provide the feedback. They assign tasks to learners to integrate behavior change on the job.

Step 3. Cultivate Internal Coaches

Now that the learning population in your target area has had firsthand experience of coaching, they are ready to learn to coach. At this point in the process coaching—as a management style—becomes embedded in the culture of your organization.

There is a distinct difference between training your managers to coach and cultivating your own coaches. Cultivating your own coaches involves transferring the capability of your coaching vendor to your coach trainees by providing your coach trainees with advanced training and certification in the coaching methodology that's worked for you. The sidebar *Assessing the Learning Needs of Coaches* can help you gain a clear understanding of what your coach trainees need to learn from the following 14 coaching disciplines, which were adapted with permission from Cynthia Thero's *The Silent Partner: Training for Coaching Mastery.*

1. Ownership of Learning.

   - Learn to state clearly to the learner their learning gap.

   - Invite acceptance and ownership of the learning needed to close that gap.

2. Change.

   - Increase the learner's discontent with his or her performance to motivate him or her to change it.

   - Make the learner aware of what better performance would be like.

   - Inform the learner of first steps he or she needs to take to change performance.

Assessing the Learning Needs of Coaches

To assess learning needs, ask trainees to fill out the self-assessment and return it to you. Be careful to ensure the confidentiality of responses to gain honest answers. Based on the themes that emerge from the responses, design coaching training to fit the needs of participants. The following is adapted from Chris Chen's *Coaching Training*.

Rate Yourself on Your Ability to:	A	B	C	D
■ *Communicate Instructions* Showing how to accomplish the tasks and clarifying when, where, and to what standard.				
■ *Set Performance Goals* Collaborating with others to establish short- and long-term goals for performance.				
■ *Reward Performance* Providing positive reinforcement to others for making progress.				
■ *Deal With Failure* Working with others to encourage them when they do not meet expectations.				
■ *Work With Personal Issues* Listening without judgment and offering emotional support for nonwork difficulties.				
■ *Confront Difficult Issues* Raising uncomfortable topics that are affecting task accomplishment.				
■ *Respond to Requests* Consulting with others on an as-needed basis. Responding to requests in a timely manner.				
■ *Follow Through* Keeping your commitments. Monitoring outcomes and providing assistance when necessary.				
■ *Listen for Understanding* Demonstrating attention to and conveying understanding of others.				
■ *Motivate Others* Encouraging others to achieve desired results and creating enthusiasm and commitment.				
■ *Assess Strengths and Weaknesses* Identifying root causes of individual performance. Defining issues effectively.				
■ *Build Rapport With Others* Showing respect for others. Acting with integrity and honesty. Easily building bonds with others. Making others feel their concerns and contributions are important.				

Answer key: One of my strengths (A); Doing OK on this (B); Need to develop this more (C); Definitely need to develop this (D).

3. Observation.

- Know how to read the learner.

- Be aware of concerns and the degree of challenge or discomfort for the learner.

4. Verbal Communication.

- Be versatile enough to adjust vocabulary and language to suit the background of the learner.

5. Nonverbal Communication.

- Possess a sound knowledge and understanding of nonverbal communication. This is one of the most important attributes for effective coaching. Because most communication is nonverbal, the ability to pick up on signals from the learner is invaluable in measuring response. Of all nonverbal communication, 70 percent is shown on the face.

6. Facilitation.

- Help the learner discuss and analyze actual or potential performance issues and identify factors inhibiting his or her performance.

- Assist the learner to utilize his or her own resources to improve performance.

7. Skill Versus Behavior Change.

- Recognize if behavior change (a chosen response to a situation based on attitude, capability, and experience) or skill change (a learned definitive set of actions taken to enact a response) needs to be addressed to change performance.

8. Clarity of Purpose.

- Provide a consistent sense of direction.

- Do not allow the learner to become sidetracked from the investment he or she has made to change his or her performance. This includes not allowing the coaching sessions to become therapy, counseling, or conversation rather than coaching.

9. Learner Support.

- Demonstrate genuine concern for the learner.

- Exhibit empathy for the learner's situation and environment; it may be contributing to the current performance level.

10. Confidence Building.

- Display commitment to the learner by presenting a professional image.

- Be approachable and maintain strict confidentiality.

11. Organization.

- Organize each coaching session to provide the learner with the best possible development experience. (See the sidebar *One-on-One Meetings* for a sample agenda and an example of a powerful type of coaching session.)

12. Discipline.

- Set clear expectations for the learner and ensure they are met.

- Structure the coaching experience to optimize learning and rigorously maintain the structure.

13. Assignments.

- Construct and assign applications that are relevant to developing the required skills and that also align with the learner's work responsibilities.

- Ensure assigned applications challenge the learner and that successive assignments become increasingly challenging.

One-on-One Meetings

One-on-one meetings are a powerful type of coaching session that move people into a proactive state and ensure that trainees have monthly performance improvement goals. One-on-one meetings bring forth communication that usually would not occur and build long-term partnerships.

The purpose of these meetings is for manager-coaches to focus on employees as individuals. They shouldn't focus on housekeeping issues, but on skills, behaviors, and professional development. The following, adapted from "Guide to Successful Executive Coaching," *Infoline* No. 250204, presents a sample one-on-one meeting agenda. Managers should include the following in their one-on-one meetings with employees:

■ *Vision Statement*
Managers should discuss and document the employee's vision and the underlying motivation beneath the vision.

■ *Job Description*
Managers and employees should work to clearly define the activities the employee was hired to perform. These are not goals, but daily tasks. Each month the job description should be reviewed and adjustments should be made as needed. Managers need to support employees in spending time wisely and help them eliminate over-commitments and low payoff activities.

■ *Monthly Increased Result*
In each monthly meeting, managers should identify and discuss a standout aspect of the employee's professional behavior. These accomplishments are an excellent way to motivate employees and help them realize that management notices their efforts.

■ *Human Development*
At the end of each quarter, managers should identify one overall strength and one overall weakness for each employee. They should then create simple plans to leverage the strength and improve the weakness during the upcoming quarter.

■ *Year-End Reviews*
By creating a proactive culture of coaching, yearly reviews will take less time, will be much more valuable, and will have greater and more personal impact on each employee. Every manager in the organization will make performance improvement a part of his or her management style. By implementing these coaching concepts, managers and employees will find that by year-end their organization has changed fundamentally.

14. Tracking and Documentation.

- Document the agreed-upon learning.

- Document work assigned, its completion, and all practice within coaching tutorials.

- Document the learner's progress and his or her investment in each tutorial and in assignments.

Who are your internal coaches? They are people in the organization who have been coached successfully, have been trained in coaching as a competency, and have demonstrated excellence in their coaching capability. They are also interested in forging a coaching path within the organization. Just be sure to maintain a re-certification schedule to ensure consistency and quality control as you bring capabilities in-house.

Step 4. Measure the Impact

As with any training and development program, an evaluation plan should be part of the picture. It's important to know if you are reaching or even exceeding your goals. Your measurement efforts should center on three things: the intent of the coaching; the growth of the individuals who participated; and the resulting business, market, and financial impact. You can collect most evaluation information with questionnaires via email or simple adaptations of existing evaluation methods currently in place. A sample questionnaire is presented in the job aid at the end of this *Infoline*. Tying the information gained from those questionnaires to financials may require some help from additional experts, either in-house or outsourced.

One of the most widely used evaluation models is Donald Kirkpatrick's four levels of evaluation, which measure:

1. Reaction to the intervention.

2. Learning attributed to the intervention.

3. Application of behavior changes on the job.

4. Business results realized by the organization due to the intervention.

Clearly state all your development objectives for all four levels. Step 1 of the coaching model presented in this *Infoline* gave you an opportunity to define your Level 4 objectives or business results. Steps 2 and 3 indicate both Level 2 and Level 3 objectives: What exactly are participants supposed to learn and how are they going to apply it? Level 1 measures the immediate reaction to the program.

Step 5. Talk It Up and Celebrate

The final critical piece to grow a coaching culture in your organization is word of mouth. Open the door for conversation by asking participants to talk about what they are experiencing. Encourage other candidates for the program to ask questions of current participants. Good buzz is the byproduct of an excellent coaching program. Do not underestimate the importance of positive word of mouth in bringing about cultural change; cultivate and leverage it as much as you can. Use existing internal communication mechanisms or create new ones to get the word out.

Snowballing along with word of mouth will be the sense of personal accomplishment. Because employees—be they senior or not—are not accustomed to personalized learning and development at this level, the sense of growth and personal accomplishment a participant experiences as a result of coaching will be obvious. It will be obvious not only by the individual who is being coached, but to anyone who works directly with that individual. Noticeable improvement in job performance is what coaching is about. If it isn't obvious, it isn't happening.

Take time to celebrate. Use the results you have measured to acknowledge success. Tap into participants who are feeling more empowered and more confident and are experiencing new or additional success. Help build forward momentum by celebrating participant outcomes publicly. Use existing organizational communications channels such as intranets, newsletters, and so forth. Celebrate the success of the *results* of the coaching. Look for testimonials that build excitement and spark the enthusiasm of others who will want to participate.

Once you have begun to experience the kind of impact coaching can have in your company, you will find a way to make it happen. Coaching as a form of professional, personalized development is by far the superior choice for development impact. It is the missing link in most current training programs.

References & Resources

Articles

Homan, Madeleine, and Linda Miller. "Ace Coaching Alliances." *T+D*, January 2002, pp. 40-46.

Olson, Merry Lee. "E-Coaching." *Learning Circuits,* September 2001.

Books

Chen, Chris W. *Coaching Training.* Alexandria, VA: ASTD Press, 2003.

Kirkpatrick, Donald L., ed. *Another Look at Evaluating Training Programs.* Alexandria, VA: ASTD, 1998.

————. *Evaluating Training Programs.* 2nd Edition. San Francisco: Berrett-Koehler, 1998.

Mitsch, Darelyn "DJ." *In Action: Coaching for Extraordinary Results.* Alexandria, VA: ASTD, 2002.

Thero, Cynthia. *The Silent Partner: Training Program for Coaching Mastery.* Denver and Sydney: The Source International, 1996.

Infolines

Darraugh, Barbara (ed.). "Coaching and Feedback." No. 259006 (revised 1997).

David, Mark. "Guide to Successful Executive Coaching." No. 250204.

Deforest, Holly, Pamela Largent, and Mary Steinberg. "Mastering the Art of Feedback." No. 250308.

Russell, Susan. "Evaluating Performance Interventions." No. 259910.

Sharpe, Cat (ed.). "Be a Better Needs Analyst." No. 258502 (revised 1998).

Coaching Evaluation Questionnaire

The following is a sample questionnaire to present to participants at the end of the coaching program. Use the data gained from these questions for the evaluation of the program as well as to improve any ineffective aspects of the program. These questions should be used in combination with questions that relate directly to the program and cover evaluation of training objectives, implementation, relevance, use of materials, and so forth.

1. What specific business measures do you feel were affected most by the coaching intervention? Please explain.

2. Are you aware of any specific financial benefits that have come as a result of coaching? If so, please describe.

3. How has coaching affected overall productivity? Answer both on an organizational and personal level.

4. What is your current level of job satisfaction? Did the coaching experience affect this in any way?

5. Have you perceived a change in the overall level of employee satisfaction as a result of the coaching intervention? Please explain.

6. Do you feel that coaching both experienced by you and provided by you is affecting the bottom line of the organization? If so, how?

7. Do you feel that coaching is affecting in some degree the company's customers and clients? If so, how?

(continued on the next page)

Job Aid (continued from the previous page)

---

8. Do you feel that your personal level of work output has improved? If so, how?

---

9. Do you feel that your work group's level of output has improved? If so, how?

---

10. Do you feel that your personal quality of work output has improved? If so, how?

---

11. Do you feel that your work group's quality of work output has improved? If so, how?

---

12. How do you feel the incorporation of coaching at the company has affected the corporate culture?

---

13. What, aside from the areas discussed above, do you perceive to be the business impact of coaching? Can you please address your response both in terms of quality as well as financial benefits?

---

14. Would you recommend this program to others?

---

15. How confident are you about your responses that relate to monetary or business benefit?

Mastering the Art of Feedback

Issue 0308

Mastering the Art of Feedback

AUTHORS

Holly DeForest
Internal Revenue Service
13915 NW 74th St.
Parkville, MO 64152
Tel: 816.891.0950
Email: frost.223@hotmail.com

Pamela Largent
Internal Revenue Service
5127 South Austin Ave.
Chicago, IL 60638
Tel: 773.581.8006
Email: lglpcl@core.com

Mary Steinberg
6223 N. Leona Ave.
Chicago, IL 60646
Tel: 773.792.2742
Email:
marysteinberg@sbcglobal.net

Contributing Editor
Tora Estep

Copy Editor
Ann Bruen

Production Design
Kathleen Schaner

Great Feedback Skills

Feedback is something we all have the opportunity to engage in, possibly on a daily basis. But why do some people have negative reactions to this common form of information exchange? The reasons vary. Most people who give feedback may not even be aware that they have done so. Consider the following common situations and see if you have done anything similar:

- thanked your manager for having the confidence to assign a major project to you

- told your spouse you appreciate him picking you up at the train station

- reminded your teenager that curfew is 10:00 p.m., not 10:30 p.m., as she seems to think

- told a co-worker that his failure to complete his portion of a report has resulted in extra hours of work for you.

Do you think of these situations as feedback? When you give someone feedback, you are identifying how you perceive a behavior and the effect this behavior has on you. Feedback tends to take two basic forms: corrective and reinforcing; and it has three basic elements: a sender, a message, and a receiver. In this equation, the message addresses a behavior the sender would like the receiver to either continue or change. Note, however, that the receiver then maintains the choice as to what to do with this information.

When you decide to give someone feedback, make sure your motivation is to help the other person grow and improve, or to strengthen your relationship. For feedback to be effective, it should not be offered to judge, to belittle, or to control; instead, it should help recipients see themselves as others see them and present them with an opportunity to learn. For managers, feedback is a way to strengthen communication with employees. For employees, effective feedback skills can strengthen relationships with colleagues. Effective feedback provides a forum for open communication. In the workplace, open communication creates opportunities for your ideas to shine forth and for your efforts to be recognized and valued. At a personal level, it can strengthen your relationships.

Feedback is a learned skill. Mastering its use can help you:

- learn continually
- strengthen your communication skills
- develop more effective relationships
- improve your decision-making capabilities
- take advantage of opportunities for growth.

This *Infoline* describes processes for giving and receiving effective feedback and shows you how to develop your feedback skills through the use of a *feedback formula*. Becoming proficient in the use of the formula requires work, but the format throughout encourages you to get involved by tapping your own experiences with feedback. If you find yourself resisting, keep in mind the positive outcomes that can result. As with other learned skills, giving and receiving feedback needs to be practiced to be done well.

Getting Started: Know Yourself

The feedback formula presented in this *Infoline* has three parts: giving, receiving, and strengthening your skills. However, before getting started, you should determine your own starting point. Complete the exercise presented in the sidebar *Feedback Effectiveness Self-Assessment* to determine how effective your current feedback skills are. The questions are designed to give you a personal reference point. The remainder of this *Infoline* will provide more detail on the questions used in the exercise and how they relate to the feedback formula.

Self-knowledge also is recognizing whether or not you tend to avoid giving feedback. If you've ever neglected to give feedback to someone when you should have, complete the following exercise. If you are one of the few who has always been comfortable giving feedback, complete the exercise imagining the perspective of someone you know who is not so at ease.

Think of a situation in which you have put off telling someone about something that bothers you. When do you think you will give the feedback?

- *When the time is right?*

- *When the person stops the behavior on his or her own?*

Feedback Effectiveness Self-Assessment

Complete the following self-assessment to identify your own strengths and weaknesses with respect to giving feedback. However, before completing the self-assessment, try to recall some recent experiences with feedback.

Recent Experiences

On a separate sheet of paper, write down your initial thoughts in response to the following questions. Answers to these questions give you the basis for understanding either your willingness to participate in or resistance to giving and receiving feedback.

● How do you react when you see or hear the word "feedback"?

● Describe your two most recent experiences with feedback (can be at work, at home, or in social settings). For each experience, identify if you were the giver, receiver, or an observer.

● If you were the giver, did the feedback result in the outcome you intended?

● If you were the receiver, was the feedback helpful?

● If you were the observer, what behaviors did you see that you would want to model? Avoid?

Self-Assessment

Looking back on these feedback situations, use this opportunity to take an objective look at your own feedback skills. For each of the following questions, answer no, sometimes, or yes. Answer as honestly as you can—you will refer back to this exercise later in this *Infoline*.

1. I express my views to others. _____

2. I pay attention to others' non-verbal cues (body language). _____

3. I become distracted when listening. _____

4. I become distracted when speaking. _____

5. I interrupt others. _____

6. I react defensively when someone gives me negative feedback. _____

7. I ask questions if I don't understand what someone is telling me. _____

8. If I have a difficult issue to raise, I write a note rather than say it directly. _____

9. Others consider me to be insensitive. _____

10. I get upset if someone disagrees with me. _____

11. I am uneasy (embarrassed) when someone pays me a compliment. _____

12. I change the subject when an uncomfortable issue is discussed. _____

13. I pretend to listen to people when I really do not. _____

14. When someone hurts my feelings, I discuss it with that person. _____

15. Others consider me to be too sensitive. _____

16. I assume silence from someone means agreement with what I have said. _____

17. I ask people if they understand what I have told them. _____

18. I express anger (disappointment) with someone in front of others. _____

19. I will ask others why someone is doing something rather than ask the person directly. _____

20. I ask for feedback. _____

- *On the person's last day of work?*

- *When the cows come home?*

- *When the person is in a bad mood about something else already, so he or she will not be angry with you?*

- *When you can send an anonymous letter?*

- *When _____
  (you fill in the reason).*

Obviously this exercise is a little tongue-in-cheek, but the point is clear. Giving feedback can be a challenging experience. What if your feedback is not welcome? There is always the chance that the receiver feels you are criticizing him or her unjustly, or that you are attacking a behavior that is either comfortable or too difficult to change. What if the recipient harbors negative feelings toward you in the future? What if you hurt his or her feelings? In other words, you could be creating a situation you never intended. In the following section, you will find a feedback process that will minimize or eliminate negative outcomes from giving feedback.

Giving Feedback

Before getting started with guidelines for giving feedback, read the sidebar *Case Study: Is This Effective Feedback?* The sidebar introduces a few characteristics of ineffective feedback. To be effective, feedback must be expressed in a manner that helps the receiver hear the message while keeping the relationship intact. To accomplish these goals, the sender must:

- show consideration
- withhold judgment
- deliver at an appropriate time
- provide freedom to change or not
- check for readiness
- check for clarity.

To illustrate these techniques, consider the example of Jay and Sarah. Jay is a customer service representative who handles customer questions and complaints over the telephone. His manager, Sarah, is responsible for occasionally monitoring his calls to determine how well he is doing. On one of these occasions, the customer asked Jay a question Jay could not answer. Jay informed the cus-

tomer that he would research the question and call him back within an hour. At this point, Sarah interrupted, "Excuse me, Jay, that question is something all of our reps should know the answer to." Sarah then proceeded to answer the customer's question herself. Naturally, Jay was embarrassed. Furthermore, this was not the first time Sarah had spoken to him like that in front of others.

Show Consideration

Feedback should consider the needs and feelings of everyone involved. One of the objectives of feedback is to help others, not to hurt them. Give feedback with care. In the example, Jay needs to let Sarah know how her comments affected him because she may not realize that her approach to the situation had a negative effect, not because he is angry and embarrassed. She may have thought that she was being helpful. Furthermore, she may be doing the same thing to others. If so, she could be having a wider negative effect, including on customers.

To show consideration when giving feedback, monitor your behavior, practice active listening, and, when warranted, show concern and caring.

■ *Monitor Your Behavior*
Pay attention to your own behavior while giving feedback. All of your attention should be directed to the communication taking place. Do not answer the phone, do not fidget, maintain eye contact, and keep your posture open.

■ *Practice Active Listening*
Listen for the content and the feeling of what the receiver says in response to your feedback. Verify that what you heard is what the other person meant by repeating it back to him or her in your own words. This is always important, but it is especially important during a feedback conversation.

■ *Express Concern and Caring*
At times you may want to explicitly express your concern and care for the receiver: "Your health is important to me. I would like to talk to you about your working so many late hours." Communicate with respect for the receiver. Choose your words carefully. Do not engage in labeling or name-calling ("you're a workaholic"). Offer feedback in the way you would like to receive it.

Before moving on to the next feature of effective feedback techniques, consider the following questions:

1. *How can Jay help Sarah by giving her feedback?*

_____

_____

2. *How can Jay show consideration for Sarah when he gives her his feedback?*

_____

_____

Withhold Judgment

To make the feedback exchange as effective as possible, do not evaluate the behavior, do not assume its intent, but do address specific behavior that the receiver has the power to change.

■ *Do Not Evaluate*
Effective feedback should describe behavior, not evaluate it. For example, do say, "The customer may have found it helpful if you had given him directions to the store." Don't say, "You did a lousy job with that customer."

Feedback that evaluates behavior can feel like a personal attack to a receiver. People have a hard time hearing the real message when they feel defensive, angry, or vulnerable.

■ *Do Not Assume Intent*
Feedback should never include an interpretation of the behavior. For example, in a statement such as, "You ignored me in the cafeteria yesterday," the speaker assumes that the other person saw her. The assumption and the way the speaker conveys it has the potential to be damaging to the relationship between the sender and the receiver.

Instead, the speaker could have said, "I saw you in the cafeteria yesterday and wondered why you didn't say hello." The speaker may have found out that the receiver did not see her, saw her but did

not want to disturb her, or was engaged in his own thoughts and needed some private time. Not assuming intent prevents defensiveness.

■ *Do Describe Specific Behavior*
Feedback should describe specific, observable behavior. This can take the form of actions seen or words heard. Telling someone that they did a good job with a customer is not as effective as saying, "That customer really appreciated it when you offered to call other stores to find the item he wanted." Describing specific behavior lets the receiver know exactly what behavior is being appreciated or discouraged.

A critical component of describing the behavior includes expressing the effect or consequences of the behavior, which can include feelings produced: "When you answer telephone calls while we are meeting, I feel unimportant to you."

Note the importance of addressing changeable behavior. When you offer feedback, describe behavior that the receiver can change. Even when you do address behavior that can be changed, be aware that many behaviors are habits, and habits are hard to break or modify.

In the earlier example, Jay wants to address the way Sarah spoke to him while a customer was listening. To set up the reason for the feedback, he should describe the specifics of the event: date, time, customer name, and customer care issue. Jay should repeat Sarah's exact words in a neutral speaking voice—adding tone or inflection to her statements is a subtle form of interpreting intent. Finally, he needs to be honest with Sarah about his feelings and tell her that he was embarrassed. If her comments raised any other emotions—anger, for instance—he needs to let her know.

Deliver at an Appropriate Time

Most of the literature on feedback states that the sender should deliver the message immediately after the behavior takes place or the next time the potential for recurrence exists. Whenever possible, this is the best approach to take. If delivered immediately, the behavior and the circumstances surrounding it will be fresh. Both parties will have a clear recollection—although not necessarily the same perception—of the event in question.

Case Study: Is This Effective Feedback?

During a team meeting, the team manager told attending members, "I received some feedback about someone that was not particularly flattering. One of the other managers said that one of you came to a staff meeting, made a presentation that got everyone stirred up, and then left without addressing the concerns he or she had raised. I want all of you to be aware of this so this does not happen again. However, I do not want to discuss this any further, as we need to continue with the agenda."

Before identifying some of the problems in this feedback situation, identify the three elements of the feedback equation: the giver, the message, and the receiver. The giver is clearly the team manager. However, the message is not so clear. What is the behavior that needs to be addressed? The fact that someone gave a presentation that stirred people up, or the fact that the receiver did not address the concerns that were raised? And who is the receiver?

What are some of the problems with the feedback presented in the case?

_____

_____

_____

_____

_____

_____

_____

_____

_____

_____

_____

Did you come up with some of the following issues?

● The intended recipient was not identified.

● The message was vague and non-specific. For example, neither the meeting in question nor the presentation was specified. The phrase "stirred up" is unclear. The concerns that were raised are not identified.

● The manager thinks she provided feedback, but all she really did was blow off steam.

● Giving individual feedback to a group could result in embarrassment to the intended recipient and does not show consideration for any of the members.

● The receiver has not been provided freedom to choose whether to change or not because the behavior described is not specific enough.

● The intended receiver was certainly not ready to receive this feedback.

● The sender did not provide anyone an opportunity to discuss the issue.

However, sometimes waiting is appropriate. For example, when you feel that either you or the receiver may lose emotional control. Emotions can cloud a person's thinking and get in the way of hearing and understanding the message. But be sure that when you decide to postpone feedback, you aren't just avoiding it. If you wait too long, you may store up a lot of issues and unload them all at once on the receiver. This can result in the receiver feeling attacked and unable to respond.

Another reason to postpone giving feedback is that the physical setting may not be appropriate. If you are with a group or out in public, it may be inappropriate to give your feedback—especially the corrective variety. Some people are embarrassed to receive reinforcing feedback in front of others, so be sensitive to the person you are dealing with.

Now that you know when an appropriate time to deliver feedback may be, answer the following questions:

1. *Should Jay give Sarah feedback now or later? Why?*

_____

_____

2. *If later, when might be an appropriate time?*

_____

_____

Here is one interpretation of our fictional scenario: Jay is embarrassed and angry. So Jay needs time to calm down. If possible, he should talk to Sarah by the close of the next business day to prevent the incident from happening again.

Jay must not wait too long to deliver this feedback, because Sarah has behaved this way in the past. When he does, he needs to be careful not to drag up a lot of old incidents. Doing so will make Sarah feel that she is being attacked, which will prevent her gaining anything beneficial from the feedback.

Provide Freedom to Change or Not

The decision to change behavior rests solely with the receiver. Each individual has a personal style—a unique way of being him- or herself. It is important at this stage to acknowledge differences. When you give feedback, the recipient learns how his or her behavior affects you. Acknowledging differences sends the message that sameness is not the goal; harmony is. Under these conditions, the feedback helps the receiver decide if the effect of his or her behavior is what he or she had intended. The choice to act on the feedback or to ignore it belongs ultimately to the receiver. Therefore, let the person know of the consequences of not changing. Consequences can be positive or negative:

- "If you continue to produce results like these, I will recommend that you receive a raise."

- "If you do not learn to use the new software, we will not be able to continue to provide you with employment."

Remember, you can't demand that someone continue or suspend a behavior. If you do, be prepared for resistance, or permanent damage to your relationship. Although Jay wants to offer feedback that is corrective—he would like Sarah to not embarrass him in front of customers—he cannot realistically expect or demand that this happen. Sarah has to decide whether she will change.

Check for Readiness

Feedback should be given and received only when both the sender and receiver are ready—mentally, emotionally, and physically. Feedback works most successfully when the receiver can clearly hear the message. Much of the published theory stresses that the feedback should always be solicited, or at least that one should ask whether the receiver wants to hear some feedback. This assumes an ideal situation in which people ask for feedback and are ready—mentally, emotionally, and physically—to receive it.

However, situations are not always ideal. It is often necessary to deliver feedback whether or not the receiver wants to hear it. If your child crosses streets without looking for oncoming traffic, or your spouse drives too fast, you are probably not going to ask if they are ready and willing to hear your feedback. Not if you value safety! If you are a manager, and one of your employees constantly arrives late or does not return your telephone calls, you probably should not wait until they ask about how they are doing.

When you decide to give feedback even if you sense the receiver does not want to hear it, consider your motivation. The impetus for the information exchange should be to help the other person grow and to maintain or improve your relationship. Giving feedback simply because you are angry is not really feedback—it is sounding off.

Complete this readiness check in the Jay and Sarah scenario:

1. *What is Jay's motivation for giving feedback?*

_____

_____

2. *Should Jay check with Sarah to find out if she would like to hear his feedback or should he impose on her?*

_____

_____

Jay wants Sarah to know what effect her behavior has on him and his working relationship with her. However, because he has no authority over her, and safety is not an issue, he should first ask her if she is willing to hear some feedback.

Check for Clarity

Sometimes the sender should check with the receiver to make sure the intended message matches the one received. This is particularly important when giving negative feedback or when emotions are running high. Remember that people perceive things differently. A receiver's past experiences with corrective feedback may cloud his or her ability to hear your feedback for what it is: your perception of certain behavior(s) and its effects on you. To ensure that the two of you are on the same track, you can ask him or her to repeat the information for you, or you can restate the feedback in a different way. Clarity helps produce more favorable outcomes.

Also encourage the receiver to check with other people to see if they share your perceptions. Remember, the decision to act on the feedback rests with the receiver, but encouraging them to verify or confirm with others will aid this process.

How can Jay increase the possibility that Sarah will hear the feedback the way he intends? After he tells her exactly what she said and how it affected him, he could repeat the consequences in a different way. He also could ask if she understands how and why he was embarrassed and if she can restate what he has told her.

Giving effective feedback is a skill you must prepare for. If Jay tried to convey a message to Sarah when he was extremely embarrassed and angry, the result could be very different from the one he truly wanted. By taking some time to prepare for it, the potential for a positive outcome increases dramatically.

Receiving Feedback

The other side of the feedback coin is receiving feedback. Soliciting feedback can seem risky. It may be difficult to open yourself up to potential criticism, or perhaps you feel awkward about receiving complimentary feedback, especially in public. When you learn about others' perceptions of you, you may not like the message. Even if you aren't the person you want to be, hearing someone else suggest that you could or should be different can be painful.

Although the feedback process requires participation from both the sender and the receiver, being on the receiving end means you may not always have an opportunity to plan your approach to the situation. Often, what you hear catches you off guard. The sidebar *Are You Ready to Receive Feedback?* presents some questions that will help you understand your responsibilities as the receiver.

Receiving feedback does not have to be painful. Like giving feedback, this is a learned skill with its own set of techniques. Many of these techniques are the same as in giving feedback. Here are some pointers to help you survive, and benefit from, receiving feedback:

■ *Show Consideration*
As previously noted, the objective of feedback is to help people. Keep this in mind when you are on the receiving end. No one should offer feedback for the sake of hurting your feelings or damaging your self-confidence, and your responses should mirror those standards.

■ *Monitor Your Behavior*
Giving feedback and showing care and concern for the growth of others may be a risk for some people. You can make the process easier for the person giving you feedback by exhibiting certain behaviors:

● expressing your feelings honestly, but without getting heated

● letting the person know if you are ready to hear the message and if you believe the sender has your best interests at heart

● sharing your thoughts and feelings about the feedback you receive.

Are You Ready to Receive Feedback?

For each of the following questions, identify the answers you believe to be correct. There may be more than one right answer per question.

1. The objective of receiving feedback is to:

   a. Enhance your personal growth.

   b. Strengthen relationships.

   c. Get you to change to please other people.

2. You always consider the giver's feelings because:

   a. It is not nice to be unkind.

   b. He or she is smarter than you and deserves respect.

   c. He or she is showing care and concern for you by sharing his or her perception of your behavior.

3. You should start mentally rehearsing your response to the giver as soon as you know what they want because:

   a. It will make you look smarter.

   b. If you do this, you will not focus on what is being said.

   c. You should always be prepared.

4. When you receive corrective feedback, you should rationalize your behavior because:

   a. It will make the sender realize that his or her perceptions are wrong.

   b. The feedback makes you defensive, and that is an honest emotional response.

   c. You shouldn't do this because you may lose an opportunity to learn.

5. You should ask for specific examples to:

   a. Help you understand exactly what behavior the giver is discussing.

   b. Put the sender on the spot.

   c. Confuse the issue.

6. You should postpone receiving feedback when:

   a. You like yourself as you are and don't want to listen.

   b. The giver will probably forget about it if you wait.

   c. The giver appears to be angry.

7. When you receive corrective feedback, you must change your behavior because:

   a. If you do not, the sender will not like you anymore.

   b. Other people can see you as you really are.

   c. You do not have to; you have a choice.

8. You may want to check with others when you receive feedback to:

   a. Determine the effect your behavior has on them.

   b. Prove that the sender is wrong.

   c. Prove that the sender is right.

9. You should ask for clarification if you have any questions about the feedback in order to:

   a. Ensure that what you heard is what was meant.

   b. Give you more time to justify your behavior.

   c. Give the sender a chance to change his or her mind.

10. When you solicit feedback from someone, you should:

    a. "Fish" for compliments.

    b. Cut off the giver if you don't hear what you want to hear.

    c. Be specific about the behavior that you want feedback on.

Key: 1a and b, 2c, 3b, 4c, 5a, 6c, 7c, 8a, 9a, 10c.

This honest exchange can help build trust between the two of you and result in a stronger relationship.

■ *Practice Active Listening*

When someone takes the time to share his or her perceptions of your behavior, practice active listening to hear both the content and the feeling in what is being said. Confirm that what you are hearing is what the sender intended. If you do not understand something, ask for clarification.

When you listen to others, it is natural to comment (out loud or mentally) about your experiences or opinions related to the topic at hand. If you share this aloud, you will interrupt the speaker and redirect the focus of the conversation away from the original purpose. Doing so could also make the sender unwilling to share additional information with you. However, if you keep your conversation internal, you may be too busy listening to yourself and miss the important points of the feedback. To avoid this situation, direct all of your attention to the communication taking place: Do not fidget and do not let your mind wander. Do maintain eye contact and, if appropriate, take notes.

■ *Withhold Judgment*

Listening and focusing on the feedback you receive is an effective way to learn about the effect you have on others. This learning cannot take place if you become defensive or try to justify your actions. Keep in mind that the speaker is sharing perceptions of your behavior with you, telling you how he or she experienced your actions. Keep in mind that the sender is not assuming any intent on your part.

■ *Do Not Rationalize Your Behavior*

Just as the person giving you feedback should not attribute motivation to your actions, you should not try to rationalize your behavior by saying, "I really didn't mean it that way." Two people may have different viewpoints or perceptions of the same incident. If that difference creates a problem, using the feedback process can provide an opportunity for discussion.

■ *Ask for Specific Details*

Feedback should describe specific, concrete behaviors. When possible, words should be quoted directly. Although hearing your actions described through the eyes of another may be uncomfort-able, you should ask for specific examples that will help you understand what behaviors prompted the feedback.

■ *Ask for Postponement*

Sometimes you may not be ready to receive feedback. If you feel emotional and fear you may lose control, then you should allow yourself time to calm down. Let the person know you are willing to hear what they have to say, but that now is not a good time for you. Also make this request if you suspect the other person may become emotional or it appears that they are acting out of anger.

Make certain you are not simply stalling in the hope that the effect of your behavior will diminish, and/or the messenger will change his or her mind about sharing his or her perceptions. This strategy not only keeps you from an opportunity for personal growth, but it also has the potential of backfiring. Sometimes when an individual waits to deliver feedback, the person has time to dwell on the perceived behavior. When the moment finally comes to talk about the situation, it may be blown out of proportion or involve other unresolved issues. If possible, when you postpone receiving feedback, establish a mutually acceptable time in the near future.

■ *Maintain Your Ability to Choose*

On the receiving end of feedback, you are still in control of whether or not you change your behavior. Feedback is a description of the sender's perception of your behavior, the effect your behavior has on him or her, and the consequences of continuing your behavior. Period. You will not always agree with the feedback you receive from others. No one should demand that you change, nor should anyone try to impose his or her values and standards on you. You cannot be expected to change to meet everyone's personal likes and expectations—that takes a chameleon.

■ *Make a Choice*

The decision to accept the feedback as valid or not clearly rests with you. You have the option of checking with others to obtain their perceptions of your behavior or to validate the feedback. You may think the feedback has raised an issue that you need to think about, and you may wonder if others feel the same. But even if they do, you still have the choice to act on the feedback or ignore it.

The fact that you are the one who decides whether or not to make a change is very important. Remember that one of the objectives of giving feedback is to help others grow. When you are the receiver, keep this objective in mind. Listen carefully to the information you are receiving. Clarify that what you are hearing is what the sender wanted you to hear. When appropriate or feasible, check with others to validate what you have heard. Once you have done all of this, weigh the information for yourself and determine whether you want to act on it or not.

■ *Check for Readiness*
When you solicit feedback, you are clearly ready mentally, emotionally, and physically. This is the ideal situation in which you are in a place where you can hear what is being shared with you and can act on it.

More often than not, however, you will receive unsolicited feedback. Sometimes the need to share is overwhelming, and the sender tells you whether you want to hear it or not. The question is, should you listen? That depends on the situation. If someone is forcing feedback on you for the wrong reasons—he or she is angry or feels like "dumping" on you—you may want to postpone the exchange. In such a situation, let the sender know you are not willing to hear what they have to say at this time. Schedule a time to continue the discussion. Be honest about your perception of his or her motivation and be firm in your resolution not to participate in the present discussion.

■ *Determine Consequences*
Sometimes the sender has a legitimate need or reason to share information with you. This is especially true in situations that involve the personal safety of yourself or others and is also commonly the case when the person has some degree of authority over you or responsibility for you—such as a parent, a manager, or an instructor. In these situations, the decision about acting on the feedback is still yours, but be sure to clearly understand the consequences of your decision.

■ *Check for Clarity*
When you receive feedback, ensure that you understand the information being shared. Request specificity and validate the feedback by asking for examples of specific instances when you have demonstrated the behavior under discussion.

■ *Ask Questions*
Because people do not always express their thoughts and ideas in the same manner, it is easy to jump to conclusions—especially in the case of corrective feedback. Take the time to summarize your understanding of what you heard. Keep in mind that one of the objectives of feedback is to strengthen relationships. Attributing incorrect motivation or intent may have the opposite effect: It can result in a breakdown in trust between you and the sender and cause permanent damage to the relationship.

Developing Your Feedback Skills

To incorporate the skills involved in giving and receiving feedback, you need to practice the skills. Hands-on experience is vital in mastering new skills. As for most people, giving or receiving effective feedback probably does not come naturally to you. What does come naturally, however, are the behaviors you have developed and practiced for years. Review your *Feedback Effectiveness Self-Assessment* and determine whether your check marks are where you want them to be. If they are, perhaps the behaviors listed are habits you want to practice and reinforce. But if the check marks are not where you want them to be, you may have habits that need to be modified or broken.

Modifying or breaking habits may threaten your comfort level. Complete the exercise in the sidebar *Breaking a Habit* at right. Pay close attention to your reactions. The reactions you experience during the exercise are similar to the feelings you would have while learning any new skill, whether it is skiing, dancing, using a new software program, or applying the feedback process. To develop new skills, you need to break or modify some habits, which is often hard to do.

Look at the words you used to describe the risk-free task of writing with your opposite hand. You may also use these words to describe the feelings you have when you practice a new way of giving or receiving feedback. Take the following steps to modify or break some habits and develop your skills using the feedback process.

Step 1: Set Goals

Do you need to develop or modify your feedback skills? If so, an excellent way to start making those changes is to set goals and write them down. Writing down your goals serves as a reminder of what you want to do, makes the goals easier to modify or share with others, and makes them more tangible and specific. Remember to try to write goal statements that are specific, measurable, and achievable.

Step 2: Gather Facts

To meet your goals, identify habits to keep. These can often help you in modifying or breaking the habits that stop you from giving or receiving effective feedback. Complete the following exercise to identify habits and what to do with them.

Under the appropriate heading, list your habits related to giving or receiving feedback.

1. *Keep*

_____

_____

2. *Modify*

_____

_____

3. *Break*

_____

_____

Breaking a Habit

Complete the following exercise. Pay close attention to your feelings and thoughts while you complete the exercise.

Sign (do not print) your full name below as you would normally:

_____

Now, put your pen or pencil in the opposite hand and sign (do not print) your full name again:

_____

What words come to mind to describe how it felt to sign your name with the opposite hand?

_____

For most people, writing with the opposite hand is a new behavior that requires breaking a comfortable habit. When asked how it feels to use the opposite hand, most describe the experience as awkward, difficult, uncomfortable, funny looking, time consuming, and so on. When asked to perform this exercise, a frequent initial response is "I will not be able to do it" (but this is rarely, if ever, true).

Did you use any of these or similar words to describe using your opposite hand to sign your name? Did you think you might not be able to do it?

Step 3: Ask for Feedback

The next step in the process is to see if your opinion truly reflects your skills in giving or receiving feedback. One way to check out what you think about your habits is to ask others for feedback. Asking for and receiving feedback gives you the opportunity to hear others' perceptions of your feedback habits. They may see things you are not aware of.

Step 4: Identify a Support Network

A support network is a group of people who can help you achieve your goals. Take the example of learning to ski. Your instructor can serve as both teacher and constructive critic. You may have a friend, also a beginner, with whom you can laugh as you tumble down the hills. More advanced skiing friends can serve as role models. Other friends, acquaintances, or ski resort personnel can serve as advisors on places to ski, equipment to purchase, and so forth. In other words, you have numerous options for advice on just about every aspect of learning and refining a skill. You also can form a support network to help you learn to use the feedback process. Use the sidebar *Who Is In Your Network?* at right to identify people to make up your support network. If you have only one or two people listed, consider expanding your network. The wider your network, the broader the range of experiences you can draw from.

Step 5: Take a Risk

Your supporters provide an opportunity to practice giving feedback. Give feedback to the people you have listed on why you chose them as part of your support network. Find out if they are willing to assist you. But remember that feedback receivers always have a choice. If they choose not to be part of your support network, learn the reasons why. This experience may seem risky, but it is ripe with opportunity for growth and learning.

Once you have found people who agree to act in these support roles, think of ways they can help you. Suggestions you may want to consider include the following:

- Ask the goal setter to look at the goals you have set. Are they realistic? Attainable?

- Ask the constructive critic to fill out the *Feedback Effectiveness Self-Assessment* based on his or her perceptions of you. Do not share your answers until he or she has completed the assessment. Ask the constructive critic to explain and provide examples of his or her answers. This is a good opportunity for you to learn something about yourself.

- Ask the coach to listen to how you plan to give feedback to someone and seek advice on your approach. However, be careful to maintain confidentiality.

Step 6: Learn Continually

In addition to developing your support network, you have other sources from which to elicit help. For example, you can take seminars on communication issues that apply to developing your feedback skills, such as active listening, conflict resolution, and assertiveness. If you take a seminar, choose one where you will have the opportunity to practice what you learn in the course. More sources include books and articles, some of which are presented in the reference section of this *Infoline*.

Step 7: Take Small Steps

Mark Twain said, "Habit is habit, and not to be flung out of the window by any man, but coaxed downstairs a step at a time." In other words, you don't have to apply everything you have learned all at once.

Taking the information you gleaned from identifying the feedback habits you want to modify or break, rank them in order of priority and concentrate on only one or two to begin with. Modifying other habits may become easier when you make the first changes at the top of your list.

You have opportunities to practice your new skills daily. Pick some safe areas for your first small steps. For example, compliment a salesperson for good service; send back a meal that was not prepared as you asked; or choose a minor issue you need to speak about with a co-worker, or friend, or spouse. Don't start with anything too serious.

Step 8: Lighten Up

Even with practice and the best intentions, things often don't turn out exactly as you want. When this happens, contact the person you chose as your comedian; humor can help you move forward. Another way to move forward is to develop an action plan. The job aid presents action plans for both

Who Is In Your Network?

Fill in the names of people who either currently serve or could serve in the roles of network advisors. Draw from both business and personal relationships. (The same names might crop up in more than one category.)

Role Model	Who have you seen give or receive feedback that resulted in a positive exchange of information?	
Coach	Who can give you advice on methods of giving or receiving feedback?	
Goal Setter	If you have trouble setting goals, who can help you?	
Constructive Critic	Who gives you honest feedback?	
Comedian	Who makes you laugh?	
Cheerleader	Who can celebrate your successes with you?	

giving and receiving feedback. Each plan also comes with an assessment to help you analyze your experiences.

As the feedback process becomes more familiar, you will not have to prepare as much for every encounter. Giving and receiving effective feedback will become second nature as you practice good habits. However, when you have an extremely difficult situation, completing an action plan will make the process less difficult.

References & Resources

Articles

Berman, Mark L. "Are You a Seeker or an Avoider?" *T+D*, December 2002, pp. 38-42.

Blodgett, Paul C. "Six Ways to Be a Better Listener." *Training and Development,* July 1997, pp. 11-12.

Clark, Kathryn F. "Say It Again, Sam." *Human Resource Executive,* December 1997, pp. 54-57.

Clarke-Epstein, Chris. "Truth in Feedback." *T+D*, November 2001, pp. 78-80.

Drucker, Peter. "Managing Oneself." *Harvard Business Review,* March/April 1999, pp. 64-74.

Harris, Richard M. "Turn Listening Into a Powerful Presence." *Training and Development,* July 1997, pp. 9-11.

HRFocus. "How to Improve Your Leadership Ability." January 2000, pp. 9-10.

Imperato, Gina. "How to Give Good Feedback." *Fast Company,* September 1998, pp. 144-156.

Joinson, Carla. "Employee Sculpt Thyself, with a Little Help." *HRMagazine,* May 2001, pp. 60-64.

Kiger, Patrick. "Frequent Employee Feedback Is Worth the Cost and Time." *Workforce,* March 2001, pp. 62-63, 65.

Koonce, Richard. "Are You Getting the Feedback You Deserve?" *Training and Development,* July 1998, p. 18.

Morris, Linda, ed. "How Effective Are We as Listeners?" *Training and Development,* April 1993, pp. 79-80.

People Management. "How to Provide Effective Feedback." July 1996, pp. 44-45.

Swinburne, Penny. "How to Use Feedback to Improve Performance." *People Management,* May 31, 2001, pp. 46-47.

Tyler, Kathryn. "Careful Criticism Brings Better Performance." *HRMagazine,* April 1997, pp. 57-62.

Walker, Carol A. "Saving Your Rookie Managers from Themselves." *Harvard Business Review,* April 2002, pp. 97-102.

Books

Aronson, Eliot. *Small Group Communication: A Reader,* 4th edition. Dubuque, IA: W.C. Brown, 1984.

Atwater, Eastwood. *I Hear You: A Listening Skills Handbook.* New York: Walker, 1992.

Bennis, Warren. *The Planning of Change.* New York: Holt, Rhinehart, and Winston, 1961.

Blanchard, Kenneth. *The One Minute Manager Meets the Monkey.* New York: William Morrow, 1989.

Brownell, Judi. *Building Active Listening Skills.* Upper Saddle River, NJ: Prentice Hall, 1986.

Bushardt, Stephen, and Aubry Fowler. *The 1989 Annual: Developing Human Resources.* San Diego, CA: University Associates, 1989.

Cushman, Donald P., and Dudley D. Cahn. *Communication in Interpersonal Relationships.* Albany, NY: SUNY Press, 1985.

Fisher, Roger, and William Ury. *Getting to Yes.* New York: Penguin, 1983.

Hanson, Phillip. *The 1975 Handbook for Group Facilitators.* San Diego, CA: University Associates, 1975.

Hathaway, Patti. *Giving and Receiving Feedback: Building Constructive Communication.* Menlo Park, CA: Crisp Publications, 1998.

Jamison, Kaleel. *The Nibble Theory and the Kernel of Power.* Mahwah, NJ: Paulist Press, 1984.

Maurer, Rick. *Feedback Toolkit: 16 Tools for Better Communication in the Workplace.* New York: Productivity Press, 1994.

Poertner, Shirley, and Karen Massetti Miller. *The Art of Giving and Receiving Feedback.* Urbandale, IA: Provant Media, 1996.

Poley, Michelle Fairfield. *Mastering the Art of Communication.* Mission, KS: SkillPath Publications, 1994.

Rubin, Irwin M., and Thomas J. Campbell. *The ABCs of Effective Feedback: A Guide for Caring Professionals.* San Francisco: Jossey-Bass, 1997.

Stone, Douglas, Bruce Patton, and Sheila Heen. *Difficult Conversations: How to Discuss What Matters Most.* New York: Penguin, 2000.

Towers, Mark. *The ABCs of Empowered Teams.* Mission, KS: SkillPath Publications, 1994.

Tulgan, Bruce. *Fast Feedback,* 2nd Edition. Amherst, MA: Human Resources Development Press, 1999.

Whiteman, Gilbert. *Effective Listening.* Old Saybrook, CT: Business and Legal Reports, 1987.

Infolines

Butruille, Susan G., ed. "Listening to Learn; Learning to Listen." No. 8806.

Darraugh, Barbara, ed. "Coaching and Feedback." No. 9006.

Feedback Action Plans

Take the opportunity to put what you have learned into action. Two action plans outline processes for giving and receiving feedback. Each plan ends with an assessment for you to take notes on how the exchange went.

Action Plan for Giving Feedback

Apply the feedback process and its elements when you want to give feedback. Answer the following questions as completely as you can on a blank sheet of paper.

The Situation

Describe the current situation that you want to give feedback about.

The Feedback Process

- Who is the intended receiver for the feedback?

- What is the information you wish to have an exchange about?

The Feedback Elements

- Describe how you can show consideration for the receiver.

- Do you feel confident in your ability to stay focused and practice active listening? How do you plan to do that?

- What is the specific, changeable behavior that you want to address?

- What are the consequences if the receiver does not change his or her behavior?

- How will you give this feedback?

- How will you deal with the fact that the receiver may or may not change his or her behavior? (Remember that change is up to him or her.)

- What is your motivation for giving this feedback?

- Create some questions that you can ask to ensure your feedback is received correctly.

Reaction

- Describe your reaction to the thought of giving this feedback.

- Who are the members of your support network who can help you if necessary?

- What information from your *Effective Feedback Self-Assessment* can help you in this situation? (Remember to consider habits that help you in your communication with others as well as any habits that you should be wary of.)

Assessment

After delivering the feedback, take some time to assess the experience:

1. What went well?

2. What was most challenging?

3. What did not go so well?

4. Did you consider the feedback elements of your action plan? If so, which ones were of the most use? If not, which ones may have helped?

5. Did you modify or break any habits?

6. What did you learn about your attitude about giving feedback?

(continued on the next page)

Job Aid

Action Plan for Receiving Feedback

Apply the feedback process and its elements when you would like to receive feedback. Answer the following questions as completely as you can.

The Situation

Describe the current situation about which you would like to receive feedback.

The Feedback Process

● Who will you request feedback from?

● What information do you wish to have an exchange about?

The Feedback Elements

● How can you show consideration for the sender?

● Describe how you plan to stay focused and practice active listening skills.

● List the specific questions that you want to ask about the situation.

● How will you receive this feedback?

● How will you deal with the fact that the sender may not agree with your decision about how to deal with his or her comments?

● What is your motivation for asking for this feedback?

● How will you prepare yourself—mentally, physically, and emotionally—to hear the feedback?

● Are you willing to change your behavior? Modify it? Not change it? What does your answer depend on?

● What questions can you ask to help the sender state the feedback?

Reaction

● At the thought of receiving this feedback, how are you reacting?

● Who in your support network can help you if necessary?

● What information from your *Effective Feedback Self-Assessment* can help you in this situation? (Remember to consider habits that help you in your communication with others as well as any habits that you should be wary of.)

Assessment

After receiving the feedback, take some time to assess the experience:

1. What went well?

2. What was most challenging?

3. What did not go so well?

4. Did you consider the feedback elements of your action plan? If so, which ones were of the most use? If not, which ones may have helped?

5. Did you modify or break any habits?

6. What did you learn about your attitude regarding the receipt of feedback?

Mentoring

Issue 0004

Mentoring

AUTHORS:

Beverly Kaye, Ph. D.
Beverly Kaye & Associates, Inc.
3545 Alana Drive
Sherman Oaks, CA 91403
Tel: 818.995.6454
Fax: 818.995.0984
Email: Beverly.Kaye@csibka.com

Devon Scheef
Scheef Organizational
    Development & Training
4840 Coyote Wells Circle
Westlake Village, CA 91362
Tel/Fax: 805.494.0124
Email: DevonScheef@cs.com

Editor
Cat Sharpe Russo

Managing Editor
Sabrina E. Hicks

Contributing Editor
Ann Bruen

Production Design
Leah Cohen

The ROI of Mentoring

It is ironic that in this time of technological achievement, the lifeblood of corporations is the accumulated insight of the people who choose to give their gifts of talent and commitment to any given organization. So, the question is this: How do we ensure that the intellectual legacy of our people continues?

A large portion of the answer lies with mentoring initiatives. Mentoring is a powerful, dynamic process—for both employees and organizations. To share wisdom is to share life experience. No matter which methodology is used, mentoring has the potential to elevate corporate dialogue from the mundane to the truly transformational.

The case for mentoring is compelling. According to an emerging workforce study done by Louis Harris & Associates, 35 percent of employees who do not receive regular mentoring are likely to look for another job within 12 months. In contrast, just 16 percent of those with good mentors expect to leave their jobs. Through mentoring programs, protégés develop vision and expertise, and mentors become reinvigorated, knowing that they are leaving a legacy to their organization, profession, and community.

Once an organization has accepted the value of a mentoring program, what approach is the best? While still popular, one-to-one mentoring is no longer viewed as the only or best approach. Many organizations find that group mentoring and virtual mentoring are attractive alternatives or supplements to traditional mentoring. Based on information contained in a previous *Infoline* on mentoring, this issue expands that focus and provides additional mentoring ideas. Here you will find an overview of the three approaches to mentoring, as well as techniques, guidelines, and tips to make your mentoring programs successful.

The Business Case for Mentoring

Among other trends reflected in the changing workforce is a growing employee commitment to careers, rather than jobs. Beginning with their first job out of college, today's employees are looking ahead to a solid career, and any individual job may be little more than a convenient stepping stone to a more ambitious end. Because of that, employers stand a better chance of retaining top-performing employees if they take an active interest in their careers—and even help shape those careers through mentoring initiatives.

Career Development: Tradition With a Twist

A key benefit to mentoring programs is that they offer something other career development programs do not: individual attention. In a complex organization, it is particularly beneficial for an employee to learn how the system operates from someone who is better educated or more experienced. It is also worth noting that when a mentor relationship works, it is the easiest way for an organization to support career development; once in place, it usually no longer requires much involvement from the organization.

Traditionally, organizations are interested in grooming employees to take over jobs of increasing responsibility. On another level, they might be concerned with retaining the bright young graduates who are still "testing the waters" but could easily take their skills and enthusiasm elsewhere if they are not quickly involved with the excitement, goals, and—most important—people of the organization. The more specific the overall goal, the easier the mentoring program is to design and the better chance the organization has of receiving a return on its investment.

Employers stand to gain as much as employees through such efforts. Among other things, mentoring programs can help resolve such organizational problems as the premature departure of young professionals, the stagnation and boredom of solid performers, or the lack of qualified people to fill senior management positions vacated by retirees.

Succession Planning Initiatives

Organizations often look toward a formalized mentoring program as a means of instituting a management continuity system at a variety of levels. Some use the program to groom middle management for senior-level jobs. Mentoring programs are an effective means of increasing the political savvy, exposure, and visibility middle managers need if they are going to succeed in top-level management positions.

Why We Mentor

Mentoring is a tool to accomplish the following goals:

- Attract and retain high performers.
- Upgrade employee skills and knowledge.
- Promote diversity of thought and style.
- Develop leadership talent.
- Preserve institutional memory.
- Create inclusion.
- Develop a line of succession.
- Foster a collaborative environment.
- Ease the transition to new assignments.
- Strengthen corporate competitive advantage.

Because many organizations are challenged by ever-evolving work environments, the implementation of such a succession, or replacement, planning program requires using change management strategies that put the right people in the right places at the right times. To find those employees who have the skills to meet organizational challenges, the planning process entails the following elements:

- identification and analysis of key positions

- assessment of candidates against job and personal requirements

- creation of individual development plans

- selection of candidates

To meet the goals of their succession planning programs, organizations are asking managers to coach and mentor in more intensive ways than they have in the past. Mentoring helps develop future executives through structured activities that allow employees to acquire leadership skills as a part of their natural rate of development.

Types of Mentoring Programs

Mentoring can take at least three forms, and many variations of each are possible depending on the organization's needs. **One-to-one mentoring** uses mentoring partners, traditionally called protégés and mentors. Historically, this relationship was seen as rather patriarchal, with a powerful mentor responsible for guiding the career of a junior up-and-coming employee. The updated view of one-to-one mentoring is that of two partners, each with areas of expertise and contribution, who work together to achieve the development or learning goals of the protégé partner. The new view of one-to-one mentoring acknowledges that mentors often gain as much from the relationship as the protégés.

Group mentoring is a format in which small groups of people commit to jointly support and pursue one another's learning goals. The group has a learning facilitator, who takes on the role of group mentor. In addition, each group member is considered a mentor to the others, serving as feedback giver, supporter, and ally. This mentoring method leverages the power of group motivation and knowledge exchange. It is an appropriate model for many of today's fast-paced and flexible organizations that rely on knowledge networks and include everyone in the decision-making process.

Virtual mentoring is a form of one-to-one or group mentoring that is conducted by telephone, email, and video conferencing. Once considered a "last resort" mentoring method, it is growing in popularity because of geographic considerations. While it overcomes the challenges of distance, it requires special rigor and disciplined implementation to compensate for lack of face-to-face contact.

One-to-One Mentoring

Despite all their advantages, one-to-one mentoring programs are not easy to establish. To set up a mentoring program you need to be familiar with program components, mentor selection, and what mentors and protégés do.

Program Components

There are five essential components of mentoring programs.

1. Determine the purpose of the mentoring initiative and set specific goals. Frequently cited outcomes include high potential development, leadership development, support for diversity initiatives, knowledge transfer, and retention of key individuals.

2. Identify and match mentors and protégés. Select participants based on fair, attainable, and known criteria, and make sure that matching mentors and protégés is voluntary. Experts have found that the best matches occur based on the development needs of the protégés. Some companies find cross-functional matching valuable as well.

3. Train mentors and prepare protégés. Good mentor/protégé matches alone do not guarantee success. Improve chances for successful mentoring by training mentors how and when to apply skills such as empathetic listening, conflict resolution, flexible leadership, assertiveness, providing feedback and positive reinforcement, motivating, and using effective instructional techniques. Prepare protégés by helping them define their goals for the mentoring relationship.

4. Monitor the mentoring process to make sure that protégés are achieving their goals. The monitoring phase offers opportunities to identify poor matches and allow participants to request specific persons to replace their current mentor or protégé.

5. Evaluate the program. Base your program evaluation on the overall objectives for the mentoring initiatives.

Selecting a Mentor

Mentors find their roles to be rewarding and developmental, but they must be seasoned employees who fulfill specific criteria. Here are items to consider when selecting mentors:

Mentoring Myths

There are several common myths about mentors:

- All mentors are good communicators.

- Mentors control the next career step.

- Mentors have the latest information available on the organization.

- It is the mentor's job to keep the protégé's boss informed.

- A mentor should have information on special career path possibilities.

- People should have the same mentor for their entire careers.

Job Performance

- Are prospective mentors recognized as effective leaders, and have they performed well in leadership roles?

- Are they considered role models of character and values consistent with their leadership competencies?

- Do prospective mentors support the organization's vision and goals?

- Do they develop subordinates well?

Business Acumen

- Do prospective mentors have a long-view perspective? Are they comfortable with strategic business outlook planning and thinking?

- Do they deal well with the inherent ambiguity and complexity of any organization? Are they role models of flexibility and change management?

What Protégés Do

Protégés bring their own personalities and perspectives to the mentoring relationship. Their fresh outlook and enthusiasm can make a real contribution to the organization, as they and their mentors develop their relationship. These are the characteristics found in good protégés:

Proactive Learner

Nowhere is the notion of "active learning" more important than in mentoring relationships. While the mentor is a respected and valuable resource, it is the role of the protégé to grasp learning opportunities, take learning risks, and engage the mentor as an active development partner.

Change Agent

The best mentoring relationships are action oriented and emphasize doing, trying, and practicing versus telling, listening, and passive learning. The role of change agent means that the protégé realizes that growth and development are goals of the process. Indeed, the protégé's role is to change based on this learning relationship.

Contributor

A hallmark of a successful relationship is that the mentor learns as much from the protégé as the protégé does from the mentor. A key role of the protégé is to share ideas and expertise with the mentor, and view the relationship as one of reciprocal learning.

Interpersonal Skills

- Do prospective mentors have a history of positive relationships with a broad scope of individuals?

- Are they seen as trusted resources in their own organization?

- Do they have a history of freely sharing expertise and insight with others?

Learning Capacity

- Are prospective mentors aware of their strengths and weaknesses? Are they willing to talk about these with others?

- Are they personally committed to continuous growth and receptive to new approaches and ideas?

What Mentors Do

Every mentor brings unique experience and expertise to the relationship. Here are the roles most mentors perform:

Guide. A guide takes you through a journey, shows you a path, and helps you see important things along the way. This role can be accomplished in two forms. The *wise owl* offers perspective about what is going on in the organization; while the *teacher* helps people teach themselves by asking the right questions, throwing out ideas, and keeping conversation moving. These mentors lead with questions, share their views freely, and reflect on their own journeys.

Ally. An ally can help by offering honesty and friendship while helping others understand how they are seen in the organization. The role can be one of a *sounding board*, where the mentor creates an environment for venting feelings and frustrations. Or the ally can take the form of a *straight talker*, where the mentor provides honest and candid feedback from his or her vantage point. Allies tell it like it is, feel comfortable when others are venting, and freely offer their own feelings and views.

Catalyst. A catalyst may use ideas and knowledge from his or her own experiences to stimulate others to explore the culture and environment that surrounds them. This mentor can be an *entrepreneur*, helping the protégé to see the organization in a new light, or a *creative motivator*, stimulating the person to discuss feelings, ideas, visions, and creative concepts. Catalysts know the inner workings of the organization, think of themselves as creative or idea persons, and get excited when they see others get excited about new possibilities.

Savvy Insider. The savvy insider knows the ropes. Insiders understand how things really get accomplished in the organization. They can be *people connectors*, putting protégés in touch with people in the organization who can take their learning to another level, or they can be *information providers*, supplying specific data that comes from their connections and activities.

Advocate. The advocate actively seeks to propel the protégé's growth and helps him or her develop action plans. Advocates may be *champions*, using their positions to help protégés gain visibility and exposure, or serve as a *powerful voice*, taking action on one or more of the protégés. These mentors go to bat for their people, let others take responsibility and share credit, and enjoy strong credibility and the respect of their peers.

Tips for One-to-One Mentors

Here are some ideas for achieving success in the mentoring relationship:

■ Get in Gear

Every mentoring relationship needs two elements. First, what are the protégé's goals for the relationship, and what are your own—what do you want to learn or achieve as well? Second, what role does the protégé want you to play? Are you comfortable with that role? Explore these questions at your first, and most important, mentoring meeting—it is the foundation for the relationship.

■ Recognize the Power of Feedback

Mentors provide the gift of feedback. By sharing unbiased perceptions in a kind and honest way, mentors have tremendous impact. Be sure to provide coaching points, and recognize growth and change. Feedback given in the spirit of helpfulness and progress is appreciated and acted on, as long as it is specific and direct, solicits the protégé's input, and points the way to change in the future.

■ Be Yourself

Be straightforward about your own strengths and weaknesses. By doing so, you model how a successful person deals with reality. Offer your own lessons learned, struggles, and successes. Being a mentor does not mean being perfect. Many protégés report that their mentors helped them by disclosing how they had handled difficult aspects of their own personalities.

Conversation Starters for Mentors

At first, it may be difficult for mentors who are new to the role to get started in the relationship-building process. Here are a few suggested ways to get the conversation going:

● Which assignments in the past have provided you with the most challenge? The least challenge? Why?

● Tell me about an accomplishment of which you are particularly proud.

● What are your most important values? Which values are met and not met at work?

● What makes you unique? What about your values, interests, competencies and skills, personal traits, and style?

● What part of your education or work experience has been the most valuable to you over the years?

● What actions have you taken to manage your career? What assistance may I provide?

● What lessons have you learned from your successes and failures?

● What is your biggest challenge in trying to balance your work life and personal life?

■ Be a Question Coach

Mentors do not have all the answers, but they can help their partners self-discover. Use questions to help others reflect on their experience and draw out key learning points. The fast-paced action orientation of the business day does not allow much time for reflection, so promote insight by asking questions such as these: "What did you learn from this situation?" "How might you approach this situation in the future?" "What patterns are you noticing about yourself?"

■ Shine a New Light

Mentors have the luxury of being distant from their protégé's work problems and trials. Use this distance to provide the "big picture" as a context for daily ups and downs. Take the long view, and teach your protégé to do the same.

■ *Let Actions Speak Louder Than Words*

Ask your protégé to accompany you on projects that will expand his or her point of view. Look at your own job for situations that could provide learning experiences. Most people learn by doing, so bring the protégé along. Afterward, spend time debriefing the events and relating them to the protégé's development. Share your thought process regarding how you handled or acted in the situation. In the process, the protégé may have some valuable feedback to contribute.

Group Mentoring

Today's organizations are flat, sparse, team based, and self-directed. They must constantly learn new ways to serve customers and beat competitors. Employees are required to look everywhere, even outward, not just upward. In these environments, structuring one-to-one relationships may be the wrong way to go. Such relationships only strengthen patriarchy, and the notion that someone "else"—at a higher level—must have the answers. Furthermore, copying the one-to-one relationships that work so well in the informal system gives us a different animal when we try to "formalize" them. So, why replicate? Why not invent something totally different?

A group approach, whereby a mentor works with a group of protégés, sets very different dynamics in motion. Protégés are responsible for the group agenda—setting it, requesting what they need for their development, and working together. Peers recognize how much they can learn from one another, and group mentors, when freed from the responsibility of coming up with an agenda, can respond more candidly to real concerns and issues. All participants feel better about the process and learn more as a result.

Mentors look forward to the group meetings. With shared agendas, they learn too. Some bring their own current organization issues to these meetings, to elicit the fresh viewpoints of their protégés who have a different status and tenure in the organization. Many group mentors do not look upon this as the added burden they felt in earlier one-to-one efforts.

The group mentoring concept has a number of pluses. It places a successful organization veteran with a group of four to six less-experienced protégés. As a group they do the following things:

- exchange ideas
- analyze development issues
- receive feedback and guidance
- build team-development skills
- build interpersonal interaction skills
- become a "learning group"

The Learning Group

The mentoring group should be assembled with care. Participant qualifications include not only demonstrated ability to perform, but also interpersonal skills and a willingness to learn from others.

Group composition. The ideal protégé group consists of four to six high-performing employees who are seen as making important contributions to the organization currently and in the future. Typically, their names are on the succession-planning lists. They have expertise the organization does not want to lose—whether the expertise is technical, managerial, or administrative.

In selecting high-performing people for a protégé group, it is important to consider the interaction and the synthesis of the group as a whole. Diversity in position levels, functions, gender, race, and career goals serves several purposes. A diverse protégé group creates a unique opportunity for the members to learn the perspectives of people in different positions and areas of the organization. It also helps create a peer network of contacts. In addition, when people in a group do not think alike, valuable interaction is more likely. But achieving diversity in a small group is usually deliberate. The members must be selected with diversity in mind.

Mentoring Do's and Don'ts

The difference between mentoring success and failure lies in the ability to retain intellectual capital and integrate learning continuously. Here are some do's and don'ts for successfully rolling out a mentoring program:

Do	Don't
Look at employee retention rates, the percentage of senior managers who will reach retirement in the next five to 10 years, and current bench strength; then develop objectives.	Develop a mentoring program because it is popular or because you have read that it works for other organizations.
Set long-term goals that will help make your organization a better place to work, increase productivity, make people more savvy about managing their careers, connect people, increase diversity, and build trust and communication.	Develop a mentoring program without setting goals.
Benchmark the practices of other successful mentoring programs. Consider the limited use of outside consultants to advise and provide feedback to the program developers.	Develop a mentoring program that relies solely on internal resources.
Publicize the program in a variety of forms and forums. Conduct briefings, enlist champions, and create mentoring resource centers.	Expect employees to flock to the program without an aggressive internal marketing plan.
Carefully screen protégés and mentors to assess their level of interest and commitment. Pair participants who can and want to help reach learning goals.	Develop a program that mandates relationships or is limited to certain employees, such as high-potentials.
Provide training and coaching to participants about creating specific and appropriate learning goals, building trust, communicating, and defining roles and responsibilities.	Expect people to know how to mentor and be mentored—even senior-level executives who have had significant mentors in their lives need guidance.
Encourage mentoring partners to meet face-to-face and connect via telephone or email at least once a month. Recommend that they plan at least one event outside of the office during their relationship.	Let more than three or four weeks go by without contact between mentoring partners, or the relationship may falter.
Make continuous improvements to your program based on what you learn along the way. Use surveys and exit interviews to assess effectiveness.	Rest on your laurels.

Adapted from "Play '20 Questions' to Develop a Successful Mentoring Program," by J.G. Lindenberger and L.J. Zachary in Training & Development, *February 1999, © ASTD.*

Organizing Mentoring Groups

When forming mentoring groups, take into consideration the following guidelines:

- Diversity makes a difference. Select groups with diverse racial and gender representation to foster different ways of thinking about careers and success.

- Group mentors do not necessarily need to be the very highest-level executives in the organization. Choose people who are about two levels above the protégés.

- Group mentors should be outside the protégés' functional chain of command.

- Don't forget the protégés' immediate managers. Their roles are crucial too. Plan some meetings that include the protégés' managers, in order to help clarify those roles.

- Give group mentors some ideas for getting dialogue started—questions to ask, concepts to discuss, and experiences to share. But mentors are not in charge of the process. They should encourage the group to set the agenda.

Learning needs. Protégés need many broad opportunities for growth to attain their potential. Development assignments outside the group setting are a vital program component. Such assignments provide an excellent laboratory for a research and development manager who has not had much experience in a business unit. Or, a budget officer who needs field experience in what it takes to manage a profit center. Many protégés have never managed teams, run meetings, negotiated contracts, or planned client presentations. Consequently, they need opportunities to round out their repertoires. Group members must be willing to experiment. Testing new waters should be a stimulating challenge, providing grist for group meetings.

The learning continues when group members come together again to discuss the meaning of their on-the-job experiences. But the key is to make the learning deliberate. Ask group participants to take on specific development assignments that will offer growth opportunities in the workplace. Such assignments fall into the following three categories:

1. Platform. These assignments enable group members to learn new skills in a temporary work assignment or short-term project constructed specifically for them. After the assignment is completed, the "platform" is dismantled.

2. On-the-job. These assignments enable group members to try out new skills and responsibilities while working at their jobs.

3. Dedicated. These assignments enable group members to gain exposure and experience in different areas of the organization. The members are accountable for the work they do while on the assignment, and they must live with the consequences.

Managers and mentors need to continually debrief the learning embedded in these assignments.

Group action. Typically, a protégé group meets with its mentor each month for several hours. The agenda should accommodate any topics or concerns, and anyone should be permitted to initiate a dialogue. The leader and group members share the responsibility for learning every step of the way. In *The Fifth Discipline*, Peter Senge suggests that through an open framework of shared responsibility, groups are able to pursue dialogue rather than discussion. Discussion involves:

- attempting to influence others
- seeking solutions
- determining actions
- making decisions
- gaining consensus
- maintaining hierarchy

Dialog, which is critical to the group model, entails the following elements:

- thinking more freely at deeper levels
- talking about beliefs
- exploring ideas and gaining insight
- adding knowledge
- stretching oneself
- diverging toward varied interests

The Group Mentor

The ideal group mentor is someone concerned with his or her own learning, the learning of others, and the future of the organization. The group mentor should be a senior person on the technical or management track, preferably at the manager or director level. The mentor's experience must be broad (acquired at different organizational levels), and his or her insight should stem from having done the job.

Specifically, a group mentor's track record should include the following things:

- success in his or her field
- contact with a wide variety of people
- vast accumulated experience
- substantial power
- history of fostering employees' development
- control of substantial resources
- broad organizational experience
- success in managing teams
- reputation for competence

It is crucial for group mentors to be sensitive to diversity. They must approach diversity issues with candor and understanding, especially when differences related to gender, race, or ethnicity arise in the learning group. Group mentors also must have, and be able to pass on, appreciation for the paradox of organizational life, which is not necessarily rational, formula driven, or goal oriented. It is full of variables with competing and conflicting demands. This awareness and admission can help people deal with ambiguity just when they thought they had things figured out.

Tips for the Group Mentor

To make a group mentoring process successful, do the following things:

■ Ask the Right Questions
This is often more important than giving the right answers. Opening the conversation so that the group can take charge of the process is essential to success. Do not push them to look for answers to problems and issues, but rather to look for all the various options and consider what they really think about the issues. Preparation is a critical factor in making a group meeting successful. Simply jotting down four or five questions that will get the group thinking can be your best prework.

■ Listen More Than You Talk
Do not feel that just because you are the leader of the group, it is your responsibility to do most of the talking. Once the group has jelled, members should be able to generate dialogue themselves, and you should not need to spend much of your time talking. It may be easy to get into the trap of being seen as the guru or the leader of this small group and always being there to provide insight and advice. Yet for true learning to take place, it is necessary for you to hold back and allow the group to find their own answers and solutions. You are more of a facilitator of this process.

■ Let the Group Create the Agenda
If group members feel that they are responsible for what is being discussed at each session, they will have a much greater sense of ownership in the process. This, in turn, will stimulate attendance because the sessions are of their own making. You can guide and assist members in the process of creating the agenda, but do not let this be your sole responsibility.

■ Do Not Have All the Answers
Many questions and issues will come up in this group for which you do not have the answers, and there is no reason you should assume that you must have answers for every situation. It will be far more interesting for everyone if the group brainstorms answers or ways to obtain answers together, rather than looking to the learning leader. You do not want to create a student-teacher environment where there is a built-in sense of inequality. The

Mentoring in Action

Many organizations have been successful in establishing mentoring programs. Here are just two examples:

Chemical Company

Begun originally by one business unit as an effort to gain vertical parity for its women and minorities and develop leadership capabilities, group mentoring gradually spread throughout a global chemical company. Approximately 30 protégés moved through the year-long program each time it was offered. Protégé groups included six to eight high-potentials from diverse locations. Each group was assigned to a mentor who met with the group once a month for a minimum of two hours.

Mentors were selected by senior management. Protégés were those tapped for succession planning and continuity planning. Groups developed their own agendas and asked their mentor for the kinds of interaction and discussions they felt were important. Managers of the protégés met with mentors at the beginning of the process and kept in touch on an individual basis after that. All groups were brought together four times during the year to join in a learning community and hear from other senior leaders. Groups reported that the interaction with their peers was as important in their learning as the interaction with their mentor.

City Government

When the engineering group of a large California city saw that it needed to develop not only its future leadership but also its middle managers, it launched its own group mentoring effort. Protégés self-selected into the program by completing an application describing their interest in the process and talking about their career goals. Members of the protégé group selected mentors they thought demonstrated a concern for development. All protégés attended a career development class and then used the subsequent meetings with their mentors to discuss various aspects of this learning. Mentors attended a brief training session, followed by get-togethers to learn more about each other's experience in the mentor groups. Groups met for a year, decided their own agendas, and also decided whether or not to continue once the year had ended.

group should feel collegial, recognizing that answers grow out of its collective intelligence, and work together rather than exclusively.

■ *Give Advice Through Storytelling*
Often the best way to give examples is to use the lessons of your own experiences. This will increase your credibility and breathe real life into your suggestions so that the group can identify with you on an intimate level. You can make the dialogue richer by considering articles that the group has read in advance of the meeting. But if the conversation becomes theoretical or didactic rather than personal, it will not have the same learning potential. Encourage the group to tell stories and give individual examples related to their readings and assignments so that they personalize the learning.

■ *Have Something Up Your Sleeve*
Do not assume that just because you are not responsible for the agenda you should not have some ideas for group dialogue ready to interject. For the most part, conversation will come easily as the members of the group get to know one another and the issues with which they are most concerned. If the easy flow of dialogue gets jammed up, however, you will want to be prepared to get things moving again.

The Manager

Because protégé group activities go beyond group meetings, it is crucial that the managers of the protégés be committed to making the group experience a success. Some managers may view learning groups as tugging at the allegiance of their own direct reports, taking them away from job tasks and work groups. To that end, managers should receive orientation or training on the benefits of the mentoring process. An orientation leads managers through several activities that teach them how to help employees think through a development assignment.

Managers explore their roles in facilitating development conversations and providing feedback and coaching. They also link high-performing employees to organizational information and networks, helping them to shape goals and process learning on an ongoing basis. Development-minded managers enrich the process by encouraging members

Mentoring Strategies

When deciding to harness the benefits of informal mentoring activity, organizations should take the time to plan management strategies that guarantee results. These are the issues they should consider:

Business Case for Mentoring

What are your reasons for developing the program? What business impact do you want to achieve? What success indicators will tell you that the mentoring initiative is succeeding? (Consider both quantitative and qualitative measures.)

Organizational Concerns

What is your organizational history with mentoring programs? How have previous mentoring efforts been perceived? How will this history affect how you implement and communicate the current initiative? Do you have organization-wide cooperation and support from top management? Will you request organization-wide input or advice from a limited number of experts and decision makers? Does the organization have positions for the new talent it develops in mentoring programs?

Communication

What will you name this mentoring initiative? How will you present the program? What will you say about its purpose, objectives, goals, mechanics, and benefits? What are the benefits to the organization and the program partici-

pants? How will you publicize the program? What resources do you have (memos, discussions, meetings)? How will you regularly communicate the purpose, progress, and results?

Roles and Responsibilities

Who will be the process owner? Who will be the day-to-day manager? What other resources and roles are needed?

Implementation

How will you select participants for the program? What will the selection criteria entail? How will you present these criteria to interested candidates? Will participation be voluntary or mandatory? Why? How will the program foster and support mentor-protégé relationships? Will it provide opportunities for mentors and protégés to meet and exchange views and opinions so they can assess their own suitability? Or will the program assign mentors to protégés?

Evaluation

How will you evaluate the results and outcomes of the program? When will you make adjustments to ensure accomplishment of program goals? Is the mentoring program the best way to impart skills and knowledge and to develop human resource potential? What are its advantages over other training methods?

to explore new ways of contributing to the job while still monitoring their continued responsibility. Such managers understand their role in terms of day-to-day authority and skill building.

As partners in the process, managers perform the following functions:

- Provide personal feedback to learners on values and mindsets that arise in group meetings.

- Cultivate people's capabilities for their current and future jobs.

- Help craft and debrief challenging learning assignments in partnership with learning leaders and learning group members.

- Endorse experimentation, applaud new approaches, and permit mistakes.

- Ask questions to encourage discussion on what participants are learning and how.

Mentoring Guidelines

Use the following guidelines for organizations setting up programs, mentors working with protégés, and protégés seeking mentoring relationships.

Organizations

☐ Get top management support of the program. Managers should endorse and be willing to fund the program as well as give mentors, protégés, and learning groups time away from the job to meet and form relationships.

☐ Make the mentoring program part of succession planning, or a larger career or management development effort to help employees.

☐ Start with a short program—six months at most—to accomplish specified learning goals without imposing a long-term, burdensome commitment.

☐ Minimize the dropout rate by making the program voluntary and by establishing clear expectations.

☐ Publicly announce the criteria for selecting program participants. Selection criteria should be fair and attainable so as not to invite the resentment of those who feel they have been unfairly excluded.

☐ Select mentors with high levels of expertise, rank, and power. Select protégés who have basic skills and capabilities, but most important, the desire to learn from mentors.

☐ Give mentors and protégés an orientation that addresses the concerns, expectations, and benefits to participants and the organization.

☐ Allow for diverse mentoring styles, providing structure but permitting flexibility. Prevent problems by specifying responsibilities of mentors, protégés, and their immediate supervisors or managers.

☐ Document the progress of the mentoring program using evaluation instruments, meetings, reports, and logs, and use this documentation to recommend maintaining, expanding, or eliminating the program.

Mentors

☐ Expect to invest considerable time and effort. Like any other strong relationship, the one between mentor and protégé or learning group requires a solid foundation of mutual trust and understanding.

☐ Be prepared to initiate the relationship; protégés often are apprehensive about approaching senior advisers.

☐ When the time is right, let protégés or learning groups go. If they are gradually given more independence to act and make decisions on their own, protégés will be prepared mentally for separation.

☐ Have realistic expectations of the relationship. Do not expect lifelong gratitude; some protégés may consider this a business arrangement to which they owe improved job performance only.

Protégés

☐ Look for a mentor among the ranks of middle and senior managers. Observe work and communication styles to select the kind of mentor who would be right for you.

☐ Do not wait to be chosen. Express your interest by asking middle and senior managers for advice.

☐ Know what you want from the relationship, based on your current situation. Think about your competencies, the skills you would like to develop, and your long-range career plans.

☐ Know what is expected of you in the relationship. Besides providing mentors with respect and psychological support, as your relationship develops into one of mutual assistance, you will be returning the mentor's help by acting as his or her agent.

☐ Have realistic expectations. Relationships may not last a lifetime and most cannot fulfill *every* need, because individual mentoring styles vary as do degrees of mentoring.

Virtual Mentoring

Cross-site or distance mentoring often involves alternative communication such as telephone, email, and video conferencing. Whichever methods you choose, you will want to use some strategies to compensate for less face-to-face time. Communication research shows that it takes about 25 to 30 percent more time to build a personal relationship when you build it at a distance. That is because you miss the gestures, body language, and subtle communication of direct contact. The *good* news is that people involved in distance mentoring report high satisfaction because they often develop better listening skills and plan their time more carefully than face-to-face mentoring partners.

Tips for Virtual Mentoring

To make virtual mentoring programs successful, consider the following suggestions:

- Pay special attention to outcomes and objectives. Be clear and precise about the relationship's purpose.

- Exchange photos. If you are not familiar with each other's sites, send some photos of your facilities, work areas, co-workers and anything else that would help your partner get to know you.

- Exchange "artifact" boxes. Package up and send items that will help your partner understand your site's products and your job. Use your imagination.

- Establish a "mentor hotline time." This is periodically designated time dedicated to mentor-learning partner conversation.

- Keep commitments. If you view conversations as "just a telephone call," it is easy to cancel or postpone them. Follow through on plans and activities. Dependability contributes to strong partnerships.

- Exchange information that paints a "whole picture" of each person's work environment on a routine basis. For example, share regular status reports.

- Do not begin by replacing teleconferencing with email. Email is very useful, but early on you will want to hear each other's voices, and the spontaneity associated with live conversation is important.

- Combine communication methods. For example, use email to supply detailed information in conjunction with a planned teleconference or project review. Send a follow-up email after a telephone conversation.

- Listen with a third ear. Be sensitive to tone of voice as a substitute for seeing body language.

- Ask "why" and "how" questions to obtain deeper understanding in conversations.

- Connect at conferences or organization-sponsored events.

- Create a mentoring group at your site for people who have distance mentors. Form a collaborative group to support mutual development.

- Plan field trips to your partner's site when you have opportunities to be near or at his or her location.

Putting It All Together

While the time-honored practice of mentoring has always been with us, today it is a dynamic tool for employee development. Whether you select one-to-one mentoring, learning groups, or virtual mentoring, know that relationship learning forges an environment that reduces learning curves and development cycles.

Yes, there is time investment. And mentoring in any form requires careful preparation and fit with business objectives. The payback comes not just in rewards for the organization, however, but also in personal dividends for the participants. Use the ideas and tools in this *Infoline* to unleash the potential for you and your organization.

References & Resources

Articles

Benabou, Charles, and Raphael Benabou. "Establishing a Formal Mentoring Program for Organizational Success." *National Productivity Review,* Spring 1999, pp. 7-14.

Coley, Denise Bolden. "Mentoring Two by Two." *Training & Development,* July 1996, pp. 46-48.

Gunn, Erik. "Mentoring: The Democratic Version." *Training,* August 1995, pp. 64-67.

Jossi, Frank. "Mentoring in Changing Times." *Training,* August 1997, pp. 50-54.

Kaye, Bev, and B. Jacobson. "Mentoring: A Group Guide." *Training & Development,* April 1995, pp. 22-27.

———. "Mentoring: A New Model for Building Learning Organizations." *OD Practitioner,* volume 28, number 3 (1996), pp. 35-44.

———. "Reframing Mentoring." *Training & Development,* August 1996, pp. 44-47.

Kaye, Bev, and Devon Scheef. "Shared Brain Power." *National Business Employment Weekly,* Nov. 23-29, 1997, pp. 11-12.

Lindenberger, Judith G., and Lois J. Zachary. "Play '20 Questions' to Develop a Successful Mentoring Program." *Training & Development,* February 1999, pp. 12-14.

Messmer, Max. "Mentoring: Building Your Company's Intellectual Capital." *HR Focus,* September 1998, pp. S11-12.

Robinson, S. "Mentoring Has Merit in Formal and Informal Formats." *Training Directors' Forum Newsletter,* May 1990, p. 6.

Scandura, Terri A. "Mentorship and Career Mobility." *Journal of Organizational Behavior,* March 1992, pp. 169-174.

Simmons, Kathy. "Growing a Successful Mentor Program." *Executive Update,* December 1999, pp. 42-45.

Tyler, Kathryn. "Mentoring Programs Link Employees and Experienced Execs." *HRMagazine,* April 1998, pp. 98-103.

Van Collie, Shimon-Craig. "Moving Up through Mentoring." *Workforce,* March 1998, pp. 36-42.

Van Slyke, Erik J., and Bud Van Slyke. "Mentoring: A Results-Oriented Approach." *HR Focus,* February 1998, p. 14.

Books

Bell, Chip R. *Managers As Mentors.* San Francisco: Berrett-Koehler, 1996.

Caruso, Richard E. *Mentoring and the Business Environment.* Brookfield, VT: Dartmouth Publishing, 1992.

Fritts, Patricia J. *The New Managerial Mentor.* Palo Alto, CA: Davies-Black, 1998.

Huang, Chungliang Al, and Jerry Lynch. *Mentoring: The Tao of Giving and Receiving Wisdom.* New York: Harper San Francisco, 1995.

Jeruchim, Joan, and Shapiro Jeruchim. *Women, Mentors and Success.* New York: Fawcett Columbine, 1992.

Kaye, Bev. *Up Is Not the Only Way.* Palo Alto, CA: Davies-Black, 1997.

Kaye, Bev, and B. Bernstein. *MentWorking™—Building Relationships for the 21st Century.* Scranton, PA: Career Systems International, 1998.

Kaye, Bev, and B. Jacobson. *Learning Group Guide.* Scranton, PA: Career Systems International, 1998.

Kaye, Bev, and Sharon Jordan-Evans. *Love 'Em or Lose 'Em.* San Francisco: Berrett-Koehler, 1999.

Kram, Kathy E. *Mentoring Relationships at Work.* Lanham, MD: University Press of America, 1988.

Murray, Margo, and Marna Owen. *Beyond the Myths and Magic of Mentoring.* San Francisco: Jossey-Bass, 1991.

Peddy, Shirley. *The Art of Mentoring.* Houston, Texas: Bullion Books, 1998.

Senge, Peter. *The Fifth Discipline.* New York: Doubleday, 1990.

Wickman, Floyd, and Terri Sjodin. *Mentoring: A Success Guide for Mentors and Protégés.* New York: McGraw Hill, 1997.

Zeldin, Michael, and Sara S. Lee, eds. *Touching the Future.* Los Angeles: Hebrew Union College, 1995.

Zey, Michael G. *The Mentor Connection.* Homewood, IL: Dow Jones-Irwin, 1984.

Infolines

Callahan, Madelyn R., ed. "Alternatives to Lecture." No. 8602.

———. "Design Productive Mentoring Programs." No. 8609 (out of print).

Gibson, Richard. "Selecting a Coach." No. 9812.

Slavenski, Lynn, and Marilyn Buckner. "Succession Planning." No. 9312 (revised 1998).

Younger, Sandra Millers. "Learning Organizations: The Trainer's Role." No. 9306 (revised 1999).

Program Outline/Planner

When you are charged with setting up a mentoring program for your organization, use this outline as a guide. In it you will find the questions you need to address in order to have a successful program.

1. State the objectives of the mentoring program:

_____

_____

2. List the benefits of the mentoring program for each of the following:

a. Organization:

_____

_____

b. Mentor:

_____

_____

c. Protégé:

_____

_____

3. Which mentoring method(s) can help you achieve your goals?

☐ One-to-one mentoring

☐ Group mentoring

☐ Virtual mentoring

4. Who are the key stakeholders in the mentoring initiative, and what will their involvement look like?

Stakeholder	Involvement
_____	_____
_____	_____
_____	_____

5. Consider the following questions concerning the structure of your mentoring program:

a. What criteria will you use to select mentors?

_____

_____

b. What criteria will you use to select protégés?

_____

_____

c. What role do you see for the managers of the protégés?

_____

_____

d. How will you orient mentors, protégés, and managers to the mentoring process and prepare them to be successful?

_____

_____

(continued on the next page)

Job Aid

e. How will you "match" mentors and protégés?

_____

_____

f. What plans do you have to follow up on the process and gather periodic input from all participants?

_____

_____

g. How will you recognize and reward all those involved?

_____

_____

6. How will you present the benefits and selection criteria (bulletin board, employee newsletter, and so forth)?

_____

7. How will the program foster mentor/protégé relationships? List ways of providing support for the participants (program guidelines, weekly meetings, councils, and so forth).

_____

_____

8. List the positions that the organization has for the protégés. Are there enough? Will the organization create new ones?

_____

_____

9. Consider the following when deciding on evaluation factors:

a. How will you evaluate the program? State your method(s)—questionnaires, surveys, interviews, and observations.

_____

_____

b. How did the program affect protégés?

_____

_____

- Attitudinal effect: _____
- Behavioral effect: _____
- Accomplishments: _____

c. How did the program affect mentors?
- Attitudinal effect: _____
- Behavioral effect: _____
- Accomplishments: _____

d. How did the program affect the organization?
- Overall performance rating: _____
- Productivity: _____
- Condition of corporate climate: _____

Interview Skills for Managers

Issue 0206

Interview Skills for Managers

AUTHOR

Eric F. Grosse, Jr., Ed.D
Prince George's Community College
301 Largo Road
Largo, MD 20774
Tel: 301.322.0699
E-mail: grosseef@pg.cc.md.us

Eric Grosse, is Dean of Business, Management and Technology at Prince George's Community College. The *International HR Journal*, the Greater Washington Society of Association Executives, and the USDA Graduate School have published his works. He has presented workshops for ASTD and the American Evaluation Association, among several other industry groups.

Editor
Stephanie Sussan
ssussan@astd.org

Copy Editor
Ann Bruen

Production Design
Kathleen Schaner

Infoline Consultant
Stewart Hickman

Interviewing Skills

Managers who have little or no experience conducting interviews often believe their chances of hiring the best candidate for a job are about as good as throwing double sixes on a single toss of the dice.

There are ways, however, to turn the apparent obstacles into opportunities to hire or promote excellent talent. By carefully selecting and properly using one or more interviewing techniques, any manager can lay the groundwork for a successful new hire or promotion.

Whether determining the suitability of a job applicant for an open position or deciding whom to promote, there are three questions a manager conducting the interview should ask before summoning the first candidate:

1. What will make a candidate suitable for this job?

2. What are the signals that a candidate may be appropriate for this job?

3. What are the signals that a candidate may *not* be appropriate for this job?

By answering the first question ahead of time, it becomes possible to answer the other two during the interview. The key to answering the first question lies in understanding your organization's core culture—what it does and does not value, where it wants to go, and how it plans to get there—and then applying those insights to the interviewing process.

Once you answer the first question, you must choose the type of interview to conduct. There are seven types of interviews:

1. Patterned interviews.

2. Semi-structured interviews.

3. Nondirective interviews.

4. Stress interviews.

5. Group interviews.

6. Board or panel interviews.

7. Behavioral event interviews.

In addition, there is an interview format that should be followed when an employee leaves an organization. If properly handled, exit interviews can provide a wealth of information about what's not working well in an organization.

This issue of *Infoline* explores the art and science of interviewing, with a focus on how different interview formats work. This issue also will discuss interviewing as part of the career advising process, as many promotion decisions arise from career advising. Case studies, interviews, checklists, and a job aid are provided to complete the process of turning a "toss of the dice" into a well-conceived and executed managerial decision.

Step 1: Understand Corporate Culture

The most critical preparation a manager should do prior to conducting an interview is to understand his or her organization's core culture. An organization's core culture is what sets it apart from its competitors. For example, one organization's culture may be very competitive; a mild-mannered person would not fit well into this culture.

Managers who understand their organization's core culture screen résumés to see which candidates reflect similar values—backed up by appropriate job experiences and education—and which candidates do not. For example, if an organization's core culture is to put the customer first at all times, every candidate considered ought to offer evidence, first through a job résumé and then validated through an interview, that customer service is first on their mind. An appropriate interview question to screen for a customer-friendly mindset might involve asking how the candidate would handle an overbearing customer who demands a refund when corporate policy prohibits it.

Jonah's Interview

What can go wrong in an interview? A look at this hypothetical case study will set the stage.

As a recently promoted manager, Jonah Devins was asked to coordinate a series of interviews for three open positions in the HR Department of a high-tech company. One of the open positions was the director's job.

Because he already was overwhelmed by his regular job responsibilities, Jonah decided that he would simply read the job description on the corporate intranet and spend a few minutes before an interview reading the applicant's résumé and job application. Because he knew he had a "gift of gab," he figured that the interviews would be opportunities to have pleasant conversations with interesting people and that he could then provide some general feedback to management, who would make the hiring decision.

Although he had asked the administrative assistant to send the first candidate in after he had finished his lunch, the candidate appeared about midway through his tuna sandwich—just as he had started reading about her work experience.

"Hi, I'm Jonah Devins, Director of Administration. Sorry for the mess here, but I understand you're interviewing for the HR Director's job. You seem awfully young, and do not seem to have any experience with technology, so could you give me a brief summary of your relevant work experience?" he began, as he tried to clean up his half-eaten lunch.

"Well, yes, I am interviewing for that position, and most of my HR experience was obtained during my master's degree program in ISD," replied the candidate. *"Your ad in the newspaper didn't specify I had to have experience in technology."*

"I didn't see that particular ad, but I'm sure the HR Department just overlooked our requirement that candidates for any position in this company must have five years' experience in a high-tech environment and a college degree. By the way, what's ISD?" Jonah asked.

After providing a definition of ISD, the candidate began to discuss her past employment history. She also mentioned that she had recently married and was expecting her first child in about four months.

"So you're pregnant? I guess that means you'll be requesting maternity leave. You should know that most managers in this company don't grant any leave during the first six months of employment," Jonah said.

"Really?" she responded. *"When I called your HR Department, they said they complied fully with the Family and Medical Leave Act."*

"Well, I'm just telling you what the common practice is around here. I guess if you have trouble with how we work here, you might want to reconsider your interest in this position," he said.

"No, I'm sure about my interest. I'm wondering if we could return to the job itself—do you know if the HR Department here has made the shift to performance consulting?" she asked.

"I'm afraid I don't know what performance consulting is," he responded. *"But I think I've received enough information from you. If you don't have any further questions, thanks for your time and we'll contact you shortly,"* he added, hoping to push her out the door so he could prepare for the next candidate—and finish his lunch.

"Well, I'm sorry you're in a hurry. Perhaps we could reschedule this interview when you have a bit more time. I feel I need to understand more about this position, as well as how your company handles maternity leave," she responded.

"I've told you all I know. Again, thanks for applying for the job. We'll be in touch." With that, he rose to shake her hand and escort her out of his cubicle.

Based on the information in the sidebar to the left, *Jonah's Interview*, it seems unlikely Jonah will ever know whether the candidate he interviewed was suited to be the director of his company's HR Department. Besides the questions he asked—and those he failed to ask—he neglected to obtain important information about his own company before calling in the first candidate.

When you adopt a core-culture approach to interviewing, specific job experiences and education requirements (such as those stated by Jonah) become much less important. What is important is education and job experiences that directly address the candidate's *behavior and mindset*—whether these were gained while the candidate was in high school, the military, or in his or her previous job.

Finally, organizations that regularly communicate their core culture see to it that both job fit and culture fit receive attention in the interview process. To do otherwise virtually ensures that managers—such as Jonah—arbitrarily will overemphasize *job fit* (as he did by demanding to see relevant work experiences) and ignore *culture fit* (as he did by failing to learn basic facts about contemporary practices in human resources development prior to conducting the interview).

To ensure that both job fit and culture fit receive attention in the résumé-screening process, look at job competencies. In her book, *Recruiting, Interviewing, Selecting & Orienting New Employees*, Diane Arthur identifies four primary categories of job competencies:

- measurable skills
- knowledge
- behavior
- interpersonal skills.

Screening résumés for the presence of required competencies in each of these four categories will help ensure a good job fit. However, it is only when a manager pays attention to what is found in a fifth category—attitude—that he or she can assess whether the candidate demonstrates a good cultural fit. The *Competency Assessment Worksheet,* found at the back of this issue, provides a tool that can help any manager determine how a candidate measures up in each of the five competency categories.

Step 2: Ask Competency-Based Questions

Completing the *Competency Assessment Worksheet* will document evidence from a candidate's résumé that he or she is, potentially, suited to the job *and* the organization. Such evidence can be tested and validated primarily during the employment interview.

The key to making maximum use of worksheet data is to ask competency-based interview questions that link directly to one of the five categories. A comprehensive example is presented below.

Position: Training and Development Director

Competency Category: Measurable skills

Key Responsibilities & Requirements:

- align the training function with business strategies

- develop core leadership practices that are integrated into all training programs

- ensure that all employees in the organization can develop and manage their own career plan.

Evidence Indicating a Significant Strength

- Three years' experience in running a training function in a start-up technology company

- one year as a member of this corporation's senior management team.

Evidence Indicating a Moderate Strength

- completing a master's degree in Human Resource Development (degree expected in three months).

Evidence Against

- none.

Competency-Based Questions to Ask

- Describe the relationship between the training function in your current job and the corporation's business strategies.

- Tell me about your responsibilities as a member of your company's senior management team. What particular skills do you feel you contribute to the team?

Competency Category: Knowledge

Key Responsibilities & Requirements

- use training to improve employee productivity

- increase the number of employees who meet learning objectives at the end of each learning opportunity

- use training to develop more competent managers

- ● use information on training and development to support business objectives.

Evidence Indicating a Significant Strength

- none.

Evidence Indicating a Moderate Strength

- completing an MS degree in Human Resource Development (degree expected in three months).

Evidence Against

- résumé highlights a number of training courses designed, developed, delivered or managed—but no indication of impact or outcomes.

Competency-Based Questions to Ask

- Tell me about a time when you were able to follow up one of the training classes you have delivered. What did you observe?

- Tell me about a class in which the participants were managers. How did you know they benefited from your course?

Competency Category: Behavior

Key Responsibilities & Requirements

- effectively motivate subordinates

- calmly operate in a turbulent environment

- demonstrate flexibility in dealing with changing business imperatives.

Evidence Indicating a Significant Strength

- three years' experience running a training function in a start-up technology company

- coordinated two corporate-wide downsizings over 18 months.

Evidence Indicating a Moderate Strength

- had to personally relocate her office three times in nine months because of a merger and two subsequent downsizings.

Evidence Against

- appears not to have supervised in any previous position.

Competency-Based Questions to Ask

- Tell me about a time when you needed to motivate others. How did you do it?

- What was your role in the two downsizings you mentioned in your résumé ? What did you learn from those experiences?

Competency Category: Interpersonal Skills

Key Responsibilities & Requirements

- communicate with senior managers

- think strategically

- persuade a largely older workforce to become lifelong learners.

Evidence Indicating a Significant Strength

- membership on senior management team

- served as a literacy volunteer with senior citizens for two years.

Evidence Indicating a Moderate Strength

- none.

Evidence Against

- none.

Competency-Based Questions to Ask

- Tell me about a time when you felt you were particularly successful as a literacy volunteer. What happened?

- Describe an occasion when you had to solve a problem without having any guidelines. What happened? How did you feel about the outcome?

Competency Category: Attitude

Key Responsibilities & Requirements

- strong commitment to customer service

- strong commitment to designing performance measures and using them to improve performance.

Evidence Indicating a Significant Strength

- none.

Evidence Indicating a Moderate Strength

- none.

Evidence Against

- none.

Competency-Based Questions to Ask

- Tell me about a time when you felt you provided superior service to a customer. What was required? How did you react? What was the outcome?

- Describe one experience you've had with performance measurement. What were the specific facts? How did you react? What was the outcome?

Beyond Competency Questions

Competency-based interview questions should compose of no more than 70 percent of any interview. A good rule of thumb for the remaining 30 percent is to address the following areas:

● setting the candidate at ease; opening the interview—no more than 10 percent

● explaining the organization's core culture—up to 10 percent

● answering a candidate's questions—up to 5 percent

● wrapping up the interview and outlining the next steps—no more than 5 percent.

Managers can obtain valuable information when working in each of these other areas. For example, notice the candidate's body language as you begin the interview. Does he or she appear tense (tightened body muscles, inability to make or sustain eye contact, low voice), even after you've attempted to put him or her at ease? Is he or she more eager to talk, ask questions, or listen? Does he or she appear overly eager to impress you?

As you explain your core culture, check for visual cues that he or she understands what you are saying. Does he or she seem to relax and become more involved in the interview as you proceed? Does he or she ask questions? Are the questions fairly basic or do they indicate that the candidate has thought about these topics before?

Be sure to structure the interview so that the candidate knows he or she is permitted—and encouraged—to ask questions. After presenting the corporate core culture, for example, you might say something like: "I know I've gone through our culture, mission, and values pretty quickly. Let me stop for a minute or two and answer any questions you might have."

A candidate who has followed your presentation and indicates through his body language that what you said resonates is more likely to ask questions. If in the interest of time you move too quickly into competency-based questions, however, you are unlikely to leave enough time for the candidate to form and ask questions. By waiting just a few minutes for the questions to develop, you will obtain valuable information about the strength of this candidate's fit with your culture.

When wrapping up the interview and outlining the next steps, be as specific as possible—but do not over-commit. While it is strongly recommended that you answer a candidate's questions about who else is in competition for this job, when a final decision will be made, and what the next steps are, you are unlikely to have all of that information available. Even if you do, there is a fine line between being frank and open about the other candidates and not compromising either their chances or those of the candidate you just finished interviewing.

Objective Vs. Subjective Data

During an interview, you will receive both *objective* and *subjective* data from a candidate. *Objective data* is anything that can be substantiated with factual evidence (such as items contained in a résumé, direct quotes made by the candidate, or clear and unambiguous body language). *Subjective data* is the personal feelings and impressions you receive during the course of conducting the interview. While both types of data will be valuable as you assess the candidates, both require caution when they are used to determine a candidate's suitability for a job.

Objective data obtained through the interview will need to be matched against information found in the *Competency Assessment Worksheet*. In general, you will be looking to see if the interview supports what the résumé states, contradicts the résumé, or offers entirely new information. Candidates whose objective, verified data indicates a close match with the position's key responsibilities and requirements probably will clear the first hurdle on the way to a job offer. Although verification can and should be sought between résumé data and interview data, it is important to remember that checking references is an important part of establishing verification as well.

While it is tempting to use only objective data to quantify each candidate's match-up against the job fit and culture fit, it is important to understand what taking this approach loses. Numerical ratings and subsequent rankings tend to rely on the use of terms such as *outstanding*, *poor*, or *above average*. Unless elaborate steps have been taken before the interview to obtain agreement as to exactly what these terms mean, it is highly unlikely any two people will agree how to apply them to a pool of equally qualified candidates. In addition, if you conduct interviews over several days, your understanding of what the terms mean may change as you move farther away from that first candidate.

Using *subjective* data to evaluate candidates can be quite valuable, but should be approached with caution. All of us form impressions of people, and sometimes, these impressions are right on target. It certainly helps if you have a great deal of experience and know yourself well. But, as we saw in the case of Jonah Devins, subjective data in the hands of an inexperienced manager can lead to disaster. So the question becomes: How can valuable subjective data be recorded and appropriately used to evaluate job candidates? Here are some guidelines:

Take notes. Be sure to let the candidate know you are taking notes and that you may ask him or her to repeat a statement. Most candidates appreciate the fact that you are taking notes (it shows their comments are important) and that you notified them ahead of time. Avoid using a tape or video recorder, as these usually are too intrusive to the interview process.

Recognize and record any personal biases. You may, for example, firmly believe that only an internal candidate is suitable for this job due to its complexity. If so, record that impression in your interview write-up, as well as your reasons for holding that view.

Record unusual behaviors objectively. It is possible that a candidate exhibiting less than optimal behaviors (such as interrupting you, avoiding eye contact, or constantly shifting in a chair) is merely nervous. Applying a judgment phrase such as "candidate acted like a real know-it-all" will not fully capture the potential meaning of a behavior.

Don't respond if baited. Occasionally, a candidate will say or do something unusual just to see how you react. While this can be annoying and may signal a less than optimal candidate, now is not the time to make that judgment. Simply record the incident and your reaction.

Avoid recording unsubstantiated opinions. While you definitely will need to render your opinion as to whether a candidate should receive a job offer, it is imperative that only substantiated data (whether objective or subjective) be used. The best opportunity to voice that opinion is in a summarizing statement written as the last piece of an interview write-up, in which you weigh all data and evidence—providing specific examples as you go along—and then render your opinion.

How to Recognize Inappropriate Candidates

While it certainly is desirable that one candidate easily surface from a group of well-qualified individuals, reality usually is quite different. Knowing why various candidates are *not* suited for a job is just as important as knowing why one candidate was offered the position. Here are some ways to document how candidates failed to match up:

Record any interview statements that clearly indicate unsuitability. If the position requires significant availability after normal work hours and the candidate says he cannot work beyond an eight-hour day, note that in the interview write-up.

Record any instances where résumé evidence is directly contradicted during the interview. Even if the candidate catches him or herself and reverses again, you should be suspicious of such behavior and note it objectively.

When in doubt, ask the candidate. If the position requires regular lifting of boxes of course manuals, do not assume a diminutive female is incapable of such work. The proper procedure is to first state the job requirement and then ask the candidate if he or she would have any problem meeting it. Record his or her answer and move on with the interview.

Provide realistic job previews. Be familiar enough with the position (or know someone who is) to offer each candidate an accurate and reasonably complete picture of what this job looks like on a day-to-day basis. Many candidates, upon hearing exactly what a job entails, will tell you it is not what they had in mind. Simply record that statement and move on.

Interviewing Promotion Candidates

Interviewing candidates for a job promotion shares certain similarities with the process for interviewing candidates for other open positions—and has certain differences.

Similarities

As in interviewing other candidates, the interview process for a job promotion should begin with a completed *Competency Assessment Worksheet*. While it is always important that there is an accurate position description, these are even more critical when interviewing a candidate for a job promotion. There is nothing more embarrassing to a manager interviewing a candidate for a promotion only to learn later that the position description he or she used was so old that it was, in effect, for an entirely different job.

There is another value in starting with a completed *Competency Assessment Worksheet*. Although a manager may claim to know which employee is best suited for a promotion, many organizations post the open position throughout the workforce. Thus, the hiring manager will, in all likelihood, be able to interview those whom he or she anticipates interviewing—but the manager also must be prepared to interview other, perhaps equally qualified candidates. Completed *Competency Assessment Worksheets* keep the playing field level—and help keep the organization (and the manager) from having to appear in court to explain their hiring decision.

Differences

Perhaps the single most important difference coming into play when interviewing a candidate for a job promotion is when the promotion involves entry into management. Generally, when interviewing internal candidates for entry-level management positions, it is assumed that superior technical skills and personal ambition propelled the candidacy. Thus, such a candidate already has achieved, in all likelihood, a positive reputation in the organization.

When interviewing such an individual, it is important to balance recognition of past personal achievement—however valuable—with the known requirements of the new job. Moving into management may not necessarily be the best career choice for a superior technical performer—but losing such an individual from continued employment in the organization is an even less desirable outcome.

Know When a Candidate Should Be Promoted

Interviewing a candidate for what is clearly a "step up" position requires skills in several areas. The hiring decision made here can have a major impact on the organization, the candidate, and even the interviewer herself.

For internal candidates, the interview for a "step up" position ought to be the result of career advising that has occurred over the course of an individual's tenure with the organization. Even though an interviewer may not have been responsible for an internal candidate's career advising, questions asked during the interview should probe the nature and extent of whatever career advising has occurred.

The sidebar *Career Advising*, to the right, describes the relationship between the various steps of the career-advising process, competency categories, and possible interview questions.

While one-on-one formal interviews involving a hiring manager and a job candidate often are preferred by both parties, there are other interview formats that offer opportunities to collect better, more holistic data on job candidates. Each of the major interview types is profiled below.

Career Advising

Managers routinely conduct interviews for internal candidates interested in moving into management. The relationship of these interviews to an organization's established career-advising process can be confusing, as the agendas for the candidate and the interviewing manager are both overlapping and different.

A basic assumption is that all aspects of a person's life are interrelated; that is, the career, attitudes, and competencies have an impact on a person's philosophy of life, interpersonal relationships, self-concept, and social development. The overarching goal of career advising is the development of employees so that they are able to function intellectually, personally, socially, and professionally—within an organization where they have already enjoyed a level of success.

While the manager interviewing an internal candidate will play a role in the career advising process, that is not his or her ultimate objective. The hiring manager's objective is to find the best candidate for the job opening. While important career advice may be dispensed along the way, the manager must take care not to mislead the candidate into thinking that this position is necessarily the next step on his or her career ladder.

The key to avoiding this situation is to use competency-based interview questions that directly link a candidate's previous career advising experience to the requirements of the open job.

Career Advising Step	Purpose	Related Competency Category	Suggested Interview Question
First Interview	• establish a climate in which other interviews can continue	• none	• None—this is an area where it is possible to mislead the candidate.
	• determine candidate's interest in the position	• attitude	• "Based on your knowledge of our organizational culture, how does this position fit?"
	• lay out a plan for counseling and related activities, including diagnostic tests.	• none	• "What would you do to fix [or improve] that fit, if you held the job?"
Second Interview	• interpret diagnostic test results.	• knowledge • tangible skills	• "I see you recently completed one [or several] diagnostic tests. What do the test results tell you about how you might acquire the knowledge and skills required of a person who occupies this position?"
Third Interview	• provide occupational knowledge.	• knowledge	• "Based on what you have heard about this position, what additional information do you need to understand what is required of someone who holds the job?"

Types of Interviews

There are several types of interview formats. Each format has a distinct purpose and should be used in the appropriate situation. The following section will outline each interview format and explain the pros and cons of each.

Patterned Interviews

As an interview format, patterned interviews usually are considered the most reliable method of gathering information. Patterned interviews ask each candidate a carefully crafted set of identical questions in the same way and in the same order. Generally, ad hoc follow-up questions are discouraged, because information gathered in this manner is thought to prejudice the interviewer's opinion of the candidate. Furthermore, candidates are discouraged from volunteering information outside the scope of the patterned interview and such information, if received, often is eliminated from the candidate's interview file.

Strengths: Because of a rigid adherence to form and structure, candidate qualifications gathered through patterned interviews easily can be compared because the questions asked of all candidates are identical.

Weaknesses: It is extremely difficult to ensure identical use of a patterned interview across a large pool of candidates—and it is virtually impossible to avoid asking follow-up questions, if only to seek clarification of vague statements. There also is the possibility that important, even crucial, information about a candidate can be lost because of the rigidity of the patterned interview.

Semi-Structured Interviews

Semi-structured interviews—like the interview conducted by Jonah Devins—rely on a loose script of open-ended questions. During semi-structured interviews, the interviewer is able to improvise as the situation dictates. These types of interviews often are used for interviewing applicants when the interviewer has not had adequate time or opportunity to prepare or is only somewhat knowledgeable about the job.

Strengths: When used by a capable manager who is reasonably knowledgeable about the open position, semi-structured interviews offer perhaps the best opportunity for a candidate to convince the interviewer of his or her suitability for the position. As such, there is little opportunity for the dissatisfied job seeker to complain that the format did not permit him or her to showcase his or her abilities to the fullest extent.

This format is particularly well-suited for competency-based interview questions that can be individually tailored to each candidate's experiences.

Weaknesses: As Jonah Devins demonstrated, a semi-structured interview conducted by a neophyte manager usually is a recipe for disaster. Relying on a "gift of gab" to fill in the blank spaces that arise during most interviews can lead to vague questions that are only partly answered, leaving both the interviewer and interviewee confused and disappointed. While semi-structured interviews are the typical format in most organizations, their use should be carefully monitored and, if possible, training should be provided regularly to all managers as to when, how, and under what circumstances semi-structured interviews can be used most effectively.

Nondirective Interviews

Because they have no set format, structure, or questions, nondirective interviews generally are inappropriate for gathering information to make a selection decision. They can, however, prove to be quite useful for career counseling purposes—particularly when it has been made clear to the candidate that further consideration for the position is not an option.

Strengths: Nondirective interviews offer a powerful opportunity for a manager to provide focused career counseling to a job candidate who may approach the job's qualifications, but fall short in one or more competency categories. When such a situation presents itself, a competent and caring manager can—with the right job candidate—provide a meaningful interview experience and strengthen the organization's reputation.

Weaknesses: Fortunately, most managers intuitively sense that having no format or questions available to conduct a job interview is a sure path to disaster. Those who do find themselves in such a situation invariably will sketch a few questions and quickly turn a nondirective interview into a semi-structured interview. Once again, however, a more experienced manager is better able to make this transition than a new manager is.

Stress Interviews

Stress interviews are designed to see whether candidates can think on their feet in uncomfortable situations. It is an unusual interview format, and as such, it is rarely appropriate for obtaining the highest quality information on which to base selection decisions.

There are two types of stress interviews: *staged* and *realistic job previews*. During staged interviews the interviewer believes that by putting candidates through some amount of pain and discomfort, their true behaviors, skills, and abilities will be revealed. During realistic job preview interviews, the interviewer simulates the amount and kind of stress encountered on the job. While it is difficult to imagine a situation where staged stress interviews are appropriate, it is relatively easy to imagine situations where stress-filled realistic job previews would be highly desirable. Examples include interviews for positions in law enforcement, the emergency medicine field, and fire fighters.

Strengths: Recognizing that stress interviews are inappropriate for most selection situations—and tend only to show off an insecure interviewer's position of authority—there are few occasions when this interview type would yield valuable information about a candidate. When stress-filled realistic job previews are required, make sure to provide a well-designed stress interview.

Weaknesses: Under most circumstances, stress interviews should be avoided because they do nothing to enhance the reputation of the organization authorizing them.

Group Interviews

Group interviews are designed to allow several interviewers to obtain information about one individual simultaneously, rather than having separate interviews that require more time. The main objective is to obtain a diversity of views about a candidate and have a broader range of questions asked than would be possible with one interviewer.

The sidebar *Group Interviews* offers guidance on effectively planning, conducting, and using the group interview process.

Strengths: The diversity of views presented by group members can be extremely effective in showcasing candidates who, on paper, don't appear to be fully qualified—or might even appear overqualified. Another strength could be that while one person is conducting the interview and asking questions, another could be taking notes.

Weaknesses: A group interview process generally takes far longer than one-on-one interviewing. If time is at a premium, the position is relatively low on the job ladder, or the candidate pool is large, it is unlikely that group interviews will be a wise choice. In addition, if the group is responsible for making the selection, time must be taken to ensure that consensus is reached and disagreements are resolved.

Board or Panel Interviews

Board or panel interviews are similar to group interviews, except that a board may serve as the hiring authority and exercise supervision over the candidate once he or she has been hired. A panel is a group of individuals who have been specifically selected for a group interview assignment, rather than convened ad hoc by an overworked interviewer.

Strengths: In addition to the strengths listed for the group interview, the candidate will have the opportunity to see who his or her bosses will be.

Weaknesses: The weaknesses are identical to those listed for the group interview. Occasionally, when interview panels are used, their members may feel less than enthusiastic about participating in a process that does not seem to directly affect them. Panel member defections should therefore be expected and managed accordingly.

Behavioral Event Interviews

Behavioral event interviews (or behavioral interviews, as they also are called) have been around for about 30 years and, with a growing need faced by most organizations to hire from a diverse talent

Group Interviews

To be used effectively, group interviews require advanced planning and careful thought. The following should help you plan, conduct, and use the group interview process in an effective manner.

Choosing the Interview Group

Be sure to include at least five individuals from the following group:

☐ HR

☐ department manager

☐ candidate's immediate supervisor

☐ member of candidate's peer or work group

☐ a subordinate (if the open position is in management)

☐ a line manager

☐ an administrative support person

☐ another staff manager

Arranging Logistics

Everything is important. Be particularly aware of the following:

● Arrange for an appropriately sized room. Make sure all interviewers and the candidate can move to their chairs easily and without disrupting one another.

● Create a comfortable room layout. Determine where the candidate will be most comfortable and, at the same time, be clearly seen by all group members.

● Arrange for comfortable chairs. This is especially important if the group will be in session for several hours (or days) and interviewing numerous candidates.

● Make sure there are pads and pencils at each place.

● Arrange for water and glasses.

● See to it that there is easy access to bathrooms.

● Make all necessary meal arrangements. If the candidate has been told to expect a meal, be sure to check with both the candidate and the members of the group for special dietary needs.

Tips for Conducting the Group Interview

As with any other training activity, group interviews must be *managed* and *facilitated*. The manager doesn't necessarily need to be a group member, as long as that person understands that he or she is responsible for all logistics.

The group facilitator must be a member of the group. Whether that person is responsible for providing interview feedback is a question that must be answered prior to the group convening. Generally, the facilitator is responsible for the following:

● introducing the candidate

● summarizing the candidate's credentials

● having each group member introduce him or herself to the candidate

● laying out the agenda for the interview

● closing the interview and thanking the candidate for his or her participation.

Collecting and Summarizing Interview Data

It is vital that a data collection format be agreed on before interviewing the first candidate. While there are no right or wrong ways to do this, several issues need to be considered:

● How many of the interview questions will be *open-ended* and, thus, rely upon the note-taking abilities of the interviewer?

● How many of the interview questions will be *closed-ended* and require a check-off, yes/no response, or choosing a number?

● How will differences between interviewers be resolved (or will they be left unresolved)?

● Will interviewers reconvene after all candidates have been interviewed and review their composite data and make recommendations?

● Will the recommendations of the group be binding or advisory only?

pool, have gained in popularity since the mid-1990s. The concept behind behavioral interviews, is that your past performance is the best predictor of future performance. Interviewers (individuals, panels, boards, or groups) ask for specific examples of specific events (including events with both positive and negative outcomes) in order to draw a conclusion as to how a candidate would perform in a similar situation in their organization. The questions asked tend to be more probing, and well-trained interviewers generally don't permit candidates to answer with vague, canned, or hypothetical answers.

Conducting a behavioral event interview requires substantially more homework on the part of interviewers. Not only must the *Competency Assessment Worksheet* be completed, interviewers must gain an understanding of what separates less-than-effective performance from exemplary performance. Generally, this is done by asking exemplary employees within the organization for specific examples of how they accomplish key tasks, or by asking their supervisors.

Strengths: Many experts believe that behavioral interviews offer the best opportunity for candidates to showcase their accomplishments and for interviewers to hire the best individual for the job. By faithfully adhering to the principles of the behavioral interviewing process for all candidates, only meaningful, highly focused interview questions will form the basis of the hiring decision.

Weaknesses: In some instances, eliciting specific behavioral events from top performers requires too many resources to make the process worthwhile. In other situations, the pace of change in an organization makes past success of limited relevance to defining current or future success factors—or the organization may simply be looking to move in an entirely different direction. When such circumstances exist, behavioral interviewing may be too cumbersome or inappropriate for the hiring situation at hand.

Exit Interviews

Perhaps the least discussed kind of interviewing occurs when an individual leaves an organization—either voluntarily or by request. Known as *exit interviews*, discussions with an employee on his or her way out can provide valuable information about the health and well being of an organization, as well as offer the employee an opportunity to vent about how he or she has been treated.

Although generally handled by an organization's HR Department, data obtained from an exit interview needs to be provided to the responsible unit(s) where the employee worked.

Strengths: Exit interviews often are viewed as the first step toward uncovering issues of unfair treatment of employees. Often, employees who feel they have been treated improperly will signal their intent to pursue legal action during an exit interview; on the organization's side, an astute interviewer occasionally can defuse such a situation by actively listening to the employee's charges and providing the organization's response.

Weaknesses: Because of the occasional unpleasantness associated with interviewing someone who is being asked to leave an organization, many exit interviews are nothing more than very brief one-way conversations. In such situations, the opportunity to gain information about what is not working well in the organization is lost.

Reliability and Validity of Interviews

Interview *validity* refers to whether interview questions map to specific competencies listed on the *Competency Assessment Worksheet*. To ensure maximum validity, there needs to be a one-to-one correspondence between interview questions asked and underlying competency.

To ensure interviewer *reliability*, all interviewers need to use interview questions that are designed this way. It is only when this mapping has been documented and used by all interviewers for a particular candidate can it be said that the interview data for that candidate is reliable and valid, or consistent with the competencies deemed essential for the job.

According to David Cherrington in *The Management of Human Resources* Instructor's Manual, the "unreliability of employment interviews is created by several factors that reduce the consistency of the information obtained from them. . . . The mood of the interviewer may be different at different interviews, the questions asked in the interview may differ, the mood of the interviewee may be different, the topics discussed will change each time—in short, because each interpersonal interaction is unique and can never be exactly duplicated." Cherrington suggests the following steps for increasing the reliability of interviews:

- Ask systematic and well-structured questions and avoid vague, open-ended questions that invite the candidate to provide hypothetical answers.

- Make sure that permissible responses can be clearly defined and properly categorized during the candidate assessment process that will occur later on.

- To the extent possible, consider developing a rating scale that can be used to sort and rank responses against "best in class" (this is made considerably easier if behavioral interviewing techniques have been used).

Reliability is a necessary but not sufficient condition for developing high-quality interview questions. Establishing reliability ensures consistency; establishing interview *validity* ensures that the questions asked map to the appropriate competencies.

There are four types of validity that can be used to rate the quality of proposed interview questions. They are described below.

1. Face validity. An interview question has high face validity if it appears to a candidate to measure what it is supposed to measure. For example, Joshua Devins' request that the candidate for the HRD Director's job provide a "brief summary of his or her relevant work experience" doesn't have high face validity because it is too vague. An improved question would have focused on one of the specific skills required by the HRD Director.

2. Content validity. An interview question possesses content validity when a group of recognized content experts or subject matter experts has verified that the question assesses an appropriate competency for the particular job or position. Content validity must be established before the interview begins; it is too late to attempt to establish it during the interview itself.

3. Concurrent validity. Concurrent validity refers to the ability of an interview question to correctly classify qualified and unqualified job candidates. Establishing concurrent validity is the "holy grail" of interviewing, and as such, much is at stake when attempting to design questions that have concurrent validity. Perhaps the best approach is to rely on the research involved in separating exemplary from non-exemplary performers prior to doing behavioral interviewing.

4. Predictive validity. Predictive validity in interviewing refers to the ability of specific questions to predict future success on the job. The only sure way to establish predictive validity is to interview the hired candidate and ask him or her which interview questions provided the most accurate gauge of what the job actually involves.

How to Chose the Type of Validity

While it is critical to establish the validity of all interview questions, it is not practical to design interview questions to reach all four types of validity. Generally speaking, the following guidelines should work in most situations:

1. Because it is relatively easy to establish, cost effective, and offers a solid defense in case of adverse legal action, establishing each question's *face validity* should be a requirement for all interviewing.

2. Establishing concurrent or predictive validity, while certainly desirable, can be time-consuming. Consequently, most organizations rely on *content validity*, believing that questions with high content validity offer the highest value for the time and cost involved in developing them.

Do Your Homework

Ultimately, the key to a successful interview process is for the manager to do his or her homework. This entails having a strong understanding of the corporate culture, completing the *Competency Assessment Worksheet,* and determining the most appropriate interview method for your needs. Lastly, the manager needs to find a keen balance between job fit and culture fit. Once those tasks are successfully completed, the manager is sure to find the best candidate for the job.

References & Resources

Books

Arthur, Diane. *Recruiting, Interviewing, Selecting & Orienting New Employees*. Third edition. New York: AMACOM, 1998.

Cherrington, David J. *The Management of Human Resources* (Instructor's Manual). Fourth edition. Englewood Cliffs, NJ: Prentice Hall, 1995.

Harris, Jim, and Joan Brannick. *Finding & Keeping Great Employees*. New York: AMACOM, 1999.

Pace, Wayne R., Philip C. Smith, and Gordon E. Mills (eds.). *Human Resource Development: The Field*. Englewood Cliffs, NJ: Prentice Hall, 1991.

Shrock, Sharon A., and William C.C. Coscarelli. *Criterion-Referenced Test Development*. Washington DC: International Society for Performance Improvement, 1996.

Articles

Linkage, Inc. "Building Competency-Based Selection, Performance and Learning Systems" Participant guide for the *Building Competency-Based Selection, Performance and Learning Systems* workshop. Contact Linkage Educational Resources at 617.862.3157 for additional information.

Saphiere, Dianne Hofner. "Online Cross-Cultural Collaboration." *Training & Development*, October 2000, pp. 71-72.

Job Aid

Competency Assessment Worksheet

This worksheet should be completed after reviewing a job candidate's résumé. It will serve as a reference for asking interview questions and as a guide for assessing candidates against our criteria in each competency category.

CANDIDATE: _____   INTERVIEWER: _____

DATE: _____   INTERVIEW LOCATION: _____

POSITION: _____

POSITION DESCRIPTION AVAILABLE: ☐ yes   LAST UPDATED: _____
☐ no

Competency Category	Key Responsibilities & Requirements	Evidence Indicating a Significant Strength	Evidence Indicating a Moderate Strength	Evidence Against
Tangible or measurable skills				
Knowledge				
Behavior				
Interpersonal skills				
Attitude				

Motivating Employees

Issue 0510

Motivating Employees

AUTHOR

Sharlyn J. Lauby
ITM Group, Inc.
1530 Seabay Road
Fort Lauderdale, FL 33326
Tel: 954.217.2165
Email: slauby@itmgroupinc.com

Sharlyn J. Lauby is president of Internal Talent Management. Prior to starting ITM, Lauby held several senior-level human resources positions in the hospitality, transportation, entertainment, and business services industries. She has designed and implemented successful programs for employee retention, customer satisfaction, and corporate communications.

Lauby, a recognized Senior Professional in Human Resources (SPHR), is a recipient of the Women's Circle of Excellence Award presented by the Greater Fort Lauderdale Chamber of Commerce. She also was named one of the "2004 Heavy Hitters in Human Resources" as compiled by the *South Florida Business Journal*.

Managing Editor
Tora Estep
testep@astd.org

Editor
Sabrina E. Hicks

Copy Editor
Ann Bruen

Editorial Consultant
Beverly Kaye

Production Design
Kathleen Schaner

Manager, Acquisitions and Development, ASTD Press
Mark Morrow

Employee Motivation

Lee Iacocca once said, "When I must criticize somebody, I do it orally; when I praise somebody, I put it in writing."

That's one method to motivate employees, but different needs motivate different people. Some employees crave power, others want money. Some employees desire constant praise, others want to be left alone. It's crucial for managers to figure out what motivates each employee.

Motivation is defined as a psychological force that determines the following:

- The direction of a person's behavior: This refers to the many possible behaviors in which an employee could engage. For example, an employee who knows what to do to satisfy a customer's needs should not have to ask for his or her manager's permission to act.

- A person's level of effort: Effort refers to how hard people work. Some employees exert a high level of effort to provide superior customer service.

- A person's level of persistence in the face of obstacles: Persistence refers to whether, when faced with roadblocks and obstacles, people keep trying or give up. If an employee did not have a customer's order in stock, for example, would he or she give up and apologize to the customer, or would the employee persist and locate the order at another store?

This issue starts where *Infoline* No. 259108, "How to Motivate Employees," starts: with a primer on motivational theories that have been updated and expanded. Based on these theories, this *Infoline* then presents ways to integrate motivation into the workplace, strategies to motivate employees, and common mistakes managers make.

Motivational Theories

Several motivational theories exist that can provide insight into how best to motivate employees, whether you are a manager or a trainer of managers. View the following theories as complementary, each focusing on a different aspect of motivation. By considering all of the theories together, you garner a valuable understanding of the intricacies associated with motivating a workforce.

Maslow's Hierarchy of Needs

Psychologist Abraham Maslow proposed that all people seek to satisfy five basic kinds of needs:

- physiological
- safety
- belongingness
- esteem
- self-actualization.

Those needs constitute a hierarchy of needs, with the most basic or compelling needs at the bottom (see the sidebar *Maslow's Hierarchy of Needs* for an illustration and ideas on how to use the hierarchy to motivate employees). Maslow argued that a person must have his or her lowest-level needs met before he or she would strive to satisfy needs higher in the hierarchy. Once a need is satisfied, it ceases to operate as a source of motivation. The lowest level of unmet needs in the hierarchy is the prime motivator of behavior. If or when that level is satisfied, the needs at the next highest levels in the hierarchy motivate behavior.

Herzberg's Motivation-Hygiene Theory

Researcher Frederick Herzberg proposed a theory that focuses on two factors:

1. Outcomes that can lead to high levels of motivation and job satisfaction.

2. Outcomes that can prevent people from being dissatisfied.

According to Herzberg's Motivation-Hygiene Theory, people have two sets of needs: motivation needs and hygiene needs.

■ *Hygiene Needs*
Associated with the physical and psychological context in which work is performed, hygiene needs refer to extrinsically motivated behaviors performed to acquire material or social rewards, or to avoid punishment. The consequences of an extrinsically motivated behavior are the source of the employee's motivation, not the behavior itself. Hygiene needs are satisfied by pleasant and comfortable working conditions, pay, job security, good relationships with co-workers, and effective supervision.

Maslow's Hierarchy of Needs

Psychologist Abraham Maslow proposed the idea that everyone seeks to satisfy five basic kinds of needs: physiological, safety, belongingness, esteem, and self-actualization. The most elemental of an individual's needs are physiological: food, drink, shelter, and sexual satisfaction. The second step up the hierarchy is the need for safety, for shelter, and for protection from physical and emotional harm. The third level of needs are social ones—for love and a sense of belonging from parents, siblings, or extended families. The next level of need is for esteem. Needs here are both internal (for example, self-respect and autonomy) and external (for example, status and attention). Finally, an individual works to gain self-actualization, which is a "knowing" about life and its meaning for the individual and a sense that she or he fits into the paradigm. Ways that managers can satisfy these employee needs follow:

■ *Physiological*
Provide a compensation system that enables an employee to buy food and clothing and to have adequate housing.

■ *Safety*
Provide job security, adequate health benefits, and safe working conditions.

■ *Belongingness*
Promote good interpersonal relations and organize social functions, such as company picnics and holiday parties.

■ *Esteem*
Grant promotions and recognize accomplishments.

■ *Self-Actualization*
Give employees the opportunity to use their skills and abilities to the fullest extent possible.

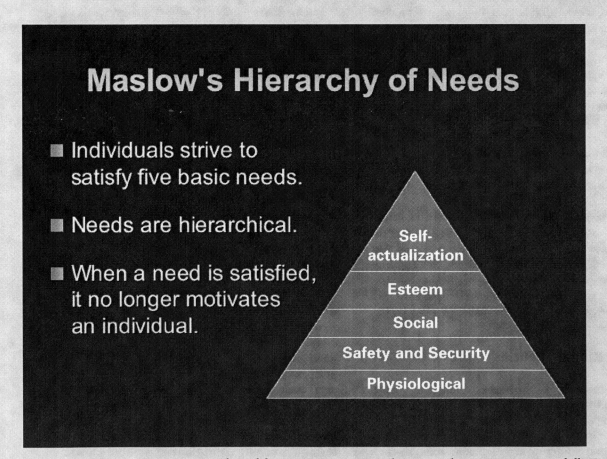

Adapted from Maureen Orey and Jenni Prisk's Communication Skills Training.

Herzberg's theory contends that when hygiene needs are not met, workers will be dissatisfied. However, satisfying hygiene needs alone does not lead to highly motivated employees or high levels of job satisfaction within a workforce. For motivation and job satisfaction to be high, an employer must meet motivation needs.

■ *Motivation Needs*

Motivation needs are related to the work itself and how challenging that work is. Outcomes such as interesting work, autonomy, responsibility, growth and development on the job, and a sense of accomplishment and achievement help to satisfy motivation needs. Intrinsically motivated behavior, therefore, is behavior that the employee performs for its own sake; the source of motivation is actually performing the work. Some ways to motivate intrinsically are to provide opportunities for growth and achievement and to recognize people's achievements.

You can motivate people in three manners: intrinsically, extrinsically, or both. It depends on a variety of factors:

- personal characteristics such as personalities, abilities, values, attitudes, and needs

- the nature, or characteristics, of the job

- the nature of the organization—its structure, culture, control systems, human resources, and reward systems.

McClelland's Theory

Psychologist David McClelland extensively researched the following needs:

- achievement—the extent to which an individual has a stong desire to perform challenging tasks well and to meet personal standards for excellence

- affiliation—the extent to which an individual is concerned with establishing and maintaining good interpersonal relations, being liked, and having the people around him or her get along with each other

- power—the extent to which an individual desires to control or influence others.

To some degree, you'll notice the presence of each of those needs in all employees; yet, in the workplace, the level of importance of each need depends upon the position occupied by an employee:

- A high need for achievement and power is an asset in frontline and middle management.

- A senior-level manager needs to possess a strong desire for power.

- A high need for affiliation, contrarily, may not be desirable in senior-level managers. That need might lead them to try too hard to be liked by their employees, rather than doing all they can to ensure that employees' performance is as high as it can and should be.

McGregor's Theory X and Theory Y

In his 1960 management book, *The Human Side of Enterprise,* Douglas McGregor influenced the history of organizational management when he proposed the two motivational theories by which managers perceive employee motivation. He referred to those opposing motivational theories as Theory X and Theory Y. Each theory assumes that management's role is to organize resources—including people—to best benefit the company. However, beyond that commonality, the theories are quite dissimilar.

■ *Theory X*

A manager who ascribes to Theory X assumes the following:

- Work is inherently distasteful to most people, and they will attempt to avoid work whenever possible.

- Most people are not ambitious, have little desire for responsibility, and resist change.

- Most people are self-centered and prefer to be directed. They must be closely controlled and often coerced to achieve organizational objectives.

- Most people are gullible and unintelligent and have little aptitude for solving organizational problems.

Here, motivation occurs only at the physiological and security levels of Maslow's hierarchy. Theory X assumes that the primary source of most employee motivation is monetary, with security a strong second.

Under Theory X, management approaches to motivation range from hard to soft. The hard approach relies on coercion, implicit threats, micromanagement, and tight controls—essentially an environment of command and control. The soft approach, however, is to be permissive and seek harmony in the hope that employees, in return, will cooperate when asked. However, neither of those extremes is optimal. The hard approach results in hostility, low output, and extreme employee demands; the soft approach results in a workforce with an increasing desire for greater reward in exchange for diminishing work output.

You might think that the optimal approach to management would lie somewhere between those extremes. McGregor, however, asserts that Theory X management styles hinder the satisfaction of higher-level needs. The only way that employees can attempt to satisfy higher-level needs at work is to seek more compensation; thus, they focus on monetary rewards. Consequently, in a Theory X environment, people use work to satisfy their lower needs; they seek to satisfy their higher needs during their leisure time.

McGregor suggests that a command-and-control environment isn't effective because it relies on lower-level needs for motivation. In modern society, those needs are mostly satisfied, so they no longer act as motivators. You would expect employees in such an environment to dislike their work, avoid responsibility, have no interest in organizational goals, resist change, and so forth, thus creating a self-fulfilling prophecy. From that reasoning, McGregor proposed an alternative: Theory Y.

■ *Theory Y*

In strong contrast to Theory X, a Theory Y manager makes the following general assumptions:

- Work can be as natural as play if the conditions are favorable. Under those conditions, people will seek responsibility.

- People will be self-directed and creative to meet their work and organizational objectives if they are committed to them.

- People will be committed to their quality and productivity objectives if rewards are in place that address higher needs such as self-fulfillment.

- The capacity for creativity spreads throughout organizations.

- Most people can handle responsibility because creativity and ingenuity are common in the population.

Under those assumptions, employees have an opportunity to align their personal goals with organizational goals by using their need for fulfillment as the motivator. Employees can be most productive when their work goals align with their higher-level needs.

The higher-level needs of esteem and self-actualization are continuing needs in that they are never completely satisfied. As such, it is through those needs that you can best motivate employees.

McGregor stressed that Theory Y management does not imply a soft approach. Recognizing that some people may not have reached the level of maturity assumed by Theory Y, he suggests that those employees may need a system of tighter controls that a manager can relax as each employee develops. For more tips on applying Theory Y management, see the sidebar *Applying Theory Y Management* at right.

Vroom's Expectancy Theory

Yale School of Management professor Victor Vroom proposed the Expectancy Theory of motivation. This theory has evolved into one of the most popular work motivation theories because it focuses on all three parts of the motivation equation: inputs, performance, and outcomes. Its premise is that motivation is high when employees believe that high levels of effort lead to high performance, and high performance leads to the attainment of desired outcomes. Expectancy Theory identifies three major factors to determine a person's motivation:

■ Expectancy

Expectancy refers to the probability that a person's effort will yield a reward. For example, how motivated would you be to prepare for a test if you thought that no matter how hard you studied you would earn a "D"? Employees are motivated to put forth a high level of effort only if they think that doing so leads to high performance. In other words, for people's motivation to be high, expectancy must be high.

■ Instrumentality

Instrumentality refers to a person's perception that they will actually get the reward. Managers must ensure that employees receive the rewards that they are promised. Employees are motivated to perform at a high level only if they think that high performance will lead to—or is instrumental in attaining—outcomes (rewards). Outcomes can be pay, job security, or a feeling of accomplishment. Employees must have both high expectancies and instrumentalities, but the theory acknowledges that people differ in their outcome preferences.

■ Valence

Valence refers to how important the outcome is to a person. To motivate, you must determine which outcomes have high valence for your employees and ensure that those outcomes are provided when employees perform at a high level.

An example of Vroom's Expectancy Theory can be found in organizations where sales activity has a direct correlation to sales results. While commissions or bonuses might provide a basic reward, companies will often create additional incentives (or interim rewards) to recognize the link between effort and performance. These incentives are commonly introduced as short-term programs to sell a particular product or service.

Additionally, many companies also are turning to employee incentive programs where points or company money is issued, so employees get the opportunity to select the reward that suits them best. An individual might save his or her points to get a watch or expensive item for him- or herself or to purchase items for his or her children. The premise of these programs is to provide what is important to the employee.

Applying Theory Y Management

If Theory Y holds true, you can use these management principles to improve employee motivation:

■ Decentralization and Delegation

Decentralizing control and reducing the number of management levels creates an environment in which managers have more subordinates. Thus they are forced to delegate some responsibility and decision making to their employees.

■ Job Enlargement

Broadening the scope of an employee's job adds variety and opportunities to satisfy ego needs.

■ Participative Management

Consulting employees in the decision-making process taps their creative capacity and provides them with some control over their work environment.

■ Performance Appraisals

Requiring employees to set objectives and participate in the evaluation of those objectives allows them to feel involved in the appraisal process.

Properly implemented, a work environment such as the one described above results in a workforce that is highly motivated because employees work to satisfy their higher-level personal needs through their jobs.

Adams's Equity Theory

Your employees' perceptions concerning the fairness of their work outcomes relative to their work inputs is the focus of the Equity Theory. Formulated in the 1960s by workplace and behavioral psychologist J. Stacy Adams, this theory suggests that motivation is influenced by the comparison of one's own outcome-input ratio with the outcome-input ratio of another person or group of people. Note that Adams stressed that perception, rather than objective outcomes a person receives or the inputs a person contributes, is what is important in determining motivation in this case.

Avoiding Inequity

Managers are charged with the responsibility of making sure that inequity does not occur within their work teams. They can incorporate interpersonal activities or procedural skills into their daily interactions to help employees feel that equity exists in the workplace.

Interpersonal Activities	Procedural Skills
Team management: Allowing employees to work on projects as a team can break down barriers.	Ethical behavior: Conducting oneself in an appropriate manner can build trust in employees.
Participative management: Including employees in the decision-making process can allow them to provide valuable input.	Consistency: Being aware of things that have been done in the past, so the scales don't tip too far in one direction or another, can forestall the perception of arbitrariness.
Empowerment: Giving employees the freedom to make decisions can boost their self-esteem (not to mention improve customer relations).	Inclusiveness: Being nonjudgmental and unbiased and appreciating the differences each person brings to the workplace provides individuals with a sense of fair treatment.
Management by objectives: Having employees and management mutually agree upon goals can help employees get to the next level.	Accountability: Being responsible for one's actions and taking ownership of activities provides individuals with the sense that what they do is important.

This theory is based on the assumption that employees ask two questions about their work:

● What do I receive in return for what I give?
● What do others receive for what they give?

The Equity Theory contends that employees create mental ratios about their work situations in order to answer those questions. Equity occurs only when employees believe that the ratio of their outcomes received (pay, benefits, job satisfaction) to their inputs given (education, knowledge, experience, effort) is equal to the same ratio of a "comparison other" (who may or may not be like the employee).

Inequity, however, occurs either when employees believe they are receiving less or more for their efforts than the comparison other. According to this theory, balance is important, and employees are uncomfortable with either of those two imbalances. For some examples of how to avoid inequity in the workplace, see the sidebar *Avoiding Inequity* at left.

When imbalance is perceived, employees might

● work less because they believe others are overcompensated

● work harder because they believe that they are overcompensated in relation to others

● convince others to work less hard to restore equity

● convince others to work harder to restore equity

● reassess their perception of equity

● change their comparison other.

Self-Efficacy Theory

Self-Efficacy Theory relates to a person's belief about his or her ability to perform a behavior successfully. Even with the most attractive consequences or reinforcers hinging on high performance, people are not going to be motivated if they do not think that they can actually perform at the required high level.

Similarly, when people control their own behavior, they are likely to set difficult goals that will lead to outstanding accomplishments, but only if they think that they have the capability to reach those goals. Thus, self-efficacy influences motivation both when managers provide reinforcement and when workers themselves provide it—the greater the sense of self-efficacy, the greater the motivation and performance.

Eleanor Roosevelt once said: "No one can make you feel inferior without your consent." The following are some things managers can do and encourage employees to do to improve the situation:

- Mentoring. Peak performance requires skills and abilities. Help employees develop the skills and attitudes that they need to succeed.

- Behavior modeling. You've all heard the old saying, "practice what you preach." Well, it's true . . . if you want others to act a certain way, you need to practice that behavior yourself. Making sure that you have a positive outlook and self-image can have a significant effect on yourself and the people you come into contact with.

- Setting achievable goals: It is important to set realistic, achievable goals and work toward accomplishing them. It is equally important to celebrate successes. As you get more comfortable with goal setting, you can introduce stretch goals.

- Take compliments graciously: Learn to accept "thank you" and "great job" with grace. Some people just don't want to believe the nice comment. Smile and say thank you in return.

Skinner's Behavioral Reinforcement Theory

According to psychologist B.F. Skinner, people learn to perform behaviors that lead to desired consequences and learn not to perform behaviors that lead to undesired consequences. Translated into motivation terms, Skinner's theory means that employees will be motivated to perform at a high level to the extent that they obtain outcomes that they desire.

This theory provides four tools—positive reinforcement, negative reinforcement, punishment, and extinction—that you can use to motivate high performance and prevent workers from engaging in behaviors that detract from organization effectiveness.

■ Positive Reinforcement

Giving employees the outcomes that they desire when they perform behaviors that contribute to organizational effectiveness is considered positive reinforcement. Those outcomes are the rewards that a person desires such as pay, praise, or a promotion. One example of an inexpensive reward system is provided in the sidebar *Positive Reinforcement: The CandyGram.*

■ Negative Reinforcement

Negative reinforcement also can encourage behaviors that contribute to organizational effectiveness. Managers might choose to use negative reinforcement to eliminate an undesired outcome when a specific behavior is performed. Examples of negative reinforcement include management criticism, unpleasant assignments, or job-elimination threats. When negative reinforcement is used, employees are motivated to perform behaviors because they want to stop receiving the undesired outcomes.

■ Punishment

The act of administering an undesired or negative consequence when a dysfunctional behavior is performed is punishment. Punishments take various forms: pay cuts, suspensions, discipline, and termination. They also can have unintended side effects such as resentment, loss of self-respect, and a desire for retaliation. Managers should use punishment only when necessary.

■ Extinction

Extinction is the process of eliminating whatever reinforces an undesired behavior. For example, if you have a co-worker who likes to come into your office and talk about nonwork topics, what can you do? While you like the person and enjoy the conversations, those breaks put you behind schedule, and you have to work late to catch up. By acting disinterested in the nonwork topics, you discourage the behavior.

Positive Reinforcement: The CandyGram

In *Getting Them to Give a Damn,* author Eric Chester specifically addresses recruiting and retaining a younger, emerging workforce. But he presents at least one idea that will work for employees of any age.

The North Carolina Department of Environment and Natural Resources encourages employees to participate in "CandyGram," a nominally priced recognition program. To recognize a co-worker, employees attach a note to one of the following edible items:

LifeSavers candies	For a person who has been a real "lifesaver"
Strawberry jam	For a person who has helped you out of a "jam"
100 Grand Candy Bar	For a person who saves you a lot of money
Nestle Crunch Bar	For a person who was there for you during "crunch" time
Zero bar	For a person who completes a project with no mistakes—or "zero" errors
Mr. Goodbar	For a person who possesses a great attitude
York Peppermint Patty	For a person who is invaluable—"he or she is worth a mint!"

Adapted from Eric Chester's Getting Them to Give a Damn.

Managers can get into trouble if they use only positive reinforcement and refrain from negative reinforcement. It is important for a manager to identify the right behaviors to reinforce. An effective manager will ensure that the reinforced behaviors are ones over which employees have control and that the behaviors contribute to organizational effectiveness.

Ways to Integrate Motivation Into the Workplace

When examining your workplace environment, you'll discover two influences that have a great effect on the motivation of your employees:

■ *Management*
Instead of coming from some nebulous ad hoc committee or corporate institution, the most valuable recognition comes directly from one's manager. The sidebar *Rewarding Employees* at right provides examples and options of ways managers can reward their employees.

■ *Performance*
Employees want to be recognized for the jobs they were hired to do. The most effective incentives are based on job performance—not on nonperformance-related praise such as attendance or attire.

These influences should be considered when integrating motivation into job design, performance feedback, pay-for-performance systems, and relationship-building initiatives.

Job Design

J.R. Hackman and G.R. Oldham's job characteristics model explains in detail how you can make jobs more interesting and motivating for your employees.

According to Hackman and Oldham, every job has the following five characteristics that determine how motivating workers will find that job. These characteristics determine how employees react to their work and lead to such outcomes as high performance and satisfaction, and low absenteeism and turnover.

Rewarding Employees

Research into why talented people stay in organizations is the basis for the following ways to show your employees that you appreciate them:

■ Private Time With You

Have lunch with an employee and ask questions like:

- What can I do to keep you on my team?
- What might make your work life easier?
- What can I do to be more supportive or help you?

■ Frank Talk About the Future

Hold a career conversation in a quiet, private place—off-site, if possible. Ask the following questions to start:

- What do you enjoy most about your job? The least?
- Which one of your talents haven't I used yet?
- What jobs do you see yourself doing in the future?

■ Representing the Company

Give employees the chance to attend an outside conference or seminar designed for their affinity group.

■ Professional Growth

Let employees choose from a list of potential projects, assignments, or tasks that could enrich their work.

■ Recognizing Family

Give employees a prepaid phone card during the holiday season, or give a free pass for X number of days or hours off to attend children's school programs or sport activities.

■ Professional Interests

Give a subscription to an employee's favorite business magazine and satisfy employees' need for information.

■ Submit to Pruning

Ask the employee with whom you never agree to engage in some straight talk about how you might work together better. Listen carefully and don't defend yourself. Then take a step toward changing at least one behavior.

■ A Unique Perk for Fun

Give an employee a "kicks" coupon that entitles him or her to spend up to X amount of money to take a break or have some fun at work. It could involve the entire team.

■ A Priceless Introduction

Ask the employee for the name of someone in the organization that he or she would like to meet, chat with, and learn more about. Provide an introduction and encourage the employee to decide how to spend the time.

■ A Personal Trainer Session

Consider a gift certificate for an employee to have a lunch with you or another mentor of his or her choice.

■ A New Door

Brainstorm an opportunity hit list with an employee about growing, learning, and stretching in some way. Prioritize the list and then open the door!

■ Blending Work and Passion

Have a "Passion Breakfast" for all employees, a team, or one-on-one. Ask, "What do you love to do?" "At work?" "Outside of work?" Brainstorm and commit to helping them build more of what they love into their workday.

■ An Exception to the Rules

Give a "Bend the Rules" pass that involves and encourages going against the status quo. Bend as much as you can when employees make their requests.

■ Genie in a Bottle

Ask an employee to write down six ways he or she would like to be rewarded. Anything goes. The only rule is that half of the ideas have to be low or no cost.

■ A Chance to Download

Give 12 coupons for listening time—one for each month, in which an employee can talk about anything for 20 minutes. Your job isn't to understand, just to listen.

■ Honoring Values

Over a cappuccino, glass of wine, or cup of tea, try asking one of your employees any of these questions:

- What do you think makes a perfect day at work?
- Looking back, what has satisfied you the most?
- What does the word success mean to you?

Take notes and read them back to the employee. What did you both learn about his or her values?

■ The Starring Role, For Once

Give an employee a chance to lead a project you've been hoarding for yourself (you know which one). Offer the spotlight, yield, coach when necessary.

Adapted from Beverly L. Kaye and Sharon Jordan-Evans's "The ABCs of Management Gift-Giving," Training & Development, December 2000.

1. Skill Variety.

The extent to which a job requires an employee to use a wide range of different skills, abilities, or knowledge is referred to as skill variety. For example, the skill variety required by the job of a research scientist is higher than that required by the job of a food server.

2. Task Identity.

Task identity refers to the extent to which a job requires a worker to perform all the tasks necessary to complete that job from the beginning to the end of the production process. For example, a crafts worker who takes a piece of wood and transforms it into a custom-made piece of furniture, such as a desk, has higher task identity than a worker who performs only one of the numerous operations required to assemble a television.

3. Task Significance.

The degree to which a worker feels his or her job is meaningful because of its effect on people inside the organization (such as co-workers) or to people outside the organization (such as customers) is task significance. A teacher who sees the effect of his or her efforts in a well-educated and well-adjusted student enjoys high task significance compared with a dishwasher who monotonously washes dishes as they come to the kitchen.

4. Autonomy.

Autonomy refers to the degree to which a job gives an employee the freedom and discretion needed to schedule different tasks and to decide how to carry out those tasks. Salespeople who have to plan their schedules and decide how to allocate their time among different customers have relatively high autonomy compared with assembly-line workers whose actions are determined by the speed of the production line.

5. Feedback.

The extent to which performing a job provides a worker with clear and direct information about how well he or she has completed the job is feedback.

For example, an air traffic controller whose mistakes result in a midair collision receives immediate feedback on job performance; whereas a person who compiles statistics for a business magazine often has little idea of when he or she makes a mistake or does a particularly good job.

Hackman and Oldham argue that these five characteristics influence an employee's motivation because they affect three critical psychological states. If the employee feels that his or her work is meaningful and that he or she is responsible for work outcomes and for knowing how those outcomes affect others, the employee will find the work more motivating, be more satisfied, and thus perform at a high level.

Managers can use the following tips when designing structure and jobs:

- When deciding which type of organizational structure to use, carefully analyze an organization's environment, strategy, technology, and human resources.

- When creating a more formal structure, meticulously define the limits of each employee's job, create clear job descriptions, and evaluate each worker on his or her job performance.

- When creating a more flexible structure, enlarge and enrich jobs and allow workers to expand their jobs over time. Encourage workers to work together and then evaluate both individual and group performance.

- When using the job characteristics model to guide job design, recognize that you can enrich most jobs to make them more motivating and satisfying.

Performance Feedback

Performance management is the process used to identify, encourage, measure, evaluate, improve, and reward employee performance at work. As a feedback process, it serves an important role for both motivational and informational purposes, as well as acts as an improver of manager-employee relations. For example, supportive feedback can lead to greater motivation, and feedback discussions about pay and advancement can lead to greater employee satisfaction with the process.

One of the biggest challenges managers face is how to handle an employee's reaction to feedback. That is especially true when confronting poor performance issues. If you remember that detailed and specific feedback is more likely to result in increased performance, you'll ease the situation for both you and the employee.

When conducting performance feedback sessions, focus on the following:

● Create a supportive environment for employees to address concerns.

● Open the channels of communication for productive two-way dialogue.

● Build and maintain trust and respect with your employee.

Pay-for-Performance Systems

In *Keeping the People Who Keep You in Business,* author Leigh Branham reviews the role money plays in retaining the right people. He explains that while surveys rank pay behind factors such as meaningful work, meeting challenges, and opportunity for advancement, compensation places people in a socioeconomic niche. It determines what they can and cannot buy. That makes compensation an emotional and important issue.

Managers and executives should look at compensation not as a way to drive performance but rather as a message to employees about what results they value. In 2000, Branham writes that about two-thirds of small- and medium-size companies offered some kind of variable pay, such as profit sharing or bonus awards, to their employees, compared with less than 50 percent in 1990.

Four linkages are needed to connect performance with rewards:

● Valuable results are measured.
● Measured results are accomplished.
● Accomplished results are rewarded.
● Rewarded results are valuable.

Many companies have switched to variable pay options as a way of updating their compensation practices. Here are some types of variable pay in use today.

■ *Special Recognition Monetary Awards*
This method awards cash payouts to recognize unplanned, significant individual or group contributions that far exceed expectations. They are most effective if given when the contribution is fresh in the minds of all employees and with visible fanfare.

■ *Individual and Group Variable Pay*
These programs are designed primarily for employees or teams who do not normally participate in incentive compensation programs (that is, technical positions, telecommuters, and so forth). For positions or projects that do not have a lot of interaction with others, this method of variable pay is also valuable.

■ *Lump Sum Awards*
If you want to reward individual employee performance when base pay is already above the competitive market rate for the job, create a lump sum awards program. This program allows an organization to reduce annual payroll and still reward top performers.

■ *Stock Options*
These plans offer employees the opportunity to purchase their for-profit common stock at some time in the future at a specific price. Stock options serve to tie employees to the organization because ownership tends to cause employees to be more aware of how their organization is performing.

You can use the described options as complements to existing pay structures to enhance performance and retention. Your company executives must evaluate the current pay practices and business goals, and decide to what degree they want to reward results. The key word here is *results*. Rather than rewarding employees for seniority, bigger budgets, and larger staffs, these plans focus on the achievement of outcomes. Some examples of the use of pay-for-performance systems and their effects are described in the sidebar *Case Study: Who's Doing It?*

Case Study: Who's Doing It?

The following are some examples of pay-for-performance systems that have been used in various organizations to improve motivation:

- A national airline carrier gives each of its employees a $100 bonus check every time the carrier is ranked the nation's number one on-time airline.

- A health system made its 4,800 employees eligible to earn one to five percent of their annual salaries as a performance bonus if their business units achieved certain patient satisfaction and cost-per-discharge goals. In two years, the system had eliminated a chronic absenteeism problem, flattened its cost-per-discharge, and raised its patient satisfaction rate to the 95th-plus percentile.

- A tech company quadrupled its number of stock-option-eligible employees between 1993 and 1999. The company believes that move has helped it to significantly cut turnover among technical workers during that same period.

Adapted from Leigh Branham's Keeping the People Who Keep You in Business.

Relationship-Building Initiatives

In *The Six Fundamentals of Success,* Stuart Levine identifies the need to invest in relationships. He introduces the concept of how gestures—such as congratulating co-workers—can lead to better relationships, both personally and professionally.

A few of the key concepts that he mentions include:

■ *Give Generously*
When you give generously in relationships, you create an energy that brings good luck back to you.

■ *Talk Face-to-Face*
A *Fortune* 500 CEO tells the tale of how he walks through his entire U.S. headquarters to wish all 2,000 employees a happy holiday. He has a piece of candy at every stop. (He claims to put on 10 pounds each holiday season.) Why does he do it? He wants to thank them face-to-face. He knows that during the next year he will have to email them to ask for their support, and it helps if his employees see him as a real person.

■ *Help Team Members Get Ahead*
Having a great team makes coming to work rewarding for a manager. But attracting bright, hard-working people can be a challenge at times. The best way for you to recruit go-getters is to earn a reputation as a manager whose employees move up in the organization. To help you hire for a motivational match, use the interview questions in the job aid at the end of this *Infoline.*

■ *Coach Your Team*
Coaching your team makes your life easier in two ways: It improves the quality of work, and, as a result, your department's overall performance. Coaching elicits excellence.

Strategies for Rewarding Employees

There are two keys to rewarding your employees. First, you must understand the basic needs that motivate employees. Second, you need to continually monitor your workers to determine if their needs are being met.

Understanding Needs

In *The Manager's Desk Reference,* authors Cynthia Berryman-Fink and Charles B. Fink relate that 99 percent of employees are motivated by one of the following seven needs:

■ *Achievement*
Employees want the satisfaction of accomplishing projects successfully. They want to exercise their talents to attain success. If the job is challenging enough, employees are self-motivated. Therefore, if you provide them with the right work assignments, your employees will consistently produce.

■ *Power*
People get satisfaction from influencing and controlling others. They like to lead and persuade and are motivated by positions of power and leadership. Give your employees the opportunity to make decisions and direct projects.

■ *Affiliation*
Employees derive satisfaction from interacting with others. They enjoy people and find the social aspects of the workplace rewarding. You can motivate employees by giving them opportunities to interact with others: teamwork projects, group meetings, and so forth.

■ *Autonomy*

Employees want freedom and independence. It can be to your benefit to allow employees to make their own choices, set their own schedules, and work independently of others.

■ *Esteem*

Individuals need recognition and praise. Whenever possible, give your employees ample feedback and public recognition.

■ *Safety and Security*

Employees crave job security, a steady income, health insurance, fringe benefits, and a hazard-free work environment. By providing predictable work with little risk or uncertainty, you motivate your workforce.

■ *Equity*

Employees want to be treated fairly. You can assume that they compare work hours, job duties, salaries, and privileges with their co-workers. If they perceive inequities, employees will become discouraged.

Some ways to recognize which need is the primary motivator for an employee include considering his or her personality type based on various personality inventories, listening empathetically, or simply asking questions about job satisfiers. The sidebar *Four Nonmonetary Rewards* at right—which is based on the seven needs—describes some no-cost ways to reward your employees.

Gathering Information

On an ongoing basis, you should monitor your workforce to obtain useful information (for instance on motivation and job satisfaction) for a variety of organizational initiatives. Two ways to gather information about your workforce are surveys and focus groups.

■ *Surveys*

Employee surveys are instruments you can use to assess worker perceptions about their work environment. Use surveys to collect data on a wide variety of topics such as, but not limited to, the following:

- quality of management

- organizational strategy

Four Nonmonetary Rewards

Cash bonuses are great, but they are certainly not the only way to reward employees. In fact, other methods can be equally as effective. Here are four ways that you can recognize employees without dipping into your budget.

■ *Flexible Scheduling*

Once an employee demonstrates that he or she is a consistent contributor, relax some of the structure. Let employees exercise some judgment on when to take breaks and meals. You could expand this benefit to flexible work start times.

■ *Advancement Opportunities*

Let good employees know that you are looking out for their best interests. Continually look for promotional possibilities for your employees—even if that means letting them leave your department. Sure, you might lose a good employee, but the company still retains that good employee, and your remaining employees will know that you have their best interests at heart.

■ *Special Assignments*

Managers should give special opportunities to exceptional workers. Employees will see these opportunities as a welcome change of pace and the chance to learn new skills. Assignments can vary from sitting on a special task force to working on a new product launch.

■ *Public Praise*

Most people relish being recognized in front of their peers (however, be sure that anyone you praise publicly does enjoy that kind of recognition). As a manager, you can benefit from these moments by praising exceptional performers.

Adapted from George T. Fuller's
The Supervisor's Big Book of Lists.

- quality of work-life issues

- employee morale and job satisfaction

- effectiveness of compensation and benefit programs

- employee development opportunities

- employee retention and attrition issues

- organizational communications.

■ *Focus Groups*

Focus groups are small groups of employees that you invite to participate in a structured discussion with a facilitator. Use them as follow-up to a survey or independently to discover how employees feel about a specific program or issue. Note that for both surveys and focus groups, you must

- avoid misleading respondents about the reasons for the survey or focus group

- explain who is being surveyed and what the data will be used for

- use the data only for the reasons explained to participants

- maintain strict confidentiality if you have made that promise to the participants

- provide results to participants if you have made that promise.

Common Manager Mistakes

If you aren't getting the motivational mileage that you should as a manager, perhaps you are making one of the following five management mistakes.

■ *Misplacing Ownership*

Do you think motivation is the job of the human resources department? Although many companies give their HR departments some responsibility for formal rewards and recognition programs, that doesn't mean you are off the hook. In many situations, employees find that informal recognition from their managers for a job well done means more to them than a formal company program.

■ *Misaligning Incentives*

It is a mistake to give each of your employees the same incentive. No single action will motivate all employees. It's your job to determine the unique motivators for each employee and to provide an appropriate motivator when recognition is deserved.

■ *Saving Recognition*

It's inappropriate to save recognition for special occasions. When you observe your employees performing at a high level, recognize that success—regularly and often.

■ *Playing Favorites*

Managers should neither give handouts nor play favorites. You should not give recognition when none is warranted. That act not only cheapens the value of the incentive but also you, as a manager, lose credibility. In your interactions with employees, credibility is one of the most important qualities that you can build. Lose that, and you could lose everything.

■ *Misspeaking Praise*

When praising employees, don't just say, "Good job." Be specific so that your employees know exactly what they did to receive recognition. This simple act—providing detailed praise—helps to develop the skills and abilities of your workforce.

The mind is a muscle. If the minds of your employees go unchallenged, they will start to atrophy. Your workforce is full of creative people ready for an interesting, invigorating challenge. If you want to keep your top performers, you'll need to create new projects or opportunities for them. This *Infoline* will help you achieve that.

References & Resources

Books

Berryman-Fink, C., and C. B. Fink. *The Manager's Desk Reference.* New York: AMACOM, 1991.

Branham, L. *Keeping the People Who Keep You in Business.* New York: AMACOM, 2001.

Chester, E. *Getting Them to Give a Damn.* Chicago: Dearborn Trade Publishing, 2005.

Dell, T. *Motivating at Work.* Revised Edition. Menlo Park, CA: Crisp Publications, 1993.

Fournies, F. *Why Employees Don't Do What They're Supposed to Do and What to Do About It.* New York: McGraw-Hill, 1999.

Fuller, G.T. *The Supervisor's Big Book of Lists.* Englewood Cliffs, NJ: Prentice Hall, 1994.

Garber, P. R. *99 Ways to Keep Employees Happy, Satisfied, Motivated, and Productive.* Mystic, CT: Ransom & Benjamin, 2001.

Gostick, A., and C. Elton. *The 24-Carrot Manager.* Layton, UT: Gibbs Smith, 2002.

Jones, G., and J. George. *Contemporary Management.* 3rd edition. New York: McGraw-Hill/Irwin, 2003.

Levine, S. R. *The Six Fundamentals of Success.* New York: Doubleday, 2004.

McGregor, D. *The Human Side of Enterprise.* New York: McGraw-Hill, 1960.

Nelson, B. *1001 Ways to Energize Employees.* New York: Workman Publishing, 1997.

———. *1001 Ways to Take Initiative at Work.* New York: Workman Publishing, 1999.

———. *1001 Ways to Reward Employees.* New York: Workman Publishing, 1994.

Nelson, B., and P. Economy. *Managing for Dummies.* New York: John Wiley & Sons, 1996.

Orey, M., and J. Prisk. *Communication Skills Training.* Alexandria, VA: ASTD Press, 2004.

Woods, R. H. *Human Resources Management.* 2nd edition. Orlando, FL: Educational Institute of the American Hotel & Lodging Association, 1997.

Infolines

Austin, Mary. "Needs Assessment by Focus Group," No. 259401 (revised 1998).

Long, Lori. "Surveys From Start to Finish," No. 258612 (revised 1998).

Sharpe, Cat. "How to Motivate Employees." No. 259108 (revised 1997).

Reports and White Papers

Grensing-Pophal, L. "Engaging Employees From A to Z." SHRM White Paper, 2002.

Poe, A. C. "Doing More With Less: Motivating Your Workforce in Uncertain Economic Times." SHRM White Paper, 2002.

Ragan Communications. *The Motivational Manager.* Available through Amazon.com.

———. *The Manager's Intelligence Report.* Available through Amazon.com.

Miscellaneous

Envision Software. "Theory X and Y." www.envisionsoftware.com, 2005.

Society for Human Resource Management. "The SHRM Learning System" Module Three, Human Resource Development, 2004.

Society for Human Resource Management. "The SHRM Learning System" Module Five, Employee and Labor Relations, 2004.

Finding the Motivational Match

Employees will not stay with a company very long if they are not motivated to do their jobs. It is important to discover what motivates individuals before they even start with the organization, during the interview process. The following list of interview questions can help determine an employee's motivational match for a position.

1. Tell me about a time when you handled a project that you found satisfying. What was the situation and why was it satisfying?

2. Tell me about a time when you worked on a project that you found dissatisfying. What was the situation and why was it dissatisfying?

3. Give me examples of job experiences that you felt were satisfying.

4. Do you have short-term and long-term goals for yourself? Are they realistic? Did you accomplish them last year?

5. What kinds of things can a manager do to motivate his or her staff?

6. Describe a situation when you were able to have a positive influence on the actions of others. How did you do it? What were they able to accomplish?

7. How do you motivate yourself to do unpleasant tasks?

8. Give me an example of a time you went above and beyond what was asked of you.

9. How would you define success for someone in your profession?

How to Conduct a Performance Appraisal

Issue 9005

How to Conduct a Performance Appraisal

REVISION CONSULTANT

Stew Hickman
Director, Learning Network
Georgetown University Hospital
3800 Reservoir Road
Washington, DC 20007
Tel: 202.784.2648
Email: esh5@gunet.edu

Throughout his 23 years in the field of education, training, management consulting, and HR, Stew Hickman has helped organizations become more productive and satisfying places to work and learn. He has trained and consulted on a range of topics, from empathic listening and MBTI, to organizational culture and change management.

Editorial Staff for 9005

Author
George B. Berke, Ph.D.

Editor
Barbara Darraugh

Revised 2001

Editor
Cat Sharp Russo

Contributing Editor
Ann Bruen

Production Design
Kathleen Schaner

Assessing Performance

It is said that 80 percent of U.S. businesses use formal performance appraisal systems, yet some 90 percent are dissatisfied with the process. Can this possibly be true? Well, take a look at your own organization. Is there a performance appraisal system? Does it work well? Could it be improved? Most likely, the answer is yes.

Why is it that a few systems work well? Is it the people; is it the process; do some managers know how to conduct a good performance appraisal while others are clueless? There are many reasons, and often the reason is grounded in an organization's culture and human resources development. The fact of the matter is that people at large, managers and employees alike, are dissatisfied with current performance appraisal systems.

Let's first answer a basic question. Why do we have performance appraisal systems? There is a laundry list of reasons, but the highlights are:

- To make personnel decisions, that is, which employees will receive salary increases, training, promotions, demotions, dismissal, and so forth.

- To help employees develop and reach their potential career growth.

- To standardize within an organization how employees are rated. By providing a uniform process and criteria for rating performance, appraisals become more objective.

- To afford legal protection to an organization against employee lawsuits.

This issue of *Infoline* does not propose to give you a complete system that answers all problems. What we are trying to accomplish is to give you background and foundation guidance as well as ideas, processes, methods, and best practices for conducting performance appraisals. Use all of it or just what applies to you and your organization.

Performance Management Goals

Performance management occurs at several levels. In their seminal book *Improving Performance*, organizational development experts Geary Rummler and Alan Brache identify three levels: organizational performance management, process performance management, and individual/job performance management. (See the sidebar *Levels of Performance* for a more complete explanation of their classifications.) It is necessary to think about the appraisal of an individual employee's performance in the context of this larger picture.

The Management System

Performance appraisal, as defined above, is the process of describing, evaluating, and developing the results of a person's work effort, in whatever way the work is defined by the organization or the manager. The performance appraisal occurs in the context of the organization's performance management system, which typically is made up of the following components:

- The job description: what the jobholder will do in general terms.

- The work plan for the department: usually the link between the organizational strategy and the work objectives for the department.

- The individual goals and objectives: based on the work plan, these define the focus for the period—usually a year—and the standards to which the work should be performed.

- Development objectives: based on the appraisal, these can define areas for improvement or continued growth for the individual.

- Feedback: by which the performer gets information about how his or her work is going.

These components fit into an overall framework of planning, implementing, and reviewing. The outcome is the performance, that is, the results you want from the employee's work.

Levels of Performance

Performance management occurs at three levels. This adaptation of the Rummler-Brache model, found in *Improving Performance*, helps define each.

Level	Scope of Attention	Tools Used	Outcomes
Organization Performance Management	● Organizational goals and measures. ● Department goals and measures. ● Resource allocation. ● Management of interface between departments.	● Strategic planning process. ● Resource allocation process. ● Integration process.	● Horizontal integration of department goals. ● Success in achieving the strategy.
Process Performance Management	● Process goals and measures. ● Resource allocation. ● Management of interface between process steps.	● Operating procedures. ● Networks. ● Client relationships.	● Processes are owned. ● Processes are measured and managed. ● Processes work well.
Individual/Job Performance Management	● Individual performance goals and measures. ● Management of interface between tasks.	● Performance planning (goal setting). ● Feedback. ● Performance review. ● Professional development. ● Compensation management. ● Incentive plan.	● Individual strategic contribution. ● Sought behaviors are exhibited. ● Individual commitment, competence, and development.

The Management Cycle

The diagram depicted in the *Performance Management Cycle* on the next page, shows the iterative nature of the work. Traditionally, the cycle takes a year, but some organizations speed up that cycle to effect quick adjustments in response to customer demands, changing market conditions, or other contingencies. The cyclic principle is the same, however, and is predicated on one thing: goal clarity. If the outcome is clear, you stand a chance of getting there.

So, it all starts with the development of goals for performance—the outcomes you want to see. Performance goals can be written toward four general outcomes:

1. Improving an aspect of the person's work that is not meeting expectations.

2. Maintaining the current level of performance.

3. Enhancing some aspect of the work the person is doing but needs to do better.

4. Developing an additional skill.

A performance goal should contain the following elements: a verb, a result, and a measure (usually quality, quantity, or time). See the sidebar *Performance Goal Components* for examples of these elements.

Developing Performance Criteria

Accurate measures of performance are critical to any performance appraisal system. These measures are based on the organization's overall objectives. An understanding of the mission is then translated into a knowledge of the relationships between the desired results, the means to accomplish the results, and the work to be done. The criteria for measuring results become the performance standards.

Performance standards are more than just job descriptions. While job descriptions detail the components of a task or job, performance standards define how well it must be done (an ideal measure), or when a task is performed in an acceptable manner (a satisfactory measure). Effective standards have the following characteristics:

■ *Standards Are Job Based, Not Person Based*
Standards are different from goals or objectives. Performance standards are determined for job categories, while goals or objectives are set for specific employees. For example, a manager with three administrative assistants may have one standard for the position, but different goals for individual assistants.

■ *Standards Are Achievable*
Most employees in a job category should be able to meet a standard.

■ *Standards Are Understood*
They must be understood and, if possible, agreed upon by both the supervisor and the subordinate.

■ *Standards Are Specific and Measurable*
If possible, standards should be set in objective quantifiable terms: numbers, dollars, or percentages. These standards measure results. If is often just as important to measure the means through which the ends are accomplished. These subjective measures rate an employee's ability to organize time, communicate, assist others, manage people, follow directions, and apply technical skills.

■ *Standards Are Time Oriented*
The standards should state what needs to be accomplished by what time.

■ *Standards Are Written*
Both the supervisor and the subordinate should have a copy of the job standards.

■ *Standards Are Subject to Change*
Performance standards should be reviewed periodically and changed if necessary. Changes in significant job factors, such as the introduction of new equipment, new methods, or new materials, may cause a review. Managers should not, however, change standards because an employee is not meeting them.

Performance standards have dual purposes: They give employees a guide to behavior needed to accomplish desired job results; and they provide a basis by which a person's performance can be fairly appraised.

Performance Management Cycle

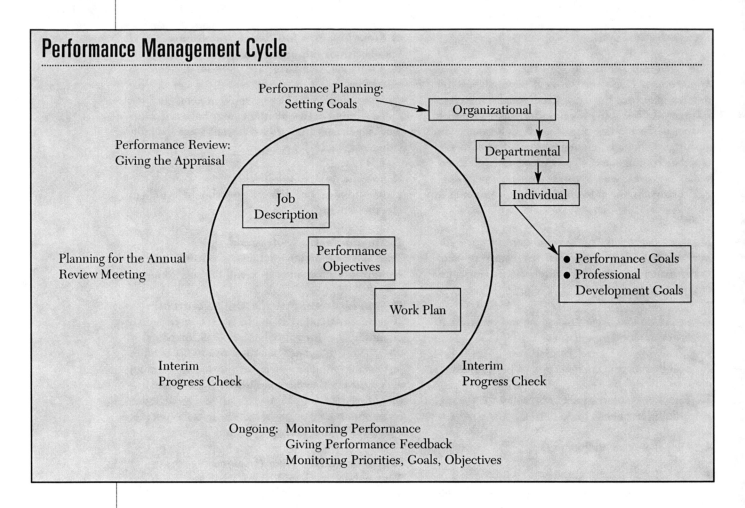

Performance Planning:
Setting Goals

Organizational

Departmental

Individual

Performance Review:
Giving the Appraisal

Job
Description

Performance
Objectives

Work Plan

● Performance Goals
● Professional
   Development Goals

Planning for the Annual
Review Meeting

Interim
Progress Check

Interim
Progress Check

Ongoing: Monitoring Performance
Giving Performance Feedback
Monitoring Priorities, Goals, Objectives

Job Analysis

A thorough analysis of job content is the first step in developing performance criteria for an effective appraisal system. Job analysis is defined as the systematic collection of job-related information for each individual job, including what is to be done, how it is to be done, and why it is to be done. Common methods of job analysis include these:

Task analysis. This quantitative approach uses questionnaires and interviews with employees to determine the component tasks that make up a job. Job analysts then assign ratings based on abilities, personal traits, and physical demands required of a worker in performing the tasks.

Critical incidents. Job knowledge experts outline important dimensions of a job and describe behavior that comprises poor, average, and exceptional performance of a particular dimension.

Job elements. This qualitative approach uses job-knowledge experts to generate skills, knowledge, abilities, and other worker characteristics required to perform a job. These elements are then ranked to gain consensus on the most important aspects of the job.

Appropriate Appraisal Formats

The second step in developing an effective appraisal system is the selection of an appropriate format. Measurements of performance fall into two general categories:

1. Objective measurements, which include attainment of preset numerical data such as units of work output or sales revenue targets.

2. Subjective measurements, which are based on human judgment.

Subjective measures are much more complicated than objective measures. Several approaches to subjective rating systems are discussed below.

■ Relative Rating Systems

Relative rating systems compare one employee with others in his or her job category or department. Relative rating systems include:

- Simple rankings that rate workers from highest to lowest, best to worst.

- Alternation method that requires the rater to list all employees and then choose the best, then the worst, second best, second worst, and so forth, until all employees have been ranked.

- Paired comparisons that provide the advantage of one-employee-to-one-employee comparisons. In paired comparisons, the rater compares one person with every other employee and counts the numbers of times that person is rated superior.

- Forced distribution that converts standard scores into a normal statistical distribution. Although it helps control central tendency (rating everyone in the middle) and leniency errors, it assumes that employees conform to a normal distribution.

■ Absolute Rating Systems

Absolute rating systems describe a particular employee without reference to other employees. Among the forms of absolute ratings systems are these:

Narratives. The narrative essay is the simplest type of absolute review. The supervisor writes about an employee's strengths, weaknesses, and potential and adds his or her suggestions for improvement. Well-written narratives provide detailed feedback to employees. Essays are, however, almost totally unstructured and provide only qualitative information.

Performance Goal Components

Performance goals should contain the following elements:

A Verb	A Result	A Measure (Quality, Quantity, Time)
To increase	...the number of tests administered in the Research Clinic	...from X to Y by no later than [date].
To continue	...to provide the same level of customer service, despite a reduction in resources	...as indicated by meeting the published standards.
To investigate	...the feasibility of installing a new XXX system	...at a cost not to exceed $[amount]. Complete by [date].

Behavioral checklists. Behavioral checklists detail behaviors desired in a particular job category. The supervisor is asked to check any behavior that applies to the employee being evaluated. This approach makes the evaluator an *observer* of behavior rather than a judge. To make the approach more evaluative, items can be scaled using attitude scale construction methods. For example, a descriptor can be followed by a weight. A numerical ranking is achieved by adding the weights of the responses.

Forced-choice system. This behavioral checklist was developed to reduce leniency errors and to establish objective standards of comparison between employees. In a forced-choice system, checklist items are arranged in groups from which the supervisor chooses statements that best describe the employee. A special scoring key determines an overall rating. Forced-choice scales are developed according to either the degree to which a statement differentiates effective from ineffective workers (discriminability) or the degree to which the quality described is valued (preference).

Halos, Horns, Pitfalls, and Biases

One way to reduce subjectivity is to become aware of what feelings and opinions you carry into a review discussion. As you read these descriptions, think of specific discussions you have had with staff members for which that description might be accurate. This analysis will help you be more aware of some areas where you need to be more objective.

Halo Effect

This is the tendency of a supervisor to overrate a favored employee. It can happen for the following reasons:

Effect of past record. Good work in a previous rating period tends to carry over to the current period.

Compatibility. People who please are sometimes rated more highly than they deserve.

Effect of recency. A person who does outstanding work immediately prior to the evaluation may be able to offset an entire year of poor performance.

The one-asset person. An employee with certain characteristics—an advanced degree, a glib talker, or an impressive appearance—may be ranked higher than an excellent worker without these attributes.

The blind spot. In this case, the supervisor is blind to certain defects because he or she also possesses them.

The no-complaints bias. "No news is good news" may account for too much.

The high-potential person. The supervisor considers the future possibilities for the staff member rather than what that person has actually accomplished.

Horns Effect

This is the tendency to rate an employee lower than circumstances warrant. Some causes of this are as follows:

The boss is a perfectionist. High boss expectations lead to an employee rating lower than might be warranted.

The employee is contrary. Some bosses find it difficult not to become irritated with employees who disagree often with them.

The oddball effect. The maverick or nonconformist may get low ratings just because he or she is different.

Membership in a weak team. Sometimes a good player on a weak team ends up with lower ratings than if that employee were on a high-performing team.

Guilt by association. A person who is friends with someone who is perceived as a troublemaker may also be perceived as a troublemaker.

The dramatic effect. This is the opposite of the recency effect, whereby one recent goof offsets an entire year of good work.

Personality traits.

Self-comparison. The employee does not do the job the same way the supervisor did when he or she held that same job.

Other Pitfalls

Some other inaccurate reviews may be a result of the following elements:

Stereotypes. This pitfall involves basing appraisals on fixed conceptions of performance rather than on actual performance. Requiring supervisors to apply objective criteria to performance will discourage stereotyping.

Subjective standards. These "standards" have different meanings for different people. This confuses the definition of *standards* with that of *goals and objectives*.

Central tendency. This ignores individual performance differences and rates all employees the same.

Leniency bias. Supervisors who give employees the benefit of the doubt, exaggerating positives and eliminating negatives, are guilty of leniency.

Opportunity bias. This bias exists when an employee or group of employees are rated higher or lower than warranted because of outside circumstances.

Controlling Biases

The following guidelines will help you reduce error rates and bias in performance appraisal plans:

Develop and use goals and standards throughout the performance period.

Be aware of your own potential biases and remain objective.

Keep notes on specific performance throughout the year and reference this information during the discussion.

Keep forms simple. Complex forms that attempt a "complete" evaluation only serve to frustrate managers and allow their biases to overpower their objectivity.

Use other raters. Design in the use of raters other than direct supervisors to increase the number of inputs to the performance appraisal system.

Build in subjective ratings. Leave some space for the evaluation of traits such as creativity and integrity or other traits that are especially valued by the organization.

Don't pretend it is easy. Let your managers know that it takes a certain amount of time and effort to perform a fair and accurate employee evaluation, more time than they probably are currently spending.

Critical incidents. Critical incidents are reports by knowledgeable observers of things an employee did over a period of time that were especially effective or ineffective in accomplishing parts of his or her job. Critical incidents provide data on an employee's unique way of going about his or her job. It is a natural for performance evaluation, because the supervisor can focus on actual job behavior rather than on personality. In addition, critical incidents provide a wealth of information on job and organizational problems in general and are of great help in establishing training objectives.

The supervisor should go one step further and outline, as specifically as possible, what satisfactory performance looks like. This is particularly important for standards around soft areas such as teamwork and customer service.

The Appraisal Process

Once you have completed the "homework" of establishing standards and choosing measurement formats, the actual appraisal process is simple. Its simplicity is based on objective observation—a focus on behaviors rather than personalities.

First, the standards and rating systems must be explained to the employee. For example, a supervisor should explain to employees that the standards are conditions that should exist at the *end* of a specific time, usually a year, and that they will be rated on an "unsatisfactory, satisfactory, exceptional" scale.

During the defined time period, the supervisor should periodically review actual performance against the standards. This review allows for adjusting standards—if they were set too high to too low—as well as keeping employees posted about how they are doing. Keeping workers informed during the year eases much of the anxiety of an annual performance appraisal.

Appraisal Checklist

In his *Performance Management Workbook,* E. James Brennan recommends the following guidelines when conducting performance appraisals. They cover the entire process—before, during, and after any appraisal.

☐ Cover one thing at a time.

☐ Compare the actual results with the standards.

☐ Appraise on the basis of relevant, accurate, and sufficient information.

☐ Be honest and be prepared to discuss questionable items.

☐ Keep the appraisal open to employee input.

☐ Avoid comments on age, race, sex, or national origin that may violate discrimination laws.

☐ Keep written and oral appraisals consistent.

☐ Remember that the appraisal is the supervisor's opinion and is based on his or her observations.

☐ Make written appraisals available to employees.

☐ Identify areas for improvement and specify remedial actions.

☐ Support the employee's effort to improve.

☐ Give the employee feedback about improvement and performance needs.

☐ Never imply the existence of communications that have not been made.

☐ Provide a right of appeal.

☐ Have employees acknowledge the evaluation. They may not agree with it, but they should understand it and what it was based on.

Following this process makes the performance review much easier. During this year-end discussion, the supervisor and employee can discuss documented performance and plan new performance objectives and standards for the coming year. The performance review then becomes a job-related discussion that confirms the employee's understanding of his or her job duties; checks for problems in the work environment; produces information for rewards; provides feedback; and evaluates work results.

A performance appraisal will be sound if it complies with the following guidelines:

● Its purpose is well defined.

● It is founded on relevant and accurate information.

● It is complete—no important information has been overlooked.

Before attending an end-of-the-year performance review, the employee needs to know the following things:

● Why he or she is being judged.
● What the judgment is based on.
● How the results of the evaluation will be used.

Knowing this information will help make the employee less defensive at the beginning of the performance review.

The Performance Review

The performance review itself requires a great deal of managerial or supervisory skill. A poorly done review can antagonize and demoralize a good employee; a well-planned review can be exhilarating and motivating for both the supervisor and the subordinate. Part of the difficulty of a performance review is that it is expected to accomplish what may be conflicting goals. The performance review should be used to do the following:

- Review a full year of performance, comparing actual results and how they were achieved with previously agreed-upon performance goals and standards.

- Give recognition and reinforcement to the employee who is doing good work.

- Identify any area where performance does not meet expectations and mutually agree on steps to take to improve performance in that area.

- Identify areas for growth and enhancement based on the department's future needs balanced with employee interests.

- Summarize information pertaining to the employee's knowledge, skills, behaviors, accomplishments, and so forth that is used for salary decisions.

These sometimes-conflicting objectives put the supervisor in an extremely difficult position. If the employee hears only that he or she did not get the expected salary increase, discussion of other job-related areas (including the need for improvement) may have to be postponed until another meeting. The supervisor can take steps to ease this dilemma, however, by doing the following things:

Decide on the best time for the review to take place. This means a time when both parties can spend time together without interruption.

Decide on the best place for the review. This is often a neutral private office.

Prepare the facilities. Seating the employee on the other side of the supervisor's desk puts the employee at an immediate disadvantage. Instead, try placing the chairs side by side and have coffee or water available.

Gather information and materials. Have the prepared appraisal forms ready, along with any backup information that may be needed.

Plan the opening. A friendly approach—first discussing sports events, inquiring after family, or commenting on the weather—will assure the employee that he or she has not walked into a lynching party. Remember, however, that the opening needs to be something the supervisor is also comfortable with. If the supervisor has never discussed personal matters, this is probably not the time to inquire after family members.

Plan the approach. There is no right or wrong approach to a performance review. For example, the supervisor could list job strengths first or use the performance appraisal form as a discussion guide.

Plan the conclusion. Know when and how to conclude the review, including what agreements are required from the subordinate. Remember that the objectives the review needs to accomplish may require more than one meeting.

Guarantee no interruptions. This requires coordination and careful location choice.

Communication is the key to an effective performance review. How the results of the review are presented may override the results themselves. Supervisors should take a nonevaluative stance; their job is to improve performance, not comment on personality or lifestyle.

One way to avoid evoking defensive behavior from employees is to take an open, nonjudgmental or nonblaming stance. Many confrontations can be avoided by describing a problem in an impersonal way and encouraging the employee to work with the supervisor toward a solution. For example, telling an employee that he or she is tactless and undiplomatic is tactless and undiplomatic. A kinder, gentler, and more effective way of stating the same thing is, "Some people interpret your candor as hostility."

Roles During Performance Review

Basically, these are the areas that supervisors and employees are responsible for during performance appraisal meetings.

Supervisor	Employee
Review employee's performance.	Be prepared to discuss work accomplishments for the year.
Write summary of key points.	
Communicate review to next-level manager prior to review discussion.	Be prepared to discuss your self-assessment of performance results—including strengths and steps needed to improve performance.
Hold discussion with employee and reach agreement, if possible, on key points and performance rating.	Participate actively in discussion.
Work with employee to resolve differences over rating.	Make improvements agree upon in the performance review discussion.
Identify areas for development with employee.	Sign review to indicate that the review has been discussed.
Identify performance problems and, with employee, develop a plan for improving performance.	

Another way to sidestep defensive behavior is to show the worker that the supervisor has some empathy for the person's situation, rather than being disinterested about the evaluation's effect on the employee. A comment like "That's one way to look at it" does not indicate that the supervisor is open to any discussion. A statement such as "I get the feeling you didn't feel confident about the original plan" will lead the way to discussion.

These methods emphasize analysis of an ongoing problem rather than judgment or evaluation. The analysis should encourage the participation of the employee in solving a work- or job-related problem, rather than assessing blame for lack of outcome. Among the benefits that accrue from a non-evaluative approach are these:

● improved creativity in solving problems

● less supervisory reluctance to discuss employee performance problems

● an employee's clearer understanding of why and how he or she needs to change work behavior

● the growth of cooperation between individual employees and an increase in group motivation

● greater employee self-reliance.

See the sidebar *Roles During Performance Review* for further guidelines to follow.

Make It Legal

The conduct of performance appraisals is often the basis for legal action by disgruntled employees. Subjective supervisory ratings, especially, have been examined by federal courts for violating sections of the Civil Rights Act of 1964. The following areas require careful consideration and legal advice to avoid running afoul of federal or state laws and regulations:

1. Any procedure, including formal or informal performance appraisal, that is used to make any personnel decision (including hiring, transfer, promotion, or dismissal) is covered by federal regulations.

2. Title VII of the Civil Rights Act does not require proof of intent to discriminate in order to prove discrimination. Disproportionate numbers of majority or minority members in specific job categories are considered *prima facie* evidence of discrimination. Any performance appraisal system that results in differential promotion or dismissal of groups of employees may be discriminatory.

3. Employers are solely responsible for validating the performance appraisal system that they use. If an employee shows that evidence of discrimination exists, he or she does not have to prove that the performance appraisal system is invalid.

4. Validity requires empirical evidence showing that the use of the performance appraisal is valid for the purpose for which it is being used. The valuation procedure itself has standards:

   - The data must be representative of both potential and current employees.

   - Tests must be given under standardized conditions.

   - The criteria must be work related and free from factors that would unfairly depress scores.

   - The performance appraisal system must be valid for all minority groups as well as for the population as a whole.

   - The relationship between the performance measure and work performance must be both statistically and practically significant—that is, related to profitability, product, or other specific organizational indices.

Changing Appraisal Systems

To help avoid the quagmire of federal and state laws and regulations, consult a labor attorney when devising a new or revising an existing performance appraisal system. In general, employers should have a formal performance appraisal system that uses actual job performance whenever possible. Supervisory ratings of job performance are second best. To meet the criteria imposed by recent court cases, the performance appraisal system should have these characteristics:

- The performance ratings should be job related.

- The variables rated should be developed through job analysis.

- Raters must be able to observe the performance they are to rate.

- Ratings should not be based on raters' evaluations of vague, subjective factors.

Suggestions for Reviews

The following suggestions will help supervisors conduct effective performance reviews:

Coach on results. The emphasis in performance appraisal must remain on performance. Coaching on results is another way of focusing on the desired outcome, rather than a personality trait or behavior. Remaining impersonal in criticism—noting, for example, that a production standard has not been met—is the best way to reach the employee.

Get down to cases. Employees need concrete information on what is expected from them. Supervisors should give employees specifics about performance problems, rather than generalized criticism. Remember that "softening" the criticism by being vague or beating around the bush only leads to confusion and misunderstanding.

Determine causes. Simply reporting that a problem exists and asking what will be done about it eliminates a powerful potential source of information: What is the cause? Consideration of causes encourages a problem-solving rather than a judging atmosphere, while uncovering information that may be helpful in solving department-wide problems.

Make it a two-way process. The performance review is often thought of as a "telling" process, in which the supervisor tells his or her subordinate what is wrong. Supervisors can overcome an employee's reluctance to speak up during the interview by simply asking questions and listening to the response.

Set up an action plan. Deciding on appropriate action flows naturally from discovering the cause of performance shortfalls. The supervisor and subordinate should consider several possible actions to correct a problem area or cause; concentrate on one or two specific actions; be specific about who, what, and when; provide for follow-up; and put the plan in writing.

Provide motivation. Once the necessary actions have been defined, the supervisor should emphasize the benefits to the subordinate of achieving the necessary results. Benefits include advancement, pay increases, additional responsibility or status, or simply the sense of a job well done.

- Care should be taken through the choice of measures, through training, and so forth, to ensure that ratings are not biased by prejudice against protected groups.

- Ratings should be collected and scored under standardized conditions.

Defending Appraisal Systems

Here are the factors that need to be built into a reasonable and defendable performance appraisal system:

- Performance standards are a part of job descriptions.

- Standards are based on job analysis, and employee knows standards in advance.

- Standards are based on realistic, and preferably agreed-upon, performance.

- Employee gets feedback on performance from supervisor regularly throughout the year.

- Employees can comment on their ratings.

- Supporting documentation exists that bears on the performance problem.

- Training is available to qualify for promotion.

There are other factors to consider, such as these:

- One rater should not be able to control an employee's career.

- There must be a review process.

- The rater should be familiar with the employee's performance.

- Safeguards should exist to prevent discrimination.

After the Appraisal

One reason why appraisal systems fail to meet expectations and cause such dissatisfaction to employees is that once the annual appraisal has been completed, it's as though everything about the appraisal gets put aside until the following year.

Use the appraisal as a template for follow-up during the course of the subsequent year. Instead of having just annual reviews, devote an hour or so for each employee every six months, preferably each quarter, to review that employee's performance and progress. This will be of great benefit to the manager because it allows the manager to observe and record specific examples of performance as they occur, rather than trying to remember back over a year's worth of time. More important, the interim review gives the employee an opportunity to change behaviors and performance outcomes. It also allows employees to gauge their own success on a more regular basis.

Best Practices

Several organizations have developed creative performance-management techniques that have resulted in effective talent and potential assessments. Review these best practices and see if some of them can be applied to your organization's performance appraisal system.

- Link performance appraisal to your organization's mission, vision, and corporate strategy.

- Take performance appraisals seriously, and use them to transform the culture of your organization. Let employees know exactly what is expected of them if they are to succeed, and insist that managers maintain consistent standards for everyone. The process of rooting out poor performers and rewarding excellence fosters an environment of continuous improvement.

- Identify and assess the core competencies that are critical to the success of your organization. Then develop descriptions of the behaviors that demonstrate mastery of these competencies. Create an evaluation scale based on the frequency of these behaviors, as they are observed by the employee's rater. Establish a rating vocabulary that is as nonjudgmental as possible, but at the same time, encourage supervisors to be truthful in their assessments.

- Train managers in appraisal skills: behavioral observation and employee development; confronting unacceptable performance; persuading; problem solving; and planning.

- Recognize that the only way for employees to get better at what they do is for their managers to provide candid, timely evaluations. The most valuable kind of feedback is contained in daily interactions, not in once-a-year written evaluations. At the same time, encourage employees to participate in their own development by deciding what kind of feedback is most useful to them.

- Identify high-potential employees and develop them quickly. Move average performers out of the way—and poor performers out of the organization—to make room for talented employees to grow.

References & Resources

Articles

Barrier, Michael. "Reviewing the Annual Review." *Nation's Business,* September 1998, pp. 32-34.

Baumgartner, Jerry. "Give It to Me Straight." *Training & Development,* June 1994, pp. 48-51.

Cyr, Robert. "Seven Steps to Better Performance Appraisals." *Training & Development,* January 1993, pp. 18-19.

Eckes, George. "Practical Alternatives to Performance Appraisals." *Quality Progress,* November 1994, pp. 57-60.

Grote, Dick. "Painless Performance Appraisals Focus on Results, Behaviors." *HRMagazine,* October 1998, pp. 52-58.

————. "The Secrets of Performance Appraisal: Best Practices from the Masters." *Across the Board,* May 2000, pp. 14-20.

Hall, James L., et al. "What We Know About Upward Appraisals of Management: Facilitating the Future Use of UPAs." *Human Resource Development Quarterly,* Fall 1996, pp. 209-226.

"How To: Provide Effective Feedback." *People Management,* July 11, 1996, pp. 44-45.

Kikoski, John F. "Effective Communication in the Performance Appraisal Interview." *Public Personnel Management,* Summer 1999, pp. 301-322.

Kunreuther, Robert. "Stepping Through the Appraisal Looking Glass." *Journal for Quality & Participation,* October/November 1994, pp. 28-31.

Lee, Chris. "Performance Appraisal: Can We 'Manage' Away the Curse?" *Training,* May 1996, pp. 44-59.

Longenecker, Clinton O., and Nick Nykodym. "Public Sector Performance Appraisal Effectiveness: A Case Study." *Public Personnel Management,* Summer 1996, pp. 151-164.

Martin, David C., and Kathryn M. Bartol. "Performance Appraisal: Maintaining System Effectiveness." *Public Personnel Management,* Summer 1998, pp. 223-234.

McMahon, Gerard. "A Lovely Audience." *People Management,* March 25, 1999, pp. 60-61.

Ramsgard, William C. "Designing Performance Appraisal the Right Way: The CAM Process." *Performance & Instruction,* July 1994, pp. 14-18.

Segal, Jonathan A. "Evaluating the Evaluators." *HRMagazine,* October 1995, pp. 46-50.

Zigon, Jack. "Making Performance Appraisal Work for Teams." *Training,* June 1994, pp. 58-63.

————. "Performance Appraisal Lessons from Thirteen Years in the Trenches." *Performance & Instruction,* July 1994, pp. 3-13.

Books

Beatty, Richard W., et al., eds. *Performance, Measurement, Management, and Appraisal Sourcebook.* Amherst, MA: HRD Press, 1995.

Cadwell, Charles M. *The Human Touch Performance Appraisal.* 2d edition. West Des Moines, IA: American Media Publishing, 1994.

Grote, Dick. *The Complete Guide to Performance Appraisal.* New York: AMACOM, 1996.

Jerome, Paul J. *Evaluating Employee Performance.* Irvine, CA: Richard Chang Associates, 1997.

Kirkpatrick, Donald L. *How to Improve Performance through Appraisal and Coaching.* New York: AMACOM, 1985.

Lecky-Thompson, Roy. *Constructive Appraisals.* New York: AMACOM, 1999.

Mager, Robert F., and Peter Pipe. *Analyzing Performance Problems.* 3d revised edition. Atlanta: Center for Effective Performance, 1997.

Moglia, Tony. *Partners in Performance.* Menlo Park, CA: Crisp Publications, 1997.

Murphy, Kevin R., and Jeanette N. Cleveland. *Understanding Performance Appraisal: Social, Organizational, and Goal-Based Perspectives.* Thousand Oaks, CA: Sage Publications, 1995.

Rummler, Geary A., and Alan P. Brache. *Improving Performance: How to Manage the White Space on the Organization Chart.* 2d edition. San Francisco: Jossey-Bass, 1995.

Tracey, William R., ed. *Human Resources Management and Development Handbook.* 2d edition. New York: AMACOM, 1994.

Checklist: Preparing a Performance Review

Here are some suggestions for "getting it all together" before an annual performance review meeting.

1. Remind the employee of the performance review process:

☐ Identify potential dates for the meeting.

☐ Review with the employee how to prepare for the meeting (for instance, do you want him or her to do a self-appraisal first, to come prepared with a list of accomplishments?)

2. Determine sources for performance data: Compile a list of sources of data about the employee's performance (the performance plan; feedback from clients, internal customers, peers; accomplishment reports).

3. Review and analyze the data:

☐ Analyze the data gathered from a variety of sources.

☐ Avoid personal biases.

☐ Assess performance against each performance goal.

☐ Support each observation with examples and specific details.

4. Determine rating: Calculate overall rating for the entire year (or portion of year, if appropriate).

5. Prepare to summarize at the end of the meeting:

☐ What are the strengths?

☐ What are the areas for improvement?

☐ What are the implications for professional or career development activities for the next year?

6. Communicate to the next-level manager:

☐ Share written review.

☐ Share rationale for rating.

☐ Solicit views from next-level manager and ask to support your decision.

7. Confirm the performance review data.

Job Aid

Checklist: Conducting a Performance Review

Here are the steps to follow when conducting a successful performance review.

1. Open the meeting:

☐ Establish rapport.

☐ Explain the purpose of the review.

2. Create dialogue:

☐ Encourage the person to talk.

☐ Listen; don't interrupt.

3. Review the goals and standards: All feedback should refer to these goals and standards.

4. Keep feedback objective: Feedback should focus on behaviors, actions, and performance, not personality.

5. Discuss accomplishments:

☐ Solicit person's view first.

☐ Supplement person's view with your view.

6. Discuss areas for improvement:

☐ Solicit person's view first.

☐ Supplement person's self-feedback with your view.

7. Discuss performance rating.

8. Discuss future performance cycle in light of strengths and areas for improvement.

9. Develop a plan for training or professional development for the next year.

10. Summarize meeting.

11. Agree on follow-up or progress checks, as appropriate.

Succession Planning

Issue 0405

Succession Planning

....

AUTHOR

Sandra Hastings, Ph.D
Sandra Hastings Associates
17 Hebron Rd.
Bolton, CT 06043
Tel: 860.643.0624
Email: SLHastings@aol.com

Sandra Hastings in a nationally known author, consultant, trainer, and president of Sandra Hastings Associates. She has helped organizations of all sizes implement award-winning organizational changes.

CONTRIBUTING AUTHORS

Marilyn Buckner, Ph.D.
National Training Systems, Inc.
4800 East Conway Drive, NW
Altanta, GA 30327
Tel: 404.843.1953
Email: drbruckner@aol.com

Lynn Slavenski
Equifax, Inc.
1550 Peachtree Street
Altanta, GA 30309
Email: lynn.slavenski@equifax.com

Managing Editor
Tora Estep

Contributing Editor
Stephanie Sussan

Production Design
Kathleen Schaner

**Manager
Acquisitions and Development**
Mark Morrow

Revised 2005

Succession Planning

In today's ever-changing world of mergers, acquisitions, downsizes, shrinking markets, and flattening organizations, many organizations are asking:

1. Do we have qualified people ready to fill key positions now and grow the business in the next three to five years? (Short-term emphasis.)

2. Will we have a sufficient number of qualified candidates ready in five to ten years to fill key positions? (Long-term emphasis.)

Adding to the urgency of the above questions is the reduction in the workforce that is quickly approaching as the baby-boomer generation nears retirement. This could mean:

- lost productivity

- lost knowledge, experience, and institutional memory

- a limited pool of employees qualified to replace retirees

- a limited pool of potential candidates because of a national decline in the number of workers in the 25-44–year range

- stiff competition with other organizations to keep workers who are not retiring from seeking opportunities elsewhere.

These losses are equivalent to a sports team losing talented players. To avoid getting caught with the ball and no one left on your team who knows how to play, your organization should prepare a succession plan.

What is Succession Planning?

Everyone talks about succession planning, but what exactly is it? As you would expect, the primary component of a succession plan is the identification of replacement personnel. At its simplest, it is the determination of who will fill a job when it opens. At its best, replacement identification includes an evaluation of the quality and readiness of the named successors.

Ultimately, succession planning is a long-term strategic initiative that ensures that the right staff are in the right jobs at the right times. It ensures the continued effective performance of an organization by establishing a process to develop and replace key staff over time. It also helps your organization answer key questions such as:

- Who will move into this human resource position when Kay retires?

- John could move into any one of these three director positions. If he accepts one, who will replace him in his current position? Is this the best position for John?

- How can we keep Sally from leaving us if she doesn't get the promotion?

- How can we get more female and minority employees into key positions?

If your organization carries out succession planning correctly, you will be able to confidently say that you are well prepared for the future! This *Infoline* presents a model that will help you do just that in four simple steps: establish the scope of the plan; create the plan; implement the plan; and monitor, evaluate, and revise the plan (see the sidebar, *Four Phases of Succession Planning*). And, keep in mind, that there are myriad software solutions out there that can help you with each of these phases. (See the sidebar, *Technology Can Simplify Succession Planning*, for more information.)

Phase 1: Establish the Scope

Generally, HR staff leads a succession-planning effort with staff input. When you establish the scope of a succession plan, be sure to:

- review your organization's strategic plan

- analyze attrition data and retirement projections

- identify external factors

- define parameters of the plan.

Four Phases of Succession Planning

Succession planning is completed in four phases, as illustrated in the figure below.

Phase 1. Establish the Scope

1. Review the organization's strategic plan.
2. Analyze attrition data and retirement projections.
3. Determine external factors.
4. Define the scope of succession planning.

Phase 4. Monitor, Evaluate, Revise

1. Monitor progress and make necessary interventions.
2. Evaluate implementation and revise the plan based on lessons learned and new succession-planning issues.

Phase 2. Create a Succession Plan

1. Identify job functions.
2. Identify staffing levels needed and related KSAs.
3. Determine availability of staff.
4. Conduct gap analysis and establish priorities.
5. Create a workforce plan with strategies and measures of success.

Phase 3. Implement the Plan

1. Communicate the succession-planning process.
2. Implement strategies.

Review the Strategic Plan

Succession planning builds on an organization's strategic plan, which outlines how the organization will reach the measurable goals and objectives that support its mission and vision. The strategic plan shapes business strategy with information from customers, aligns employees' behavior to the organization's mission, and turns employees' intentions into actions.

Review your company's strategic plan to identify current and future priorities. These will determine how your staff is distributed across departments and divisions, define functional responsibilities, and create technology to support delivery of the organization's products and services. You need to understand these priorities to identify where retirement and general attrition will have the greatest impact on your organization.

Analyze the Data

Succession planning requires an analysis of retirement projections, attrition patterns, and the anticipated effects of retirement and attrition.

Determine the number of employees who are 50 years of age or older. (See the sidebar *Retirement Analysis* for tips on how to do this.)

Then, you should determine how many 50+ individuals might retire in the next 5, 10, and 15 years. Be sure to review the eligibility requirements of your organization's retirement plan. Also, survey employees to determine their retirement goals (see the job aid, *Workplace Planning Questionnaire*, at the end of this *Infoline* for a sample questionnaire).

The next step is to analyze the current patterns of attrition to make projections. Gather the following statistical data for the past one to five years and break it down by age, education level, race, and gender:

- number of current employees
- number of new hires
- number of voluntary separations

Technology Can Simplify Succession Planning

There's no doubt that the advent of Learning Management Systems and other learning and performance software tools have simplified the life of the busy training and performance professional. These complex systems coordinate everything from training registration to assessment to learning data to curriculums.

But the technology doesn't end there. These systems often can help you optimize your succession planning by tracking performance, identifying skill gaps, and noting employee qualifications and education.

And the good news is it doesn't have break your organization's budget. Many of these systems leverage off of your existing IT infrastructure. The first step is to see if your current system can be adapted to include succession-planning data. If it does, it's just a matter of working with your technology group to optimize the software to your needs. If, however, you decide to embark on a new system, keep the four phases in mind when selecting the appropriate software (refer to the diagram at left).

- number of involuntary separations
- number of other separations (for example, disability or death)
- average length of employment
- turnover rate
- reasons for attrition.

Identify External Factors

Assess how any external factors affect staffing levels. The goal is to determine how to focus your succession-planning efforts, given the context in which retirement and staff replacement are taking place.

Retirement Analysis

The following example presents a three-step method to analyze retirement projections. Use it to paint a picture of the retirement outlook in your organization in the next 5, 10, and 15 years.

1. Start by determining the number of employees more than 50 at various staff levels:

    ● Executive staff (chief officers, vice presidents): 23 of 28

    ● Management staff (directors, administrators, managers, and supervisors): 56 of 83

    ● Frontline staff: 182 of 396.

2. Next, divide each group more than 50 into three age ranges (50-54, 55-59, and 60+). Using the example of management staff from above:

    ● Twenty-seven of the 56 (48 percent) are 50-54.

    ● Twenty-one of the 56 (38 percent) are 55-59.

    ● Eight of the 56 (14 percent) are 60+.

3. Finally, create tables for each staff level group that identifies department, number of employees in department in total, employees in 50+ age ranges, and total number of employees 50-60+. Include reports for each office, division, or department as necessary. The following example is an abbreviated version of a frontline staff table.

Department	Total	50-54	55-59	60+	Total 50-60+
Workforce development	3	1			1 (33%)
Sales	7	3	1		4 (43%)
Finance and HR	5	1			1 (20%)
Building services	2	1			1 (50%)
Information technology	7	3	0		3 (43%)
TOTALS	24	9	1	0	10 (21%)

Define Plan Parameters

It's important to ensure that you can accomplish your goals within a reasonable timeframe. To do this, narrow the succession-planning process to a manageable scope. Decide which is better: Starting with a small project and building it over time, or starting with a large project.

Phase 2. Create the Plan

When conducting your planning, create a bottom-up approach—either specific positions or a pool for similar positions—whereby managers at lower levels make initial recommendations as to who can be replacements for direct reports. Then, have each higher level of management review the recommendations and make revisions. Together with management, take the following steps to create your succession plan:

● identify job functions

● identify staffing levels needed and related knowledge, skills, and abilities (KSAs)

● determine what staff members are available

● conduct a gap analysis and establish priorities

● develop a workforce plan that includes measures of success.

Identify Job Functions

Job functions are major responsibilities of programs or departments that have specific outputs and outcomes for internal and external clients. Given the scope of the succession plan that you have established, identify which functions you will need to staff. Consider existing functions, as well as future functions.

To assess current and future staff needs, answer these questions:

● What services or products may be discontinued or outsourced?

● Which functions will remain unchanged?

- How will the organization enhance or change existing services or products?

- Will the enhancements involve significant changes in the work process?

- What functions, if any, will be consolidated?

- What new services or products will be offered?

- What technological changes will be made or introduced?

- Is a reorganization needed? Does the current structure make sense given future needs?

- Are there plans to open new offices or close existing offices?

Identify Staffing Levels and KSAs

Once you know which functions are important to the succession plan, determine staffing needs by identifying critical KSAs and the number of staff needed with each KSA or competency set. You need to ask:

- What KSAs are needed to perform the targeted management functions?

- What KSAs are needed to perform the targeted frontline functions?

- What job classifications or titles could provide incumbents with the needed capabilities? What job classifications or titles could provide the needed capabilities if requirements were modified or incumbents developed?

- What competencies do not fit within the existing structure of the organization? Which of these competencies will require the development of a new title?

- What are the projected workload volumes for each job title?

- What staffing levels are needed by competency or title, level, and geographic location? Will you want to change supervisor-staff ratios?

- How will the organization ensure diversity?

- How do technology, budget, work process, and service delivery changes affect competencies and staffing levels?

- Will the organization provide alternative work schedules? If so, how will these changes affect staffing and/or recruitment?

Determine Staff Availability

In this step, you will determine how many staff will be available after the anticipated attrition of the target population, and assess the skill sets of remaining employees.

To calculate staff supply, use this three-step process:

1. Calculate the number of employees. Group the total number of employees by the following categories: title, grade, organization, location, skills or competencies, and other.

2. Calculate the attrition pattern. Sum the number of employees likely to retire, resign, die, transfer, or obtain an interdepartmental promotion by title, grade, organization, location, skills or competencies, and other.

3. Describe the projected workforce based on expected attrition without hiring replacements. To understand what the workforce might look like, consider the following questions:

   - What are the existing employees' competencies for each job classification?

   - What are the employee-specific competencies, including the competencies that fall outside of normal duties (for example, the ability to speak Spanish or visual design skills)?

   - What are the demographics, including occupation, title, grade level, organizational structure, and retirement eligibility?

   - What are the attrition rates for each demographic category? Factor in other variables such as the likelihood of certain employees to retire.

- What will the future composition of the workforce be, based on the existing demographics and projected attrition rates without factoring in any hiring?

Remember to review all employees to see whether they should be successors. Be sure to look at his or her:

- time in current position
- performance
- readiness for advancement
- potential to move to a new position
- development required.

After determining what the staff supply is likely to be, identify remaining employees with the skills to replace retiring staff members.

If it seems like there is a minimal supply of future talent, you should begin to beef up your organization's development programs. Unless development is a strong part of a succession-planning program, the actual replacement will not be able to move into a designated position and the high-potential employee will not be prepared.

Identify High-Potential Employees

A high-potential employee is someone who has the ability to move into—and perhaps above—a particular level, such as vice president or other key positions in an organization. To narrowly define *high potential*, look at critical competency areas for leaders. High potentials need to have management, as well as growth potential. The following factors are common denominators among those with leadership capacity:

Results driven—has completed many challenging assignments.

People skills—influences, motivates, works with a wide range of people.

Mental ability—street smart, asks insightful questions.

Lifelong learning—seeks challenging opportunities for new knowledge, learns from successes and failures.

Integrated thinking—links ideas, sees essence of problem.

Flexible—adjusts priorities, takes risks, and embraces change.

Energy—gets energy from work and energizes others.

For more about high-potential employees and a useful tool for succession planning, see the sidebars *High-Potential Definitions* and *Succession Summary Tool.*

Analyze Gaps and Priorities

Conduct a gap analysis to determine the existence and/or extent of a skill gap for each job. You can use the method used in the tables in the sidebar *Sample Gap Analysis.* Don't forget to factor in your organization's diversity goals into the analysis.

To understand the gap between supply and demand, answer the following questions:

- Are there lists of eligible candidates for the jobs your organization needs to fill?

- Will the lists still be valid when you need to fill positions? Do the candidates on the lists have the needed skills? Will the candidates still be on the list when you need to fill the positions?

- Do you conduct exams for any of the positions? If so, when will the next exam be given? How will the exam cycle affect the organization's ability to appoint or hire qualified applicants?

- If there is no appropriate job title that provides the competencies needed for a future position, to what extent does the projected workforce provide these competencies? Consider the estimated number of qualified people based on likely job titles and estimates of the number of people who would pass a qualifying exam.

- How many staff would need to be recruited externally for positions filled on an open competitive basis (include adherence to Equal Employment Opportunity goals).

High-Potential Definitions

Only 5 percent of those in a salary range mentioned below should be considered high-potential employees. (This is the norm in many organizations.) The following are definitions of high-potential employees:

Potential to be a senior-level officer in any sector

- can advance two job levels within five years

- demonstrates quantifiable accomplishments

- if in field, willing to relocate

- if at headquarters, willing to get field experience (relocate) if needed to become senior officer in their career ladder

- has potential for at least 10 to 15 more years with the company.

These candidates should have the following characteristics:

- people skills

- management skills (decision making, planning and organization, leadership, oral communication)

- background, knowledge (understand business, technical knowledge, experience)

- traits such as results orientation, ability to deal with change, flexibility

- willingness to move from sector to sector.

Potential to be at least regional or staff executive

- can advance two job levels within five years

- if in field, willing to relocate

- if at headquarters, willing to relocate if needed in their career ladder

- demonstrates quantifiable accomplishments.

These candidates should have the following characteristics:

- people skills

- management skills (decision making, planning and organization, leadership, oral communication)

- background, knowledge (understand business, technical knowledge, experience)

- traits such as results orientation, ability to deal with change, flexibility

- willingness to move from sector to sector.

Potential to be general manager, department head

- same criteria as above

In some cases, sectors also will provide definitions of sector high-potential employees.

Succession Summary Tool

The position is listed first on the form because it is the focus of the planning process. You can collect optional pieces of data, such as Social Security or other employee identification numbers that are used to retrieve information electronically.

A job-function code identifies the type of job that an incumbent occupies or can fill in the future. This code is helpful if the system is expected to do candidate searches for similar positions. The probability of vacancy (PV) rating alerts the organization if a manager will be leaving in less than one year. The successor(s) are listed on the right of the form with their potential (PO), readiness (RE), and performance (PR) ratings.

Division: _____

Department: _____

Unit: _____

RATING MANAGER (Manager of Unit)	JOB FUNCTION CODE _____ SUCCESSION NAMES	PV	PO	RE	PR
POSITION: NAME: ID#	(List candidates in order of preference.) 1. NAME: ID# 2. NAME: ID# 3. NAME: ID#	___ ___ ___	___ ___ ___	___ ___ ___	___ ___ ___

DIRECT REPORT POSITIONS	JOB FUNCTION CODE SUCCESSION NAMES	PV	PO	RE	PR
POSITION: NAME: ID#	(List candidates in order of preference.) 1. NAME: ID# 2. NAME: ID# 3. NAME: ID#	___ ___ ___	___ ___ ___	___ ___ ___	___ ___ ___

Note: If you do not have an ID# for a person on the list, please contact your personnel or human resources representative for assistance.

PROBABILITY OF VACANCY

1. Within 12 months
2. Within 1-2 years
3. Beyond 2 years

POTENTIAL

1. Advance 2-3 levels
2. Advance at least 1 level
3. Move to a lateral position

READINESS

R. Ready now
F. Ready 1-3 years
Q. Promotability within 5 years is questionable
? Too early to evaluate

PERFORMANCE

1. Exceptional
2. Exceeds expectations
3. Meets expectations
4. Does not meet expectations
X. New in Position

JOB FUNCTION CODES

01 Finance/Accounting
02 Contracts Administration
03 Sales
04 Account Management
05 Public Relations & External Affairs
07 Human Resources
08 Security
09 Data Processing
10 Library
11 Purchasing
12 Material Handling & Distribution
13 Facilities & Plant Maintenance
14 Communications & Administrative Services
15 Executive Support & Planning & Business Development
16 Publications
17 Technical
18 Technical Support
20 Airplane Operations
21 Manufacturing Managers
23 General Managers & Executives
40 Legal

Sample Gap Analysis

The following tables present an example of a gap analysis. The numbers were created for purposes of illustration.

Projections of Need for Sales Managers in 2021		New York Office	Atlanta Office	Phoenix Office	Total
Today's supply (January 2004)	Job title (for example sales manager)	45	23	17	85
Projected (based on trend data):					
Transfers or resignations		-8	-3	-1	-12
Retirements		-12	-9	-7	-28
Other separations (death, dismissal, other job)		-5	-3	-2	-10
Future supply (January 2021)		20	8	7	35
Future demand (January 2021)		43	25	16	84
Gap (to be filled by sales staff)		-23	-17	-9	-49

Projections of Need for Sales Managers in 2021		New York Office	Atlanta Office	Phoenix Office	Total
Today's supply (January 2021)	Staff	216	73	65	354
Projected (based on trend data):					
Transfers or resignations		-13	-8	-10	-31
Retirements		-42	-9	-18	-69
Promotion to Sales Supervisor (assuming acceptance of promotions)		-23	-17	-9	-49
Other separations (death, dismissal, other job)		-15	-7	-6	-28
Future supply (January 2021)		132	32	22	177
Future demand (January 2021)		215	85	80	380
Gap		-92	-53	-58	-203

- What's the number of staff who will no longer be needed because of restructuring and changes in job functions?

You'll identify primarily three types of gaps:

1. Excess staff performing obsolete or declining functions or functions that you can outsource.

2. Inadequate supply of qualified staff for positions that likely will go unchanged.

3. Inadequate supply of staff with skills for positions that may require a change in classification.

After analyzing the gaps, consider the direction of the organization to prioritize staff gaps in the succession plan. To complete this step of the process you will want to identify:

- the staffing gaps that do not require a large commitment of resources

- the benefit of addressing the remaining anticipated staffing shortages

- the implications if you do not address all of the staffing gaps.

Considering your answers to these questions, prioritize each of the job titles or functions by need and get executive input and approval for establishing staffing priorities.

Create a Workforce Plan

Now that you have prioritized job titles and functions, create solutions to staffing shortages. As you identify actions to address skill gaps, you also may uncover associated costs (for example, staff resources). Reorder your priorities if costs seem excessive relative to the likelihood of success.

Develop implementation strategies for each goal in your project plan. To create the implementation strategies you will want to:

- research best practices of other organizations

- familiarize yourself with the topic

- ask for employee input on the topic

- brainstorm potential solutions by evaluating pros and cons of each option

- identify barriers and recommendations to eliminate barriers.

Some solutions for staffing shortages are presented in the sidebar *Staffing Shortage Solutions*.

Create measures of success for each implementation strategy you decide to pursue. Define success and determine outcomes that will demonstrate attainment of goals by developing measures for each specific outcome. Create interim measures of success to be used for monitoring progress, as well as final measures of success.

Measures of success are critical because you will use them to communicate to staff and executives the value of the work done by the succession-planning team. Without measures you cannot prove accomplishments and ensure continued support for the team's work.

Phase 3. Implement the Plan

In the implementation phase, you will communicate the succession-planning process and implement the strategies defined in it.

Communicate the Plan

Because communication of a major initiative can define its success, sharing information about the plan is critical before, during, and after implementation.

It's also important to remember that employees determine the significance of an initiative by evaluating the communication associated with the initiative. To emphasize the importance of the initiative, create a communication plan that ensures continued, visible information about the status of the strategic-planning effort. Remember that consistent, visible support from management will encourage employees to support the initiative. To gain support, everyone in management must "walk the talk."

The sidebar, *Communication Plan,* presents a sample communication plan, while the following is a list of components you may want to make part of the plan:

- a message from the CEO (for example, a written letter or email, a speech, or a video)

- meetings with all staff to explain the project, including the timeline

- regular updates for all staff through letters, meetings, emails, or intranet postings

- opportunities to ask or get answers to questions during implementation.

In the introduction to the succession plan (done by executive staff and management staff), include the following elements:

- introduction: background, goals, assumptions, description of current state of the organization, and description of need

- description of the project: sequence and dates of activities, connection between activities and the organization's strategic plan, avenues for feedback, milestones, and methods to measure progress

- explanation of the benefits (to the organization, as well as to individual workers)

- discussion of potential common concerns

- review of critical stakeholders (each person in the organization is a critical stakeholder)

- expectations and commitments

- conclusion

- questions and answers.

Whenever you communicate with staff, use feedback loops to determine how your communication plan is working. Ask what the staff thought about the message, and if they thought the medium and timing was appropriate. Also, ask if other media should have been used and if other groups have been missed or other questions need to be answered.

Implement Strategies

When you roll out the succession plan, consider the following tips and tasks.

■ *Get Top Management Support*
A sense of urgency is the single most important factor in successful succession planning. To establish succession planning as a priority, tie it to the organization's strategic plan and get resources assigned to the project. Executives and directors will want to determine the best way to get the initiative off the ground and maintain its momentum.

■ *Conduct Management Review Meetings*
Review meetings keep the succession-planning effort in the minds of top management and give them the opportunity to shape the process. In addition, the senior management team will want to incorporate discussion of the succession-planning process in staff meetings.

■ *Put Development First*
Successful succession planning will result in desired outcomes only if high-potential employees develop their KSAs. Ensure that development of staff is a key priority for all departments, divisions, and offices.

■ *Move People Effectively*
Transition to new jobs must be well planned and well executed for replacement strategies to be effective. Ensure that all managers are involved and supportive of interdepartmental assignments.

■ *Engage Key Stakeholders*
Ensure acceptance for the succession-planning process by engaging individuals representing key stakeholder groups (for example, unions). Before you implement specific strategies, communicate the following:

- what you plan to do and what you plan to produce (for example, training, articles, intranet site, new job classifications)

- the implementation schedule, including due dates for drafts, revisions, final products, and so forth

- the benefits to employees and the identification of who will be affected and how

Staffing Shortage Solutions

To develop your staffing solutions, consider these actions and strategies.

Position Classification Actions

These actions include:

- streamlining job duties for more efficiency
- modifying titles to incorporate new duties
- creating new job titles
- redesigning titles to accommodate new work patterns
- reallocating titles to meet emerging business needs.

Recruitment and Selection Strategies

These include actions to recruit and hire qualified candidates. To enhance your current competitive hiring process:

- determine the strengths of your organization
- ask staff to identify reasons they like their jobs
- research best-practice recruitment strategies
- incorporate strategies that successful organizations use (for example, online recruitment and effective interviewing techniques)
- create a comprehensive recruitment strategy to ensure that your organization is the "employer of choice"
- create strategies to re-employ retirees for part-time and/or temporary work, evaluate candidates for all job openings, and recruit minorities and women.

Retention Strategies

Once you've hired the best, you'll want strategies to keep them. To build a formal retention plan:

- develop an effective orientation program
- ensure managers and supervisors can facilitate transition into the organization through the assignment of buddies, frequent meetings with the new employee, and training
- implement a reward and recognition program that acknowledges the work of exceptional employees and appeals to all workers

- assign interesting and challenging work
- reduce negative workplace practices
- provide benefits that increase loyalty (for example, wellness program, flextime, free parking, training, and tuition reimbursement)
- research and implement best practice retention ideas
- provide opportunities for all staff to continually enhance skills and increase learning.

Organizational Interventions

Organizational interventions could include:

- permanent redeployment of staff
- temporary assignment of staff
- new organizational structure
- job shadowing for key jobs before an individual retires
- establishment of mentoring programs
- mandatory training for employees in key positions.

Knowledge Transfer Strategies

Create formal and informal processes to capture the knowledge of experienced workers before they leave. Knowledge management strategies include:

- apprenticeships, internships, and traineeships
- best practices
- communities of practice
- documentation of processes
- document repositories
- expert interviews
- job aids
- knowledge audits
- knowledge fairs
- knowledge maps and inventories
- learning games
- lessons learned debriefings
- mentoring
- on-the-job training
- storytelling
- training.

Staff-Development Strategies

Because filling key positions that open up due to retirement and changing business needs is an ongoing problem, develop career-development strategies that routinely prepare replacements for staff in key positions.

Provide skill-building opportunities (formal and informal) for all staff through a variety of job assignments, training sessions, self study, coaching, job shadowing, job enrichment and rotation, and so forth.

In addition, use a standardized career-development process to ensure all employees know how to develop the skills necessary to be considered for lateral and promotional opportunities.

Devote significant time to creating training options that ensure staff have the skills to fill future positions. Some actions to consider when designing training opportunities include:

- identifying competencies (general and job specific) for executives, management, and front-line staff
- prioritizing training options based on the organization's strategic goals and objectives
- determining the best way to train
- committing training funds for training needed to promote staff readiness for future job openings
- getting employee input about potential career options
- designing career-development programs for employees
- assessing the skills of high-potential employees.

- the individuals responsible for implementation of various strategies

- the schedule for information to be shared with employees, including the medium of communication.

■ *Anticipate Staff Reactions*
Be ready to respond to questions and barriers that arise at all points during the implementation process.

■ *Get Nay Sayers on Board*
Involve them in the process. Have them identify solutions to pitfalls that they identify.

Finally, frame the implementation of succession strategies as "continuous improvement" and communicate what worked and what will be improved during each step of the process.

Phase 4. Monitor, Evaluate, Revise

Once you have implemented the succession plan, monitor progress, evaluate the implementation and revise the plan as needed.

Monitor Progress

To monitor the implementation process, you need to:

- review progress at predetermined points in time (which should be part of the implementation plan)

- determine if the succession plan is on track to meet timeline objectives; if not, have the succession-planning team determine how to get back on schedule

- measure interim results as required, analyze results, and make changes in the work plan as necessary

- report progress to your organization's executives on a regular basis

- create and administer regularly scheduled communication briefings to keep staff informed and answer questions to clarify the project.

Communication Plan

The table presents a sample communication plan.

What	How	When	Who
Launch the initiative	Memo to staff	Before the start of the implementation phase of the project	CEO; public relations office; directors, managers, and supervisors
Communicate progress	Newspaper article interviewing succession team members Staff meetings Newspaper articles Regular intranet updates Answers to staff questions shared Report of attainment of milestones Interview with succession-planning team	Weekly, monthly, and daily as necessary	CEO; public relations office; directors, managers, supervisors, and succession planning team

Evaluate and Revise the Plan

Because succession planning will become an ongoing part of your organization's business plan, you need to evaluate the effectiveness of the succession plan and make revisions as appropriate.

You'll need to consider several continuous improvement issues. For example, have there been unanticipated changes in the external environment that affect decisions about staffing needs? If so, what were the changes and how will you need to change the succession plan to reflect the new reality?

Is staff retiring at the rate anticipated or is there a difference between retirements and projected retirements? If there's a difference, how do you need to change the succession plan to ensure staffing readiness?

Will your organization achieve its goals given the current pace of the succession-planning effort?

Does feedback from staff indicate that they understand the succession-planning effort or do you need to revise your communication efforts for this initiative?

Do formal evaluations of the succession-planning process suggest modifications that need to be made to improve efficiency?

Are the staff replacing retirees able to assume their new job responsibilities without having a negative effect on their direct reports and the organization? Or is your organization experiencing a brain drain in key positions that was not addressed in the original plan? If a skill gap exists, what adjustments will the organization need to make to eliminate the problems now and in the future?

Finally, determine if your organization met the goals of the succession plan and achieved the planned measurable results. If it didn't, what corrections will you need to make to attain the goals and objectives of the succession plan? After all, the implementation of a successful succession-planning program will help ensure that your organization is ready to deal with the constantly changing workplace of the future.

Books

Ahlichs, Nancy. *Competing for Talent: Key Recruitment and Retention Strategies for Becoming an Employer of Choice.* Palo Alto, CA: Davies-Black Publishing, 2000.

Arthur, Diane. *Recruiting, Interviewing, Selecting, and Orienting New Employees.* 3rd Edition. New York: AMACOM, 1998.

Beazley, Hamilton, Jeremiah Boenisch, and David Harden. *Continuity Management: Preserving Corporate Knowledge and Productivity When Employees Leave.* Hoboken, NJ: John Wiley & Sons, 2002.

Blank, William E. *Handbook for Developing Competency-Based Training Programs.* Englewood Cliffs, NJ: Prentice-Hall, 1990.

Duane, Michael John. *Customized Human Resource Planning: Different Practices for Different Organizations.* Westport, CT: Quorum Books, 1996.

Green, Paul C. *Building Robust Competencies: Linking Human Resource Systems to Organizational Strategies.* San Francisco, CA: Jossey-Bass, 1999.

Harris, Jim, and Joan Brannick. *Finding and Keeping Great Employees.* New York: AMACOM, 1999.

Kaye, Beverly, and Sharon Jordan-Evans. *Love'em or Lose'em: Getting Good People to Stay.* San Francisco, CA: Berrett-Koehler, 1999.

McCall, Morgan W., Jr. *High Flyers: Developing the Next Generation of Leaders.* Boston, MA: Harvard Business School Press, 1998.

National Academy of Public Administration. *Building Successful Organizations: A Guide to Strategic Workforce Planning.* Washington, D.C., 2000.

————. *Building the Workforce of the Future to Achieve Organization Success.* Washington, D.C., 1999.

Rothwell, William J. *Effective Succession Planning: Ensuring Leadership Continuity and Building Talent From Within.* 2nd Edition. New York: AMACOM, 2001.

Rothwell, William J., Robert K. Prescott, and Maria W. Taylor. *Strategic Human Resource Leader: How to Prepare Your Organization for the Six Key Trends Shaping the Future.* Palo Alto, CA: Davies-Black, 1998.

Rumizen, Melissie Clemmons. *The Complete Idiot's Guide to Knowledge Management.* Madison, WI: CWL Publishing, 2002.

Wenger, Etienne, Richard McDermott, and William M. Snyder. *Cultivating Communities of Practice.* Boston, MA: Harvard Business School Press, 2002.

Articles

Byham, William C. "How to Create a Reservoir of Ready-Made Leaders." *T+D.* March 2000, pp. 29-32.

Rothwell, William and Rich Wellins. "Putting New Competencies to Work For You." *T+D.* May 2004, pp. 94-101.

Websites

Census Bureau. Available at http://www.census.gov.

Colorado. Available at http://www.state.co.us/gov.

Department of Commerce. Available at http://www.bea.doc.gov.

Department of the Interior. Available at http://www.doi.gov/hrm/doiwfp.html.

Department of Labor (Bureau of Labor Statistics). Available at http://www.bls.gov.

Department of Transportation (DOT). Available at http://www.dot.gov.

General Accounting Office (GAO). Available at http://www.gao.gov/.

Georgia. Available at http://www/gms.state.ga.us.

Health and Human Services (HHS). Available at http://www.hhs.gov.

Internal Personnel Management Association. Available at http://www.ipma-hr.org/.

Kansas. Available at http://da.state.ks.

Minnesota. Available at http://doer.state.mn.us.

New York. Available at http://www.cs.state.ny.us/

Office of Personnel Management. Available at http://www.opm.gov/workforceplanning/index.htm.

South Carolina. Available at http://www.state.sc.us/ohr/workforce01/wfplanmenu.htm.

Washington State. Available at http://www.wa.gov.

Workforce Planning Questionnaire

During the next 15 years more than 50 percent of our employees will become eligible for retirement. Whether or not all these employees choose to retire, the organization wants to plan for the inevitable changes in the workforce. Specifically, we want to provide opportunities for employees who don't want to retire but might like a more flexible work schedule, as well as opportunities for individuals to obtain the education and training needed to assume new positions.

To help us achieve these goals, we ask you to complete this questionnaire so that we can more accurately assess the workplace needs of all employees. Thank you for helping us get a snapshot of what the future workforce might be. Once the data has been compiled, we will share the results of the survey with all staff.

Job title_____

Check the appropriate boxes:

1. My position is:

☐ administrative support staff (receptionists, secretaries, administrative assistants)
☐ frontline staff (deliver service to customers and support direct service to customers)
☐ director
☐ supervisor
☐ manager

2. I am eligible to retire in:

☐ the next five years
☐ the next 10 years
☐ the next 15 years

3. I plan to retire in:

☐ the next five years
☐ the next 10 years
☐ the next 15 years

4. I would like to have the following new position in five years:

☐ Supervisor
☐ Manager
☐ Director
☐ Executive
☐ Other (specify) _____

5. I would like to have the following new position in 10 years:

☐ Supervisor
☐ Manager
☐ Director
☐ Executive
☐ Other (specify) _____

6. I would like to have the following new position in 15 years:

☐ Supervisor
☐ Manager
☐ Director
☐ Executive
☐ Other (specify) _____

Answer the following question only if you are eligible for retirement in the next 15 years.

7. When I am eligible for retirement I would like to:

☐ Retire
☐ Work fewer hours (part time)
☐ Have a flex schedule (for example, work four days and have three days off)
☐ Other (specify) _____

Change Management

Issue 9904

Change Management

AUTHOR

Stella Louise Cowan, M.Ed.
Tel: 313.393.0050
Fax: 313.393.0051
Email: Indybridge@msn.com

Stella Cowan has worked in training design and delivery and organizational development for more than 14 years. Her work experience is vast—ranging from acting as a learning systems consultant to a leadership education specialist. She now operates a business in instructional design. Stella is also an adjunct professor in management at Spring Arbor College and Baker College.

Editor
Cat Sharpe

Associate Editor
Sabrina E. Hicks

Production Design
Anne Morgan

ASTD Internal Consultant
Phil Anderson

Change: The Inevitable Reality

Organizations are under siege by a relentless business environment—relentless due to its ability to change at an exponential rate. As a result, negative realities such as the following persist:

- shrinking market share
- increasing customer demands
- continuing inefficient, obsolete processes
- altering workforce due to demographic changes.

Creating solutions to harness these changes and providing practitioners to guide the helm of change are hot topics for people like us in the training or human resources (HR) profession. Organizations need change practitioners who can not only conceive of the broad, *aerial* strategy but also break down this strategy into specific action-oriented activities that move the change forward (that is, operationalize the strategy). We call this the *ground* view.

You must have an aerial, big picture view of your organization's approach to change. This big picture falls flat, however, if you do not operationalize it. Listed below are the key players in managing the change for your organization:

- organizational development specialist
- trainer
- HR expert.

Although there is no magic elixir to ease organizational change, certain tactics can help you manage your organization's change efforts. Use this issue of *Infoline* as a primer on change management tactics and the skills needed to facilitate change and implementation roadblocks. This issue includes a number of tools, hands-on examples, and models for change practitioners to use as resources and ideas. With the continued increase in mergers, downsizing, and reengineering, these tools are beneficial because possessing a high level of such change practitioner skills is extremely valuable and marketable.

The Broad or Aerial View

The emphasis of this *Infoline* is the tactical side of change management; however, we must start by taking a look at a typical broad view. The *Six-Phase Change Strategy Model* sidebar on the following page represents the phases of change along a continuum. It shows that progress can be forward or backward, depending on what is going on in the organization.

You must remember that change is incremental relative to both the redesign or reengineering of processes and the transformation of employee attitudes and behaviors. Attitudes and behaviors such as sliding trust, increasing disengagement, and growing fear are challenging to manage and require most of the actions described in the six steps of the model. The change manager (whether he or she is an organizational development specialist, trainer, or HR practitioner) supports forward movement through programs and active advocacy of change. The bottom line is that successful change demands a multipronged approach.

The Dynamics of Change

Having a broad, aerial view for the change process is just the first step. You need perspective on the challenge of moving each employee through the different phases of change acceptance, which we will refer to as the Adaptation/Acceptance Spectrum (consult the sidebar by that title). Keep in mind this phrase: "Change is a process, not an event." Change takes time and typically occurs in overlapping increments—plus, it does not occur as a result of a single effort.

Change is an emotional experience for those involved, and people adjust to change at different rates. It can bring pain, confusion, uncertainty, guilt (for change survivors), and even excitement for those who see personal advantages in it. Understanding the characteristics of each phase of the Adaptation/Acceptance Spectrum helps you manage the change in your organization.

Six-Phase Change Strategy Model

This model depicts each phase as an independent item. It is important to remember, however, that the actions involved are not necessarily independent of one another. Some can occur concurrently. For example, monitoring impact (phase 4) and responding to feedback (phase 5) should occur at almost all points. In addition, actions like training and communications are common threads, punctuating most of the phases.

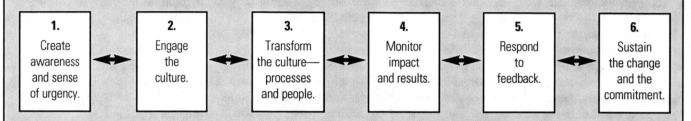

The Six Phases

Phase 1: Create awareness and a sense of urgency. Communicate information on the need for change on a consistent and timely basis. Communicate a clear vision for the organization's future. Share the business case for the specific change strategies selected. Share the financial picture and financial recovery plan to the extent possible.

Phase 2: Engage the culture. Implement programs like town meetings, merger or integration hot lines with prerecorded updates, support circles, and cross-division and cross-level change leadership councils. Create avenues for employee input and involvement.

Phase 3: Transform the culture—processes and people. Implement specific actions such as training, coaching, job counseling, redesign of performance system, and restructure of job roles.

Phase 4: Monitor impact and results. Obtain and analyze data on employees' adaptation to the change, effect of the change on meeting customer requirements, and degree of progress on system or process modifications.

Phase 5: Respond to feedback. Make ongoing, appropriate adjustments to the change strategies and tactics.

Phase 6: Sustain the change and the commitment. Ensure that you align HR systems like recruitment, rewards, training, and involvement to carry the new culture forward. Ensure management systems (like decision making and communication) reflect the new culture. Ensure the physical structure of the organization is consistent with the needs of the new culture.

Phase 1: Thrusting into the Unknown

For the most part, people like the comfort and perceived certainty of their current state. Managing their move from rejection to acceptance (and ideally to embrace) takes time and depends on the stimuli prompting the change. As shown in the sidebar on the following page, change begins for employees with the act of "thrusting" them into the unknown or uncertain. The unknown or uncertain can be any number of events:

● a new procedure
● a change in job responsibilities

● a change in reporting relationships
● a change in business practices
● the loss of a job.

People tend to freeze or become paralyzed in this phase of the spectrum.

The literature and theories on involvement indicate that people are more likely to resist change in which they have no input, which is disturbing because people are usually put in a new situation unexpectedly and without their input or involvement. Input or involvement engenders a sense of ownership of the situation. Such ownership does not mean that

Adaptation/Acceptance Spectrum

The purpose of the graphic below is to provide change managers with some perspective on the different phases employees encounter as they accept change.

Reject/Resist   **Accept**   **Embrace**

Phase 1
Thrusting into
the unknown
or uncertain

Phase 2
Searching for a lifeline
back to normalcy

Phase 3
Learning/incorporating
new behaviors, people,
and skills into one's
environment/world

Phase 4
Feeling
surefooted

Phase 5
Arriving back
to normal

© 1998, S. Cowan.

employees who are required to change expect to be the decision makers. But it does mean this: They want you to consider their ideas, and they want you to inform them about events leading to decisions affecting them.

Even if the situation of change cannot be avoided, letting them know ahead of time can lessen the resistance. When it comes to communication and involvement, more is better. To manage the fear of the unknown and lessen resistance, tactics such as the following will help as you communicate change:

- regularly scheduled voice or email messages on the state of the change

- cross-functional reengineering teams with rotating membership

- periodic focus groups to solicit ideas

- change readiness or climate surveys.

Phase 2: Searching for Normalcy

Despite communication and involvement, the "searching for a lifeline back to normalcy" phase can be difficult and long lasting. Employees may understand the change and feel involved to some degree, but grabbing that lifeline is no easy task.

Even at this stage, people are still somewhat frozen or paralyzed by change. Your role in change management is pivotal in constructing the lifeline.

The lifeline consists of support actions needed to facilitate release from the frozen state. This does not imply that there is a quick fix. But support actions like the ones described below can help the thaw.

Coping skills. Effective coping techniques are important for managing change. Coping techniques include the following:

- implementing stress and grief management (typically, people experience loss and go through the stages of grief when responding to a drastic change like job elimination)

- handling ambiguity

- confronting fears.

Facilitator-led workshops, counseling, videotapes, and audiotapes are formats for teaching coping skills. Employee assistance providers can also support this effort. Keep in mind that coping skills are valuable through the entire change cycle. Change is a process, and as it unfolds it brings new disruptions to handle.

Decision making. If jobs are relocating or changing substantially and employees have the opportunity to decide whether they want to relocate or retrain, the quality of their decision making is important. That is why items like a worksheet or pamphlet containing the pertinent decision factors and tips for reaching the best personal decision are valuable. They help employees feel as if they have some control over their circumstances.

Emotional support. You cannot underestimate the value of emotional support. People need understanding and empathy (not to be confused with sympathy). They need to know that although you cannot necessarily fix their pain, you can relate to it. Moreover, people need to connect with others experiencing similar circumstances.

Support groups, either in person or virtual, can address this need. The groups can be informal or facilitated. The group format provides an arena for expressing and receiving empathy and for divesting emotionally. Employees that benefit particularly from the group format are the survivors of downsizing. Very often, these people suffer from *survivor's guilt* and need their own special emotional support.

Career or job planning. Today, more than ever, people need to be adept at career or job planning. One of the most difficult changes for people can be workforce transition (that is, movement of people to different jobs, elimination of jobs, or transfer of jobs). People are sometimes wedded to their job with no concept of how to transfer their skill sets to a different job. Understanding the concept of transferring skill sets opens up new opportunities for the individual and the organization. In fact, from the organization's viewpoint, redeployment of resources can be a strategic option.

Getting to "Normal"

The road from phase 3 ("learning/incorporating new behaviors") to phase 5 ("arriving back to normal") requires a host of actions. However, it bears repeating that there is no magic formula. The information described under the next sections, "Change Management Skills" and "Operationalizing the Change Strategy," speak to those actions.

Change Management Skills

Successful change management weaves together two key threads:

1. People considerations (for example, emotions associated with job or work elimination or survival).

2. Process considerations (such as restructuring of tasks and responsibilities).

Change is a two-sided coin that involves both people transformation and business strategy innovation. Sometimes, however, the emphasis on reengineering the processes and systems eclipses the people side. This is a mistake. The human or high-touch side of change management is a necessary ingredient. An effective change manager, therefore, is a combination of strategist, process consultant, diagnostician, and *humanist*. Characteristics of a successful change manager include the following:

● appreciates that organizational change unearths interpersonal or emotional issues (that is, the "people" side of change)

● understands the implications of change to production and management systems

● knows how to take in, sort through, and frame information in a way that creates a foundation for a change strategy

● can build an appropriate strategy that integrates the "people" and the "process" side of change management

● can operationalize the broad strategy into specific tactics.

More specifically, the 12 groups of behaviors described in the *Implementation Skills* sidebar at right are key to success at change management. The behaviors are particularly relevant to the critical objective of balancing people transformation with business innovation or process redesign.

Implementation Skills

Having a sound, detailed plan; top leadership support; the resources; and the manpower for your organization's change is ammunition for success. But to win the battle, you need certain skills to implement the change effectively. While there is no definitive list of skills for change managers, the list below is applicable to fueling an atmosphere of change and implementing appropriate change tactics. Also, depending on your organization's particular change situation (for example, wide scale versus limited or targeted change, merger versus spin-off of a division or business segment), the frequency and extent you use the skills may vary.

Skill Sets	Behaviors
1. Thinking Analytically	● Evaluating data or information systematically to identify surface, as well as underlying, causes of problems (for example, performance gaps or process misalignment). ● Assessing the impact of solutions and making appropriate modifications.
2. Seeing the "Big Picture"	● Looking beyond details to see the overarching goals and results. ● Understanding the impact of business decisions on the entire change strategy. ● Making appropriate modifications to the general strategy based on business decisions and customer input.
3. Thinking Out-of-the-Box	● Designing new or innovative ways to address organization initiatives and customer needs.
4. Using Technology	● Using existing or new technology to design products, create solutions, deliver programs, and market services.
5. Using Human Relations	● Working collaboratively with others to build understanding and trust and to achieve common goals. ● Establishing and maintaining rapport with individuals and groups.
6. Learning Continuously	● Being self-directed and persistent in pursuing new information, technology, and ideas.
7. Creating Partnerships/ Networks	● Building ownership and support for change among affected individuals or groups.
8. Thinking Holistically	● Recognizing that an organization is a living, breathing entity. ● Identifying the parts of an organizational process or operation. ● Understanding how the parts fit together and the impact of misalignment of one part on another. ● Understanding the impact of modifying one part on another.
9. Using Project Leadership Methods	● Acting as a lead contact or focal point for components (for example, program, intervention, or event) of the change strategy. ● Directing the activities of others contributing to the component. ● Overseeing project deadlines, deliverables, and customer expectations. ● Adapting to constraints and unexpected roadblocks.
10. Leveraging Power/ Influence	● Establishing and using a power base through unique knowledge or expertise or through alignment with power brokers in the organization.
11. Creating Solutions	● Customizing or designing solutions that best fit the problem. ● Implementing the solutions. ● Tracking the impact of the solutions and making adjustments as appropriate.
12. Responding to Clients	● Interpreting client needs and expectations through various actions (for example, feedback system, survey, and consistent in-person contact). ● Developing effective solutions (for example, coaching, training, or intervention) to close the gap if needs or expectations are not met.

As is evident by the 12 groups of behaviors, in your role as a change practitioner you will wear many hats. These hats or skill sets serve different but related purposes and complement each other.

■ *Analyzing and Designing Hat*

The hat for analyzing issues and designing appropriate solutions represents foundation skills:

- thinking analytically
- thinking "out-of-the-box"
- learning continuously
- creating solutions.

These skills allow you, through tactics like surveys, focus groups, observation, and data collection, to see and design the best solution fit for change-related problems. They help to develop and make use of instruments like the *Performance/Issue Analysis* sidebar and the *Change Management Planning* job aid (parts I and II) to achieve this. These types of tools help you ask the right questions and organize the information in a way that creates a visual framework of the problem.

■ *Strategy Hat*

Seeing the big picture, thinking holistically, and responding to clients are important when deciding what broad strategies to use in the change plan. It is simply a matter of identifying factors in the business, economic, political, and social environment (like those shown in the sidebar bottom left). You must also realize that customer demands drive the need for change and dictate the required response to it.

■ *Change Agent Hat*

Everyone in the organization is in essence a change agent. Change management is not one department or one person; therefore, building a network of advocates and champions is critical. You should not underestimate the value of good press or word-of-mouth advertising. It creates needed momentum. To create that momentum, skills such as using human relations techniques, creating partnerships, and leveraging influence are desirable for your change management role.

■ *Technology and Leadership Hat*

Using technology and project leadership methods are two skills that can prove to be your best friends in fostering change. Technology can support creative change programs or solutions, such as performance coaching through videoconferencing or virtual brainstorming using bulletin boards on an intranet.

Virtual brainstorming is a creative way to foster idea sharing across geographic and department boundaries because there is not always the opportunity to meet in person. It can also foster involvement and network building. The actual brainstorming process would involve posting questions or needs on the intranet bulletin board. Employees would place responses to questions or needs (adding to each other's ideas) on the board either independently (that is, asynchronous postings) or employees would be online at the same time for a designated period (that is, a synchronous chat). The responses could be in narrative form, lists, or even mind maps. Creativity would be the key, and visual images (words or pictures) stimulate creativity. The responses would remain on the intranet as information resources.

Finally, in your change management role you will orchestrate a number of wide-ranging activities such as the following:

- breaking large tasks down into specific activities
- ensuring adequate time for those activities
- conducting a cost analysis.

Big Picture/Holistic View

External Environment
- competitors
- government regulations
- societal changes (for example demographic shifts)
- globalization
- expanding technology
- decreasing product appeal
- growing niche markets
- politics

Internal Environment
- formal and informal communication
- financial picture
- decision making
- rewards
- predominant leadership style
- selection and promotion
- training and development
- performance measurement and feedback

Performance/Issue Analysis

Use the performance/issue analysis tool to map out a problem from a holistic viewpoint. It will help you to determine what systems or processes in the organization have an impact on the problem and to what degree. This process is key to ensuring that you identify the real causes of the problem and understand the full effect of those causes.

Date: **Change Consultant:**   **Client:**   **Problem Category:**

Stakeholders	**Process** What are the processes involved in the performance issue— jobs, roles, tasks, procedures, and so forth?	**People/Departments** Who are the people or departments affected by the performance issue?	**Picture of Ideal Environment** What would things look like if the problem did not exist? 1._____ 2._____ 3._____	**Value** What value does fixing the problem add to the bottom line?

Organizational Systems and Processes	**Lack of Solution Fit (Y/N)**	**Degree (high, medium, low)**	**Relationship to Problem/Issue**
Communication			
Training and Development			
Rewards and Recognition			
Performance Management			
Selection and Promotion			
Customer Input			
Employee Involvement			

© 1997, S. Cowan

Change Management Tactics

A dictionary might define "tactics" as maneuvers, procedures, or schemes—and all three apply within the context of change management. Tactics are the individual actions you use to ignite, maintain, and revitalize (if necessary) the change process. Listed below are some sample tactics you might consider using in your change efforts.

Meetings
- all-employee meetings—scheduled on a regular basis or as needed
- leadership meetings—scheduled on a regular basis or as needed
- quick focus sessions (for example, lesson-learned session after project completion or team intervention)
- department huddles (that is, impromptu, informal department gatherings for giving information, celebrating, or reinforcing morale).

Telephone Coaching
- performance, career, or process coaches can use
- potential coaches include human resources (HR) staff, internal subject matter experts (SMEs), and external consultant experts.

On-Site Coaching
- performance, career, and process coaches can use this tactic with groups or individuals
- potential coaches include HR staff, internal SMEs, and external consultant experts.

Communication Vehicles
- newsletters
- department bulletin boards
- intranet bulletin boards
- all-employee letters.

Telephone Hot Line
- employees submit questions, share challenges and successes, and request information.

Training
- classroom, on-the-job, or self-instructional (for example, workbook, video, CD-ROM-based) training for technical or behavioral issues
- knowledge/information partnerships
- learning contracts
- action plan for transferring learning
- peer teaching.

Tools and Models
- help develop skills transfer knowledge and provide a means for applying learning (for example, a communication debrief and the Four Point Coaching Model presented later in this issue).

Nerve Center
- group containing key personnel, technology, and resources for deploying and coordinating change leadership tactics across the organization.

Survival Kit
- application-oriented tips and resources for coping through an organizational change.

Recognition Day/Week
- leadership and co-worker acknowledgement of employee contribution
- banners, certificates, and profiles in the organization's newsletter recognizing achievements
- non-monetary rewards such as flextime, compressed workweek, special assignment, resources or technology, and special partnerships.

Being able to manage these types of activities well is why project leadership skills are beneficial in a change management position.

Operationalizing the Change Strategy

The change management strategy starts from the big picture view, which is very broad and incorporates a number of initiatives. Operationalizing the strategy simply means breaking down the broad and wide into action-oriented activities (for example, programs, processes, or events) that move the change forward. The change practitioner can embrace these activities and measure progress and success more easily.

While all of the tactics listed in the above sidebar are effective in facilitating change, a few deserve some additional attention:

- tools and models
- training and coaching.

Tools and Models

The organization's employees are the bedrock of successful change tactics. As harbingers of the new culture, they must believe in the vision and use job behaviors that support realization of it. Obviously, changing performance or job behavior is not an exact science. It requires, among other factors, a way to perform the following:

- create common practices
- communicate those practices
- support application of those practices.

One such way is developing or adopting appropriate performance tools and models. A performance tool is a logical, straightforward learning or application aid (such as the *Communication Debrief* on the next page). A performance model is a succinct, easily applied example of a process or procedure (see the *Four Point Coaching Model* sidebar for an example and design tips).

Both models and tools provide a mental picture, which provide a more assessable framework for analysis or discussion. They also present a structured way of digesting information and perform the triple duty of teaching, coaching, and reinforcing.

Teaching. The boxes in the Four Point Coaching Model—observe, individualize, encourage, and track—represent separate subject areas for training in the classroom. Organize activities or exercises around each area. You can also design each area as a mini, stand-alone training module (possibly 45-90 minutes).

Coaching. Use the coaching questions on the communication debrief to guide discussion, identify challenges, and determine development needs during individual coaching sessions.

Reinforcing. The call-outs in the communication debrief make it easy to review and reinforce the application tips.

The idea is to pass the knowledge along while creating a sense of independence. This act builds the change tactics infrastructure, which is an important part of transforming the culture.

Training and Coaching

Training and coaching are interrelated essential parts of the infrastructure. With the redesign of jobs, the reengineering of whole processes, and the introduction of new technology, a need definitely exists for training employees. Training can occur in the classroom or on the job, but it also includes self-instructional training and performance coaching. No matter how you decide to provide it, training should be *application oriented*. This means that the instructional strategy focuses on how to apply the classroom concepts on the job.

To ensure that training transfers to on-the-job application, include a process and worksheets on application planning in your training programs. Design your instruction to place less emphasis on conveying concepts and more emphasis on creating experiential learning opportunities (for example, simulations, role plays, learning games, and behavior modeling).

The *Leader As Change Facilitator* sidebar is an example of an application-oriented program. The theme of the program is "Be a change *instigator* not a change *spectator*." A segment from W. Mitchell's powerful book *It's Not What Happens to You, It's What You Do About It* is included as pre-reading. The program is a one-and-a-half-day classroom experience with follow-up coaching for the implementation activities. A pre-training survey is administered (preferably in person) to gather the following information from the leader:

- department's key customers
- methods for collecting customer data
- methods for communicating with staff.

Both the survey and follow-up coaching, which can be in person, by telephone, or by email, help establish a partnership between you and your customers. Through activities like these, you increase your sensitivity to your customers' world (that is, their requirements, issues, and challenges).

Communication Debrief

Below is a sample of a communication debrief, which is a leader development tool. Use it as an example of how to learn from your meeting experience.

Action: Something you did—like not refocusing the group when it went on a tangent in the middle of the meeting. Unchecked tangents can kill the momentum and consume valuable time.

Date: Communication Topic:

How did the meeting go overall?

What action or statement would I repeat? Why was the action or statement effective?

What action or statement would I *not* repeat?

Why was the action or statement ineffective? How would I change it?

Briefly summarize the results of the meeting.

Base the debrief checklist on your task actions and use it to help you reflect on the way you conducted the meeting.

Debrief Checklist

Statement: Something you said such as, "Ron, it's silly to feel anxious about the new job roles." Minimizing how someone feels makes that person defensive and less open to the message or purpose of the meeting.

☐ Did I begin by describing the **purpose** (for example, communicate a new policy) and desired **outcome?**

☐ Did I **address questions** or concerns about the purpose or outcome (for example, whether or not the new policy being communicated would also be provided in writing)?

Whether or not you need to obtain information from the person depends on the nature of the meeting.

☐ Did I **obtain information** needed to meet the purpose?

☐ Did I **provide clarity** or background information on issues related to the purpose (for example, the criteria used to make a policy decision)?

☐ Did I **deliver the complete message** or information? Did I verify whether the group understood the message?

☐ Did I develop **next actions** (if required), with input from the group?

Not all meetings require actions, resources, or deadlines as outcomes. For those that do, try to involve the group members (that is, solicit their input and ideas) in developing these items. When people are involved they are more receptive and feel ownership of the outcomes.

☐ Did I identify **resources,** with input from the group?

☐ Did I set **deadlines** for completion of actions, with input from the group?

☐ Did I **restate** the outcomes at the end of the meeting?

☐ Did I **check for unanswered questions** or concerns before concluding? Did I answer or make arrangements to get answers to the group later?

☐ Did I **thank the group** for participating in the meeting?

© *July 1998, S. Cowan*

Four Point Coaching Model

Observe and respond to coaching opportunities.

- Pay attention to behaviors, actions, and feedback that indicate a need for coaching (for example, customer or peer complaints, procrastination, or expression of uncertainty about handling project).

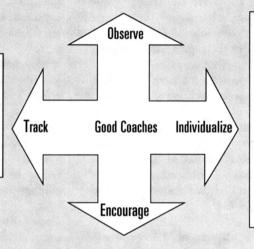

Track performance and provide feedback.

- Reinforce desired performance.

- Identify ineffective performance and suggest alternative actions.

Individualize the coaching style based on who is being coached and the particular circumstances of the coaching opportunity.

- Consider the person's abilities, experience, willingness, work style, and confidence level—*the who.*

- Consider the deadline, resources, complexity of the task, impact of the task, logistics, organizational priority, and so forth—*the circumstances.*

Encourage initiative and ownership, and offer support and guidance.

- Ask open-ended question to solicit input such as ideas, actions, and solutions.

- Provide expertise, experience, knowledge, and direction.

- Balance the "asking" and the "providing."

© *July 1998, S. Cowan.*

Implementation Roadblocks

Just because senior leadership has decided that the organization needs to change, it does not mean automatic success. Implementation roadblocks manifest themselves in many ways. No matter how well designed your overall strategy is or how skilled you are, you will likely confront some of the following roadblocks.

Lack of vision. When the corporate vision or specific business strategies are unclear, people are sometimes unsure about how they should interpret changes.

Lack of leadership support. The change manager is often the chief advocate of the change process. This role includes injecting the sense of advocacy into the rest of the organization—particularly leadership. Actions that are essential for success must first be present in leaders. They must model the behaviors needed to bring about change in both process and culture. Only top leadership can provide the sanctions of time and resources necessary for change. They must also remove obstacles to change that are out of the realm of direct reports. Problems occur when senior leadership says one thing, but their behaviors suggest the opposite.

Lack of HR systems alignment. Hiring people with the right abilities and attitude, rewarding people for the right behaviors and outputs, and training people in the right skills are all part of aligning the systems to provide what you need to redesign the culture.

History of poor implementation. When an organization has a history of poorly implemented strategic plans, people tend to expect very little when new change efforts are announced.

Insufficient time. If insufficient time is allocated for implementation, there will be large maintenance cost after the change.

Environment of low risk taking. Overly punishing errors or rewarding the mere absence of errors promotes an environment of low risk taking. High risk taking should be the desired behavior in an organization undergoing change.

Lack of clear communications. If information about change is allowed to filter down the organization in an unmanaged fashion, it becomes diffused, less specific, and interpreted in arbitrary ways.

Lack of resistance planning. All major changes, even ones that have positive implications, encounter resistance. People are not necessarily resisting change but rather the disruption caused by change.

Poor management of resistance. When resistance does not surface, it is often because it has been denied or quashed. When overt resistance is not acknowledged and managed properly, the resistance often goes "underground." The results are covert resistance:

● slowdowns
● malicious compliance
● outright sabotage.

Lack of synergy. Forgetting that an organization's various operations are interdependent can lead to initiating changes in one place and encountering resistance from people and functions in another place.

Poor follow-through. Many organizations reward people with a lot of fanfare for starting big projects, but they fail to follow through to see that the project was finished or that it achieved the desired results.

Roadblocks like these just prove that the world of change management is unpredictable, exciting, and challenging. During change, addressing both the process needs *and* the people needs of your organization is a complex—but necessary—balancing act.

As the change manager, you and the committed, visible support of top leadership are the primary catalysts of this balancing act. Your ability to translate broad strategy into action-oriented tactics lays a pathway for creating real systems and behavioral change. Moreover, thriving on the excitement, enduring the challenges, and expecting the unpredictable are the hallmarks of a successful change manager.

Leader As Change Facilitator

Below is an example of the course design for an application-oriented program. The theme for this program was "Be a change *instigator* not a change *spectator*." Use this example to help you design your own application-oriented programs that facilitate change.

Section	Title	Content
Introduction/ Ice Breaker	**Change is like …**	Ask participants to stand beneath one of the four flipchart titles (listed below) that best describes their feelings about change. • Change is like a roller coaster ride—*It is both exhilarating and frightening.* • Change is like a new pair of shoes—*It is tight and uncomfortable until you break it in.* • Change is like a hot fudge sundae—*It is delicious and satisfying and leaves you eagerly anticipating the next one.* • Change is like a hailstorm—*It is fast and furious and you just have to ride it out.* Once participants are gathered beneath the flipcharts, ask them to chat for a minute about their reaction to recent changes in their lives. Next, ask them one-by-one to introduce themselves (for example, name, department, job/responsibility, and reason they stood beneath that particular flipchart) to the large group.
Opening Activity	**What, why, and how**	Through use of poster boards, summary information sheets, question and answer time, and an appearance from someone in senior leadership, address the following questions: • What is changing? • Why is it changing? • How will it benefit the organization? • How can it benefit the organization's employees?
Learning Outcomes	**Goals**	Asking these questions is critical in setting a framework for the learning and application process. Discuss the fact that a certain amount of ambiguity comes with dramatic organizational change—not all questions can be answered. • Understand change in general. • Understand implications of the change or transition for the organization. • Understand leader's role in facilitating change or transition. • Develop a plan for helping staff manage change or transition.
Department Environment Maps		Through an interactive exercise using the department environment maps that were created during pre-training sessions, participants should realize the following: • They have similar challenges. • They share customers, technology, and resources. • They have common goals. • They can be a resource to each other.
Supervisor's or Manager's Role	**Change— personal view**	Examine the personal view of change through an activity involving a three-part instrument: • Change grid (What does change look like? How does it affect me?). • Change pulse (How do I feel about the change? Where am I on the change Adaptation/Acceptance Spectrum?). • Change implementation (What can I do to adapt/accept this change? What can I do to facilitate the change?).
Management Behaviors	**Eight keys**	Examine the eight keys of management leadership (listed below) and, using an assessment process, determine development needs relative to the eight keys: • listening • collaborating • recognizing/rewarding • presenting information • communicating one-on-one • coaching. • supporting • clearing the way
Action Planning		Complete a plan for transferring the learning to the job (for example, what will be done, when, who needs to be involved, resources, benefits, and so forth). The training department sets up a coaching schedule for continued support during implementation.

© July 1998, S. Cowan.

References & Resources

Articles

Barrier, Michael. "Managing Workers in a Time of Change." *Nation's Business*, May 1998, pp. 31-34.

Buchel, Mary. "Accelerating Change." *Training & Development*, April 1996, pp. 48-51.

Carrig, Ken. "Reshaping Human Resources for the Next Century—Lessons from a High Flying Airline." *Human Resource Management*, Summer 1997, pp. 277-289.

Caudron, Shari. "Rebuilding Employee Trust." *Training & Development*, August 1996, pp. 18-21.

Cook, Julie. "Tackling Large-Scale Change." *Human Resource Executive*, May 20, 1997, pp. 44-46.

Cutcher-Gershenfeld, Joel, et al. "Managing Concurrent Change Initiatives: Integrating Quality and Work/Family Strategies." *Organizational Dynamics*, Winter 1997, pp. 21-37.

Demers, Russ, et al. "Commitment to Change." *Training & Development*, August 1996, pp. 22-26.

Denton, D. Keith. "9 Ways to Create an Atmosphere for Change." *HRMagazine*, October 1996, pp. 76-81.

Frady, Marsha. "Get Personal to Communicate Coming Change." *Performance Improvement*, August 1997, pp. 32-33.

Kramlinger, Tom. "How to Deliver a Change Message." *Training & Development*, April 1998, pp. 44-47.

Orlikowski, Wanda J., and Debra J. Hofman. "An Improvisational Model for Change Management: The Case of Groupware Technologies." *Sloan Management Review*, Winter 1997, pp. 11-21.

Prickett, Ruth. "House Proud." *People Management*, November 12, 1998, pp. 43-45.

Rough, Jim. "Dynamic Facilitation and the Magic of Self-Organizing Change." *Journal for Quality and Participation*, June 1997, pp. 34-38.

Schneider, David M., and Charles Goldwasser. "Be a Model Leader of Change." *Management Review*, March 1998, pp. 41-45.

Smith, Dick. "Invigorating Change Initiatives." *Management Review*, May 1998, pp. 45-48.

Strebel, Paul. "Why Do Employees Resist Change?" *Harvard Business Review*, May/June 1996, pp. 86-92.

Topchik, Gary S. "Attacking the Negativity Virus." *Management Review*, September 1998, pp. 61-64.

Trahant, Bill, and Warner W. Burke. "Traveling through Transitions." *Training & Development*, February 1996, pp. 37-41.

Books

Barger, Nancy J., and Linda K. Kirby. *The Challenge of Change in Organizations: Helping Employees Thrive in the New Frontier*. Palo Alto, CA: Davies-Black, 1995.

Carr, Clay. *Choice, Chance & Organizational Change: Practical Insights from Evolution for Business Leaders & Thinkers*. New York: AMACOM, 1996.

Hambrick, Donald C., et al., eds. *Navigating Change: How CEOs, Top Teams, and Boards Steer Transformation*. Boston: Harvard Business School Press, 1998.

Jeffreys, J. Shep. *Coping with Workplace Change: Dealing with Loss and Grief*. Menlo Park, CA: Crisp Publications, 1995.

Maurer, Rick. *Beyond the Wall of Resistance: Unconventional Strategies That Build Support for Change*. Austin, TX: Bard Books, 1996.

Mitchell, W. *It's Not What Happens to You, It's What You Do About It*. Partners Publishers Group, 1997.

Smith, Douglas K. *Taking Charge of Change: 10 Principles for Managing People and Performance*. Reading, MA: Addison-Wesley, 1996.

Infolines

Carr, Don Aaron. "How to Facilitate." No. 9406 (revised 1999).

Koehle, Deborah. "The Role of the Performance Change Manager." No. 9715.

Smith, Warren. "Managing Change: Implementation Skills." No. 8910 (out of print).

Titcomb, T.J. "Chaos and Complexity Theory." No. 9807.

Change Management Planning

This job aid has two parts. Part I provides descriptions of when particular change tactics are most appropriate. Part II provides space for you to list the various components of your program and to select the change management tactics you think best support each component. The purpose of the descriptions and the worksheet is to support designing the best overall strategy for a specific change-related problem.

Part I.

Tactic	Application
Education	Appropriate when looking to close a **knowledge gap** or **skill deficiency** that requires college or technical education (such as the completion of a degree or certificate).
Training	Applies when **job processes** or **job technologies** have changed and internal training programs are available to meet the need. Local colleges and training firms offer technical, skills, and interpersonal training.
Coaching/ Counseling	There are four types of coaching or counseling: ● **Performance coaching** closes gaps in the quality or production of an individual's or a group's work outputs. It can involve reviewing examples of desired outputs, reinforcing strategies for producing desired outputs, and giving constructive feedback on outputs. ● **Career coaching** is useful during workforce transition situations (such as job transfer, elimination, or redesign). It can involve skills assessment, résumé writing, cover letter writing, job searching tips (internal or external), and education planning. ● **Process coaching** supports groups working on their flow-charting of processes, identifying redundancies, and recommending improvements or changes. It is also an appropriate analysis activity when reengineering organizational systems. ● **Human relations coaching** provides support, insight, or guidance in handling inter-group or team relations, change adaptability, or communication issues.
Interviewing	Useful if you are collecting sensitive information, if the questions are mainly open ended and less suited for a written survey, or if there is a need for the interviewer to interact with the interviewee during the interview. Can be done in person or by telephone. In-person is desirable when hearing the information and seeing the person providing the information is beneficial to the outcome (for example, better opportunity to establish rapport or build relations and to observe the interviewee's behavior).
Mentoring Program	Useful if you want to **impart leadership knowledge** and **experience** to the culture. Appropriate for addressing **diversity issues** around change by establishing special programs for underrepresented groups. Can be an informal or formal program.
Tool or Model	Helpful in situations where a **job aid** can contribute to improving performance or can provide support in applying a process. Can supplement formal training, be used as a guide when coaching, and is an effective method for enabling employees to perform independently.
Intervention	Involves using activities (such as team building, role clarification, or structured feedback) to influence behavior, stop certain behaviors, or increase awareness. The goal is to get a group back on track and can involve one activity or a series of activities designed to meet a specific need.
Assessment or Survey	Aids with **collecting employees' opinions** or **attitudes** about change (for example, change readiness survey or team participation survey).
Focus Group	Useful to **obtain sensitive information,** debrief after an incident to channel emotions, debrief after completion of a project for lessons learned, or assess employees' readiness for or adaptation to change. Can be intact or cross-functional groups.
Communication	Used to inform, educate, motivate, or influence. Newsletters, email, voicemail, all-employee letters, banners, and bulletin boards are examples of communication vehicles. Appropriate during change (for example, a merger) because **employees need and want to be informed** of what is happening and motivated to stay engaged. A communication vacuum leads to half-truths, innuendoes, and lies. Communication during all phases of change is necessary. Timeliness, honesty, and consistency are key.

(continued on the next page)

Job Aid

Action Planning	Helpful in transferring classroom learning to the job, applying a process to a situation, and implementing individual or group performance development activities.
System Alignment	Involves changing systems (such as compensation, performance review, training, and selection/promotion) to support the type of culture the organization wants to build. For example, if your organization wants to create a culture of entrepreneurial thinkers, the design of its compensation system might include a reward (such as a bonus) for developing and successfully implementing ideas that grow the business. Elements like employee empowerment, risk-taking, and trust would have to be a part of this culture. You would also need an infrastructure of resources, tracking methods, and reporting. (This is actually more of a strategy than a tactic.)

Part II.

	Appropriate Change Management Tactic					
Project Components	**Education**	**Training**	**Coaching/ Counseling**	**Interviewing**	**Mentoring Programs**	**Tool or Model**

Project Components	**Intervention**	**Assessment or Survey**	**Focus Group**	**Communi- cation**	**Action Planning**	**System Alignment**